Hidden Riches

Hidden Riches

TRADITIONAL SYMBOLISM FROM

THE RENAISSANCE TO BLAKE

---

by Désirée Hirst

And I will give thee the treasures of darkness, and
hidden riches of secret places, that thou mayest know
that I, the Lord, which call thee by thy name, am the
God of Israel.   ISAIAH 45:3

BARNES & NOBLE, INC · NEW YORK
Publishers · Booksellers · Founded 1873

First published in 1964 by
Eyre & Spottiswoode (Publishers) Ltd
22 Henrietta Street, Covent Garden, WC2
© *1964 by Désirée Hirst*
Published in the United States in 1964
by Barnes & Noble, Inc
105 Fifth Avenue, New York 3

To my Parents

Printed in Great Britain by
The Shenval Press, London, Hertford & Harlow

Contents

*

Plates

*

The following acknowledgments are due for the illustrations: to the Trustees of the British Museum for Plates 1, 2, 4a, 4b, 4c, 5, 6, 7a, 7b, and 8. Acknowledgment is also due for the facsimile of Blake's Crucifixion from *Jerusalem* (Plate 3), which is reproduced by permission of the publishers, the Trianon Press.

Figures

*

Preface

*

During the many years of research necessary to assemble the material for this book I have always been able to draw on the special knowledge of a number of distinguished scholars. It is not easy for anyone but an experienced Hebraist to make progress in an understanding of the Jewish Mystical Literature of the Kabalah, but for ten years I profited by the readings from the Kabalah given by Rabbi Dr Lehman at Oxford. And also from the vast learning of Professor Scholem who holds the chair in Jewish Mystical Studies at the Hebrew University at Jerusalem. In the same way C. H. Josten, Curator of the Museum of the History of Science at Oxford, has always been willing to place his authoritative knowledge of seventeenth century England at my disposal, and Dr Walter Pagel, who has made an exhaustive study of Paracelsus and J. B. Van Helmont, has never failed to take a helpful, encouraging interest in the progress of my work.

M. François Secret of the Ecole des Hautes Etudes at the Sorbonne, possibly now the greatest authority on the Christian Kabalah in the Renaissance, has always extended the utmost courtesy and given many valuable pointers. The Librarian of Dr Williams Library, London, kindly put at my disposal Christopher Walton's fascinating collection of books and manuscripts on William Law and his sources, and the Librarian of the Chetham Hospital Library in Manchester also helped me to gain access to books from the John Byrom collection there which had been in store.

Finally much constructive criticism, interest and advice has come from Professor Nevill Coghill and Sir Maurice Bowra at Oxford, Professor Geoffrey Bullough of King's College,

London, the Editor for the New York Public Library, David Erdman and Professor Foster Damon. I also remember with appreciation discussions on Blake with the late Rev Heming Vaughan and with the novelist, Joyce Cary. A grant for research was also received through the kindness of the late Mrs Spalding. To all the students attending my London University Extension lectures on Blake I am indebted for their stimulating observations and suggestions.

D.H.

List of Leading Characters

*

Agrippa von Nettesheim, Henry Cornelius, 1486–1535. Scholar and soldier in the service of the Emperor Charles V. Popularizer of Neo-Platonic, Hermetic and Cabalistic ideas and symbols.

Blake, William, 1757–1827. Artist and poet. His symbolic system draws on the tradition which is the subject of this book.

Boehme, Jacob, 1575–1624. Prosperous burgher of Gorlitz whose contacts with circles interested in mysticism, and individual visionary experiences, impelled him to build up his own theosophical system.

Brooke, Henry, 1738–1806. Dublin artist. Nephew of the playwright and novelist of that name. Friend of John Wesley. Admirer of William Law's mystical theology and collector of records of visionary experiences who kept up a wide correspondence.

Clarke, Richard, 1719?–1802. Anglican clergyman, friend and follower of William Law. Correspondent of Henry Brooke. Student of Hebrew, well versed in the Kabalah and in Neo-Platonic symbolism. Universalist.

Dürer, Albrecht, 1471–1528. Artist and engraver. Absorbed in speculations on harmony, perspective and the philosophy of Art.

Everard, John, 1575–1650? Theologian and provocative preacher. Translator of mystical, Cabalistic and Hermetic works.

Ficino, Marsilio, 1433–1499. Philosopher and scholar engaged in translating Greek texts on Platonism, Neo-Platonism and Alexandrian Hermeticism under the patronage of the Medici family at Florence.

Fludd, Robert, 1574–1637. Physician. Pre-occupied with Alchemy, the Kabalah, Rosicrucianism and Neo-Platonic theories of cosmic harmony. Involved in controversies with the astronomer John Kepler and the learned Franciscan, Marin Mersenne.

Giorgio, Francesco, 1460–1540? Learned Franciscan of the Venetian convent of the Order of Friars Minor. Deeply versed in the Jewish Mystical tradition of the Kabalah and in Neo-Platonic theories of cosmic harmony. His books were widely influential.

Glanvill, Joseph, d. 1680. Theologian and believer in re-incarnation. His books, inspired notably by Origen, attracted the attention of Henry More.

Helmont, François Mercure van, 1618–1699. Physician and medical scientist, preoccupied with Alchemy, Neo-Platonism and the Kabalah. Contributed to Christian Knorr von Rosenroth's compilation, the *Cabbala Denudata*.

Law, William, 1686–1761. Anglican theologian particularly concerned with Mysticism, admirer of Jacob Boehme. A Non-Juror, he led a retired life without the ecclesiastical preferment his brilliance would otherwise have commanded.

Milton, John, 1608–1674. Poet and pamphleteer. Influenced by the thought of Samuel Hertlib, John Dury and Comenius, whose philosophy, permeated with Neo-Platonism and Cabalism, was the inspiration of the English Revolution.

More, Henry, 1614–1687. Leading Cambridge Platonist. He was also interested in Descartes' philosophy and in the Kabalah. Contributed to Christian Knorr von Rosenroth's compilation, the *Cabbalah Denudata*.

Paracelsus; Philippus Aureolus Theophrastus Bombastus von Hohenheim, 1493–1541. Physician and philosopher. Responsible for important discoveries and for the rise of modern chemistry out of alchemical experiment. Instigator of an entire literature tinged with Gnosticism and Neo-Platonism.

Pordage, John, 1607–1661. Anglican clergyman and physician. Popularizer of Jacob Boehme's thought in England. Author of serious Behmenist studies and originator of the Philadelphian Society.

Postel, Guillaume, 1505–1581. Mathematician and orientalist. Professor at the Collège de France. Later a Jesuit priest, though expelled from the Society for the eccentricity of his theory of knowledge. Translator and commentator on major Cabalistic texts.

Reuchlin, Johann, 1455–1522. Hebraist. Author of works on the Kabalah, on the Talmud, and of a Hebrew grammar.

Swedenborg, Emanuel, 1688–1772. Swedish scientist. An export in mining engineering, astronomy and the anatomy of the brain, gifted with powers of extra-sensory perception. He became absorbed in religious speculation and his teaching was drawn on for the foundation of the New Church.

Introduction

*

The understanding of a traditional symbolism provides an essential key to many kingdoms of the mind. We seldom stop to consider, for instance, how we are made free of the republic of letters, the architect's domain, the musician's world, or how we communicate with the scientist, the theologian or the mathematician. It is usually only when there is a failure of communication that such questions begin to impose themselves. Yet to arrive at an appreciation of any of these disciplines, in order that communication may take place, a language of symbolism must be learnt. While it is still unfamiliar to us we are bound to be mystified, achieving only scattered glimpses into the other's mind, even if he be a genius. This mental confusion is especially evident when a strange civilization is first encountered. While any foreign language begins by sounding like Double Dutch, even to the highly educated European Oriental and African cultural forms are often meaningless, their music being no more than an unpleasant sound, and the inspiring complexity of Hindu temple architecture, for example, nothing but an uncomfortable mass of writhing figures.

At the same time we forget how much we take for granted that makes our own literature and art bewildering to outsiders. For those brought up in the Christian West certain presuppositions inform the imagination from an early age. The world is seen as finite; having a beginning and an end. The succession of events is stretched out between the Creation and the Last Day. Even those who do not read the Bible accept a pattern which rests on Genesis on one end and the Judgment on the other, and with it the whole procession from Alpha to Omega, hardly aware the while that this is the source of their vision of life. Without that broad outline such Western concepts as Progress and Evolution have no meaning. No one could read *The Divine Comedy* or *Paradise Lost*, or look at the Sistine chapel murals intelligently without bearing this pattern in mind. Yet it is one that makes no particular appeal to a Hindu who takes for granted that the universe itself is eternal, and that to expect movement towards a goal, or even an explanation of creation, is folly. It is significant that to many Indians even Western music, perhaps the most refined of all the arts of our civilization, seems at first bombastic and materialistic.

Even within our own civilization, which we think we understand, there are elements that are hardly grasped at all. Without taking the trouble to explore these, our appreciation of even the most towering geniuses must remain very circumscribed. A great deal eludes us while we think we have correctly interpreted the work as a whole. The result is unsatisfying, or if the mind is satisfied, it is being content with too little. Sometimes, also, the thought behind the masterpiece is far more strange than would appear on the surface; even in direct contradiction to many of our usually accepted values. It is as though we were in the exact position of men and women who tried to read Proust, James Joyce, Virginia Woolf or Eugene O'Neill, in a world where all trace of the psychological theories which have so much affected the twentieth century, had been lost.

When, for instance, many readers are faced with the phenomenon of William Blake they find themselves equally lost. There are many critics even, as a recent commentator, Margaret Rudd, has pointed out, who

> would like to possess the key to Blake's mythological labyrinth, for it seems to contain something of extraordinary power and significance. But to find the key seems too great an effort.

I am convinced that to discover that key there is no escape from a journey into the past, a return to Blake's origins. His was a voice speaking even in his own time, from the past, but for the future. The men of the eighteenth and nineteenth centuries were heirs to many treasures from the past and of these none has been so much misunderstood as the art and philosophy of the Renaissance. The extent to which the ideas and symbolism of Leonardo da Vinci, Michelangelo, Botticelli, the Medicis, Palladio and the great humanists, Ficino, Erasmus and Colet, for instance, are actually misinterpreted by us for lack of a full grasp of their symbolic language, in fact through a failure in communication, has been emphasized by Edgar Wind in his study, *Pagan Mysteries in the Renaissance*.

The minds of these thinkers were dominated by concepts derived, it is true, from the ancient world, by a kind of Neo-Platonism blended with Hebrew symbolism, but they were, nevertheless, sincere Christians, only too anxious that the Pagan wisdom should be baptized. Professor Wind has given a detailed survey, among other things, of the way in which Pico della Mirandola, Ficino's brilliant pupil, hammered out a scheme by which these apparently Pagan elements were supposed to be harmonized with Christian orthodoxy. And he insists that we make a grave mistake in thinking that the substitution of Pagan mythological figures in Renaissance art for Christian ones, their interchangeability, as it were, betrays 'a profound secularization'. While portraits of the Madonna might sometimes resemble a Venus, statues and paintings of Venus just as often resemble a Madonna or a Magdalene. The classical subjects were chosen for their inner spiritual sense, which, used allegorically, could not be said to conflict with the Christian faith in any way. The impetus of this special imaginative effort lasted well into the seventeenth century and had definite after-effects upon the eighteenth century also. Few, in fact, of the major achievements in poetry, music, philosophy, architecture or medicine were unaffected. Nor were the politicians and theologians of the time left untouched. They either derived part of their inspiration from this source or were provoked by a reaction from it. And in England the group of Anglican theologians known as the 'Cambridge Platonists', and the great divine William Law with his followers were among those most deeply influenced.

However, any examination of the question of William Blake's sources must inevitably be an extremely complex matter. To begin with there is the problem of what is meant by 'source'. In considering, say, Shakespeare's sources, one might discuss the theme of the plots to his plays; whether they come from English historical chronicles, or Italian novella. Information on such points can be very enlightening, but a far more profound problem is involved when one investigates Shakespeare's probable religious loyalties, whether he absorbed the spirit of Montaigne, or if *Love's Labour's Lost* really reflects the philosophical pre-occupations of the New Learning, as has been suggested in Muriel Bradbrook's *The School of Night*. Or what vision is being expressed in that very significant romance, *The Tempest*. A man's vision of life, the values by which he means to be judged, are clearly more important than the framework of his stories or even the characters he writes of, or paints.

It has been suggested that many of the fables used in Blake's myths, and many of the characters that people them, were drawn from the eighteenth century translations of the Neo-Platonic Greek writings brought out, with extensive commentaries, by Thomas Taylor. This thesis has been ably presented by George Mills Harper in his critical study *The Neo-Platonism of William Blake*, and of course by Kathleen Raine. It is most unlikely that the works of Thomas Taylor made no impact upon Blake, especially in view of Taylor's close contacts with Blake's sculptor friend Flaxman. Indeed Taylor was conspicuous in the late eighteenth century and early nineteenth, for his eccentricity and his Neo-Paganism, and George Harper has shown his influence upon the Romantic poets Wordsworth, Coleridge, Shelley and Keats and on Charles Lamb, Thomas Love Peacock and Leigh Hunt. His work was admired by such outstanding Greek scholars as Dr Copleston, Provost of Oriel College, Oxford, and Dr Adam Clarke. His curious and elaborate books may very well have furnished Blake with a convenient mine of legend and mythological characterization to draw upon. And an understanding of these intricacies helps

4

greatly to illuminate the complexities of Blake's own system.

Nevertheless the spiritual giant who dominated the eighteenth century was not Thomas Taylor but William Law. Perhaps the most outstanding of all Anglican divines, Law was a Christian Platonist in the style of the seventeenth century Cambridge Platonists, and because of his enthusiasm for this tradition he was deeply influenced by the Lutheran mystic, Jacob Boehme, whom he recognized as working within it. A devoted admirer of that long train of Catholic mystics who were inspired by the type of Neo-Platonism that stems from St Augustine and the Areopagite, he found Boehme, whose Paracelsian friends had helped to shape his symbolic system, the only Protestant mystic who could compare in stature with these earlier figures. The values which William Law's circle of followers upheld during the middle and later years of the eighteenth century, also informed William Blake's thinking during his whole working life. This is not to say that Taylor's version of this philosophy had no effect on Blake's mind. It is most probable that many of the shifts of emphasis in plot and character within the myth of Blake's prophetic books derive from the works of Proclus, Plotinus and Porphyry, and of Plato himself, as presented and interpreted by Thomas Taylor. And a man can hardly borrow quite so heavily without being considered influenced. George Harper mentions, for instance, 'Blake's Twenty Lost Years'.

> During this time, according to his own account, he was sympathetic to, and deeply absorbed in, reviving the ancient art of the Greeks.

He admits, however, that upon his visit to the exhibition of art at the Truchsessian Gallery, Blake underwent an interior experience which altered his whole outlook.

> Suddenly, on the day after visiting the Truchsessian Gallery of pictures, I was again enlightened with the light I enjoyed in my youth, and which has for exactly twenty years been closed from me as by a door and by window-shutters.

He suggests that he went through a crisis which was really a spiritual one and this I think is precisely the truth. During the twenty years of darkness during which Blake had felt fettered, he had passed through a depression similar to the corresponding one in Ficino's life when he struggled to reconcile his Christianity with his Platonism. After the visit to the Gallery he found himself released from any compulsion to revere Greek thought in itself and he was able, openly, to stand by his real loyalties which belonged to a tradition that was deeply Biblical in origin; that had used classical thought as an important element, but blended it with scriptural strands and always insisted on the Eastern origins of Greek inspiration, its dependence on the more profound Wisdom of the Orient.

Indeed several years earlier than this incident, in a well-known letter to John Flaxman, dated 12th September 1800, Blake gives in verse his spiritual autobiography, listing all the major influences that had affected his development, in lines which cannot be too often repeated.

> Now my lot in the Heavens is this, Milton lov'd me in childhood
>   & shew'd me his face.
> Ezra came with Isaiah the Prophet, but Shakespeare in riper years
>   gave me his hand;
> Paracelsus & Behmen appear'd to me, terrors appear'd in the
>   Heavens above
> And in Hell beneath, & a mighty & awful change threatened the
>   Earth.
> The American War began. All its dark horrors passed before my
>   face
> Across the Atlantic to France. Then the French Revolution
>   commenc'd in thick clouds,
> And My Angels have told me that seeing such visions I could not
>   subsist on the Earth,
> But by my conjunction with Flaxman, who knows to forgive
>   Nervous Fear.
>
>   (Keynes, p. 799)

Thomas Taylor and the Greeks are conspicuous by their absence.

It is, however, well known that Blake's later 'Lambeth' books show signs of some kind of loss of faith or failure of nerve on his part. During this period he seems almost anti-Christian and clearly passed through disillusionment and bitterness. This may well have been the time when Blake was most fully under the influence of Taylor's works. But they did not satisfy him, any more than Swedenborg's system could. And he did not even make the open acknowledgement to them that he accorded to Swedenborg, 'the Samson shorn by the Churches'. The values which animated Blake's work as a whole are indeed Neo-Platonic ones; but in them the Christian Platonism of William Law and his predecessors is united with that reverence for the great prophets of the Bible which animated them all, and especially for the mystical writers, of whom the author of the Ezra Apocalypse is an example venerated by Jews and Christians alike. From the seventeenth century onwards the minds of those who lived in this intellectual climate turned more and more towards the towering figures of Paracelsus and Jacob Boehme, and Blake was naturally affected in addition by the outstanding poets of English Literature. Finally, the two most profound political upheavals of his day, the American War of Independence and the French Revolution, were bound to make an impact, as well as the personalities of his closest friends. Blake has given the whole story in so many words.

Another problem which must be taken into account in any consideration of Blake's sources is his own insistence on different levels of vision.

> Now I a fourfold vision see,
> And a fourfold vision is given to me;
> 'Tis fourfold in my supreme delight
> And threefold in soft Beulah's night
> And twofold Always. May God us keep
> From Single vision & Newton's sleep!
>
> (*Ibid.*, p. 818)

Everything that Blake wrote or painted has several meanings. There is no conflict between the political, the mythological,

7

the scriptural and the personal allusions which may often be found in a single line. The number of 'sources' is correspondingly multiplied. Indeed I have become convinced that Blake delighted to use names, symbols, fables and characters that could be found in a number of quite different lines of thought, cultures and aspects of life, just as he enjoyed play on words, as James Joyce did later on.

To make matters still more complicated, many of the thinkers who belonged to the tradition Blake seems to have drawn on, including some who are most likely to have influenced him, were in the habit of using certain phrases from, for instance, scripture, as slogans; catchphrases, with a meaning additional to the purely biblical one. Examples are the 'Covering Cherub' from Ezekiel, into which a cabalistic significance could be read, and the 'Ever-Lasting Gospel' from the Apocalypse which became the watchword of those religious radicals who followed on from the Medieval Joachimite movement. This last reappeared as the title of a book by Paul Seigvolk, translated into English in 1753 and influential among the disciples of William Law. The truth is that all these people spoke a common language which has its own associations. (The 'Ever-Lasting Gospel' is an expression for a teaching held to usher in the overthrow of the Church and State in its present form.) And it is necessary first to learn this language and to catch its special nuances before Blake's full message becomes apparent.

At the same time I would not suggest that Blake was inevitably informed on the works, or even the names, of all the figures I have surveyed in this study. Since this language was common to them all one cannot be sure which particular author Blake was influenced by, or whether he was not drawing on several, or upon some source not named here at all. No one can say what really happened in the past, as all critics ought occasionally to remember. These people simply used the same symbolism, they had a similar cosmic vision, and an understanding of them helps towards an understanding of Blake, and of the tradition as a whole. What I am personally convinced of is that the imagery present in Blake's poetry and art cannot be accounted for except on the understanding of heavy borrowing on his part. Coincidences, independent parallelisms and the supposition of great minds thinking alike simply will not explain what is there.

But while all this is borne in mind one also has to realize Blake's intense consciousness of the political scene around him, the sensitivity to contemporary events that has been ably demonstrated by David Erdman. Likewise his feelings as an artist, jealous for the dignity of his vocation, and for his integrity as a craftsman; one whose livelihood had been threatened by the industrial revolution and the consequences of the wars with France. His deep debt to the Bible, in the purely straightforward sense of plot and character, apart from any special meaning placed upon it, must never be forgotten. And the extraordinary prominence of the Atlantis legend in the eighteenth century, a preoccupation of Voltaire's for instance, the cult of Celtic and Scandinavian mythology, especially the resurrection of the Druids in full panoply, must be considered too. The late eighteenth century saw the beginning of archeology proper and the beginning of the serious study of Indian and further Eastern languages and religious philosophy in this country. Blake knew Sir Charles Wilkins's translation of the *Bhagavadgita* for he painted him as the subject of a lost drawing, *The Bramins*. And he was well versed even in the lesser English poets, both of his own time and earlier, apart from his studies of the classics, and later of Dante. None of this can safely be overlooked. Then, again, the picture I have given of the traditional symbolism coming down from the Renaissance is naturally a very partial one; merely a sidelight on an enormous subject. It is necessary to get all this in proportion before sensible judgments on Blake's sources can be passed.

Above all it is important to form a balanced estimate of the eighteenth century, the age which was formative to Blake. At first glance the polite Regency world described in Jane Austen's novels could not seem more remote from the fantastic universe of William Blake. But that society was only a single aspect of life in Regency England. There was also the world of the Radical thinkers, of Tom Paine, Joseph Priestley and William Godwin. There was the entire world of the Methodist revival. And there was the world of serious minded men and women whose interests really extended back beyond the Augustan age, into the atmosphere of the seventeenth century, who, like the revivalists, realized, as William Law had done, the condition of the Church of England.

> We live starving in the coldness and deadness of a formal, historical, hearsay religion.

We can get glimpses of what was stirring in that age by looking at a letter from a figure not without significance in Blake's story, the Rev Jacob Duché, who later became chaplain to the Female Orphan Asylum at Lambeth and at whose house the early followers of Swedenborg were accustomed to meet. This letter belongs to a time when Duché was still in America – for he only took up his London appointment when forced to flee from the displeasure of George Washington. But he is already deeply concerned by the shallow spirituality of the Anglican Church of the day and has already encountered the enlivening influence of William Law, that great Non-Juror whose influence permeated the later eighteenth century to a degree which has not yet been guessed at. The experience described in Duché's letter we shall see repeated over and over again. Here is the letter itself.

Mr. Duché to Mr. Paine

Philadelphia Dec. 18th. 1767

My dear Sir,

I thank you sincerely for your kind and affection^e letter. I had allmost given over any expectation of the favour, but was determined to venture one letter more to extort, if possible an answer from you. Since I had the pleasure of reading your Kempis, your discourses & excellent answer to Warburton, I determined to push as far as modesty would permit, for a correspondence with you. Your letter, therefore was in every respect favourable to my wishes; and I flatter myself that I shall be indulgenced with a continuance of your favors. My heart has for some years been deeply sensible of a fallen state & I long groaned for deliverance from the bondage of my Earthly Life. I saw clearly that Physical & Moral Evil were predominant in the present state of things, and that the whole human race were involved in a situation which I could not reconcile, with the Wisdom, Goodness & Justice of God in creating them. The Christian Religion seemed to me covered with darkness & difficulty, I read most of the deistical writers, and most of the answers to them. I was sometimes a deist & sometimes a Christian. I never could understand the doctrine of the Trinity, & had an irreconciliable aversion to the Systematical Notion of atonement & satisfaction. A wrathfull God whose anger could only be appeased by the blood of His own Son pour'd out in behalf of Sinners allways appear'd to me next to blasphemous. And I often thought that the Omon [Amon?] of Egypt was a better deity than such a one, and yet I could meet with no Christian writer, who did not make this monstrous Tenet the very basis of his whole system. Providence at length brought me acquainted with Mr Law's writings; and here the grand desideratum was found. His address to the clergy was the first of his books that fell into my hands. I took it up with much prejudice in my mind against the author, whom I had always heard spoken of as an Enthusiast. But I had not read half the Pamphlet before my heart was visited with such sensations as I never felt before. My mind which had hitherto been unsettled, dark, doubting, & yet anxious to find the Truth, became serene calm & sweetly composed. I seemed as if I had got into another World, with a new set of objects a new set of Ideas, notions & sensibilities. I was happy beyond expression. I had found My God. I had found my Redeemer, I had found the Origin & source of my disorder, & the only means of consolation & a perfect cure. Since this blessed period all my doubts & difficultys have left me. I see plainly that there is no other Road to Heaven, but that which was trod by Jesus Christ himself, the same process must every Individual of our fallen race pass thro' before we can ascend with him to the Heaven of Heaven's – A painfull process 'tis True, – self denial, mortification, total contempt of the World, and death of the outward Life, are the only method by which we are to be divested of our fallen, and clothed with, our redeemed Life. The purifying fire, light & spirit of Heaven, must consume the Animal

Nature and change it into a cloud of Glory, a white robe & a house not built with hands. This new body can only be imparted to us, by an emanation from the heavenly flesh and blood of Jesus and thus alone it is that he atones & satisfies & appeases a wrath in us and not in the Everblessed God of Love. –

I have taken the liberty to lay my sentiments in this short confused manner before you, that you might see whether they correspond with your own, & how far the mystical writers have contributed to satisfy my mind, by directing me to a right pursuit of Truth. I had all the advantages of a liberal education, that this Country and England together can afford, having begun my studies at the College in this city & finished them in the usual way at Clare Hall in the University of Cambridge. I was allways dissatisfied with the Philosophy of our Schools, and the Metaphysic's tho' a favorite study appeared to me quite superficial in the way they are commonly taught. I now see in what points they fail'd, and how far short they stopped in their enquiries after Truth. They had no ground & bottom to stand upon, and in Metaphysics as well as divinity they greatly erred in the very first setting off. – For what true Philosophy or sound divinity could be expected from two such senseless & absurd Opinions, as are universally maintained in all the modern systems. Viz. a world created out of nothing and a wrathfull God. But I will say no more.

A copy of Duché's letter has been preserved in the correspondence of a Dublin artist, contemporary with Blake, Henry Brooke, who was himself greatly drawn to William Law's doctrines and who kept in touch with other like minded men and women wherever he could manage to discover them. All his correspondents were in revolt against the deadness of religion in their own day. They either had known Law personally, or come upon his writings after his death with relief and amazement. They persevered in studying those authors who had been Law's inspiration, especially the mystical writers and in particular Jacob Boehme. Some turned towards Jewish mysticism and others became Swedenborgians. All showed a keen interest in visionary experience and, above all, a respect for the prophetic faculty close to Blake's own. Some of these people were clearly very learned, although they were seldom in anything but rather humble circumstances. So that it is scarcely surprising to find that recent Blake scholarship has shown how he, too, was quite uncommonly well read. This was understood in his own lifetime. His young friend Frederick Tatham was hardly exaggerating when he maintained of Blake,

> His mental acquirements were incredible; he had read almost everything in whatsoever language, which language he always taught himself. . . . It is a remarkable fact that among the volumes bequeathed to the author of this sketch, the most thumbed from use are his Bible and those books in other languages.

Serious students of Blake have understood this for many years. Professor Foster Damon's early study showed how much Blake was indebted to his predecessors, how Neo-Platonic was his bent of mind. But in spite of the massive work of such commentators as Northrop Frye and Kathleen Raine, the extent of Blake's knowledge, the fulness of his mental equipment is still not absolutely realized. For many he is still, as T. S. Eliot put it, 'a wild pet for the supercultivated'. And William Blake, whom a just critic must rightly call a 'mental prince', is sometimes thought of as a simple, almost unlettered man, practically uneducated and without contact with the formative tradition of European culture. He is therefore credited with an originality, or rather a kind of originality, which in fact he did not possess. The truth is exactly the opposite. Blake's mind was amazingly receptive and indeed received a flood of impressions which can be traced in his own creations and which he drew from his very wide and painstaking study of literature and art. True, Blake may be said to have suffered from the defects of the self educated; the haphazardness, the singularity. But he was very far from being uneducated. (Samuel Palmer wrote of his linguistic prowess, 'W.B. *was* mad about languages.') Though, in his reading at any rate, he was no one's pupil, his freshness and force partly spring from this fact. In addition, the effects of drawing upon a tradition, of knowing a particular language of thought, have continually to be recalled. Once a certain currency is established, a vast fund of information on the part of those using the tradition is scarcely needed. An imaginative grasp is all that is absolutely essential. One has only to think of the thousands of painters who have used religious symbolism without necessarily being profound theologians; of the way science fiction writers have actually anticipated, through sheer power of vision, new discoveries whose technical details they could not have understood. Artists and poets have always been able to work with material in this way.

In any study of William Blake's poetry and art, however, there are other problems than those springing from the obscurity and depth of the sources he drew upon. Even taking the symbolism he used as both subtle and piercing, used for the exploration of mental regions almost beyond the scope of human intellect, the matter is still more personal than that, a question of emotion, not simply thought. Blake's very strength and honesty turn men away from his work. It demands too much. But those who have responded to that demand come through with an exhilaration which springs from facing the bitter truth. Did Blake in his turn learn from others who had passed through the same ordeal? I think the answer is, yes. To trace out this learning we must ourselves voyage into many strange regions of the mind. And these, though curious, have their own value. The laws that govern them are far from irrational and they provide us with clues to the hidden places of the soul. If there is obscurity perhaps this comes from the attempt to reach the unfathomable, to penetrate the secrets of the spirit, to measure divinity itself; an attempt doomed to failure but not less valiant for that. The dark world of Jacob Boehme, for example, is not entirely an unholy place. Out of that darkness comes treasure. The wise men of the East, in their turn, brought precious gifts.

CHAPTER I

Traditional Symbolism in the Renaissance

*

The key to William Blake's 'mythological labyrinth', as to much else that is rich and strange in our civilization, is, I have suggested, to be found in a conception at the heart of Renaissance thought; the idea that an all embracing truth might be discovered in the depths of antiquity which was restated by the Christian faith, but had always existed. To appreciate, for instance, Blake's symbolic values it is necessary to embark upon a voyage of discovery, a journey back in time. To say that at the time of the Renaissance men became intoxicated with their rediscovered Classical Heritage may be a commonplace. The process of rediscovery had been going on for such a long time that the dividing line between the Medieval period and the Renaissance proper can scarcely be traced. The one shades off into the other. But at the same time there seems to have been a peak of enthusiasm at the end of the fifteenth and beginning of the sixteenth centuries. The results of this excitement spread from Italy to France, Germany and the Low Countries, and England in particular during the sixteenth and early seventeenth centuries. They affected the whole of life: Theology, Politics, all the Arts, and they created the beginnings of modern Science.

There were two sides to this intense interest in the Greek and Latin classics. One was a passion for perfection of form. Linguists and grammarians longed to be able to write Latin prose in the style of Caesar or Cicero. Poets experimented with metre and verse form. Artists explored the possibilities of perspective and with doctors investigated anatomy. Politicians wished to discover the rules of government and soldiers read

Caesar's commentaries to learn strategy. Musicians turned to the Universal Harmony which was supposed to underlie creation and to be mirrored also by Architecture and Poetry. At the courts the first ballets visibly demonstrated this cosmic order. But there was another side which concerns us more nearly and this was connected with Theology.

The chief attraction of the salvaged Greek and Latin texts to many minds lay in those ideas contained in them that could be made to reinforce the truths of Christian doctrine. These foreshadowed or confirmed the witness of Scripture, and proved that God had never completely deserted the human race. The philosophy of Plato particularly lent itself to this pattern. In his teachings, as in those of his precursor Pythagoras, could be found a belief in the Immortality of the Soul and in another, greater, world, that this one shadows forth, a conception of the harmony of creation that seemed to the men of the Renaissance to be very Christian. So they turned to a whole literature with enthusiasm; a literature composed of the works of Plato himself, of those of earlier authors supposed to have influenced him, particularly the works ascribed to 'Orpheus', to the Neo-Platonist writers, to the writings attributed to the mysterious figure 'Hermes Trismegistus' and to what were known as the 'Sibylline oracles'.[1] The greater artistry of Homer, Virgil or Cicero was less important to these minds than this type of mystical speculation, partly pre-Christian, partly post-Christian.

One firm belief persisted. The Greeks and Romans were merely intermediaries. Wisdom is from the East. The Greeks received this Wisdom from Egypt or from Babylonia, Persia or

[1] A full treatment of this theme is given by D. P. Walker in his article 'The *Prisca Theologia* in France', *Journal of the Warburg and Courtauld Institutes*, Vol. XVII, 1954, pp. 204 ff. As Mr Walker explains (see also 'Orpheus the Theologian', *Journal of the Warburg and Courtauld Institutes*, Vol. XVI, 1953, pp. 204 ff.), the mysterious Orpheus, to whom the Orphic hymns and fragments were attributed, was regarded as a philosopher more ancient than Pythagoras and Hermes Trismegistus was identified with the Egyptian God-King Thoth.

further east. Originally it may have come from the Jews, or to the Jews, perhaps from the Egyptians through Moses. Whatever was the case, this Wisdom was soon corrupted by shallow subtlety of the Greek mind or the crass materialism of the Roman. It degenerated into an anthropomorphic mythology, an unwanted polytheism, which could make the classical authors misleading. It is surprising how often this attitude appears throughout the Renaissance, receiving, perhaps, its definitive form in the words Milton put on to the lips of Christ in *Paradise Regained,* Book IV.

> . . . All our Law and Story strewed
> With hymns, our Psalms with artful terms inscribed,
> Our Hebrew songs and harps, in Babylon . . . declare
> That rather Greece from us their arts derived –
> Ill imitated while they loudest sing
> The vices of their dieties and their own . . .

This suspicion of Greek and Roman thought is, indeed, always united with a deep respect for Hebrew learning, and the important part played by Hebrew studies in the development of the Renaissance outlook. The respect for Holy Writ traditional from Medieval times was reinforced by the Reformation. And this respect was extended to the Hebrew language itself; the sacred tongue, language of God's own choice. Beyond the text of the Bible this was likewise applied to Jewish commentaries and interpretations of the Old Testament. The Rabbis were felt to have treasured a store of learning, handed down from the time of Moses himself, and part of this was not only a particularly pure source of Wisdom but was, obscurely, a tremendous source of power too. There are, accordingly, continual references to the word 'Kabalah' – a word which means 'tradition', something received, and which can be spelt in a number of ways; 'Kabbalah', 'Quabalah', 'Cabbala', for instance. And these allusions are intermingled with appeals to classical authorities. The traditional Jewish doctrine on the 'hidden meaning' of the Bible which had been 'received' from one generation to another, was often found to harmonize very neatly with Neo-Platonic speculation and both are tinged with a philosophical Idealism which can sometimes hardly be distinguished from Gnosticism.

In general the name Kabalah covers a literature which emerged during the Middle Ages, mostly written in a peculiar Aramaic dialect and consisting of commentaries upon the Old Testament; with the famous *Zohar* or *Book of Splendour*, making its appearance in thirteenth century Spain, at its centre. The word itself began to be used about the eleventh century and before the *Zohar* there were two books definitely belonging to the system. The *Sepher Yetzirah*, or *Book of Creation*, attributed traditionally to Abraham, is usually dated between the third and sixth centuries, while the *Bahir* belongs to the twelfth century. As far back as the *Ezra Apocalypse*, a book included in the Old Testament Apocrypha usually bound up with the Authorized Version in old Bibles, the idea of a secret revelation concealed for the few, appears. Chapter fourteen shows the prophet Ezra giving instructions that the twenty-four books of the Biblical canon may be proclaimed to all, but announcing that there are seventy other books, which must be hidden; 'deliver them only to such as be wise'. The *Book of Enoch*, too, has a cosmogony using many images which later reappear in the *Zohar*. Then we find Philo reporting that the Essenes had a two-fold philosophy which they guarded; 'the contemplation of God's being and the origin of the universe'. The Jewish *Book of Jubilees* also bears traces of the system which was developed in the *Zohar* much later. The chief aim of the tradition as it developed was, indeed, to throw light on the mystery of why God chose to create the world, why He awakened from a kind of divine repose to creative activity, and how the gap can be bridged between a completely transcendent Godhead and a finite universe. It seems to have arisen from an obscure dissatisfaction with the type of monotheism presented by the official Jewish religion to the ordinary believer, and a wish, at the same time, to avoid a descent into pagan polytheism.

There is no doubt that the orthodox Jewish position was in

some ways compromised by the system, and for this reason the Kabalah always had to withstand a certain amount of hostility; an opposition which increased greatly in the eighteenth century and later. The work of Professor Scholem, who now holds the chair of Jewish Mysticism at the Hebrew University in Jerusalem, and of his fellow scholars, has brought about a much more serious understanding of the tradition within Jewish circles than existed for several generations. Professor Scholem has shown that in Talmudic times the cult of the 'Ma'aseh Bereshit', the history of Creation, and the 'Ma'aseh Merkabah', the history of the Divine Throne, was very prominent – the one based on Genesis and the other on Ezekiel's vision. In his *Major Trends in Jewish Mysticism* he has brilliantly traced out how from the contacts of this movement with Gnosticism, taking place in the early centuries of the Christian era, the Kabalah proper developed. It remained what it had originally been for the Essenes, a mystical doctrine concerning God and his relation to the universe, to be revealed only to those minds fit to receive it. Professor Scholem gives this way of thinking the name of 'theosophy', but is careful to define his use of the expression.

> By theosophy I mean that which was generally meant before the term became a label for a modern pseudo-religion, i.e. *theosophy* signifies a mystical doctrine, or school of thought, which purports to perceive and describe the mysterious workings of the Divinity. . . . Theosophy postulates a kind of divine emanation whereby God, abandoning his self-contained repose, awakens to mysterious life. . . . Theosophists in this sense were Jacob Boehme and William Blake . . .[1]

Together with an immense respect for Jewish tradition went a curiosity over and interest in other Eastern religions. They may have been Pagan but after all Wisdom is from the East. The idea of some original revelation which survived in that part of the world was strong. Although it was not easy for the men of the Renaissance to gain full or accurate knowledge of

[1] G. Scholem, *Major Trends in Jewish Mysticism*, p. 206.

Hinduism, Buddhism or Persian religion they treasured all the information which came down to them through Classical sources or from travellers. The Indian 'Brachman' or 'Gymnosophist' was a venerable figure in their estimation, to be ranked with the Persian mage, the Egyptian sage, or the disciples of Pythagoras. Paragraphs citing these august personages appear regularly in the literature of the time, whenever support is needed for some piece of Neo-Platonic or Cabalistic doctrine. And local patriotism was strong enough to bring about the introduction of Western sages into the list; the Druids being very useful for this purpose. Indeed since the time of Annius of Viterbo, at the end of the Middle Ages,[1] the prestige of the Druids had been rising and they were particularly popular with people like the French who could claim descent from them. Above all, beneath the laudable curiosity about earlier religions and Eastern beliefs can be discerned a serious attempt to find the element of truth basic to all creeds; in fact a genuine syncretism.

One of the first examples of these lists of authorities which became so typical of this movement of thought is to be found in the presentation of the *Corpus Hermeticum* in Marsilio Ficino's translation of 1463, where Ficino traces the doctrines of Hermes Trismegistus through Orpheus, Aglaophamus, Pythagoras and Philolaus down to Plato himself. Ficino, of course, accepted Trismegistus as a real person and his enthusiasm for this type of literature gained him the support of Cosimo de Medici who established him in a villa at Careggi near Florence, in 1462, giving him access to his important

---

[1] The Dominican friar, Giovanni Nanni da Viterbo, flourished from 1432–1502, and was much esteemed by the Popes Sixtus IV and Alexander VI. Two books of his appeared in 1498, one in Rome and the other in Venice, supposed to be based on fragments left by Berosus, a Chaldean scholar of Alexander the Great's time, and Monetho, an Egyptian historian contemporary with him. They are entitled: *Commentaria fratris Joannis Annii Viterbensis . . . super opera diversorum auctorum de Antiquitatibus loquentium*, and *Autores Vetutissimi Nuper in Lucem editi*. They were widely popular but soon began to be challenged by scholars.

collection of manuscripts in Greek.[1] But the real inspiration of Cosimo de Medici's passion for Neo-Platonic and Hermetic literature was his earlier encounter with that strange character who is known by the name of 'Pletho'. Georgius Gemistus, from Mistra, the site of ancient Sparta, was in the train of the Emperor John Palaeologus when the latter came over to Italy for the general council of 1439. The meetings were transferred from Ferarra to Florence by Pope Eugenius IV. In Florence the self styled 'Pletho' (from 'Plethon', signifying 'the full'), made a great impact. Cardinal Bessarion himself became his pupil and we have it on the evidence of Ficino that the lectures Pletho gave in Florence determined Cosimo de Medici to found his Platonic academy.

The truth about Pletho's own beliefs is a matter of speculation. On one hand it has been pointed out that it is unlikely a man known to hold unorthodox views would have been chosen to negotiate with the Latin church on such crucial points as the procession of the Holy Spirit; for on this question Pletho's contribution to the council was important.[2] On the other, the reports made on Pletho's championship of metempschychosis and polygamy, by his opponent Georgios Scholarios, known as 'Gennadios', the Patriarch of Constantinople, come from a fair critic, 'a reasonable and even respectful one', as Nesca Robb remarks in her *Neoplatonism of the Italian Renaissance*.[3] Moreover she is justified in saying that an examination of Pletho's book, translated into French and published in Paris under the title *Traité des Lois* in 1858, leaves a feeling of suspicion that Pletho was very far from being an orthodox Christian.[4] It seems

---

[1] Ficino's career has been well sketched out in P. O. Kristeller's *Philosophy of Marsilio Ficino*, New York, 1943, and in the introduction to Sears Reynolds Jayne's edition of Ficino's commentary on the *Symposium* of Plato, University of Missouri Studies, Vol. XIX, 1944, pp. 13 ff.

[2] For instance G. Ruggiero, 'Storia della Filosofia': *Rinascimento e Riforma*, Laterza Baii, Vol. I, p. 117.

[3] Nesca Robb, *Neoplatonism of the Italian Renaissance*, p. 47.

[4] *Traité des Lois*, Paris, 1858. Edited by C. Alexander, with Greek text and Latin translation.

probable that Pletho had developed syncretic ideas which led him to conceive of a new religion based on Greek mythology seen through Neo-Platonic eyes. What is certain is that in his youth he had spent some time at the Moslem centre of learning at Brusa, where he absorbed Zoroastrian doctrines from a teacher of Jewish origin, Elisseios. (Pletho's book on Zoroaster appeared in Paris in 1538.) Also that respect for him in Italy remained very great. Although Pletho had been buried at Mistra after his death there in 1450, five years later his bones were translated to the church of S. Francesco at Rimini by Sigismonde Pandolfo Malatesta, who had just had the church built for him by Leon Alberti.

At any rate it is true that indirectly the impetus for the establishment of the Medician Platonic Academy came from Georgius Gemistus, known as Pletho, and it was from him that Ficino took the way of thinking expressed in his *Corpus Hermeticum*. The Renaissance habit of linking together such names as Zoroaster, Hermes Trismegistus, Orpheus and Pythagoras here clearly has its origin, and as time went on the names of Moses, the Areopagite, St Augustine and the Alexandrian Neo-platonists were added to the list. But one must join with the influences coming in from the Byzantine East those surviving from the Platonic tradition which had been nurtured all through the Middle Ages, at the great Abbey of St Victor, for instance, and which had culminated in the speculative daring of the brilliant German Cardinal, Nicolas of Cusa, who taught the doctrine of the coincidence of opposites and explored the workings of the intuitive faculty.[1] In the same way the true nature of the Florentine Academy has to be understood. Though the imposing style of 'Academy' is used, it was in fact a very loose association of scholars working under the auspices of the Medici family, inspired by Ficino's enthusiasm. Lectures and discussions were held at the Careggi villa centring on Plato's works and those of Plotinus, and such men as

[1] Nicolas of Cusa (Nicolaus Khrypffes), *Prohemium*, Strasbourg 1490.

Alamano Donati, Francesco da Diaceto, Lorenzo de Medici and Cristoforo Landino belonged to the circle. Although Ficino certainly gave many public lectures in Florence, he was never a teacher at the University there. But at the same time his influence was far wider than most university lecturers ever attain. Paul Kristeller, in his masterly study of Ficinian Neo-Platonism, has shown how Ficino's correspondence guided scholars, not only in Rome and Venice, but in Germany, France, Belgium, Poland and Hungary.[1] After his death his ideas were used by philosophers like Patrizi, Bruno and Campanella, while the French Protestant thinker Lefèvre d'Etaples and the physician-philosopher Symphorien Champier were both affected by them. The same is true of Marguerite de Navarre and her circle, while Dean Colet in England clearly betrays the traces of the Ficinian Platonism in his thought which was to form an element of so much English poetry from the time of Spenser onwards.

A particularly charming example of Ficino's own spirit is to be found in his version of Plato's *Symposium*, based on an actual renewal of Socrates' banquet with his disciples taking place at the suggestion of Lorenzo de Medici on the 7th November, traditionally Plato's birthday. Dissertations on the speeches made by Socrates' original guests were delivered by appropriate characters from among Ficino's disciples. Pausanias' speech, for example, was designed to be delivered by Antonio degli Agli, bishop of Fiesole, as the leading theologian present. Ficino himself who had studied medicine as well as philosophy, modelling himself on his father, a physician named Diotifeci, was to figure as the physician Erismachus. While Thomas Benzi took the part of Socrates, Christopher Landino the role of Aristophanes in his capacity as poet, and so on. When the time appointed for the commemorative feast arrived the bishop and doctor were obliged to hand over to substitutes, being called away on their cure of souls and bodies.

---

[1] P. O. Kristeller, *Philosophy of Marsilio Ficino*, p. 19.

But with that variation, the banquet, we are told, went forward as planned.[1]

Yet the truth is that Ficino's temperament was a strange one and he obviously faced many difficulties in life. We are told by his biographer Corsi that Ficino's appearance was most unattractive, his shoulders being slightly humped, his arms and hands long and dangling, with a bright red face and a bad lisp in his speech. For someone whose thought was almost totally concerned with love, his own relationships were on the whole distant, possibly because of an extreme sensibility. It has been suggested that his enthusiasm for a career in Platonist scholarship, once Cosimo de Medici invited him to take it up, is explained by his personal characteristics. In his introduction to Ficino's commentary on the *Symposium*, Sears Reynolds Jayne remarks that they may

> amply explain why he was willing, indeed eager, to sacrifice his whole life to a single work, to become, as it were, a translating machine, maintained and supplied with raw materials by the Medici family.[2]

However this may be, it is true that Ficino admitted himself inclined to melancholy, and of a 'Saturnian' disposition. As his life drew on he grew more and more preoccupied with the problems of reconciling Platonic philosophy with Christian orthodoxy, eventually taking priestly orders himself and being made a canon of the cathedral of Florence in 1487. What always remained the characteristic of Ficino's thought, however, and of his followers (especially that of the brilliant young scholar Pico della Mirandola), was the syncretic ideal. Professor Wind in his enlightening study, *Pagan Mysteries in the Renaissance*, has expressed very accurately this ideal.

> . . . if the nature of the pagan gods were understood in the mystical sense of the Orphic Platonists, and the nature of the Mosaic Law in the hidden sense of the Cabbala, and if the nature

[1] Marsilio Ficino, *Sopra L'Amore*, Florence 1594.

[2] Sears Reynolds Jayne, *Marsilio Ficino's Commentary on Plato's Symposium*. Text with Translation and Introduction.

of Christian Grace were unfolded in the fulness of the secrets which Saint Paul had revealed to Dionysius the Areopagite, it would be found that these theologies differed not at all in substance but only in name. A philosophy of tolerance was accordingly worked out in the form of a hidden concordance which seemed to confirm the statement of St Augustine: 'The thing itself, which is now called the Christian religion, was with the ancients, and it was with the human race from its beginnings to the time when Christ appeared in the flesh: from when on the true religion, which already existed, began to be called Christian.' [1]

And not only does Professor Wind demonstrate the hold this belief had on the minds of the Florentine Platonists and those scholars influenced by them, but he has most convincingly shown how the great artists of the day caught the same fervour and made it the moving spirit of their painting, sculpture and architectural designs. They, too, wished to do honour to the 'True Religion'. This truth, so it was believed, Plato, the Moses of the Gentiles, possessed, and it was to be found among the Indian Brahmins, the Egyptian Hierophants, as well as uttered by those prophetesses, the Sibyls, and by the wise men of the West, the Druids; whilst all the time it had flourished among God's own people, the Jews, and with them not so much in their written law as in their mystical tradition. Such was the theory, and it accounts for the presence of the Sibylline figures in the Sistine chapel, mingled with scriptural personages, for the popularity of that gruesome episode, the flaying of Marsyas, an important element in the cult of Dionysius, which Raphael treated in his *Apollo and Marsyas* and Michelangelo presents through his representation of St Bartholomew, the 'flayed apostle' in his *Last Judgment* (incidentally a self-portrait), where the saint holds his own skin, the 'old man' that he has put off. And above all, this conception explains the inner meaning of the group of the Three Graces, constantly used by Renaissance artists.

In his study of Botticelli's *Primavera*, Professor Wind has given a striking example of the imagery of the Graces employed

[1] Edgar Wind, *Pagan Mysteries in the Rennaissance*, pp. 26–7.

to convey a special truth. As in all representations of the Graces, from the fresco at Pompeii, also reproduced in his book, down to the medals struck by Ficino, or Pico della Mirandola, one figure faces backwards, looking from time towards eternity. For Botticelli the three symbolize Giving, Receiving and Returning. It is Chastity that stands between Beauty and Joy, in tension with Pleasure, yet reconciled to Joy by Beauty. And the main theme of the painting celebrates the earthly Venus, a more matronly figure than the naked Heavenly Love revealed in the *Birth of Venus*. In fact the picture might be taken as a study in the processes of generation. With an almost Blakean touch a glowing, Spring-like figure is ushered in by Nymph and Zephyr as it were from the 'Northern Gate', whilst at the opposite side stands Mercury, or intellectual contemplation, touching the clouds with his wand. This masterpiece is only one example of the way in which Renaissance artists deliberately adopted classical imagery, not out of any worldly paganism, but in order to present profound spiritual truths. Botticelli, who had been a friend of the reformer Savanarola and is said to have shown him, with his disciples Domenico and Silvestro, embracing angels in the heavens at the bottom of his *Nativity* painting, had very serious preoccupations with such truths.

To Ficino the pattern of the Graces was particularly significant. He had developed a complex doctrine of divine love by which it traces a circle 'through the phases of Pulchritudo, Amor and Voluptas. The first of them issues from God as a kind of beacon, the second enters into the world which it moves to rapture, and the third returns to its maker in a state of joy'.[1] The Graces naturally made perfect symbols for this conception; and it was a conception soon challenged by Ficino's most brilliant young disciple, Pico della Mirandola who, under the influence of the main tradition of Neo-Platonic thought, favoured the 'Negative Way', the path of the mystic who adopted the name of Dionysius the Areopagite. As Pro-

[1] Edgar Wind, *op. cit.*, p. 50.

fessor Wind puts it, 'Pico suspected Ficino's optimism of a Narcissus-like Self-love through God'. He rejected Ficino's original symbolism of the Graces as Beauty, Love and Joy, substituting one where they represent, Beauty, Intellect and Will. According to this pattern Beauty is from the Heavenly world, and the powers of Intellect and Will turn towards her. But in the ultimate ecstasy Pico claimed the three would disappear into one. Ficino, on the other hand, maintained that 'union with the ultimate need not always entail extinction'. Here it is Ficino who is the more Christian. The very essence of Ficino's doctrine of Love is expressed, for instance, in his summary of Diotima's discussion with Socrates in his commentary on the *Symposium*.

> This, (we have supposed,) is what Diotima said to Socrates. But, my virtuous friend, we shall not only love God without limit as Diotima is depicted as commanding, but God alone. For as the eyes are to the sun, so the mind is to God. But the eye seeks not only light before other things, but the light alone. If we love bodies, the Soul, or the Angelic Mind, we do not really love these, but God in them: the shadow of God in bodies, the likeness of God in the Soul, and the Image of God in the Angelic Mind. So in the present we shall love God in everything, so that in the future we may love everything in God, for so we set out from these as living beings to see God and everything in Him, and whoever in the present will devote himself with love completely to God, will finally recover himself in God. Certainly he will return to his own Idea through which he was created. . . . True man and the Idea of man are one and the same; therefore each of us separated from God on earth is not a true man since he is seperated from the Form and Idea of himself. To this Idea divine love and piety will lead us, although we are here divided and mutilated.[1]

Here we see Ficino's attempts to unite the concept of the Platonic ladder of Being, and that of the Archetypal Ideas, with Christian values and symbols. He holds by the inherent value of God's creatures as they will ultimately be rediscovered in God

[1] Ficino's Commentary on Plato's *Symposium*, translated by Sears Reynold Jayne, Chapter XIX.

even by the soul who has uncompromisingly renounced them.

And Pico's tendencies towards Eastern mysticism as against Christian spirituality were not long in getting him into trouble. When, in 1486, he published his *Nine Hundred Conclusions*, the famous series of propositions partly Neo-Platonic, partly Cabalistic, he was immediately accused of heresy, in thirteen of them. They were the result of the enterprise he had launched into during his time at the University of Paris. Fired with the Ficinian syncretic ideal, he set about utilizing his knowledge of Hebrew and Greek to work out a common doctrine within the deepest and most mystical teachings of Christianity, Judaism and Islam. He met the accusation of heresy with his *Apologia*, confidently dedicating it to Lorenzo de Medici. All his judges, however, pronounced against him, with the exception of the former rector of the university of Paris, Jean Cordier, and an appeal to the Pope was necessary. This, indeed, was not successful until there had been a change of Popes, but in the meantime Pico acquired a new defender.

A Franciscan Minorite Friar, who used the imposing style of 'Archangelus of Burgonovo', produced a treatise with a still more imposing title: *Conclusiones Cabalisticae Numero LXXI Secundum Opinionem Propriam Ipsius Mirandulae, Ex Ipsis Hebreorum sapientium fundamentis Christianam religionem maxime confirmantes*. This work was intended to show how much the Jewish tradition confirms the Christian. Another one, an *Apologia*, was directed against Pico's opponent, Pedro Garcia, bishop of Ussel. Archangelus mentions twenty-one books of his. Four of these were later published and the manuscripts of the rest are scattered through various European libraries. The *Conclusiones Cabalisticae* and the *Apologia* were published in 1564 and 1600 respectively. The *Cabalistarum Selectiora* appeared in Ferrara in 1557, and so did a particularly interesting work, a treatise on the name of Jesus, *Dechiaratione Sopra Il Nome Di Giesu, Secondo Gli Hebrei Cabalisti, Greci, Caldei, Persi &c Latini*, with a dedication '*Alla molto Illustre Signora Taddea Malaspina*'. This consists of dialogues between Archangelus himself,

'F.A.', Signora Taddea, 'S.T.', and her young daughter Giulia, 'S.G'. and witnesses to the surprising directions in which this thought had currency at the time. Archangelus was himself the brother of the much better known Vicar of the Franciscan order, Aloysius Puteus, or Pozzo, and belonged to the Franciscan house at Borgo Nuovo.[1] For his considerable knowledge of Kabalah, Archangelus acknowledges his debt to his revered master and fellow Franciscan Francesco Giorgio, an outstanding figure who had derived much of his own thought from Ficino and Pico, and deserves more attention than he has yet received.

The main impact of Giorgio's thought upon the age came through his monumental work, the *De Harmonia Mundi*, which did not appear until 1525, with a dedication to Pope Clement VII. This depended for its inspiration upon a mixture of Cabalistic speculation and Neo-Platonic theories of the harmony of the universe. Such theories have their basis in what Koestler has described as,

> The Pythagorean discovery that the pitch of a note depends on the length of the string which produces it, and that concordant intervals in the scale are produced by simple numerical ratios (2 : 1 octave, 3 : 2 fifth, 4 : 3 fourth etc.) . . .[2]

And Koestler is right in saying that this discovery marks 'the first step towards the mathematization of human experience – and therefore the beginning of Science'. It is this concept of musical progression that is outlined in detail within 'Cantici Primi, Tonus Quintus' of the *De Harmonia Mundi*. (Giorgio even gave his book musical sub-titles.) A simple triangular figure here illustrates the progression from 1–27.

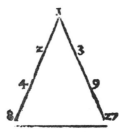

Fig. 1. *Triangle illustrating the progression from 1–27 in Giorgio's 'Musical Philosophy'.*

[1] Leon Blau, *The Christian Interpretation of the Cabala in the Renaissance*, Appendix C.
[2] Arthur Koestler, *The Sleepwalkers*, p. 28.

This is followed by a more complicated diagram with figures progressing up to the number 162.

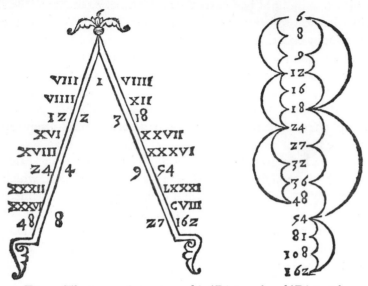

Fig. 2. *The progression expressed in 'Diapason' and 'Diapente'.*

Then follow others based on the speculations of Timoethus, Pythagoras, Ptolemy, Plato and Proclus, which, in the pattern of dividers on the one hand and elaborately enclosed brackets on the other, reach up to the figure 10368.[1]

Again Koestler has admirably expressed the way that this attitude to the universe resulted in the idea of 'the music of the spheres'.

> . . . the sun, moon and planets revolve in concentric circles, each fastened to a sphere or wheel. The swift revolution of each of these bodies causes a swish, or musical hum, in the air. Evidently each planet will hum on a different pitch, depending on the ratios of their respective orbits – just as the tone of a string depends on its length. Thus the orbits in which the planets move form a kind of huge lyre whose strings are curved into circles.[2]

[1] Francesco Giorgio, *De Harmonia Mundi*, Venice, 1536, gathering L. v.–viii.

[2] Arthur Koestler, *The Sleepwalkers*, p. 31.

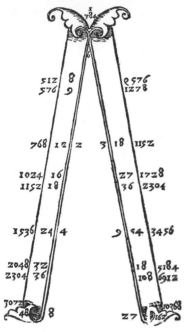

Fig. 3. *The progression, expanded to 10368, under the figure of a pair of dividers.*

Upon this lyre a vast scale was played. The musical interval between the earth and moon was supposed to be a tone; moon to Mercury, a semi-tone; Mercury to Venus, a semi-tone; Venus to Sun, a minor third; Sun to Mars, a tone; Mars to Jupiter, a semi-tone; Jupiter to Saturn, a semi-tone; Saturn to the sphere of the fixed stars, a minor third. Thus, the Pythagorean scale, using, of course, the old Ptolemaic conception of the universe, at any rate in the version Koestler quotes from Pliny, runs as follows: C, D, ♭E, G, A, ♭B, B, D. Again, Pythagoras's father, Mnesarchos, was a gem-engraver, and so Koestler points out how he early became familiar with the forms of the crystals: pyramid and double pyramid for quartz, hexagon for beryl, dodecahedron for garnet. It was certainly from Pythagoras that Plato took his use of the geometrical solids in the *Timaeus*, where four of the regular solids, pyramid, cube, octahedron and icosahedron, are identified with the elements earth, air, fire and water; while the fifth, most ethereal

31

element, the ether itself, is symbolized by the dodecahedron corresponding to the twelve signs of the Zodiac.[1]

But Giorgio was not simply concerned with abstract theoretical matters. He could apply his ideas in a strictly practical way. For instance, when an architectural dilemma had arisen over the plan for the new church attached to the Franciscan house to which Giorgio belonged, S. Francesco della Vigna at Venice, Giorgio was called in for consultation by Andrea Gritti, the Doge of Venice. Because of a controversy about the proportions of the church, which had been originally designed by Jacopo Sansovino, work on the building was at a standstill. The memorandum Giorgio submitted proving why the nave, for example, should be just twenty-seven paces long, three times nine, has been fully discussed by Rudolph Wittkower in an article on 'The Principles of Palladio's Architecture', which describes how the memorandum was placed before the painter Titian, the architect Serlio and the humanist Sansovino. Three, Giorgio explains, is the first real number because it, alone, has a beginning, middle and end. As a symbol of the Trinity it is divine.

The square and cube of 3, Giorgio goes on, contain the consonances of the universe as Plato has shown in the *Timaeus*; and neither Plato nor Aristotle, who knew the forces effective in nature, went beyond the number 27 in their analysis of the world. However, not these same numbers but their ratios are of importance and, that their ratios are to be regarded as binding the microcosm also, is evident from God's command to Moses to build the Tabernacle after the pattern of the world and Solomon's resolve to give the proportions of the Tabernacle to the Temple. Giorgio also expresses the suggested proportions of width to length of nave (9 : 27) in musical terms; it forms, as he says, a diapason and a diapente. A diapason is an octave and a diapente a fifth, 9 : 27 constitutes an octave and a diapente, a fifth if seen in the progression 9 : 18 : 27; for 9 : 18 = 1 : 2 an octave, and 18 : 27 = 2 : 3 = a fifth.[2]

[1] Plato, *Timaeus*, 55c.
[2] Rudolph Wittkower, *The Journal of the Warburg and Courtauld Institutes*, 1945, p. 69.

The kind of mentality such speculation reveals was one to which the theory of 'Man as the Measure of the Universe', put forward by the Roman authority on architecture, Vitruvius, was bound to be congenial. Giorgio quotes an exposition of what was called the 'Exempada', or system of proportions of the human body, which is evidently taken from Leon Battista Alberti's treatise *De Statua* – apparently in manuscript form, for the book was not published till 1568, when it came out in Italian.[1] This whole outlook is present in Leonardo da Vinci's Venice Academy manuscript with its famous drawing of a man, with countenance both fierce and grave, whose figure is in the formation of a Latin cross, superimposed upon one in the St Andrew's pattern.[2] Cornelius Agrippa's *De Occulta Philosophia* uses the same 'Exempada' in chapter 27, most likely in quotation from Giorgio, together with a series of illustrations of figures posed in a succession of positions; again including the Latin cross, and the St Andrew's. Likewise, this way of symbolic representation informs the influential treatise, *Divina Proportione*, by the Friar Luca Pacioli, the disciple of Piero della Francesca. The Italian painter Jacopo da Barbari, who painted a powerful portrait of Friar Luca, where he is shown tracing the figure of a pyramid, while a disciple looks on and a tetrahedron in crystal hangs beside them, was much indebted to Luca Pacioli in his turn.[3] Clearly the language of symbolism used by Giorgio in his *De Harmonia Mundi* had wide currency among this group of Renaissance artists and thinkers.

But Giorgio as a Hebrew scholar devoted much of his attention to the Kabalah and throughout the *De Harmonia Mundi* he makes continual play with the 'Mitatron', that ardent spirit, prince of all the angels, often identified with St

---

[1] Francesco Giorgio, *De Harmonia Mundi*, 'Toni Cantici Tertius' a.ii; Leon Battista Alberti, *De Statua*, Parigi 1651: see English translation by John Evelyn, *A Parallel of Antient Architecture*, London 1673, p. 65.

[2] Leonardo da Vinci, *Study in Human Proportions*, Accademia, Venice, Quaderni VI. MS. R 343.

[3] The painting is reproduced to illustrate an article, 'Le Portrait Humaniste', by Alain Jouffroy, in *Connaissance des Arts*, July, 1957.

*Fig. 4. Vitruvian figure used by Giorgio to illustrate
the 'Exempada'.*

Michael by the Christian cabalists, or even with the 'Soul of the
Messiah', who figures also in the Enoch literature. The whole
book is inspired by Giorgio's profound reverence for God as
the composer of the cosmic harmony and architect of the entire
universe. The human architect's role is to imitate the divine.
Exactly this sense of reverence animates, too, Giorgio's other
book, his scriptural commentary, *In Scripturam Sacram, et
Philosophos, tria millia Problemata*.[1] God is seen as the divine
architect, the great creator of Genesis, and this vision is supported by hundreds of references to the *Zohar*, that 'mystical
novel', as Professor Scholem has called it, and texts like the
early *Sepher Yetzirah* or *Book of Creation*; as well as to the
Sha'are Orah, the *Gates of Light*, the work of a Spanish Jew,
Joseph Gikatila. The *Zohar* is in the form of a *midrash*, or
exposition, of the weekly sections of the Torah, the Mosaic

[1] Francesco Giorgio, *Francisci Giorgio Minoritani, in Scripturam Sacram, et
Philosophos, tria millia Problemata*, Venice 1536, dedicated to Pope Paul III.

books of the Bible, used in the Jewish liturgy.[1] (Scattered through these readings are shorter and more cryptic treatises, often, like the *Idra Rabba*, or *Great Assembly*, the *Idra Zuta* or *Lesser Assembly* and the *Sepher di Tseniutha* the *Book of Conceal-ment*, obviously much older than the bulk of the book.) Giorgio has followed the general pattern of the *Zohar* – always cited with the utmost respect – in his own work. This begins with Genesis and proceeds on to a study of the Patriarchs, the history of the Jews from the time of Exodus onwards, the Law, and the 'Oracles of the Prophets'! He then continues with studies of the Gospels and of the Old Testament Wisdom literature, ending with miscellaneous matters. As the title includes the words 'et Philosophos', Giorgio freely cites Plato, Zoroaster, Proclus, Hermes Trismegistus and Origen, bring-ing in the Pagan sages and Neo-Platonic theologians according to the style set by Pletho and Ficino. A careful examination of this scriptural commentary leaves no doubt that Giorgio's grasp of the Jewish Kabalah was formidable. His references not only show a sound understanding of the Hebrew and Aramaic texts of the tradition, but they also betray a mental outlook coloured by its peculiar symbolism.

Of course Giorgio had long been notable for his knowledge of Jewish studies. The notorious Crook, Henry VIII's agent in Italy, when he was collecting evidence on the matter of the marriage with Katherine of Aragon, describes how,

> He got into the acquaintance of a Frier at *Venice, Franciscus Georgius*, who had lived 49 years in a Religious order, and was esteemed the most Learned man in the Republick, not only in the vulgar Learning, but in the Greek and Hebrew, and was so much accounted of by the Pope, that he called him the *Hammer of Hereticks*. . . . This Friar had a great opinion of the King: and having studied the case, wrote for the Kings cause, and en-deavoured to satisfie all the other Divines of the Republick, among whom he had much credit.[2]

[1] Ernst Muller, *History of Jewish Mysticism*, pp. 87–8.
[2] Gilbert Burnet, *History of the Reformation*, 1679–1715, Tom. I Book II. p. 88.

And the underlying assumptions that formed the basis of Giorgio's position, as well as his disciple Archangelus', have been well presented in Leon Blau's summary of the latter's teaching, which posited,

> ... two laws, one written, the other oral ... revealed to Moses. Thence the written law was given to the people; the oral law was handed down from generation to generation, transmitted through the seventy elders, the Prophets, and the Men of the Great Synagogue, until it reached the hands of Rabbi Jehuda ha-Nasi, who wrote down part of the tradition in the six books of the *Mishnah*. Meanwhile, however, the tradition had been known before Moses, and parts had been written in several books; one of them, *Sefer Yetzirah*, written by Abraham, has come down to us.[1]

One common-sense support to the concept of an unwritten law was the realization that it would hardly take the Almighty forty days to pass over to Moses the propositions contained on the tablets of the Law.[2] Far deeper wisdom must have been imparted to him during that time. The main text in which this wisdom was supposed to have been enshrined, and the one which left the clearest traces upon the Jewish liturgy itself, was of course, the *Zohar*. Professor Scholem has ascribed this work to the Spanish mystic, Moses de Leon. He was contemporary with Abraham Abulafia, the author of a body of writings which have been said to represent 'Prophetic Kabbalism'. But the *Zohar* is put in the mouth of the Mishnah teacher, Rabbi Simeon ben Yohai, who with his son Eleazar and various friends and disciples, are seen wandering round Palestine discussing the scriptures and life in general. The theosophic doctrine of the *Zohar* is based on the concept of the ten *Sephiroth*, spheres, or emanations, spreading out, or descending from the En Soph, the unknowable Godhead. These are arranged in three columns, or sometimes in circles. The left hand pillar, that of rigour, contains *Binah*, *Gevurah* and *Hod*; the

---

[1] Leon Blau, *The Christian Interpretation of the Cabala*, p. 26.
[2] Edgar Wind, *Pagan Mysteries in the Renaissance*, p. 25.

right hand pillar of mercy, *Hochmah, Hesed* and *Netsah*; while *Kether, Tifereth, Yesod* and *Malkhuth* form the middle pillar of mediation. As Scholem explains,

> They are called 'mystical crowns of the Holy King' notwithstanding that 'He is they, and they are He'. They are the ten names most common to God, and in their entirety they also form his one great Name. They are 'the King's faces', in other words, his varying aspects, and they are also called the inner, or mystical Face of God. They are the ten stages of the inner world through which God descends from the inmost recesses down to His revelation in the Shekhinah.[1]

The names of the different spheres are many of them taken from the titles used for God in the Hebrew Bible. Perhaps the most interesting for our purposes is that of *Elohim*, the name by which the Creator in Genesis is always called. It is likewise an expression that Blake was to use, in his prophetic books and in the *Zohar* it is applied to Binah, which heads the column of rigour and is the active force in creating the universe.

> And what is *Elohim*? *Elohim* is the name of God, which guarantees the continued existence of creation in so far as it represents the union of the hidden subject *Mi* and the hidden object *Eleh*. (The Hebrew words *Mi* and *Eleh* have the same consonants as the complete word *Elohim*.) In other words, Elohim is the name given to God after the disjunction of subject and object has taken place, but in which this gap is continuously bridged or closed.[2]

The most usual way in which the entire system of the spheres is represented is either as the Tree of Life, a tree animated in every branch by the sap of the unknowable Godhead, the En Soph, or as the Primordial Man. This being, wearing on his head Kether or 'the crown', the first manifestation of the Godhead, has the last sphere, Malkhuth, on his feet, and receives the name of *Adam Kadmon* in the *Tikkune Zohar*, one of the latest parts of the whole work. But far more valuable than abstract summaries of the *Zohar's* imaginative symbolism, one that teaches wisdom in a way expressly designed to prevent

[1] G. Scholem, *Major Trends in Jewish Mysticism*, p. 213.
[2] G. Scholem, *Major Trends in Jewish Mysticism*, p. 221.

easy popularizations, is an example of this symbolism at work. Anyone who wishes to grasp the Renaissance outlook which drew so heavily on the Kabalah, amongst other sources, must be willing to look at the material used and see what was done with it. The circles of mystics in Spain, where the *Zohar* originated, clearly had the habit of meditating on some simple object – a flower, or a candle – and drawing spiritual lessons from it, as in this example from the *Zohar*, folio 50.

Rabbi Simeon began, and said, two verses are written. 'For the Lord Thy God is a consuming fire', and it is written there 'and ye that cleave unto the Lord your God are all of you alive today'. We have explained these verses in various places and the companions have been stirred by them. Come and see, for 'the Lord Thy God is consuming fire': it has already been explained among the companions that there is a fire consuming fire; consuming it and destroying it. Because one fire is stronger than the other. And they have interpreted it. But come and see. He who wants to know the wisdom of the Holy Unity shall contemplate the flame which rises from a glowing coal or a burning candle, for the flame can only rise when it is connected with something concrete. Come and See. In the flame which rises upwards there are two kinds of light: one light white and luminous and another light with which black or blue is associated. The white light is above and rises straight upwards, and underneath is the blue or black light which is a 'throne' for the white one and that white light rest upon it. And they are bound up one with the other that all may be one. And the black light, or bearer of the blue colour, is a 'throne' of glory for the white. And this is the mystery of the blue. This blue-black throne is bound up with something else beneath, in order to burn, and it stirs it to be bound up with the white light. This blue-black light sometimes turns red, but as to the white light above – it never changes. For it is always white. The blue, however, may change into all these colours; at times blue or black, and at times red. This light is bound up with two sides. It is bound up above with the white light and it is bound up beneath with a certain thing below it which is possessed by it in order to keep it alight and be connected with it. And this light is always consuming and destroying what one puts beneath it. For thus it is with all that is cleaving to it beneath while it is resting upon it. The blue light destroys it and consumes it because it is its nature to destroy and consume. For the destruction of all is dependent on it, the death of all, and therefore it consumes everything which clings to it. But the white light which rests above, it neither consumes nor destroys at all and its light does not change. And therefore Moses said 'For the Lord thy God is consuming fire'. Consuming all that rests beneath. And therefore it says 'The Lord thy God' not 'The Lord our God' because Moses was bound up with that white light which neither destroys nor consumes.[1]

A constant use of subtly shifting repetition is obvious here. Also of paradox. Several deep truths are hinted at. God and the Godhead. God and the Throne of his Glory. The role of Moses 'bound up' with God as the representative of Israel. And the use of colour symbolism is shown: white or silver, signifying mercy; blue, punishment; and purple, judgment.

The Zoharic Kabalah was, however, followed by the Lurianic. After the expulsion of the Jews from Spain some of the mystics, who had mostly been centred round Gerona in Catalonia, moved to the town of Safed in Galilee. Among them were Moses ben Jacob Cordovero, the systematizer who grappled with what Professor Scholem has called 'the intricate conflict between the theistic and pantheistic tendencies in the mystical theology of Kabbalism', and Isaac Luria. The latter's main tenets were preserved by his disciple Hayim Vital, whose major work is the *Ets Hayim*, the *Tree of Life*; though they were given their widest currency in the works of Israel Sarug who is said to have bought some of Vital's manuscripts from his brother when he was lying ill, and whose disciple, Abraham Cohen Herrera of Florence, made a great stir.[2] Luria taught the *Tsimtsun* or retreat or shrinkage of God to make room for creation; 'the breaking of the vessels' by which Evil is accounted for by the cleansing of the ten spheres of the fragments of the 'shells' or seeds of evil mixed in them, thus externalizing these elements so that they can be overcome. And also the doctrine of the 'Edomite Kings', whose reign, 'the dominion

---

[1] This translation has kindly been provided by Rabbi Dr O. Lehman.
[2] G. Scholem, *Major Trends in Jewish Mysticism*, pp. 256–8.

of Edom' as Blake calls it, signifies earlier worlds which crashed through 'unbalanced force'.[1] But possibly even more relevant to the interests of Renaissance Christians was the work of another refugee from Spain, Don Judah Abarbanel, whose father, Don Isaac, had raised the money for Columbus's first Atlantic expedition. Practising as a doctor in Naples, Genoa and Venice, Abarbanel frequented the 'Academies of the Gentiles' and about 1501 composed the *Dialoghi d'Amore*, under the name of Leone Ebreo, which was brought out in 1535. This received a very wide circulation through being included in the famous collection of Johannes Pistorius, *Artis Cabalisticae*, published in Basle 1587. Abarbanel sought to harmonize Kabalah with Neo-Platonism, using the doctrine of 'intelligences' or spirits that move the Universe, and that of 'spheres'. Abarbanel also seized on the theory of Man's original androgyny raised in part of Plato's *Symposium*, to connect it with teachings of the same sort in the Jewish tradition. His dialogue of *Philo* with *Sophia* was translated into French, Spanish, Latin and Hebrew and must be regarded as one of the most popular works of the Renaissance.[2]

Christian interest in the Kabalah, of which Giorgio's monumental work is so remarkable an example, began, as Professor Scholem has shown, with the *Pugio Fidei* of Ramon Martín in Spain; with Pedro de la Caballeria drawing on the *Zohar* in 1450 for his *Zelus Christi*.[3] By the early sixteenth century we have to reckon with such a formidable figure as the great humanist cardinal Egidio da Viterbo, whom M. François Secret has described in a recent study as '*un des plus grands parmi les Kabbalistes chrétiens de la Renaissance*'.[4] Here he points out

---

[1] William Blake, *The Marriage of Heaven and Hell*, Plate 3. Geoffrey Keynes, *The Complete Writings of William Blake*, p. 149.

[2] Leone Ebreo: *Dialoghi d'Amore*. English translation by F. Friedeburg-Seeley and Jean H. Barnes, pp. 333–4.

[3] G. Scholem: 'Zur Geschichte Der Anfänge Der Christlichen Kabbala', in *Essays Presented to Leo Baeck*.

[4] François Secret: *Le Zohar chez les Kabbalistes Chrétiens*, Paris 1958, Introduction. *Scechina e Libellus de Litteri Hebraicis*, Rome 1959.

that this pupil of the Jewish convert, Felix Prater, translated such important texts of the Kabalah as, '*l'Hortus Nucis, le Sefer Temuna, le Reziel, le Rekananti, le Pelia*'. M. Secret has edited Egidio's own treatise the *Scechina* and has shown how he was linked with other thorough students of the subject; Theseus Ambrosius and Agostino Justiniani. How he was the protector of Elias Levi and the Austrian scholar Widmanstadt who later assembled one of the most notable European collections of texts of the Kabalah.[1] These are men whose work must be taken seriously even if they did give the tradition their own twist. Because these Christians seized on what they wanted and ignored the rest we should not take it for granted that they were ignorant. Nor was their chief aim the conversion of the Jews as is sometimes suggested. More important was the syncreticism we have been following out. The desire to find a common layer of truth in all religions and all systems.

It is no exaggeration, then, to suggest that one of the most characteristic movements of the Renaissance was the search for the 'True Religion' of St Augustine, the laying hold of the ancient original wisdom that had its special source in the East and could be found by pious study of Jewish traditional teachings on the 'unwritten Law' and of that Neo-Platonic and Hermetic literature in Greek, believed to derive from even more remote and august sources. This movement was pursued as much by churchmen as by anyone else. Its whole impulse was Christian piety. Though the speculations of a Pico or Giorgio, a Nicholas of Cusa, or Egidio were daring, they were put forward in a spirit of complete loyalty to the Church. Yet the warnings of Savonarola deserved heeding. The Dominican friar was far from hostile to the preoccupations of the Florentine Platonists. But he insisted that Christians must safeguard themselves against the degrading aspects of a revived paganism. It would be a mistake to imagine that the efforts put forth to unite a Christian idealism with the thought of the ancient world

[1] The collection of Johann Albrecht Widmanstadt is now in the Munich Staatsbibliothek.

were made without strain. The great tensions which were in fact brought into being have been well observed by the Russian thinker Nicolas Berdyaev and are due to conflicts which the Renaissance Neo-Platonists, pious men though they were, had simply not noticed.

> A pagan Renaissance is impossible in a Christian world, for ever impossible. Classic immanent perfection can no longer be the portion of the Christian soul which has been touched by transcendent longing. Decline and distortion, a dead academism are inevitable as the end of a pagan Renaissance in a Christian world.[1]

Strangely, it was precisely this 'dead academism' in Art which so much repelled William Blake and made him attack Joshua Reynolds as one of those who were 'very Anxious . . . to Disprove & Contemn Spiritual Perception'. There lies an explosive element within the Christian system which makes it equally impossible to accept this world as a self-contained perfection or to reject it in preference for a more 'real' one. The soul is asked to stretch herself from Nature to Super Nature, never to sink herself in one or fly away to the other. Those who came under the influence of the syncretic movement often tried to do one or the other. Their experiment contained within itself the seeds of its own destruction. Yet it was a most noble venture with far-reaching consequences. We shall see in how many ways William Blake's own system was moulded by this earlier language of symbolism. How completely he had grasped its message may be seen from his early print, *All Religions are One*.

> The Religions of all Nations are derived from each Nation's different reception of the Poetic Genius, which is every where call'd the Spirit of Prophecy. . . . As all men are alike (tho' infinitely various), So all Religions &, as all similars, have one source.

> The true Man is the source, he being the Poetic Genius.

A still more forthright affirmation of the same position comes in Blake's *Descriptive Catalogue*, 1809, Number V.

[1] Nicolas Berdyaev, *The Meaning of the Creative Act*, p. 234.

All had originally one language, and one religion: this was the religion of Jesus, the everlasting Gospel. Antiquity preaches the Gospel of Jesus.

Blake's own achievement, and a great many other things besides, cannot be understood without a serious and sincere consideration of the mental world that first came into being in Ficino's Florence, in the Italy of the High Renaissance.

CHAPTER II

The Tradition in Action

*

By the early sixteenth century an entirely new mental world had come into being in Europe. A world with its own language, its own landmarks, its customary symbolism. One that had roots in the ancient world, and derived much from certain aspects of Medieval thought,[1] but at the same time, a completely new world. Although it first came into being in Renaissance Italy, the intellectual excitement, the theories and symbolism which sprung out of that excitement soon spread throughout Europe. From Rome, from Florence and Venice, the influences went out, touching Germany, France, the Low Countries and then England in particular. It would be impossible here to do more than glance at some of them at work. But there are two kinds of mentality in which these influences did work with an especially potent effect. The first is the mentality of the artist, for, as Professor Wind has put it,

> When ideas are so forcibly expressed in art it is unlikely that their importance will be confined to art.

The second is that of the thinker, who in his writings, whether poetry or prose, provides material for a whole school of thought to grow; develops imagery which may then be used by scientists, artists, dramatists, poets as well as by scholars and philosophers proper. Outstanding minds of these two types

[1] Miss Yates, for example, stresses the continued influence of the great Abbey of St Victor, a traditional centre of Platonic studies throughout the Middle Ages, in her study, *The French Academies of the Sixteenth Century*. In the same way Ficino's debt to Aristotle is traced out in an article by P. O. Kristeller, 'The Scholastic Background of Marsilio Ficino', *Traditio*, Vol. II, 1944, p. 257.

from the German states of the Holy Roman Empire, from court circles in France can valuably be singled out to demonstrate the way of thought in action, and I propose to begin with a figure whose influence upon William Blake was massive; Albrecht Dürer.

Blake had a passionate devotion to Dürer as an artist. Against the patronizing passage in Sir Joshua Reynolds's *Discourses* where Reynolds quotes,

> Albert Durer, as Vasari has justly remarked, would probably have been one of the first painters of his age . . . had he been initiated into those great principles of the art, which were so well understood and practised by his contemporaries in Italy. . . .

Blake has indignantly marked a question,

> What does this mean, '*Would have been*' one of the first painters of his Age? Albert Durer *Is*, Not would have been . . .!

For Dürer as an engraver Blake had a very special sympathy, and with Michelangelo and Raphael, Dürer presented a model for Blake's theory and practice of art. He upheld the principle of Man as the Measure of the Universe and himself quotes Vitruvius,

> . . . the ancient architect, whom the Romans employed upon great buildings, says that whosoever desires to build should study the perfection of the human figure, for in it are discovered the most secret mysteries of Proportion.

This statement is to be found upon a manuscript sheet in the British Museum which bears the title 'About the proportions of Human Limbs' on which Dürer had drawn two male figures, one with limbs outstretched in a St Andrew's Cross, the other in the position of a Latin Cross.[1]

From the beginning of his artistic career Dürer had always been fascinated by these 'secret mysteries'. On both his visits to Italy, that from 1494–5 and the later one from 1505–7, he concerned himself with mastering them; and being early

---

[1] W. M. Conway, *Dürer's Literary Remains*, Cambridge 1889, p. 165.

aware that the Venetian painter Jacopo da Barbari, who followed the teaching of Fra Luca Pacioli, was in full possession of just these principles, his greatest ambition was to penetrate the depths of da Barbari's system, so that he exclaimed,

> I would rather be shown what he meant than behold a new kingdom.

Italian influences based on the Neo-Pythagorean and Neo-Platonic school of thought, transformed, in fact, this son of a Nuremberg goldsmith, brought up to work within a certain Gothic framework of angularity, after the fashion of the great Flemings, the Van Eycks – his father had been trained in the Low Countries – into a bold experimenter, the author of the *Vier Bücher von Menschlicher Proportion* and the deviser of those extraordinary drawings showing 'Man in Movement, Composed of Stereometrical Solids, with Cross-Sections at Ten Levels'.[1] If there was ever anyone who *had* 'been initiated into those great principles of the art, which were so well understood and practised by his contemporaries in Italy' it was Dürer. Moreover, his classic work on human proportion, the *Vier Bücher von Menschlicher Proportion* was drawn on by others interested in the theory of art again and again. One example of straightforward borrowing of his illustrations is to be found in a translation by Richard Haydocke, published in 1598, of *A Tracte Containing The Artes of Curious Paintinge Carvinge and Buildynge written first in Italian by Jo. Paul Lomatius of Milan*, where all the reproductions are in fact from Dürer. Then, later, Athanasius Kircher, a scholar now mainly remembered as an early Egyptologist, made use of them to illustrate the principles of the harmony and proportion he himself had derived from such authors as Francesco Giorgio.[2]

A further example of the kind of influences Dürer had absorbed from Italy appear in the special use of Pythagorean

---

[1] Erwin Panofsky, *The Life and Art of Albrecht Dürer*; plate 322 'Man in Movement, Composed of Stereometrical Solids'.

[2] Athanasius Kircher, *Musurgica Universalis sive Ars Magna Consoni et Dissoni*, Rome 1650, Tom. II, pp. 402 and 406.

geometric solids in his engravings for a book by another Nuremberg goldsmith, Wenzel Jamitzer, called *Perspectiva Corporum Regularium*. Here the Arts, and the Elements, are associated with the solids in a symbolic manner. The figure of 'Perspectiva' sits opposite 'Architectura', holding a cube and balancing a celestial globe on her knee. The section on the Tetrahedron is introduced with a title-page using firearms as its motif. The Octahedron is associated with musical instruments, while gardening implements decorate the title-page of the section on the Cube, and aquatic creatures that introducing the Icosahedron. To illustrate the Dodecahedron, two cherubs hold a terrestial and celestial globe respectively, and geometrical instruments adorn the bottom of the page.[1] In a more subtle way acceptance of the Ficinian mode appears in Dürer's famous engraving, *Melancholia I*. Ficino had laid down that a certain 'Saturnian Melancholy' was the temperamental disposition most common to genius. This view partly sprung, no doubt, from Ficino's inclination to fits of melancholy and to the fact that he was born under the planet Saturn. The superior minds Ficino envisaged as cast in this mould were those of philosophers and sages.

It was left to Dürer's fellow-countryman, Cornelius Agrippa, to suggest that the artist belonged to this category, when considering the vital role of the imagination. Of the four temperaments, the Sanguine, the Choleric, the Phlegmatic and the Melancholic, the last Agrippa says, lies more open to inspiration which operates through dreams, contemplation, and the *'furor melancholicus'* of Saturn; for this cold planet, often malignant in its influences, nevertheless symbolized 'Mind', loftier even than Jupiter, representing 'Soul'. The artist would be stimulated to creative feats by its exalted influence. The Ficinian position was of course a very Aristotelian one and it would be wrong not to remember how much Ficino was indebted to Aristotle in addition to an intense Platonism. As a Christian, indeed a priest, Ficino taught that sloth, despair and

[1] Wenzel Jamitzer, *Perspectiva Corporum Regularium*. Nuremberg 1568.

anger were vices. But still there was a kind of 'noble melancholy', and 'Aristotelian refinement of the affliction', as Professor Wind calls it, that 'became the privilege of inspired men'. We have only to consider the figure of Hamlet, over a hundred years later, to grasp the power of this conception. In the same way there was a 'noble rage' proper to the 'magnificent man', and a kind of pleasure, a *voluptas*, symbolizing the mystical union, and itself the noblest of all passions. It became the fashion for the artist deliberately to seek out the noble melancholy – this is a vogue which still persists to some degree – and Dürer seems to have done just that. At any rate, the implications behind his *Melancholia* engraving have been fully discussed along these lines by Erwin Panofsky in his study of Dürer.[1]

The influences from the Ficinian school of Renaissance Italy can be seen working themselves out even more conspicuously in the thought of Cornelius Agrippa. His controversial volume, the *De Occulta Philosophia*, which caused so much sensation in sixteenth century Europe because of its defence of Magic – the wisdom of the Magi, not the art of sorcery – is a combination of elements from Platonism, Pythagorean symbolism and the Kabalah. Its three books scrutinize three realms, or worlds; the elementary, the intellectual and the celestial world. A division borrowed from Recanati, as Leon Blau points out; the main source of Pico della Mirandola's cabalistic knowledge.[2] Blau remarks that the first book contains a survey of 'natural magic', the second is preoccupied with number symbolism, while the third discusses the Divine Names and derives much from the studies in the Kabalah of the other great German scholar to be influenced by the Florentine speculations, Johannes Reuchlin.[3] Erwin

---

[1] Erwin Panofsky, *Life and Art of Albrecht Dürer*, Chapter V, 'Melancholia I', pp. 156–71.

[2] Leon Blau: *The Christian Interpretation of the Cabala in the Renaissance*, p. 80.

[3] Johannes Reuchlin, from Pforsheim in the Black Forest, was indebted to Pico della Mirandola himself and to two Jewish teachers, Obadiah

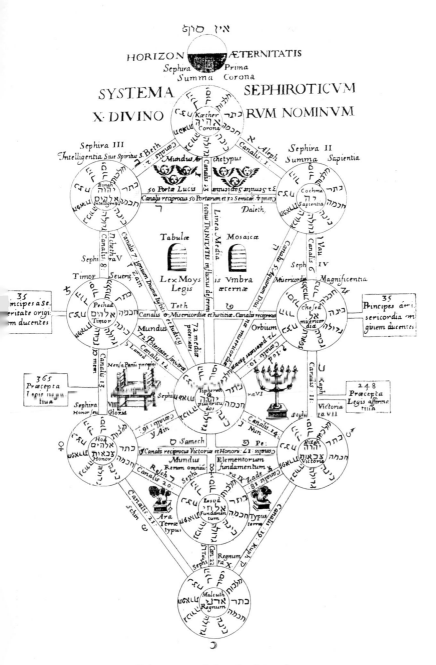

1. Diagram of the Sephiroth

From Athanasius Kircher's *Oedipi Aegyptiaci*, Rome, 1653

2. *Coelum*
Plate V of Wenzel Jamitzer's *Perspectiva Corporum Regularium*,
Nuremberg, 1568, by Albrecht Dürer

Panofsky, translating the Renaissance concepts with which Agrippa was dealing in the first book of his *De Occulta Philosophia* into modern terms explains how, Agrippa,

> basing himself upon Marsilio Ficino, sets forth the Neo-Platonic doctrine of cosmic forces whose flux and reflux unifies and enlivens the universe, and he tries to show how the operation of these forces enables man not only to practise legitimate magic – as opposed to necromancy and commerce with the Devil – but also to achieve his greatest spiritual and intellectual triumphs.[1]

These are Agrippa's own arguments, as set out in the 'Address to the Reader' which opens his *Of Occult Philosophy*. As formulated in the English edition of 1650, the one Blake most likely used, for he certainly knew the book, the address runs as follows:

> . . . a Magician doth not amongst learned men signifie a sorcerer, or one that is superstitious or divellish; but a wise man, a priest, a prophet; and that the Sybils were Magicianesses, & therefore prophecyed most cleerly of Christ; and that Magicians, as wise men, by the wonderful secrets of the world, knew Christ the author of the world to be born, and came first of all to worship him; and that the name of Magicke was received by Philosophers, commended by Divines, and not unacceptable to the Gospel.[2]

Sforno and Jacob Loans, for his knowledge of Kabalah. His first book, the *De Verbo Mirifico*, shows some inaccuracies, as Leon Blau has pointed out in his section on Reuchlin, pp. 41–60, but his next publication, the *De Arte Cabalistica*, Hagenau 1517, is much more sound. The mixture of Neo-Platonic and Cabalistic symbolism which Reuchlin used appears in the dialogues between the Pythagorean, 'Philolaus Junior', 'Marranus', a Moslem, and 'Simon of Frankfurt' a Jewish Cabalist. He leans greatly on the work of Joseph ben Abraham Gikatilia, a famous systematizer of the Kabalah, author of the popular book *Sha' Are Orah*. Reuchlin was opposed by a fanatical convert from Judaism, Johann Pfefferkorn, who caused the Cologne Dominicans to raise an enquiry into Reuchlin's orthodoxy. The case was referred to Rome by the Grand Inquisitor at Mainz where it was quashed. Though it has since come to light that the Dominicans won an appeal to Rome in 1520. The struggle helped to inspire the sixteenth century satirical masterpiece, *Epistolæ Obscurorum Virorum* of which the last part was published in 1517. Reuchlin is rightly to be commended for his scholarly defence of the Talmud and his services to Hebrew studies through the Hebrew Grammar he compiled.

[1] Erwin Panofsky, *The Life and Art of Albrecht Dürer*, p. 169.

[2] Cornelius Agrippa, *Of Occult Philosophy*, London 1651, gathering A.

These sentiments were those of Ficino himself and were endorsed by the famous Trithemius, Abbot of Sponheim, to whom Agrippa was very much indebted. Naturally, the first part of Agrippa's work continually draws on Platonic authority. On every page are phrases such as 'the *Platonists* therefore say', 'which opinion *Alcinous* and *Plato* favour'. And great emphasis is placed on the faculty of the imagination when the various temperaments, associated with the four elements, are being discussed in this examination of 'the elementary world'. Panofsky goes out of his way to explain how the first, manuscript, version had the section on imagination for its climax. Since this manuscript was copied without permission and circulated rather too freely for Agrippa's liking, he prepared a revised edition which appeared in printed form, later, in 1531. As he complained,

> . . . the work being intercepted, before I finished it, was carried about imperfect, and unpolished, and did fly abroad in *Italy*, in *France*, in *Germany* through many men's hands . . .

But the manuscript version was in some respects the most influential.

In its second part the *Of Occult Philosophy* is especially concerned with the power of numbers, after the Pythagorean doctrine, and it is here that Agrippa's classic presentation of the conception of Man as the Measure of the Universe appears. This passage sums up the very heart of the system which Ficino and Giorgio had expounded in Italy, which had so strongly affected the creative genius of the Italian Renaissance and which the influential Abbot Trithemius enthusiastically supported. The vision expressed within this system is of the 'Human Form Divine' that was the chief medium of William Blake's art.

> Seeing man is the most beautiful and perfectest work of God, and his Image, and also the lesser world; therefore he by a more perfect composition, and sweet Harmony, and more sublime dignity both contain and maintain in himself all numbers, measures, weights, motions, Elements, and all other things which are of his com-

position; and in him as it were the supreme workmanship, all obtain a certain high condition, beyond the ordinary consonancy which they have in other compounds. From hence all the Ancients in time past did number by their fingers, and shewed all numbers by them; and they seem to prove that from the very joynts of mans body, all numbers, measures, proportions, and Harmonies were invented; Hence according to this measure of the body, they framed, and contrived their temples, pallaces, houses, Theaters; also their ships, engins, and every kind of Artifice, and every part and member of their edifices, and buildings, as columnes, chapiters of pillars, bases, buttresses, feet of pillars and all of this kind. Moreover God himself taught *Noah* to built the Arke according to the measure of man's body, and he made the whole fabrick of the world proportionable to mans body; from hence it is called the great world, mans body the lesse; Therefore some who have written of the Microcosme of man, measure the body by six feet, a foot by ten degrees, every degree by five minutes, from hence are numbered sixty degrees, which make three hundred minutes;

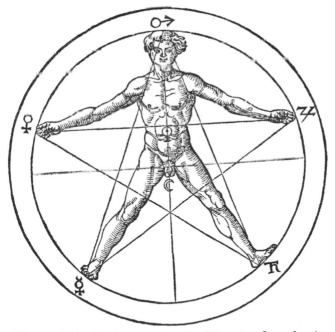

Fig. 5. Agrippa's demonstration of a Vitruvian figure forming a pentangle.

to which are compared so many Geometrical cubits, by which *Moses* describes the Arke; for as the body of man is in length three hundred minutes, in breadth fifty, in height thirty; so the length of the Arke was three hundred cubits, the breadth fifty, and the heighth thirty; that the proportion of the length to the breadth be six-fold, to the height ten-fold, and the proportion of the length to the height about two thirds. In like manner measures of all the members are proportionate, and consonant both to the parts of the world, and measures of the Archetype, and so agreeing, that there is no member in man which hath not correspondence with some sign, star, intelligence, divine name, sometimes in God himself the Archetype.[1]

Agrippa illustrates his exposition with a series of figures of a male nude posed within either a circle as in the figure on page 51, or a square, as in the following.

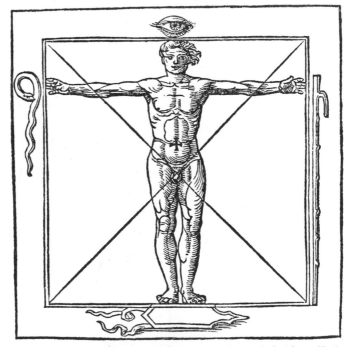

Fig. 6. Vitruvian figure set within a square, beneath the 'Open Eye', surrounded by staff, serpent and scrip.

[1] Cornelius Agrippa, *op. cit.*, pp. 263f.

These figures are placed in a variety of positions all based on either the Latin cross pattern or the St Andrew's one. They are accompanied by such symbols as the pentagram; the 'open eye', figure of the Divine presence; the serpent and the staff; the sign of the planets and of the zodiac, and an assortment of mystic numbers. Although in using the human frame according to these patterns Agrippa was working within what we have come to see as a convention belonging to a particular symbolic language, his own presentation was one that received a wide currency, since the *Of Occult Philosophy* was extremely popular, in spite of causing a furore among Princes as well as Churchmen.[1] Most likely Agrippa's version was the immediate source of Blake's peculiar preoccupation with this very arrangement of figures, which is quite a striking feature of his pictorial imagery. For example, a pencil sketch, now at the Victoria and Albert Museum, is clearly the prototype both for the line engraving 'Albion Rose', contemporary with the American War of Independence, and the colour print usually known as 'Glad Day', dated about 1794. In this connection Professor Anthony Blunt has made several suggestions. He points out that on page 65 of Scamozzi's *Idea dell' Architecttura* a Vitruvian figure appears with arms outstretched in the Latin cross position but one leg in the St Andrew's pattern,[2] Blake's figure is in exactly that posture and he may well have seen the Scamozzi illustration. But he undoubtedly knew Agrippa's series and must have pondered on the symbolism of book two of the *Of Occult Philosophy*, for this was where the names he borrowed, Tiriel and Zazel, appear; in chapter 22, within the list of Divine names belonging to the Tables of the Planets. Tiriel is the 'Intelligence' of the Planet Mercury, and Zazel the 'daemon' of Saturn.[3] And both Agrippa and Scamozzi must have had in mind the even more famous Leonardo da Vinci Venice Academy manuscript, where the Vitruvian figure consists of

[1] Henry Morley, *Cornelius Agrippa. A complete biography*, London 1865.
[2] Anthony Blunt, *The Art of William Blake*, p. 34.
[3] Cornelius Agrippa, *Of Occult Philosophy*, p. 243.

the St Andrew's pattern superimposed upon the Latin one.[1] Moreover the figure illustrating the title page of Robert Fludd's *Utriusque Cosmi*, a work likewise known to Blake, the source of some of his cabalistic imagery, is an almost precise reproduction of Agrippa's third figure, and is freely transposed in its turn, but in a reversed position, at the base of the line engraving of the plate 62 of Blake's *Jerusalem*. Again, Blake has reversed the Albion figure and placed it at the foot of the cross in the magnificent plate 76 of *Jerusalem*. Once more, in his colour print, *The Elohim Creating Adam*, the figure of the nascent Adam outstretched on the earth, is disposed on the Latin cross position. Evidently, Blake's imagination had been at work for many years on the significance of the symbolism within whose framework this kind of Renaissance thought had moved with such confidence.

When the design of Blake's paintings and engravings is considered in detail a number of rather surprising features emerge. The more Blake considered 'Gothic Art' to be 'Living Form' and complained that 'The Gods of Greece and Egypt were Mathematical Diagrams – see Plato's Works . . .' the more precisely diagrammatic his own paintings and engravings became. He uses especially the human form exactly as a mathematician might geometrical figures. And above all he had the engraver's passion for clarity, something that must have made Dürer's approach in particular always very congenial to him.

> The great and golden rule of art, as well as life, in this: That the more distinct, sharp, and wirey the bounding line, the more perfect the work of art. . . . Rafael and Michael Angelo and Albert Durer are known by this and this alone.

But the poems, as well as the pictures, reflect Blake's preoccupation with the ideas Agrippa was expounding in his presentation of Renaissance Neo-Platonic symbolism. He constantly harps on the importance of the number four, 'The

[1] Leonardi da Vinci, *Study in Human Proportions*, Accademia, Venice M.S. R.343.

Human Fourfold', in his prophetic poems; partly an echo, no doubt of such sentiments as Agrippa records

> The Pythagorians call the Number four Tetractis, and prefer it before all the vertues of Numbers, because it is the foundation and root of all other numbers; whence also all foundations, as well in artificial things as naturall, and divine, are four-square . . .[1]

And then it is very plain that Blake was acquainted with what Koestler calls 'The Universe of the Golden Chain'; the conception derived from Dionysius's *Celestial Hierarchy*, where each creature is a link in the chain of being extending from heaven to earth. The Kabalah accepts this vision completely and it reappears, of course, in *Paradise Lost*.[2] Blake's curiously ambivalent feelings about cosmic geometry, as well as his powerful imaginative handling of this kind of symbolism, is well demonstrated in a passage from the *Four Zoas*, often remarked on.

> Thus were the stars of heaven created like a golden chain
> To bind the Body of Man to heaven from falling into the Abyss.
> Each took his station & his course began with sorrow & care . . .
> . . . Travelling in silent majesty along their order'd ways
> In right lined paths outmeasur'd by proportions of number, weight
> And measure, mathematic motion wondrous along the deep,
> In fiery pyramic, or Cube, of unornamented pillar square
> Of fire, far shining, travelling along even to its destin'd end;
> . . . Others triangular, right angled course maintain.
> Others obtuse,
> Acute, Scalene, in simple paths; but others move
> In intricate ways, biquadrate, Trapeziums, Rhombs, Rhomboids,
> Parallelograms, triple and quadruple, polygonic
> In their amazing hard subdu'd course in the vast deep.
> (*Four Zoas*, Night the Second, Keynes, p. 287)

This sequence reads almost as though it were a wry comment upon the fragment bound up in Dürer's notes on art, preserved in the British Museum.

> I have heard how the Seven Sages of Greece taught a man that measure is in all things, physical and moral, the best. It was more-

[1] Cornelius Agrippa, *Of Occult Philosophy*, p. 183.
[2] John Milton, *Paradise Lost*: Conclusion of Book II.

over so highly regarded by the Most High that He made all created things in number, weight and measure. Doubtless those arts and methods which approximate most to Measurement are regarded as noblest and most honourable.[1]

The third book of Agrippa's volume stressing the cabalistic elements in this Renaissance tradition, emphasizes also that value set upon Man as the image of God which is the warrant for the intense respect for the human form always so conspicuous within it.

> Now the image of God is man, at least such a man that by a phrensie from *Venus* is made like to God, and lives by mind only, and receives God into himself. Yet the soul of man according to the *Hebrew* Doctors and Cabalists, is defined to be the light of God, and Created after the image of the word, the cause of causes, the first example, and the substance of God, figured by a seal whose Character is the eternall word. Which Mercurius Trismegistus considering, saith, that such a man is more excellent then they are in heaven, or at least equall to them.[2]

This third book outlines the very complicated and involved system by which a Christian presentation of the older Jewish Kabalah could be made. The survey begins with the various Hebrew names for God used in the Scriptures, continues with the Sephiroth and their interpretations, associates these with the Angelic Hierarchies and the heavenly spheres and then with the patriarchs. Various aspects of earthly life fall, too, under the special influence of these powers. The elements belong to the intelligence of Mars, the ruler of the Sun sponsors metals, that of Venus vegetable life, and from the sphere of Mercury comes 'elegancy and consonancy of speech'. The cabalistic meaning of the numerical values placed on the various letters of the Hebrew alphabet are also explained and above all, the book deals, not simply with angelology, but with human psychology, returning once more to the theme of man as the image of God. The psychology of mystical states is explored in particular, and there are chapters on ecstasy, the

[1] W. M. Conway, *Dürer's Literary Remains*, Cambridge 1889, p. 174.
[2] Cornelius Agrippa, *Of Occult Philosophy*, p. 508.

nature of prophecy, illustrated by reference to those heroines of the ancient world, the Sibyls, whose dark sayings were thought to have foreshadowed the coming of Christ; and the nature of love which is fully discussed, that 'Phrensie from Venus'. The whole tenor of this closing part of the *Of Occult Philosophy* is one that would have strongly appealed to Blake's own bent and it is notable that he makes use within his system of symbolism of some Divine Names that are given prominence within Agrippa's framework of Christian Cabalism; that of 'Elohim' and 'Shaddai', for example.

Cornelius Agrippa's remarkable achievement in the *Of Occult Philosophy* made a very real contribution to sixteenth century thought in countless ways. Just because it was so controversial and because of the sensation caused by its publication, the impact of the book upon lively minds all over Europe was tremendous. It reflects Agrippa's interests and preoccupations as they had accumulated over many years; the series of lectures he gave at the University of Dôle on Reuchlin's *De Verbo Mirifico*, his early study of the Kabalah, his friendship with the French physician Symphorien Champier, translator of the Sibylline oracles, his stay with Dean Colet in London, when he represented the Emperor at the court of Henry VIII while a treaty was being negotiated with François I, and above all the influence of Ficino. From the latter he took over the Platonic doctrine of a World Soul, as well as absorbing Ficino's Latin translation of the Hermetic work, the *Poemander*, which inspired a course of lectures on the symbolism of Hermes Trismegistus. These were delivered at the University of Pavia, where he had received doctorates of Law and Medicine. Agrippa's friend *Bernard*, the major-domo of Cardinal Campeggio, evidently succeeded in rousing his interest in Francesco Giorgio's immense learning also, for he wrote to him with great enthusiasm describing his encouter with Giorgio on December 28th 1532.[1] Agrippa was undoubtedly an odd personality. The title

[1] Lynn Thorndike, *A History of Magic and Experimental Science*, Vol. V, Chapter VIII, p. 130.

page to the English translation of the *De Occulta Philosophia*, describing him as 'that Famous Man, Henry Cornelius Agrippa, Knight, and Doctor of both Laws, Counsellor to Caesar's Sacred Majesty and Judge of the Prerogative Court', hardly indicates the extent of his struggles in life. He never lacked courage and most of the disasters that came upon him resulted from the basic honesty which he was unable to control and which drove him to dangerous outbursts of tactlessness. For instance, no sooner had he been established as physician to Queen Louisa of Savoy, after a nasty brush with the Inquisition on the subject of the marriages of St Anne, than he affronted the court by writing a treatise on Matrimony dedicated to Margaret of Valois, which was seen as a calculated rebuke to her for her tendency to frivolity. With salary unpaid, bereft of illusions, Agrippa produced a brilliant book, *On the Vanity of Sciences and Arts* proving how the man of parts or learning looks in vain for support from princes.[1] The publication of this provocative work was naturally taken as an insult by both the Emperor and François I. When Agrippa fled to Lyons he was thrown into prison by order of the King. Though friends begged his freedom, he died later in poverty, before he could see the *De Occulta Philosophia* through the press. (The Inquisition had earlier suppressed an edition at Cologne.) Such was the end of a strange life; one that could almost be called an exercise in bad timing. Yet there remains something endearing about this knight errant of scholarship. Despite his lack of tact, he fought bravely on many occasions for the Emperor in whose service he passed most of his career, and there is a certain charm in the picture of Agrippa charging on to the battlefield, his pockets overflowing with manuscript, while his pupils desperately try to rescue these priceless masterpieces as they fly abroad in all directions.[2] He could

[1] A full account of this, and other quarrels with his patrons, may once more to be found in Henry Morley's biography, *Cornelius Agrippa*, London 1865, and also in Joseph Orsier's *Henry Cornelius Agrippa, Sa Vie et son Oeuvre d'après sa Correspondance*, Paris, 1911.

[2] Henry Morley, *op. cit.*, p. 291.

never suppress his contempt for stupidity and pretension. By comparison with Agrippa, Blake walked warily in the world and his life was a sheltered one.

Equally rash, strange and brilliant appears the figure of another great sixteenth century supporter of the Ficinian tradition, Paracelsus. His name, together with that of the later German genius, Jacob Boehme, who was so much influenced by him, was invoked by Blake as one of his own sources and bracketed with the names of Swedenborg, Dante and Shakespeare.[1] Philipus, Aureolus, Theophrastus, Bombastus von Hohenheim, usually known as 'Paracelsus', displayed if anything, an even greater capacity for stirring up trouble than Cornelius Agrippa. Dr Walter Pagel, in his late study of the Paracelsian system, outlines the sequence of events which so often made up Paracelsus' life even at the height of his renown as a physician and philosopher.

> Paracelsus arrives. His fame immediately procures him a large audience. He effects a cure where others have failed. He finds influential friends, and is even employed with a public authority. After a short while, however, he falls foul of authorities, colleagues, pupils, and even his former friends. To avoid imprisonment or death he has to leave secretly and suddenly, forfeiting his earthly possessions.[2]

Nevertheless this prickly personality made such a huge impression on the age that he brought into being an entire literature, extending well into the following century, and inspired a whole collection of disciples to hammer out a framework of ideas which dominated the thought for generations.

This son of a physician, one William of Hohenheim – himself the illegitimate child of a member of an old Swabian family from Stuttgart, George Bombast of Hohenheim – though a

---

[1] William Blake, *Complete Writings*, edited by Geoffrey Keynes, p. 158. *The Marriage of Heaven and Hell*, plate 22.

[2] Walter Pagel, *Paracelsus. An Introduction to Philosophical Medicine in the Era of the Renaissance*, p. 17.

man of forceful originality and independent ideas, yet derived his inspiration from Ficino who was always his model. Continually accused of charlatanism by those offended by his vehement assertions, and regarded as the prince of physicians and the flower of healers by many admirers and grateful patients, Paracelsus's whole life and work seem to have been an attempt at implementing this ideal of Ficino's priest-physician.[1] By his very originality he made real contributions to medical knowledge. To his credit is his classification of miners' diseases; for Paracelsus had first-hand experience of mining problems, being apprenticed for a time to Sigmund Fueger at his mines at Schwaz and working later at the mining school at Hutenberg near Villach. And his knowledge of laboratory technique and the systematic pursuit of chemistry, in which he was a pioneer, despite the alchemical preoccupations he shared with so many of his contemporaries, owed much to what he learned at these places. All his life Paracelsus was fascinated by minerals and salts. He loved mines and spas, as much as books and the practice of surgery or medicine. Then Paracelsus's speculation on the origin of the 'stone', and his conviction that syphilis could be inherited are further examples of his perceptive genius.

In the extraordinary personality of Paracelsus we have, then, a practical man, a technician, a remarkable healer, a scholar and a profound thinker. There was, of course, the prickly personality. And Paracelsus certainly scandalized both Catholics and Protestants by his eccentric individuality. Nevertheless he was a deeply religious man. His character and doctrine cannot be properly appreciated, indeed, unless this aspect of his personality is understood. The Church buried him with honour in spite of the way he had horrified the more conventional devout, because of his great goodness to the poor, and his innate piety comes to light in the most unexpected passages of his writings. For example, Paracelsus shows unmistakable signs of a debt to the Kabalah, as well as to Ficinian Neo-Platonism with its

[1] Walter Pagel, *op. cit.*, p. 223.

emphasis on the doctrines of Plotinus.[1] Much of this may have come to him through the Abbot Johannes Trithemius, a formative influence in his education, or through Trithemius's other protegé, Agrippa. The Platonic doctrine of the World Soul was very much bound up in Agrippa's mind with his belief in a 'fifth essence' and in the presence of 'occult properties'. The purpose of true magic was to bring out these, and the element of Air is of particular importance here.

> Agrippa teaches that air concentrates into itself all the celestial influxes and . . . like a divine mirror, it reflects all things made by nature and art and all languages and speech. Penetrating into the pores of the skin, it forces all that it carries into man – to whom it appears in the form of dreams and prophecies.[2]

Paracelsus took over this notion of air, with its special powers, from Agrippa. It had its original derivation, of course, in the Hebrew concept of 'Ruach', spirit or breath. The whole argument supporting the existence of 'occult properties' and the need to draw upon them is set out with clarity in a passage from one of his earliest books, where Paracelsus at the same time praises the Kabalah and lays down the religious principles that must always guide the seeker into such mysteries.

> If we would know the inner nature of man by his outer nature; if we would understand his inner heaven by his outward aspect; if we would know the inner nature of trees, herbs, roots, stones by their outward aspect, we must pursue our exploration of nature on the foundation of the cabala. For the cabala opens up access to the occult, to the mysteries; it enables us to read sealed epistles and books and likewise the inner nature of men. . . . For the cabala builds on a true foundation. Pray and it will be given to YOU, knock and you will be heard. . . . You will gain greater knowledge than Solomon. . . . But only if you seek the kingdom of God above all else will this be granted you. The art of the cabala is beholden to God, it is an alliance with Him, and it is founded on the works of Christ. But if you do not follow the true

[1] Walter Pagel, *op. cit.*, p. 203.
[2] Walter Pagel, *op. cit.*, p. 299.

doctrine of the cabala, but slip into geomancy, you will be led by that spirit which tells you nothing but lies.[1]

For Paracelsus, as for Plato, the real world was the invisible world and the interest that the invisible world held for him was that in it, one might find traces, 'signatures' of the other. The doctrine of 'signatures' or correspondences is very evident in Paracelsus's work; he possibly derived it from the thought of Raymond Lull, the medieval orientalist, which was enjoying a vogue at the time and was one of the many systems freely drawn upon during the Renaissance.[2] But, though as a doctor the respect Paracelsus had for Nature was deep and he was more inclined to see engraved upon her world the Divine Signature, than to pit one principle against the other, as Blake sometimes did, yet there is no doubt about the sources of Paracelsus's thought. His outlook was basically Gnostic, or at any rate Neo-Platonic; and this was well understood by one of his earliest critics, Daniel Sennert, who insisted that one very characteristic Paracelsian idea was really Manichean. This was the belief that the seeds of disease, scattered all over the world, embody the evil principle that, after the Fall, invaded the seeds of purity created by God.[3] One can hardly help associating Blake's illustration to his prophecy *Europe*, usually described as 'Mildew blasting Ears of Corn', with this Paracelsian concept. The elegant figures scattering blight around them have surely a more cosmic significance than this?[4] And it is impossible to forget that Tertullian called Plato himself the 'Patriarch of the Gnostics'.

Paracelsus, at any rate, believed in a 'signature' common to all creatures which are fruits of the earth, namely the greater thickness of the original fluid matter out of which they were made, as compared with those creatures derived from water,

[1] *Paracelsus*, edited by J. Jacobi, London, 1951, pp. 207–8. Quoted from 'Herbarius', *Von der Heilwirkungen der Nieswurz*, p. 102.

[2] Frances A. Yates, 'The Art of Raymon Lull', *Journal of the Warburg and Courtauld Institute*, Vol. XVII, 1954, pp. 115 ff.

[3] Walter Pagel, *Paracelsus*, p. 204.

[4] William Blake, *Europe, a Prophecy*, Plate 9.

like crystals. And his doctrines on 'sympathy' in nature, on forces of attraction and repulsion which exist within the elements themselves, are very close to those elaborated on by Lull in his system. And though that devout follower of St Francis had no wish to foster heterodox conceptions of a war between spirit and matter, a later thinker like Giordano Bruno *did* seize eagerly upon the Lullian art for material to use in his much more definitely Monist philosophy. Then, whatever Paracelsus may have borrowed from Lull, he certainly used particular symbols from the Kabalah in quite a precise way; the image of Adam Kadmon, for instance, the Primordial, Archetypal Man who preceded the Earthly Man, Adam Protoplastes. As Dr Pagel in his explanation of this point puts it, quoting Christian Ginsburg, this

> Heavenly Man . . . even after the fall remained a microcosm whose every member corresponds to a constituent part of the visible universe. These limbs are comparable to the stars, while his skin corresponds to the sky, indicating 'secret things and profound mysteries'.

Again, one has only to think of the design on plate 24 of Blake's *Jerusalem* epic, showing the 'vegetating' of Albion, his falling into flesh; where his outstretched limbs contain the sun, moon and stars, to realize that Blake was familiar with this concept. That he knew its exact origin, too, is clear from the Preface to *Jerusalem* Chapter II, addressed 'To the Jews'.

> You have a tradition, that Man anciently contain'd in his mighty limbs all things in Heaven & Earth. . . .

Apart from his debt to the Kabalah, Paracelsus borrowed imagery from both Astrology and Alchemy, both considered highly respectable sciences in his day, though his independent mind modified this imagery considerably. For example, his belief in Man as the Microcosm convinced him that Man could influence the stars more than they could influence him. Men made their own fate and if the stars came into it at all they were not so much the cause, as the means, whereby human passions were reflected back upon the earth.[1] In the same way Alchemy, Paracelsus contended, 'is to make neither gold nor silver: its use is to make supreme essences and to direct them against diseases'. Briefly, the essence of the Paracelsian alchemic doctrine is the combination of the three principles, sulphur, mercury and salt with the conventional four elements, earth, air, fire and water, but used in a highly original way. Out of the three principles sulphur represents fire, the combustible quality of a substance; mercury, water, the volatile substance, and salt, earth, the principle of fixity. Paracelsus taught that all bodies were made of a combination of these substances, while air he believed to be a product of fire and water. Yet neither the elements nor the principles are to be taken in a materialistic sense. For 'what is visible is but the cover of the real element – alive in the thing, just as the soul is alive in the body'.[2]

Starting from their 'essence' – their 'Quinta Essentia' the 'substance of fine corporeality . . . the *life* of the object from which it is extracted in the form of a fluid' – objects evolve, in the Paracelsian system, towards their final form. And as they do, certain other forces, less concerned with the basic cosmic pattern and more with individual characteristics, come into play. For these Paracelsus had to find names of his own. There is, for instance, the 'Archeus' the individualizing principle. It is that power which in the stomach divides the nourishing elements from the waste products. Then comes the 'Vulcan', a very similar power, which forges the individual being from the reservoir of raw material available called the 'Illiaster'. As Dr Pagel explains,

'Illiaster' is a kind of primordial matter, but not matter in the ordinary corporeal sense. It is rather the supreme pattern of matter, a principle that enables coarse visible matter and all activity of growth and life in it to develop and exist.[3]

According to Paracelsus all 'Generation' springs from 'Putre-

[1] Walter Pagel, *Paracelsus*, pp. 120–2
[2] Walter Pagel, *op. cit.*, p. 93.
[3] Walter Pagel, *op. cit.*, p. 112.

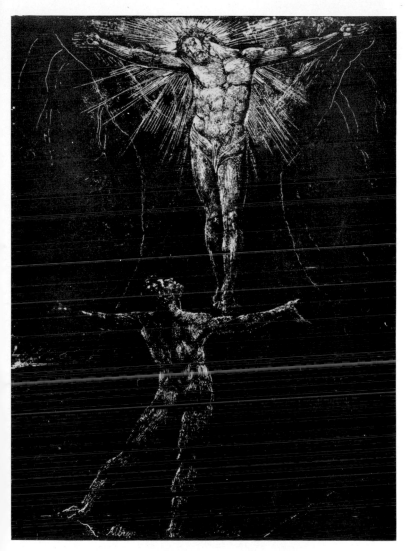

3. The Crucifixion by William Blake
From *Jerusalem*, Rinder Copy, Plate 76

4a. Henry Cornelius Agrippa
From *The Three Books of Occult
Philosophy*, London, 1651

4c. Robert Fludd
From *Philosophia Sacra*, Frankfurt, 1626

4b. Paracelsus
From *Philosophiae Magnae*, Cologne, 1567

faction'. This present creation results from a disruptive process, 'a breaking away from the original divine unity, simplicity and homogeneity'. Here a certain 'Gnostic' tendency is again evident. Then, each biological being has its own kind of time, different from 'clock time' though analogous to it, and of course each is influenced by that complicated network of affinities between plants, animals, organs, stars and even diseases known as the 'signatures' of things. And in everything created there are two bodies, the visible and the invisible. As a Paracelsian work translated into English puts it, the *Archidoxis*,

. . . every man is composed of two, viz: of a material and of a spiritual body. The materiallity gives body, blood, and flesh; but the spirituality gives hearing, feeling, smelling, touching and tastings. . . . In this therefore are the great wonders of God to be known, that there are two bodies, viz. an Eternal and a Corporal. . . .[1]

This was a not uncommon Renaissance concept[2], and the doctrine seems to pre-suppose a position like that taken up by Blake in his *Marriage of Heaven and Hell*.

Man has no Body distinct from his Soul; for that call'd Body is a portion of Soul discern'd by the five Senses, the chief inlets of Soul in this age.[3]

Above all it was Paracelsus's doctrine of the Imagination, upon which, like Agrippa, he laid much stress, that would have impressed itself most firmly on Blake's mind. Few thinkers have ever attached such an enormous importance to this faculty as did Paracelsus. Here is a characteristic passage of his on the subject.

Imagination is Creative Power. Medicine uses imagination fixed. Phantasy is not imagination, but the frontier of folly. He who is born in imagination discovers the latent forces of Nature.

[1] Paracelsus, *Archidoxis*, Translated by J.H., London 1660, p. 7.
[2] See for example D. P. Walker's survey of the doctrine of the Academies in 'The Astral Body in Renaissance Medicine', *Journal of the Warburg and Courtauld Institutes*, 1958, p. 119f.
[3] William Blake, *Complete Writings*, Keynes, p. 149. *The Marriage of Heaven and Hell*, Plate 4.

Imagination exists in the perfect spirit, while phantasy exists in the body without the perfect spirit. Because Man does not imagine perfectly at all times, arts and sciences are uncertain, though, in fact they are certain and obtained by means of imagination, can give true results. Imagination takes precedence over all. Resolute imagination can accomplish all things.[1]

No teaching could be more congenial to a mind such as Blake's, which referred to all creativity as the 'various sublime and Divine images as seen in the World of Vision'. The role of the imagination, as Dr Pagel has insisted, is related to the basic idea of Paracelsus that spirit dominates body, and is linked with the belief that there are 'two bodies in man, the visible and the invisible' with the last as the more powerful.[2] For Paracelsus not only maintained that epidemics were spread by the power of the imagination, but believed it to be a celestial force capable of lifting Man up and uniting him with the 'Primordial Man', conferring upon him even that length of life which belongs to Enoch and to all the 'Enochidai'.[3] Thus his attitude shows a mixture of magic, with what we would call understanding of the psyche. There is one particular passage in the little book *De Virtute Imaginitiva*, concerning the creative power of the imagination, which contained a description that must have read to Blake very like a self portrait.

> The power and nature of Imagination . . . you ought to know . . . cannot imagine anything, unless the things to be imagined are attracted to it by its imaginative power . . .
> By this spirit are born into the world clever and industrious people about whom I will speak here. This one or that invents such through his fancy and thinks things out with a more intent speculation than one who is vacuous, though assiduous. Thus it comes about that a man after laying aside his corporeal understanding (*ut homo intellectu corporeo exuto*) and after putting on a spiritual one, nevertheless remains corporeal in his cunning and

---

[1] Paracelsus: *Interpretatio alia Totius Astronomiae, Opera Omnia*, Tom. II, Geneva 1659, p. 670a. Translated in *The Life and Soul of Paracelsus*, by John Hargrave, p. 102.

[2] Walter Pagel: *Paracelsus*, p. 121.

[3] Walter Pagel, *op. cit.*, p. 122.

subtelty in his art. Of that mettle are excellent craftsmen and others who are born from this spirit, for it is this spirit which speculates, it is he who possesses the attractive power which is linked to the impressions. He that can penetrate there and can make his imagination sufficiently intensive, he already knows the work of the cabbalistic 'rector' and no difficulty of any kind will stand in his way.[1]

A curious phrase 'corporeal understanding', is used by Blake in his famous 'Definition of the most Sublime Poetry' when writing to his friend, Thomas Butts, on 6th July 1803, and it has puzzled many critics. The expression 'corporeal' is, of course, a favourite expression of the Neo-Platonist Thomas Taylor whose commentaries Blake probably knew well. But in the Paracelsian passage the exact concept Blake is trying to convey is actually used.

Finally there are several of Paracelsus's convictions which must have met with the heartiest agreement from Blake. Paracelsus was certain that truth was far more a matter of fruitful experience of reality than abstract thought. He had already the experimentalist's viewpoint. The logic of the Aristotelian savants he compares with the 'leaven of the Pharisees who move about in the schools, who break the power of nature and follow neither Christ nor the natural light. They are the dead who bury the dead. . . .'[2] There is, in fact, no more truly Paracelsian doctrine than Blake's well known declaration:

> I must create a System, or be
> enslav'd by another Man's;
> I will not Reason and Compare;
> my business is to create.

Then the emphasis on the fourfold nature of reality which Blake accepted so wholeheartedly is often to be found in Paracelsus's work. The concept of the number three, the figure

---

[1] Paracelsus: *Opera Omnia*, Tom. II, p. 472. A. *De Virtute Imaginativa*, Tract II. (Translation kindly supplied by Dr C. H. Josten, Curator of the History of Science Museum, Oxford.)
[2] Walter Pagel, *Paracelsus*, p. 58.

of Eternity, in its extension to four, representing Time, is as important there as it later became in Blake's system. The *Aurora*, a book attributed to Paracelsus which is one of those appearing in a seventeenth century English translation, asserts that,

> When the Quaternary rests in the Ternary (then) ariseth the light of the world in the Horizon of Eternity.[1]

And no Renaissance writer was more convinced that true wisdom was from the East, not from the conventional classic philosophers. As the *Waterstone of Wisemen*, another such translation, put it,

> Moses, Abraham, Solomon, Adam, Elias and the Magi that come from the East to Christ, were true Magi, and Divine Sophists and Cabalists; which Art and Wisdom the Grecians knew very little of, or none at all.[2]

In a word, the prejudices and presuppositions of the brilliant physician, the dispenser of what John Donne later called the 'Paracelsian Physick of the Understanding', coincided almost entirely with those of William Blake.

While the system of the Medician Academy was making the powerful impact upon the leading minds of Germany that has been traced out, the same influence was at work in sixteenth century France, especially in court circles. In fact there grew up several French academies founded in direct imitation of the Florentine original, but with a very vigorous intellectual and creative life of their own. So full and varied were their activities and with such widespread repercussions on the nation's cultural and spiritual life, and even its political preoccupations that a substantial study was needed to do justice to this subject. Miss Frances Yates's *The French Academies of the Sixteenth Century* has fully explored this fascinating subject. And she ably sums up the outlook which came to be characteristic of these groups, expressing their ideals and aspirations. These

[1] Paracelsus: *Aurora*, translated by J.H., London 1689, p. 11–12
[2] Paracelsus, *op. cit.*, p. 8.

centred round the syncretism that had been the inspiration of
Ficino's circle. And, again it was combined with a profound
Christian piety. No contradiction was considered to exist
between these two aspects of a single ideal. For,

> If the religions of all ages and nations contained hidden within
> them some spark of divine truth, the follower of Pico and Ficino
> could speak in terms of the Egyptian hieroglyph, of the *Orphic
> nox*, of *Zoroastrianism*, and yet feel himself vitally attached to the
> Christian tradition.[1]

Whether in the 'Palace Academy' founded by Henry III or the
extremely influential academy of Baïf, with its connections with
the circle of poets called the 'Pléiade', the same vision fired the
creative impulses of those who supported the aims of these
academies.

> The humanist religion dreamed of building up a system of occult
> knowledge that was common to all religions, of deepening the
> mysteries of the Church by a universal doctrine, and it was in the
> hermeticism of the academies, from the Platonic Academy of
> Florence onwards, that this wisdom was organized. Conducted
> by the divine Plato beyond the rational arguments of Aristotle,
> the academic initiate reached the level of hidden truth, only to be
> expressed in images, known under the influence of poetry and
> music, and impossible to explain, or even remember, when one
> came into a world in which the Massacre of St. Bartholomew had
> just taken place.[2]

There is evidence that Henry III, who was repelled by the
fanaticism and violence of the Spanish-inspired Catholic
League, actually attempted to approach the problem posed by
such Protestant rulers as Elizabeth of England and Henry of
Navarre through humanism. Here was common ground. Since
even Protestants held the great minds of the past in respect,
they might surely come to see that if the Church could affirm
the wisdom of Moses and Plato, a rapprochement between
Christians should not prove impossible. This policy, based on

[1] F. A. Yates: *The French Academies of the Sixteenth Century*, p. 3.
[2] F. A. Yates, *op. cit.*, p. 235.

syncretism, did in fact have some positive results. One of its supporters was the Cardinal Jacques Davy du Perron, whose book, *The Catholic Moderator*, was translated into English at his own order by the poet Henry Constable, and who later succeeded in converting Henry of Navarre.[1] But the kings of France had from the beginning of the century taken a particular interest in the type of Humanism promoted by the academies; especially in the enlightenment for Christians stored within the mystical tradition of the Jews, the Kabalah. François I had patronized the 'most Christian Cabala' of Jean Thénaud, the Franciscan Hebraist, whose exposition of *The Holy and Very Christian Cabala*, dedicated to François, was preserved among the royal manuscripts.[2] This widely-travelled Friar, whose visits to the Holy Land and other parts of the Levant are described in a rare work, *Le Voyage et Itinéraire d'Oultre Mer*, was equipped both with Hebrew and high principles. He spent much time warning his readers against magic and telling them that the holy wisdom of the Kabalah is only for those who lead good lives. Apart from the original manuscript, Thénaud undertook another at the request of the king, dated 1536, and now at the library of the University of Geneva. Then there is a prose expansion of the verse explication, beautifully illuminated on vellum, like the *Cabale Metrificé*, and now in the Bibliotheque de L'Arsenal.[3] Thénaud was fond of working with arrangements of triangles, each in gold, blue, red or purple, from which he formed such figures as '*le quadrangle d'amour*' and '*des dix cieulx*', the ten heavens. (These figures clearly bear a relation to the treatise, *Scechina*, of Cardinal Egidio da Viterbo, undertaken in 1530 at the request of Clement VII, which contains on folio 162, a demonstration of the sephiroth by means of an arrangement of triangles, and which we have noted has been edited and published by M. François Secret). Thénaud's presentation of this hidden wisdom was evidently far more

---

[1] F. A. Yates, *The French Academies of the Sixteenth Century*, p. 232.
[2] Bibliothèque Nationale: La Bibliothèque du Roi, No. 7238, olim 526.
[3] Bibliothèque De L'Arsenal: M.S. Français, No. 167.

acceptable to the French king than Cornelius Agrippa's version.

Royal patronage was also accorded to another and less gratifyingly presentable figure, rather later in the century; the amazing Guillaume Postel, whose brilliant scholarship was nowhere more deeply admired than at the court of France, yet whose eccentricities proved a perpetual source of embarrassment to all who were impressed by his learning. He is important, however, because of his lasting influence upon a further generation of enquiring minds and because the material he left behind proves his exploration of cabalistic texts to be wider and more thorough than that achieved by any of his Christian contemporaries.[1] His best known work was the translation of the earliest of these texts, the *Sepher Yetzirah*, into Latin, published in Paris in 1552. But his greatest achievement was really his extensive commentary on the *Zohar*, of which several copies circulated in manuscript. This work has been surveyed with care by M. François Secret in his recent book *Le Zohar Chez Les Kabbalistes Chrétiens*, in which he gives extracts from various sections of Postel's treatment of the *Zohar* on Genesis, arranging them in tables and collating two manuscripts; that in the Munich Staatsbibliothek and the British Museum copy.[2] The soundness of Postel's Hebrew learning and his grasp of the Kabalah is fully demonstrated in M. Secret's study. Just as Postel's wide reading, not only of the major texts of the Kabalah, but even of many minor ones is clear from the references in another of Postel's books, the *Candelabri Typici Mosis Tabernaculo Jussu Divino Expressi Brevis ac Dilacida Interpretatio*, published in Venice in 1548. The deep interest in Jewish studies which moved him was stimulated by contacts with the Belgian Hebraist André Maes, with Albrecht Widmanstadt and with Egidio da Viterbo; and his devotion to

---

[1] William J. Bouwsma, *Concordia Mundi, The Career and Thought of Guillàume Postel*, pp. 41–2.

[2] Guillaume Postel: *Zohar* MSS. Munich Staatsbibliotek, Cod. Lat 7428 (Genesis); British Museum, Sloane MSS. 1410.

Arabic learning was stirred by his discovery, on his travels in the Middle East, that many thousands of Christians who practised their religion secretly, longed for translations of the Scriptures in their own tongue. The story of Postel's fantastic life and adventures, and of his eccentric belief in a version of the medieval Abbot Joachim of Flora's prophecy concerning a new era, the age of the Holy Spirit, dominated by an 'angel-pope' has been well told in a recent book by the American scholar W. J. Bouwsma.[1] Postel imagined himself to be the 'angel-pope' whose destiny was to open this new age with large-scale conversions of the Jews and Moslems. And he met with rebuffs as a result from most of the leading figures of the age; from St Ignatius of Loyola, who discovered that he had only joined the Jesuit order because he considered it the perfect instrument for his designs, from the Emperor whose generosity he tried greatly, and from the French Court. Nevertheless by the end of his life Postel drew a wide circle of distinguished admirers round him during his retirement at the monastery of St Martin de Champs, where he reigned, an impressive figure with a long white beard, and attracted men of learning and princes to sit at his feet.

It appears that even in the monastery Guillaume Postel must have created some stir, for a manuscript from St Martin de Champs contains an exposition of the *Sepher Yetzirah*, censuring the 'great confusion regarding the distinction between the Divine Nature and that of creatures, caused by such Cabalistic works as the *Sha'are Orah*, the *Zohar*, the *Sepher Yetzirah* itself and the *Bahir*'.[2] Yet the greatest impact Postel made was really through his pupils. One outstanding figure in court circles was Guy le Fèvre de la Boderie, reputed to have studied under Postel at the Collège de France. At the age of twenty-eight he was engaged in transliterating the Syriac New Testament into

[1] William J. Bouwsma, *Concordia Mundi*, pp. 11–12; François Secret, 'Guillaume Postel et les Courants Prophétiques de la Renaissance', *Studi Francesi*, Turin 1957, III, p. 375.

[2] *Expositio Libri Jetssirae*: Bibliothèque Nationale, Hebrue 881, folio 21.

Hebrew characters and translating it into Latin, and shortly afterwards he and his brother, Nicolas, became involved in the great project for a polyglot Bible launched at Antwerp.[1] Volumes V and VI containing the brothers' contributions, included a Syriac Grammar and Dictionary, and while engaged in this labour Guy composed a highly Neo-Platonic poem, with cabalistic overtones, called *L'Encyclié des Secrets de l'Eternité*.[2] Coming back to court as secretary to the Duc d'Alençon, Guy collaborated with his brother in a French translation of Giorgio's *de Harmonia Mundi*, combined with one of Pico della Mirandola's *Heptaplus*. Guy himself also brought out a French version of Ficino's *Sopra L'Amore*[3] and, most successful of all, his patriotic French poem *La Galliàde*, which neatly turned the ancient Greek and Jewish wisdom, so sought after in the academies, to the glory of France, by representing the Druid priesthood of the Gauls as the fount of all these traditions.[4] Miss Frances Yates is not exaggerating when she suggests that this poem, using the picture of the Druids that Annius of Viterbo had so romantically painted, really mirrors the historical imagination of Baïf and his friends, who are all mentioned by name in it; not only musicians like Courville and Costely, but also the famous figures, Dorat, Ronsard, Du Bellay, Tyard, Desportes and Baïf himself.[5] The rapturous enthusiasm which greeted Guy's homage to Pythagoras, Plato, Orpheus, Zoroaster, the Brahmins and Egyptians, Hermes, Trismegistus and the Cabalists, not to forget the Sibyls, all apropos of the Druid ancestors of the French nation,[6] must have made a special

[1] For the life of the Boderie brothers see Le Comte de la Ferrière-Percy, *Les La Boderie*, Paris 1857.

[2] Guy Le Fèvre de la Boderie, *L'Encyclié des Secrets de L'Eternité* Antwerp.

[3] *Discours de L'Honeste Amour sur le Banquet de Platon, Traduit de Toscan en Français*, Paris 1578.

[4] Guy le Fèvre de la Boderie: *La Galliade*, Paris, 1578 .Also 'Par Ordre du Roi', Paris 1582.

[5] F. A. Yates, *The French Academies of the Sixteenth Century*, p. 43.

[6] For example, the Jewish Patriarchs are shown handing down a wisdom which finally descends to Dionysius the mystic, identified, of

73

impression upon Nicolas's own pupil Blaise de Vigenère, a classical scholar and historian of art who also made a close study of the Kabalah.

In turn secretary to the Duke of Nevers and 'Secrétaire de la Chambre' of Henry III, Blaise de Vigenère, when despatched to Rome in 1566 with the title of ambassador, took the opportunity of contacting rabbis and further pursued his enquiries into Kabalah. The fruits of his learning in this direction were a number of treatises like the *de la Pénitence* and *Prières et Oraisons*, published in 1587 and 1597, that reveal a sensitive Christian piety and at the same time, a close understanding of the Jewish tradition, which must have made a great appeal to Henry III's particular syncretic enthusiasms. More widely influential was his posthumous work, *du Feu et du Sel*, brought out in Paris in 1608, where the alchemical imagery used is entirely symbolic. This study, again inspired by Renaissance syncretism, appeared in an English translation by Edward Stephens, under the title a *Discourse of Fire and Salt Discovering Many Secret Mysteries, as well Philosophicall as Theologicall*, at just the date, 1649, when it might have influenced Milton, for example. Here Vigenère makes such bold assertions as the praise of Pythagoras on the first page, 'who of all pagans was undoubtedly, by common consent and approbation, held to have made more profound search and with less uncertainty penetrated into the secrets as well of Divinity, as of Nature, having quaffed full draughts from the living sources of Mosaicall tradition . . .' and he gives

---

course, with St Dennis of France, in the following passage, Cercle III:
  . . . 'Les saincts Hebrieux . . . les Chaldez:
  . . . le Trois fois grand Mercure
  Sa doctrine enseignoit fort profonde & obscure
  Aux vieux Egiptiens: ainsi aux Bacttriens
  L'enseignont Zoroastre, Orfée aux Thraciens:
  Et chez la Indiens la race légitime
  Du sainct Pere Abraham les Bracmans d'estime,
  . . . Ses symboles sacrez sous le silence encore
  Aux disciples iurez enseignoit Pythagore:
  Et le divin Platon sous énigmes voiloit
  Les mystères de Dieu qu'a Dion reveloit.'

a lengthy explication of the *Zohar* symbolism of the candle flame, arising from meditation on the text 'thy God is a consuming fire. . . .' In this the white flame denotes the Christian faith, 'designed by white water, *Apoc.* 4 : 6 and 15 : 2 (in the middle of the throne there was a Sea of Glasses, like unto Crystall) far above the Judaicall faith, red, heat with rigour and severity, designed by a pillar of fire. . . . In the secret Hebrew Theology, the red, always notes *Gheburah*, austerity; and the white *Ghedulah*, or Mercy.'[1]

A man like Vigenère, inheritor of the stored wisdom of the Christian Cabalists from the time of Pico and Giorgio, Egidio da Viterbo and Postel, may have been especially well equipped for the task of fusing Christian and Jewish streams of thought after the ideal originally held up by Ficino. But all the members of the French academies believed that the best way to reach perfection in the practice of poetry, music, art or speculative thought was to become conversant with that universal harmony which Pythagoras had set forth and Neo-Platonists and Cabalists had handed down through the centuries.[2] As Ficino explained in his *De Vita Coelitus Comparanda*, the aspirant should remember that the origins of this harmony 'is not in the harmony of the spheres, but rather in the music of the divine mind itself . . .' which 'through its effects . . . can lead the listener directly to God himself.' This mode of thought, accepted by so many of the great minds of the sixteenth century in Europe, was a lofty and inspiring one, which has enriched the world with a wealth of works of genius. If only for that reason, it deserves and repays sympathetic study.

[1] Blaise de Vigenère, *Of Fire and Salt*, London 1649, p. 12.
[2] For a study on the origins of classical ballet as inspired by these theories of harmony, see C. F. Menestrier, *Des Ballets Anciens et Modernes*, Paris 1682.

CHAPTER III

Jacob Boehme and Seventeenth-Century England

*

The symbolic language which had been adopted with so much intellectual excitement by the most original thinkers, first of Renaissance Italy, and later of Germany and France, was bound to be learnt in England also, sooner or later. By the end of the sixteenth century there are clear signs that this was beginning to happen. Spenser's mind was obviously deeply coloured by Italian Neo-Platonism. How much the themes that preoccupied Italian artists like Botticelli and Michelangelo haunted Spenser too, has been emphasized by Edgar Wind.[1] He points out, for instance, the familiar pattern of the Three Graces present in *The Faerie Queene*, Book VI, Canto X, verse 24, where Calidore sees them dance:

> Therefore they alwaies seeme to smile,
> That we likewise should mylde and gentle be,
> And also naked are, that without guile
> Or false dissemblaunce all them plaine may see,
> Simple and true from couert malice free:
> And eeke themselues so in their daunce they bore,
> That two of them still forward seem'd to bee,
> But one still towards shew'd herselfe afore;
> That good should from vs goe, then come in greater store.

Then the whole doctrine of Love, of the unfolding and infolding of Agape, is likewise traced in Book IV of *The Faerie Queene*, cantos II and X. The picture of Dame Concord with her twin sons, Hate and Love, whom she constantly strives to unite, calls to mind something close to the original Persian myth of Good and Evil as the twin sons of the Almighty, 'both

---

[1] Edgar Wind, *Pagan Mysteries in the Renaissance*, p. 33.

borne of heavenly seed' as Spenser puts it. Indeed this may be just what is behind Blake's concept of the Laocoön story. He called his pictorial version of the episode in the *Aeneid*, *Jehovah and his Two Sons, Satan and Adam*, and the serpents wreathing Men are Good and Evil.[1] Certainly Spenser, in his attempt to sound the depths of the great mystery of Love, cites Plato to support his theories, in the Proeme to the Fourth Book of the *Faerie Queene*.

> Witnesse the Father of Philosophie;
> Which to his *Critias*, shaded oft from sunne,
> Of love full manie lessons did apply,
> The which these Stoicke censours cannot well deny.

Then too, the myth of Leda and the Swan, to which Renaissance artists had applied so many meanings, is treated in Book IV, Canto X; and the secrets of the Greek mystery cults are hinted at under the figure of Venus veiled. This is Love as an Hermaphrodite, incomplete without a dual nature.

> . . . she hath both kinds in one,
> Both male and female, both under one name,
> She sire and mother is herselfe alone,
> Begets and eke conceiues, ne needeth none.

And, of course, the mythical figure of the 'mightie *Albion*', son of Neptune, possibly one of the sources of Blake's Archetypal Man, the 'Giant Albion', appears in the train of sea creatures who exort Marinell, the nymph's son, in Book IV, Canto XI. He is so powerful that this 'father of the bold and warlike people which the *Britaine* Islands hold' can bestride the Channel like a colossus. One wonders whether this seascape in the *Faerie Queene*, peopled with such superhuman beings as Phorcys, Glaucis, Amphitrite and Nereus, may have helped to inspire the long passages in Blake's prophetic books where Enion and Tharmas flee across the waters or confront one another. Blake's early poems, the *Poetical Sketches*, carry many Spenserian echoes; his 'Imitation of Spenser' is based on the

[1] Geoffrey Keynes, *Pencil Drawings of William Blake*, pl. 31. (Collection of Sir Geoffrey Keynes, dated about 1815.)

vision of Mercury in the *Mutabilitie Cantos* of the *Faerie Queene*, and then the water-colour 'Characters from Spenser's Faerie Queene' which Blake painted for the Countess of Egremont about 1809, as a companion piece to his 'Characters from Chaucer's *Canterbury Pilgrims*', must not be forgotten.

Spenser's close friend, the Cambridge don, Gabriel Harvey, shows in correspondence with the poet, a close acquaintance with the tradition of the continental academies. His disquisition on the element of fire, very much after the manner of Blaise de Vigenère, reveals Harvey's own way of thought.

> The fyer is a queynte subtile element beyonde the reatche and capacity of our divinist and most mysticall philosophers (I excepte not Hermes himselfe, whom they terme ye very perfectiste philosopher nexte unto God himselfe), and I knowe not by what extraordinary and secret meanes ye knowledge thereof should descende into the intelligible and reasonable parte, but by the ministry and mediation of owtewarde and externall sences, and be cabalistically conveyid over from age to age. . . .[1]

In the same way, as part of Harvey's elaborately rhetorial attacks on Thomas Nashe, entitled *Pierce's Supererogation or A New Prayse of The Old Asse*, he calls upon the famous men of learning of the past for aid.

> O Humanity, my Lullius, or O Divinity, my Paracelsus, how should a man become that peece of Alchimy, that can tame the Rattesbane of villany into the Balme of honesty . . .

Then too, it would have been taken as a compliment when another dramatist, George Peele, wrote of the Earl of Northumberland, the Wizard Earl who frequented the circle of Fulk Greville, Thomas Hill and Thomas Hariot and Sir Philip Sidney, with his friend Giordano Bruno, sometimes known as the 'School of Night',[2] in these terms:

[1] Gabriel Harvey, *Three Proper and wittie familiar Letters: lately passed betweene two Universitie men: touching the Earthquake in Apriell last, and our English reformed Versifying*, London 1580; Gabriel Harvey's *Letter Book*, published by the Camden Society, London 1884, p. 83.

[2] Muriel Bradbrook, *The School of Night*, p. 8. Frances A. Yates, *A Study of 'Loves Labour Lost'*, p. 95.

Renowmed lord, Northumberland's fair flower,
The Muses' love, patron and favourite,
. . . Leaving our schoolmen's vulgar trodden paths,
And following the ancient reverend steps
Of Trismegistus and Pythagoras,
Through uncouth ways and unaccessible
Dost pass into the spacious pleasant fields
Of divine science and philosophy. . . .

As far as the greatest figure of them all is concerned, William
Shakespeare, a certain naturalness and ease, a strict avoidance
of pedantry, tends to disguise the debt to this tradition which
does exist. It becomes apparent in a late play like *The Tempest*
which is practically a straightforward allegory, using alchemical imagery and a magician hero who might be straight out of
Cornelius Agrippa. (The deities who figure in the masque of
The Tempest, are those prominent in the Eleusinian mystery
cults.) But such early plays as *Love's Labour's Lost* and *The
Merchant of Venice* also abound with allusions, sometimes
humorous ones, to the system of the academies. There is a very
conspicuous passage, which perfectly outlines the theory of the
harmony of the universe followed by Francesco Giorgio and
presents a strongly Neo-Platonic scale of values, in Lorenzo's
famous speech to Jessica in Act V, scene I of *The Merchant of
Venice*.

> Sit Jessica. Look how this floor of heaven
> Is thick inlaid with patens of bright gold;
> There's not the smallest orb which thou behold'st
> But in his motion like an angel sings,
> Still quiring to the young-eyed cherubins
> Such harmony is in immortal souls.
> But whilst this muddy vesture of decay,
> Doth grossly close it in, we cannot hear it.

Venice, one must remember, was the city of Franciscus
Georgius Venetus, and of the 'many . . . Jewish Rabbins' who
supported him in his efforts on Henry VIII's behalf; not just of
Shylock.

But Joshuah Sylvester stands out amongst the Elizabethan

and Jacobean poets, courtiers and wits who show traces of a
way of thought so fashionable in Italy, France and Germany,
because he was the translator of Du Bartas' *Devine Weekes*, an
epic poem composed at the Court of Navarre in emulation of
Guy le Fèvre de la Boderie's *La Galliade*. The account of the
Creation given here contains the same general theme as *La
Galliade*, and later influenced Milton. It shows the same reverence for the ancient sages and the tradition of the Kabalah,
transposed into a biblical setting. Du Bartas's account of the
wisdom of the Magi, their understanding of the heavenly
bodies, is traced from its origins.

> First under th' Hebrewes bred and borne: Anon
> Comes to the Chaldees by adoption:
> Scorning anon, th'olde Babilonian Spires,
> It leaves swift *Tigris* and to *Nyle* retires;
> And waxen rich, in *Egipt* it erects,
> A famous Schoole; yet, firmless in affects,
> It falls in love with subtile *Grecian* wits,
> And to their hands a while it selfe commits;
> But, in renowned *Ptolemeus* Raigne,
> It doth re-visite the deere *Memphian* Plaine:
> Yet, Thence re-fled, it dothe th' *Arabians* trie;
> From thence to *Rome*: From *Rome* to *Germanie*.[1]

The theme of Du Bartas's work, which Joshuah Sylvester popu-
larized in England in a translation of considerable charm, is in
the section entitled 'The Columnes', an early version of the
'Craft Legend', so called because it was used in the 'charges' or
rules of the Freemasons.[2] It concerns Seth, and his descendant
Heber, with his two sons, Phalec and Joktan. Of Phalec it is
written in Genesis that 'in his days the earth was divided',[3] that

[1] Joshuah Sylvester, *Bartas, His Devine Weekes & Workes*, London
1605, 'The Columnes', p. 491.
[2] See for example British Museum Harleian MSS. 2054, no. 7. 'Notes
& characters with generall things which concerne the company and
occupations within the citty of chester.' *The Free Mason's orders/and
constitutions*, p. 33. ' . . . those children did know that God would take
vengeance for sin either by fire or water they writt the scieces that were
found in two pillars of stone that they might be found after the flood . . .'
[3] *Genesis* X, 21–5 & XI, 14–17.

is after the catastrophe of the Tower of Babel, there ceased to be one common language and then did 'the Lord scatter them abroad upon the face of all the earth'. Seth has left behind him, fortunately for the human race, two pillars, one of marble, the other of brick, built to survive flood or fire. Upon them are inscribed summaries of the main principles of all human knowledge, and by means of them Heber is able to point out to his sons the wonders of Mathematics and Astronomy. It is notable that the Geometry demonstrated is all of a Platonic kind.

> See heere the *Solides: Cubes, Cylinders, Cones,*
> *Pyramidos, Prismes, Dodechaedrons:*
> And there the *Spheare,* which (Worldes Type) comprehends
> In 'tselfe it-selfe; having no midst nor ends:

Part of this hidden wisdom consists in the art of reading the concealed meaning in a given Hebrew text, through understanding the numerical value of the Hebrew letters; in other words the practice of what the Cabalists knew as *Notarion* and *Gematria.* Indeed the title-page of the *Devine Weekes* in Joshuah Sylvester's translation betrays its author's cabalistic preoccupations. There is the column of rigour, surmounted by an angel with a flaming sword, opposite that of mercy, with its olive branch, and light descends from above them both from a sun which sends down its beams through the spheres of the stars and the man, to the earth. Biblical scenes ornament the whole. Its dedication is to James I, and should have proved popular, since James was so fascinated by Du Bartas's religious epic that he had translated part of it himself, and brought it out with other pieces under the title *His Maiesties Poetical Exercises at vacant houres.*[1] Indeed Du Bartas thought it worth his while to pay a visit to Scotland, to meet this Solomon among monarchs, a visit commemorated in the final section of 'The Magnificence' dealing with Solomon's Temple.[2] The fame of

---

[1] James VI of Scotland, *His Majesties Poetical Exercises at vacant houres.* Edinburgh 1591, gathering A, 3–G2.
[2] Joshuah Sylvester, *The Devine Weekes & Workes,* 1608, pt. II, p. 79.

the Scottish King had, he says,

> . . . made me venturously
> To crosse the Seas thy *Britain's* end to see:
> Where (Lord!), what saw I? nay, what saw I not?
> O King (Heav'n-chosen, for some special plot)
> Worlds Miracle, o Oracle of Princes!
> I saw so much, my Soule instructs my Senses
> A gray-beards Wisdom in an amber-bush
> A Mars-like Courage in a Maid-like blush,
> A settled Judgement with a supple Wit,
> A quick Discourse, profound and pleasing yet;
> *Virgil* and *Tullie*, in one spirit infus'd.
> And all Heav'ns Gifts into one head diffus'd.

Clearly then, by the beginning of the Jacobean period, the traditional symbolism, based upon the descent of ancient wisdom from the East, especially from hidden Hebrew lore, had been gladly welcomed by those intellectual circles gathered round the English throne. Such poets as Samuel Daniel, who named Pico della Mirandola 'the Miracle and Phoenix of the World', and John Donne, were fully aware of this way of thought,[1] and there is evidence that Inigo Jones, who was responsible for the settings of the court masques which had become so immensely popular, was a great enthusiast for that concept of universal harmony which had inspired the Italian Renaissance. So much so that his collaborator Ben Jonson was driven to an extreme reaction against the pretentiousness of his colleague's theories. At the same time the remarkable physician, Robert Fludd, took up this tradition and worked with it in a highly original way.

Nevertheless, the fact remains that a balanced picture of the development of this complex symbolism in England cannot be given without taking into account an entirely new factor, the appearance upon the scene of the German 'Theosopher', Jacob Boehme. As Paracelsus had modelled himself on Ficino

---

[1] Samuel Daniel, *Apology for Rime*, London 1603. John Donne, *Essayes in Divinitie*, Edited by E. M. Simpson, Oxford 1952, pl. I. 'Of Moses', p. 10.

and drawn upon the Neo-Platonism of the academies, so Boehme borrowed heavily from Paracelsian imagery and terminology, and absorbed a Neo-Platonic cosmic vision from a way of thought which had long been current by that time in Germany; he was also inspired by the strictly mystical writers.

The works of this man who was one of the most original and profound European thinkers of his day began to be brought out in the year of his death, 1624, and shortly afterwards his friends promoted their publication first in German, then in High Dutch, and it was not long before English translations began to appear. A series of these translations came out through several decades of the century, for which men like John Sparrow or Henry Blunden were responsible. With their fresh and ingenuous style these books made so great an impact on the English mind that vigorous groups of 'Behmenists' were soon evident and by the end of the century, with the movement called the 'Philadelphian Society', Behmenism came into existence as something rather like a separate religious sect. Since, with Paracelsus, the biblical prophets, Milton, Shakespeare, Dante, and such classical authors as Apuleius and Ovid, Boehme was one of the few earlier writers to whom Blake acknowledged a debt, giving his system prominence among the formative influences of his life—as we have seen from his letter to Flaxman[1] – the effects of his thought must obviously be traced out in Blake's own symbolism. Nor is this especially difficult for, once sought out, they are very conspicuous.

What are the main facts, then, about the life and work of this remarkable visionary and speculative thinker, Jacob Boehme? Recently the full range and subtlety of Jacob Boehme's influence has begun to be realized. He exercised, as Paul Tillich has insisted, 'an astonishing influence on the history of Western philosophy'. Tillich explains that from the publication of Schelling's famous study, *Of Human Freedom*, onwards, this influence reached out to Hegel and Schopenhauer, Nietzsche

[1] William Blake, *Marriage of Heaven and Hell*, pl. 22. Letter to John Flaxman, 12th September 1800.

and Hartmann, Bergson and Heidegger, and that Fichte particularly helped to spread it abroad.[1] Coleridge also owed much to Boehme's thought, while in our own century the great Russian thinker Nicolas Berdyaev considered Boehme had a genius for the perception of truth higher even than some gifted saints.[2] But because Boehme's system is very complex, indeed almost unintelligible, without a knowledge of its roots in the tradition we have been exploring, a widespread appreciation of his historical importance and the intrinsic value of his daring insight into the darkest mysteries has been lacking. Moreover, certain inaccurate, though romantic, myths about him still persist.

The truth is that Jacob Boehme came from substantial farming stock in Upper Lusatia, on the borders of Bohemia, and spent his life as a prosperous citizen of the nearby town of Gorlitz. Compared with many of his neighbours he was comfortably off, and had a wide circle of friends, both professional men and aristocrats, whose thought made a great impression on him. He was taught as a child by the schoolmaster of Old Seidenberg, the village where he was born in 1575; a man called Johann Leder. On settling in Gorlitz as a shoemaker, he married Catherine Kuntzschmann, the daughter of a prosperous butcher, and lived in a house he had bought from his brother-in-law, Valentin Lange. Here Boehme learnt much from the remarkable pastor at Gorlitz, Martin Moller. In his extensive study of Boehme, *Sunrise to Eternity*, Dr Stoudt has explained that the area round Gorlitz had been settled for some time by a number of families following the teachings of the theologian Caspar Schwenkfeld, whose beliefs included the deification of Christ's humanity and the glorification of his flesh.[3] Though the followers of Schwenkfeld met opposition from the Lutheran

[1] Dr Paul Tillich, Preface to *Sunrise to Eternity, A Study in Jacob Boehme's Life and Thought*, by John Joseph Stoudt.

[2] Samuel Taylor Coleridge, Pencil notes on the fly-leaf of Boehme's *Works*, British Museum copy, C. 126.k.1. Vol. I. Nicolas Berdaeyev, *The Meaning of the Creative Act*, p. 117.

[3] J. J. Stoudt, *Sunrise to Eternity*, Historical Introduction.

authorities, their influence was nevertheless felt, and since some of Boehme's friends were Schwenkfeldians, this rather ecstatic movement undoubtedly left its mark on his piety. He had inherited this Lutheran piety from his father and grandfather, both elders at the church of Old Seidenberg, and both magistrates, and it was on this foundation that Martin Moller was able to build.

When he became chief pastor in Gorlitz in 1600, Moller's first step was to organize a group within his parish under the name of the 'Conventicle of God's Real Servants' and Boehme became a member. What kind of guidance Moller must have given in this circle is clear from his own devotional works, one of which had already appeared in 1584 under the title *Meditationes sanctorum patrum durch Martin Mollerum*.[1] These writings show his heavy debt to St Augustine, to Tauler, St Bernard of Clairvaux, the French medieval mystics of the Abbey of St Victor, Ruysbroeck, Suso and Thomas à Kempis. For years, then, Jacob Boehme was exposed to the teachings of the great medieval mystics and of the fathers, transposed it is true into a Lutheran key. Moreover, he came into contact with like-minded men of all walks of life; noblemen as well as physicians, traders and craftsmen. It is scarcely surprising that his own spiritual development took a visionary turn. Two years before his first book was written in 1612, Boehme received an inner communication whereby 'according to God's holy counsel . . . he was stirred up and renewed by God. Whereupon . . . he could not put it from his mind, nor, strive against God. These (he) did . . . write secretly for himself'.[2] He had already had one illumination, on Trinity Sunday, 1600, whereby he was 'enraptured . . . by means of an instantaneous glance . . . cast upon a bright pewter dish' and thus 'introduced into the innermost ground or centre of the . . . hidden nature'.[3] The

---

[1] Also by Martin Moller: *Praxis Evangeliorum*, 1601. *Manuale Mortis*, in many editions. *Schedia Regia*, 1605.

[2] Abraham von Frankenberg, *De Vita et Scriptis*, para. 12.

[3] Abraham von Frankenberg, *De Vita et Scriptis*, para. 11.

Aurora, or *Morning Redness*, was composed simply for Boehme's own edification. But that was not how matters were to rest.

One of the members of Moller's group was a certain nobleman, Carl von Ender, a very cultivated man of an old Schwenfeldian family. He lighted upon Boehme's book and was so impressed that he caused copies of it to be prepared, which he circulated without permission. By this time there had been a change of pastor and the new incumbent, Gregory Richter, was enraged at this pretension to theologican learning on Boehme's part and had him denounced to the magistrates and temporarily banished from the city. The matter ended by his being admonished to leave writing alone. There was a period of seven years during which Boehme did not write but meditated on the problems he had discussed in the *Aurora* and absorbed a great deal from the learned men who now became interested in him. He sold his business and seems to have become a merchant in wool and linen instead, an occupation which brought him sometimes into the cities of Prague and Leipzig. The friends who influenced him most at this time included, not only Carl von Ender, but the physician Tobias Kober, the Paracelsian Johann Huser, Johann Rothe, a student of Tauler, and above all Balthasar Walther. This last was an exceptional man. He had travelled widely, having visited Greece, Syria and Egypt as well as Poland and Wallachia, had published theological writings of an esoteric kind, and had been closely associated with the Gorlitz Paracelsians. Though he was later director of the chemical laboratory at Dresden, and became physician to the Prince of Anhalt, he was at the time he knew Boehme tutor to the children of Lord Schweidnitz, Balthasar Tilke, who was himself interested in Boehme's doctrines.

The whole circle then, of which Walther was an outstanding member, lived in an atmosphere of Paracelsian alchemy, of mysticism, especially that belonging to the school of the German medieval masters, and of the Kabalah, with which, perhaps, Walther's oriental voyagings had brought him into direct contact. During this time it is certain that Boehme learnt a good deal about Kabalah and Alchemy. Boehme, for instance, takes over the 'Philosophic Globe' which figures in Reuchlin's *De Arte Cabalistica*, and a mystical use of the alphabet from the same source.[1] He shows an acquaintance with the *Fourth Book of Ezra*, or *Apocalypse of Ezra*, a part of the Old Testament Apocryphal literature which held great attraction for cabalists. There are two places where Boehme actually uses the word 'Cabala' and it seems very likely that two of his basic symbols, the 'ungrund' or primal abyss and the concept of an archetypal man, the original Adam, are derived from the En-Sof of the Kabalah and the Adam Kadmon.[2] Then Boehme follows, also, Johann Huser's edition of the works of Paracelsus, where in part three, *De Secretis Creatoris*, there is a passage associating the Sulphur, Salt and Mercury of Paracelsian alchemy, with the three stages of the Mystical way; purgation, illumination and union.[3] Then the title of one of Boehme's books, the *Mysterium Magnum*, is the Paracelsian term for a kind of 'Grand Matrix', the 'Prima Materia' of all things, whose masculine opposite is the Archeus, or 'Separator'.[4] Boehme continually draws upon the doctrines of the matrices and of the quintessence and, like Paracelsus, he believed in 'Astral' bodies. In the years when Boehme's creative gifts were lying fallow he was occupied, it is clear, in becoming familiar with this type of imagery. He was being transformed, in fact, by his learned associates into a well-read, well-informed man, even one with some degree of intellectual sophistication. The pressure brought to bear upon him by his enemy, Gregory Richter, forced him to work out his own system of thought in detail, and to stand by it without compromise.

---

[1] J. J. Stoudt, *Sunrise to Eternity*, p. 115.
[2] Jacob Boehme, *Von 117 Theosophicshen Fragen* III, 34; VI, 11.
[3] Will-Erich Peuckert, *Das Leben Jakob Bohmes*, Jena, 1924, pp. 56 & 61.
[4] Walter Pagel, *Paracelsus*, p. 91.

About 1619, Boehme seems to have received another illumination, he says,

> I was not able to comprehend that light till the breath of the most
> High did help me again, and awakened a new light in me, and
> then I obtained a better style of writing, also a deeper and more
> grounded knowledge; I could bring everything better into out-
> ward expression . . . [Letter xii. 13].

Boehme's correspondence with his friends, mainly devoted to
explaining his spiritual perceptions and system of symbolism,
grew, and he also made new friends, including Christian
Bernhard, imperial tax collector at Sagan, who supported him
through many difficulties, Abraham von Franckenberg, his
future editor and biographer, and Johann Jakob Huser, the
mint master at Glogan. Some of his most interesting letters are
addressed to the nobleman Abraham von Sommerfeld. But
soon he ceased to observe the ban against composing books
and a stream of works, in fact, issued from his pen. Balthsar
Walther was particularly active in urging him on to write and
from this period of renewed literary efforts date such treatises
as *The Three Principles of the Divine Essence*, the *Apology for
Balthsar Tilke*, the *Signaurum Rerum*, the *Mysterium Magnum* and
the *Clavis* or 'Exposition of some principall Matters', which
were all in the end nearly as current in English as in German.
The times were very troubled and the circle gathered round
Boehme helped one another in practical as well as spiritual
ways. At first Boehme's writings passed only among his
friends but eventually, on New Year's Day, 1624, some of
Boehme's highly placed friends had the boldness to publish
several of his tracts under the title *Der Weg zu Christo* ('Way of
Christ'), and it was this publication that precipitated the troubles
that marked the end of Boehme's life.[1]

His old enemy Pastor Richter was immediately scandalized.
He preached against him from the pulpit, stirred up rioting in
which Boehme's windows were smashed and had him de-

[1] J. J. Stoudt, *Sunrise to Eternity*, p. 177.

nounced to the Gorlitz council. On 23rd March, he was arraigned for disobeying the order forbidding him to write and the matter was referred to the Elector, though the members of the council went out of their way to show their respect for Boehme during the proceedings. When he returned to Gorlitz from Dresden, where his examination before the Elector took place, he had been 'only partly vindicated', as Dr Stoudt remarks, 'neither justified legally nor branded an illuminated heretic'. The last of his books were then quickly composed, for Boehme worked unremittingly until his death in November on such works as the *Table of the Three Principles*, *The Theosophical Questions* and the two beautiful devotional treatises, the *Dialogue Between an Enlightened and Unenlightened Soul*, and *Of Divine Prayer*. At his friend Frankenberg's he was 'seized with a burning fever' and asked to be brought back to his own house at Gorlitz. When he seemed beyond hope of recovery his physician friend, Dr Kober, approached the new pastor, Pastor Thomas, who had succeeded after Richter's death and a Master Elias Dietrich was sent to examine the dying Boehme upon his faith. Dietrich was completely satisfied with Boehme's comments on each article of the Lutheran creed and gave him communion. At his death a few days later Boehme was heard to remark that he heard the strains of sweet music. He blessed his family and murmured quietly, 'Now I go hence to Paradise'.[1]

The life of Jacob Boehme shines out as that of a sincere and, indeed, holy man, while his originality of thought has rarely been surpassed in the West. What exactly was the basis of Boehme's philosophy? What gave his system so great an appeal to seventeenth century English readers, and later to men like Blake and Coleridge in the eighteenth century? Perhaps the most startling doctrine Boehme developed was his concept of 'Eternal Nature'. No other system, within Christianity at least, has ever taken such an idea into account. For it has

[1] Account of Dr Tobias Kober, quoted by J. J. Stoudt, *Sunrise to Eternity*, p. 191.

nothing to do with Creation but exists in the life of Heaven before time or space have been brought into existence. It arises out of the abyss, the 'ungrund', the original, unmanifested deity, the still point where all is silence, and is expressed in three principles (which seem to be based on the pattern of Paracelsus' three alchemical principles of Salt, Sulphur and Mercury). The first two of these are defined in Boehme's *An Apology ... and Reply upon Esaiah Stiefel,* where the divine nature is shown as

> ... with the stern Fire-world, according to the Father's Property, and according to the Light and Love-world in the Sonnes Property; And yet it is, but One only substance undivided, but One God; as Fire and Light is One.[1]

From this confrontation of contraries Boehme developed his 'contrarium', the dialectical principle which informed all his thought. As Bishop Martensen – the Danish theologian best known for his clash with Sören Kierkegaard, the existentialist philosopher – has explained it,

> this contrarium is the eternal nature. The eternal Will, united with the idea, posits out of itself the eternal Nature, and thereby gains life, actuality, definition and attributes. Now, in so far as the one eternal Will enthrones itself as Lord over the *Fire*, and the Power-principle (the primary qualities), God exists as the Father. In so far as the one eternal Will enthrones itself as Lord and Bearer of the *Light-principle* which gathers into its unity the plenitude of power that proceeds out of the Father, God exists as the Son.[2]

From the interplay between these contraries proceeds the third principle; the 'Outbirth'. In fact the classical dialectical pattern of 'Thesis – Antithesis – Synthesis' comes into being. Influenced by Boehme, Hegel later revived the dialectical method and in his turn influenced Marx, with his evolution of 'dialectical materialism'. Boehme himself liked to illustrate this

[1] Jacob Boehme, *An Apology and Reply upon Esaiah Steifel,* London 1661, Englished by John Sparrow, no. 16, p. 90.
[2] Hans L. Martensen, *Jacob Boehme,* p. 61. Edited by Stephen Hobhouse.

pattern by diagrams of a dark circle touching a light one, with a third circle underneath both. The point of contact between dark and light circles is marked by the 'lightning flash', the creative spark, the flame of vitality. And this creative spark illuminates also Boehme's own great achievement, his avoidance of any crude division into 'Good' and 'Evil' by presenting instead a reaction between different kinds of Good. The whole pattern is well set out in summary form by a seventeenth century Boehme enthusiast, Edward Taylor, in his *Jacob Boehme's Philosophy Unfolded.*

> Principle 1. The Spring or Fountain of Darkness.
> Principle 2. The Vertue (or Power) of Light.
> Principle 3. The Outbirth (generated) out of the Darkness by the Power of light.

Represented by Similitudes, viz:

1. Man's Soul, giving Reason and Thoughts, signifieth the Father.
2. The Light showing the Power of the Soul and how to direct it, representeth the Son.
3. The Mind resulting from this Light, and governing the Body, resembleth the Holy Ghost.

1. The Darkness in us, which longeth after the Light, is the First Principle.
2. The Vertue of the Light, whereby we see Intellectually, is the Second Principle.
3. The longing Power proceedeth from the Mind, and that attracteth or impregnateth itself, whence groweth the Material Body, is the Third Principle.

There is an inclosure, knot or stop between each Principle. See Chap. 7 of the Book call'd, *The Three Principles*, Ver. 21, 22, 23.[1]

As well as the 'Ternary' or Three Principles, Boehme has also a 'Quaternary' which comes into being when a fourth principle is added which he calls the 'Virgin Sophia', acting as a mirror to the uncreated light of deity. Boehme's devotion to the Sancta Sophia is almost Greek Orthodox in tone, and his

---

[1] Edward Taylor, *Jacob Behmen's Theosophick Philosophy Unfolded*, London 1691; (c) 2, Preceeding the Preface.

use of the fourth element is linked with his belief, as Bishop Martensen explains, in a Heavenly Nature, as well as an earthly, temporal one.[1] And in Christian symbolism as a whole God with His creation is always expressed by the number four, which signifies completion. But again, in addition to the Ternary and the Quaternary, there exists also a set of 'Seven Natural Forms or Properties', composed, as Martensen points out, of two ternaries with a meeting point at the number four, which represents the lightning-flash. The first is the dark negative ternary, 'an unsatisfied hunger and an anxiously eager restlessness'. The second the light one, 'in which nature has surrendered its independence and is transfigured into the Light, in order to the fashioning of the eternal harmonies'. Furthermore, Boehme also posits a final set of 'Ten Forms of Fire'. These include the Seven Properties but go beyond them at each end. For instance, the first form is the 'Eternal Liberty', a concept which Boehme expands on in his *Forty Questions Concerning the Soule*, when he is discussing the Dark and Light Worlds.

> Yet we cannot say neither, that the Darkness *swalloweth* up the Light, viz the Eternal Liberty: for that which is Eternal, suffereth not it self to be *altered* or changed: but we must say, that Light and Darkness are *IN One another*.[2]

On the other end of the scale comes the Tenth Form 'the corporizing of Angels and Holy Souls' which follows upon the 'Virgin Tincture' or 'Life of Angels and Holy Souls'. The Seven Natural Properties and the Ten Forms of Fire are patterns that go back to the Seven Spirits round the Throne of God in the *Apocalypse* on one hand, and the cabalistic Sephiroth on the other. Even the Seventh Property, the Maiden Wisdom, the Virgin Sophia made actual in the world, corresponds in some degree to 'Malkhuth', the Kingdom, which is the last emanation in the descent of the Sephiroth.

But there is one doctrine among the many forceful and

---

[1] Hans L. Martensen, *Jacob Boehme*, pp. 71–2.
[2] Jacob Boehme, *Forty Questions of the Soul*, London 1655, p. 12, no. 11.

daring concepts Boehme developed which influenced William Blake more than any other; the doctrine of the double Fall, and the original androgyny of Man. According to this belief Man was originally a purely spiritual being, an angel. From that happy state he fell twice; once into matter and a division into sexes, and again into the sin of disobedience and death after the serpent's temptation of Eve. By our redemption in Christ we shall be brought back to our original bliss, however, and will rise again at the Last Day as Adam was first created. Whereas the second Fall was the result of pride and rebelliousness, exactly as in the orthodox Christian view, the first sprung more from weakness, inability to sustain the high spiritual condition to which Man was called. Adam gave way to Nature.

> ... for the properties of the Creation, which all lay in *Adam* ... awakened and rose up in its own self, and drew the free-will into it, and would needs be manifested.[1]

Before this development Man had dwelt in Paradise, containing within himself the feminine element, equally balanced between the 'Dark' and 'Light' Worlds, a Virgin image of God.

> *Adam* was a Man, and also a woman, and yet none of them (*distinct*,) but a Virgin full of ... modesty, and Purity, *viz. the Image* of God: He had both the Tinctures of fire, and light, in him; and in the Conjunction of which, the own Love, *viz.* the Virgineall Centre, stood, being the faire Paradisicall *Rose-Garden* of delight, wherein he loved himselfe; as we also in the *Resurrection* of the Dead. ...[2]

This self love, however, was transformed into a kind of 'self-lust' when Adam was first tempted. The process is described at length in Boehme's study, *Of the Election of Grace*. The qualities of Eternal Nature then demanded to be exteriorized and there occurred that materialization which William Blake contemptuously calls 'vegetation' or even, 'reptilization'. With it

---

[1] Jacob Boehme, *Of the Election of Grace*, Englished by John Sparrow, London 1655, chapter 6, no. 29.
[2] Jacob Boehme, *Mysterium Magnum*, London 1654, chapter 18, no. 2.

goes the division into sexes and the need for reproduction. The life of generation begins. After the second fall the process is complete.

> And then they became Creatures of the outward world, viz. in the outward Natural Life, framed or Imaged with a bestial form, also they became a *Carcase* or Sack of worms, to be filled with Earthly food! . . . they had clearly the *Marks* of the beastial kind, and sex; Although that beastial kind was not quite awakened, yet it was stirred up in the longing or *Lust*.

This sorry state came about, of course, through Eve's plucking of the fruit from the Tree of the Knowledge of Good and Evil, but her very existence, though necessary, constituted a betrayal of the Virgin Sophia, Adam's real love. Before the fall there had been no need for sexual reproduction. For when Man stood in the contemplation of God, as the Jewish Neo-Platonist, Abarbanel, expresses it, 'in this contemplation he remained immortal and had no need of generation'.[1] According to this vision Man was made an immortal spirit; as sexless as the stars.

Boehme's particular presentation of material creation as a fall into matter seems to have caught Blake's imagination and haunted his mind all his life. Especially the way this fall of the original Man is seen under the figure of falling asleep; a sleep unto death. For, as Dr Stoudt, commenting of Boehme's *Mysterium Magnum*, explains, as long as Man 'stood in heaven his essences were in Paradise; his body was indestructible . . . – the elements stood in awe of him'. But eventually, 'tired of unity, Adam slept and his imagination turned away from God. . . . He brought will and desire from God into selfhood and vanity; and he broke himself off from God, from his divine harmony. . . . Sleep was succumbing to this world's powers, and Adam became a slave to just those powers which previously had served him. Now the elements ruled him.'[2] In this sleep Eve was created from Adam, and all through Blake's

---

[1] Judah Abarbanel (Leone Ebreo), *Dialoghi D'Amore*, translated by F. Friedburg-Seeley & J. H. Baines.
[2] J. J. Stoudt, *Sunrise to Eternity*, pp. 264–6.

symbolism the two motifs appear of Albion, Blake's 'Ancient Man', stretched on the rock of ages in sleep, and the division into sexes, something so monstrous that the heavens shuddered at it.

The First Book of Urizen shows how,

> All Eternity shudder'd at sight
> Of the first female now seperate,
> Pale as a cloud of snow
> Waving before the face of Los.
> (*The First Book of Urizen*, Plate 18, *Keynes*, p. 231)

And the sleeping Albion is continually shown, as in the epic *Milton*, plate 15,

> . . . upon the Rock of Ages,
> Deadly pale outstretch'd and snowy cold, storm cover'd,
> A Giant form of perfect beauty outstretch'd on the rock
> In solemn death . . .
> (*Milton*, Plate 15, *Keynes*, p. 497)

It is significant that not until the very end of Blake's prophetic poetry, at the finale of his major epic, *Jerusalem*, does Albion wake from sleep, rise from the rock and walk into the heavens, to be reunited with his emanation, Jerusalem. For this particular aspect of his myth, then, Blake is clearly indebted to Boehme. But it is important to remember that Boehme never showed that bitterness towards woman which Blake often displays. He never forgets the role of the Virgin Mary, a role Blake is sometimes inclined to parody, insisting that,

> Christ has truly, in the body of the Virgin Mary, attracted to Him our human essences, and is become our brother.
> (*The Three Principles*, xiii, 41)

For Boehme believed that Woman must save Man by bringing him to a renewed communion with the Maiden Sophia.

Nonetheless, Boehme's whole system made an overwhelming impact upon Blake, especially visually, through the illustrations to what was known as the 'William Law' translation of Boehme's work. The diary of that lively figure, Henry Crabb

Robinson, a kind of Boswell to many remarkable men in the early nineteenth century, notes how much Blake was struck by these figures. His entry for 10th December 1825 records a memorable dinner party at the house of a German merchant and a distinguished connoisseur of Art, Mr Aders, and explains how the talk turned towards great men of the past and how, by Blake,

> Jacob Boehme was placed among the divinely inspired men. He praised also the designs to Law's Translation of Boehme, 'Michael Angelo could not have surpassed them'.

This translation, a compilation of all the various translations of Boehme's books which had come out separately in the seventeenth century, had been originally projected by William Law, the eighteenth century Anglican divine, and contained a mass of material left behind by William Law when he died. But the work was actually carried out by two friends of his, Thomas Langcake and George Ward, and much of the material they attributed to Law had been copied by him from the work of other Boehme enthusiasts. For instance, the beautiful translation of Boehme's treatise *Of the Supersensual Life*, contained in some copies of the 'Law' edition, is really by Francis Lee, and the very elaborate designs mentioned by Crabb Robinson were drawn up by the German Behmenist, Dionysius Andreas Freher, and copied by his disciple, the artist Leuchter, much earlier in the century. But they were first engraved for this edition, and, as David Erdman points out in his study, *Blake, Prophet Against Empire*, this was a sufficiently complicated process to have created quite a stir in the engraving trade.[1] These figures, and the explanations of them produced by Freher, have likewise all been carefully examined in Dr C. A. Muses's book, *Illumination on Jacob Boehme*.[2] The particular figures used are from a set drawn about 1727 and now in the Dr Williams Library, London. And rather inadequate extracts

[1] David Erdman, *Blake, Prophet Against Empire*, Princeton 1954, p. 10.
[2] C. A. Muses, *Illumination on Jacob Boehme*, New York 1951, pp. 44-74.

from Freher's commentaries were included with them by Langcake and Ward. The full manuscripts are in the British Museum.[1]

The designs appearing with Boehme's *Four Tables of Revelation*, at the end of volume three, are particularly interesting in that great prominence is given in them to the contrast between Man in his original state and in his fallen one, divided into sexes. The figures contain a series of flaps which open to reveal symbols of a more and more deeply interior nature. Freher's comment on the first design, showing Man's original condition, draws attention to a fact which can easily be overlooked and which must have impressed Blake. Namely, that it is dominated by the cross. This cross,

> displays itself from the Center, touching the Zodiac in its four Centural Points, and dividing the whole Circle or wheel of outward and inward Nature, or of Time and of Eternity, into four equal Parts.

The fourfold division, especially of human nature itself, became essential to Blake's own scheme. Annotating a revealing passage from the philosopher Berkeley, which presents the extreme idealist position that natural phenomena 'are only natural appearances. . . . They and the phantoms that result from those appearances, the children of imagination grafted upon sense'. Blake remarks,

> The All in Man. The Divine Image or Imagination.
> The Four Senses are the Four Faces of Man & the Four Rivers of the Water of Life.

[1] Dr Muses also explains that the entire venture was financed by Mrs Hutcheson, one of the two ladies associated with William Law in his work at Kingscliffe, and was to have comprised five volumes. But when Mrs Hutcheson died in 1781, Miss Gibbon, the other lady, refused further financial help. Eventually, however, another volume, now very rare, containing all the rest of Boehme's works, apart from the letters, was published in Dublin by a 'Mr. Holdcroft'. This was, no doubt, the son-in-law of Henry Brooke, who copied out Brooke's correspondence with fellow Behmenists into a manuscript now at the Dr Williams Library. (Walton MS. I.i.43.)

And his affirmation of 'a Fourfold vision' of course, is famous. Other features in the Tables, or explanations of them, that would have appealed to Blake are the zig-zag lightning flashes that illuminate the background to the design of the Fall. (It is notable that this motif is always present in any of Blake's pictures where there is a manifestation of the 'Dark World'. This appears in the scene of Adam and Eve's expulsion from the Garden of Eden, in the *Paradise Lost* illustrations; and in the *Job* scenes. Even in an illustration after Rubens engraved by Blake in 1780, for the *Protestant's Family Bible*.) Then the symbol of the peacock for worldliness probably struck him and the distinction made in the explanation to the third design between the 'exterior sun', and the inner, newly risen sun of man's regeneration. Another figure, 'The Tree of the Soul', in volume one, would have caught his attention. This is often coloured, and shows the tree growing up into the 'Solar World' with its Zodiac, passing through the Dark World and the Fire World, through Paradise and touching at the top the 'Light Majesty'. A ray of light from the paradisal world pierces the solar one and on the other side an off-shoot of the tree, the 'perverse will', passes through the Dark World to the Fire World. Familiarity with such patterns as this one must have encouraged Blake to use the symbolism of the right and left sides, of mercy and rigour, which derives from the Kabalah, and to develop that very diagrammatic arrangement of his pictures which is so often noticeable. For Blake's pictorial vision was a startlingly geometrical one, however much in theory he disapproved of 'mathematic form'.

The Gnostic tendency in Boehme's thought, so conspicuous in his doctrine of the Fall, yet co-existing with a deep Christianity, undoubtedly had dangerous implications that weakened the force of Boehme's message in some ways and its effects upon Blake were not entirely happy. But no-one can deny the great value of Boehme's attitude to Good and Evil. He is here at his most original. For by the use of terms like 'Astringency' he hints at the existence of a positive quality in what we usually consider evil in that side of life from which we recoil and which puzzles us. The dark world, the fire world, the element of salt, have about them a bracing quality that is admirable and has a part to play. This is no dualism in the strict sense, for such a positive quality does not represent sin, or moral evil, but rather what comes forth to contain evil, to control it and punish it, and forms a hidden source of energy for good. It is just this aspect of reality that supplies a tautness, otherwise missing; and above all it is associated with freedom, with that liberty which is the source of the Godhead itself and with which every moral being is endowed. Blake seized on this profound intuition of truth in Boehme's works and used it magnificently. The great lyric, 'Tyger, Tyger' is a testimony to this; and the perception he shows in some of the 'Proverbs of Hell'.

> The roaring of lions, the howling of wolves, the raging of the stormy sea, and the destructive sword, are portions of eternity, too great for the eye of man.
> (*The Marriage of Heaven and Hell*, plate 8, Keynes, p. 151)

Perhaps Blake's importance as an artist and prophetic writer rests more than anything else on his achievement in giving form to Boehme's vision on precisely this point.

The English public of the seventeenth century, at any rate, were well aware of the virtues of Jacob Boehme's vision. A publisher's remarks on the labours of that Edward Taylor, whose *Jacob Boehme's Philosophy Unfolded* still remains one of the best and simplest expositions of Boehme's thought, makes clear how highly such an enterprise was appreciated at the time. Thomas Salisbury explains the way the material for this book came into his hands, at the beginning of the 1691 edition of the work.

> . . . one Mr. Edward Taylor an English Gentleman, the latter part of his time he lived at Dublin, in much Privacy and Retirement where he made this his Work and Business. He died at Dublin about the year 1684. His Manuscripts were preserved by the care of a Friend, and brought over hither . . . considering the labour taken by this good Man for a Publick Benefit, we could not in

justice to the Author deceased, nor with the respect we owe to all Mankind our Brethren, suffer so good and Profitable a Work to perish under our Custody.[1]

The panegyric on Boehme with which the publisher ends his remarks is also illuminating, as an index to the high esteem that Boehme was held in by the end of the seventeenth century in England. Nowadays such praise might be regarded as extravagant but at that time both Boehme himself and the tradition he represented commanded a sort of awe. The regular publications of Boehme's works in English had ensured a respectful audience for his doctrines. Thomas Salisbury explains that he will conclude,

> . . . with a Testimony concerning the Writings of Jacob Boehme from an ingenious and learned hand. 'Whatsoever the thrice great Hermes delivered as Oracle from his Prophetical Tripos, or Pythagoras spake by Authority; or Socrates debated; or Aristotle affirmed; yea whatsoever Divine Plato prophesied, or Plotinus proved; this and all this, or a far higher and profound philosophy is (I think) contained in the Teutonick's Writings'.

Edward Taylor's work is the first example of the enduring interest in Boehme's system that was to flourish in certain circles in Ireland, especially in Dublin. And as by the turn of the century Behmenism in England had developed into something very like a religious sect it is necessary to consider for a moment how this came about.

The seventeenth century in England, was, of course, a time when sects proliferated; the age of 'Enthusiasm', *par excellence.* And some of these movements show a strong family resemblance to the tradition represented by Behmenism. A study of those which were particularly conspicuous in the Cromwellian era and shortly after, has been made by A. L. Morton in his book *The Everlasting Gospel.* His conclusions are that these groups are important for investigators of William Blake's background because they lasted on into the eighteenth century,

[1] Edward Taylor, *Jacob Boehme's Theosophick Philosophy Unfolded,* Publisher's Preface, (a) 2.

And it is certain that they persisted most strongly, as they had sprung up originally, among the artisans and petty tradesmen of the thickly peopled working-class area. These were exactly the social circles and the geographical areas in which Blake was born and in which his whole life was passed.[1]

They had a certain affinity with the group gathered round Pastor Moller at Gorlitz from which Boehme derived his inspiration. Among the Ranters, for instance, a doctrine circulated which might well have been asserted by the Schwenk-feldians of Boehme's district of Germany. A summary of Ranter doctrines by John Porter lists this statement.

First Concerning God
They maintain that God is essentially in every creature, and that there is as much of God in one creature as in another, though he doth not manifest himself so much in one as in another: I saw this expression in a Book of theirs, that the essence of God was as much in the ivie leaf as in the most glorious Angel![2]

The phrase, 'The Everlasting Gospel' again, was current among the Ranters, as among the Seekers, and the Familists, who may have inherited it from the German 'Brethren of the Free Spirit'. It was often used, as is well known, by Blake, and is the title of his last poem. The most distinctive passage where the expression occurs is the section of the *Descriptive Catalogue* where Blake takes up the characteristic attitude I have emphasized is very close to the original syncreticism of the Italian academies.

All had originally one language, and one religion: this was the religion of Jesus, the everlasting Gospel. Antiquity preaches the Gospel of Jesus.
(*A Descriptive Catalogue*, Number V, Keynes, p. 579)

The ultimate origin of the expression, as Mr Morton explains, is in the tradition stemming from the mystical abbot, Joachim of Flora, whose teachings Guillaume Postel had reverenced, and allowed to colour his whole outlook. This medieval

[1] A. L. Morton, *The Everlasting Gospel*, p. 35.
[2] John Porter, *The Smoke of the Bottomless Pit*, London 1651, p. 2.

Cistertian monk and abbot eventually became the head of a separate religious institute, after he had founded the abbey of San Giovanni at Fiore, receiving recognition in 1204, a few months before his death. His doctrines taught an age of Law, under God the Father, giving place to the age of the Gospel, 'of faith and filial obedience', under the Son, in turn to be succeeded by 'the age of love and spiritual liberty', under the rule of the Holy Spirit. And they were much affirmed by the extreme radicals among the Franciscan order, often termed the 'Franciscan Spirituals'. They continued an underground existence until the Brethren of the Free Spirit and the sixteenth century Familist sect seized upon them, and combined them with the kind of Antinomianism which saw God 'in all existing beings' and considered that under the Spirit the outward formalities of Religion were no longer binding upon 'the children of God'. According to these sects 'the dispensations of Moses and Christ were to be succeeded by that of the Holy Spirit or of Elias',[1] and it is easy to recognize in all this an atmosphere very close to Blake's own. His highest praise for his symbolic figure, Los, was, after all, to call him 'the ever-apparent Elias'. Close parallels may be traced, as A. L. Morton stresses, between Blake's *Marriage of Heaven and Hell* and the work of Abiezer Coppe the Ranter, especially in his *A Fiery Flying Roll* and his preface to Richard Coppin's *Divine Teachings*.[2] The Seeker, William Erbery, sounded the note of just that kind of patriotism Blake delighted to employ in his own symbolic system, in his book, *Call to the Churches*.

I hear a sound of the new Jerusalem coming down from God out of Heaven among you. . . . I hold forth nothing but the new Jerusalem, in which God shall gather all the Saints . . . in whom he will appear in power and glory, dwelling in the midst of them, that many Nations shall joyne to the Lord in that day; and these Northern Nations, I believe to be the first fruits of the world;

[1] Robert Barclay, *The Inner Life of the Religious Societies of the Commonwealth*, p. 415.
[2] Abiezer Coppe, *A Fiery Flying Roll*, London 1650. Richard Coppins, *A Hint of the Glorious Mystery of Devine Teachings*, London 1649.

for the Nations of them that are saved shall walk in the light of the New Jerusalem.[1]

Erbery it is that portrays the prophets as calling to God that he is 'their Husband, and they his *Hephziba* and *Beula*, that their land shall be married also to him'.[2] In this atmosphere, of course, John Bunyan lived and wrote. Blake illustrated and clearly drew upon *Pilgrims Progress*. He surely knew Bunyan's country of Beulah, stretching round the borders of Paradise. In this atmosphere the Philadelphian Society, too, grew and flourished at the end of the seventeenth century; an association of pious Behmenists who took their name from the church of Philadelphia mentioned at the beginning of the Apocalypse, signifying, as it were, a remnant of believers. It came into being round the figure of the prophetess and visionary, Jane Lead, who in her turn received the impetus for its formation from Dr John Pordage, the author of some remarkable theological studies of Boehme's works.[3] The group was supposed to be inter-denominational, for the Churches were to be regenerated from within. And certainly Pordage, as an Anglican minister, had no difficulty in reconciling his loyalties. But at the same time certain sectarian characteristics developed. Public meetings were organized and another Boehme enthusiast, Richard Roach, a young scholar from St John's College, Oxford, records in his manuscript, *Account of the Rise and Progress of the Philadelphian Society*, that,

> . . . they met in Baldwin Gardens in the House of Mrs. Joanna Oxenbridg. w. whom Mrs. A. Bathurst Combined who were Two Principal Persons in carrying on ye Spiritual Work: & both Enlightened Persons and both having great & Wonderful Experiences & Manifestations fro ye Heavenly World.
> (Bodleian MS. Rawlinson D.833, fol. 65 recto)

This Mrs Ann Bathurst was a connection of the noble family of

---

[1] William Erbery, *A Call to the Churches*, London 1653, pp. 36–7.

[2] William Erbery, *Nor Truth nor Errour*, London 1647, p. 13.

[3] John Pordage, M.D., *Theologia Mystica*, London 1683; *Treatise of Eternal Nature*, London 1681.

that name and a manuscript in three volumes describing her spiritual experiences, a kind of interior diary, forms part of the Rawlinson collection at the Bodleian Library, and the late Earl also sent a reproduction of her portrait to the Library.[1] But eventually the meetings proved too large and noisy for Mrs Bathurst.

> . . . they were constrain'd to take a Larger Place, ye room where they met not being but a Private Chamber & Mrs. Bathurst then Aged & Sickly not being able to bear so Great a Conc. & ye Disorders attending it.

Unfortunately these meetings were invaded by groups of what were called 'French Prophets' or 'Camisards', emigrées from the Cévennes war, who specialized in violent ecstatic manifestations.[2] Mrs Lead and her associates made use of Westmorland House while the rest gathered at Hungerford Market. Roach says,

> The Hungerford Meeting met with great Opposition & Violence from ye rude Multitude: and Continued for about Half a Year till Division Growing also among themselves, they were not Able to hold it any longer, & so that Party laid down their Publick Design.

But it was not only after the time that Jane Lead formed the actual Philadelphian Society that meetings were held. In the days before Dr Pordage's wife's death, she had been the heart of a group which became fired with the same strange emotionalism as the Camisards.

John Pordage was the 'son of Samuel, merchant, of London'[3] and he is listed as admitted pensioner at Pembroke College, Cambridge, in 1623, his BA degree is listed for 1626 and a

---

[1] Bodleian MSS. Rawlinson D. 1263, 1338. The Hon. W. R. S. Bathurst, FSA, uncle of the present Earl Bathurst, has explained to me that Ann Bathurst, née Gammon, born 1610, was the second wife of the third son of the eldest son of Alderman Bathurst, 1529–95, the founder of the family.

[2] See Ronald Knox, *Enthusiasm*, Oxford 1950, p. 356f; and Nils Thune, *The Behmenists and the Philadelphians*, Uppsala 1948, p. 136f.

[3] Venn's *Alumni Cantabrigiensis*, Vol. III, p. 381. See also the pedigree of the Pordage Family, Bodleian MS. Ashmole 851, f. 200.

doctorate of medicine (incorporated from Leyden university) in 1640. He married a widow, Mary Freeman, formerly Mary Lane, in 1633, who was originally from Worcestershire. And he seems to have been in orders, for in 1644 he reappears as curate-in-charge of St Laurence's Church at Reading. By 1647 he is established as rector of Bradfield, nearby. It is significant that Bradfield was one of the richest livings in the country at that date and the circumstances under which Pordage received his preferment are mysterious.[1] It had been held by Richard Baylye, President of St John's College, Oxford, who had succeeded Archbishop Laud as Vice-Chancellor of the University and Baylye was personally removed from his offices by the fourth Earl of Pembroke, who sided with the Parliamentarians during the Civil War. It may have been through Pembroke's influence that Pordage gained the living. His son Samuel was certainly steward, later, to the Fifth Earl. Or it might have been through the influence of Elias Ashmole, then living in the area and a great admirer of Pordage's skill in astrology; though Ashmole had not yet made the marriage to Lady Mainwaring which was to give him ascendancy in Bradfield.

Amongst the circle of villagers there who became enthusiastic supporters of Behmenism Pordage was always known as 'Father Abraham' and his wife as 'Deborah'. After one extraordinary public demonstration, a pamphlet entitled *A Most Faithful Relation* was brought out ridiculing Pordage, and his enemies were eventually able to get him deprived of his living, after a sensational trial; again the occasion of a whole spate of pamphlets.[2] It is clear Pordage was suspected of some kind of possession and he is reported as rushing out of church 'bellowing like a Bull, saying that he was called, and must be gon'. Mr William Foster, one of the local gentry, whose wife seems

[1] J. Ecton, *Thesaurus Rerum Ecclesiasticarum*, London, 1742, p. 540.
[2] John Pordage, *A Just Narrative of the Proceedings of the Commissioners of Berks*, quoted in Cobbett's *State Trials*, Vol. V. *Truth Appearing thorough the Clouds of Undeserved Scandal*, Thomason Collection, British Museum, London 1665. Christopher Fowler: *Daemonium Meridianum, Sathan at Noon*, 1656.

to have been intimate with the Pordages, was the amazed spectator, and at their home was still more taken aback to find 'Mistress *Pordich* Clothed all in White Lawne, from the crown of the Head to the sole of the Foot, and a White rod in her hand'. She was surrounded by supporters who hailed her as 'Prophetess' and set about dancing country dances and 'making strange noyses'. They explained that '*It was a rejoycing, because they had overcome the Devil*' and soon Dr Pordage reappeared upon the scene, 'all in black Velvet' and Foster was pressed to bring his wife to join the company when he made excuses, 'Then said the Doctor, there as nothing can be done without her'. In spite of the disappointment 'they keep dancing of the Hayes, and Trenchmore, and expecting when they shall be taken up to Heaven every hour'.[1]

As a result of this outburst Pordage did not enjoy his prize for long. The neighbouring ministers in Reading and Abingdon who had Presbyterian leanings, Christopher Fowler, John Tickle and Simon Ford, combined to attack him on points of doctrine, and though the charges brought against Pordage before the *Committee of Plundered Ministers* were dismissed, the successful case following the uproar in Bradfield came shortly afterwards, and in 1654 Pordage was ejected.

The family did not leave the neighbourhood entirely, though, and indeed old maps still show a 'Pordage Farm' at Woolhampton[2] in this area, for according to an entry in *Calamy Revised*, for 1669, Pordage was then known as

Head of a conventicle at Reading of 'tradesmen of every parish of the toune and neere'.

A number of Oxford scholars started to be attracted to the group which seems to have met at Reading. As Roach explains,

[1] *A Most faithful relation of two wonderful passages which happened very lately . . . in the Parish of Bradfield.* Printed by James Cottrell, London, 1650. British Museum Thomason collection and Harvard Library.
[2] This information was kindly supplied by Mr Hills, lately Headmaster of Bradfield College, Berks.

This was at R. . . . where for sometime they kept up a Continual Oratory both Day & night relieving one another by turns: . . . close watch they were obligd to keep by reason yt upon ye Fresh Opening of Heavens & Powers of ye Spirit descending there was an opening . . . of ye Bottomless Pit . . . Heavenly Visions voices raptures & Enjoyments were given to enable them to Conquer & bear down ye Infernal apparitions.

In spite of these rather questionable manifestations, which illustrate the weakness of those movements that came to be included under the heading 'Enthusiasm', it is clear from Roach's account that some deeply sincere and very learned people supported Pordage's group. The Pordage family life, indeed, gained an extraordinary repute. For Richard Baxter commented as follows on

. . . Dr. *Pordage* and his Family, who live together in Community, and pretend to hold visible and sensible Communion with Angels, whom they sometime see, and sometime smell.[1]

Baxter knew of this through a young man who was living with the Pordages in 1649 and who is thought to be Abiezer Coppe himself. Mrs Pordage and their daughter Elizabeth were both buried in the churchyard of Bradfield when they died and quite a long time after his wife's death Pordage seems to have moved to London where he met fresh inspiration in the form of Jane Lead, 'whose Extraordinary Gift of Revelation y Dr gave great regard to & Attended upon'. He practised Medicine during his last years, even advertising from Holborn offering to send packets of 'scurvy grass' through the post to clients. Pordage was never lacking in enterprise. It was during the 1680s that Pordage's two important studies of Boehme's doctrine appeared. He himself died in 1681 and was buried at St Andrew's Church, Holborn.

Explaining the origin of the Philadelphians, Roach says,

It was then from some of this Inward Mystical Way in England that ye Philadelphian Society had its Rise: & that with a fresh Concurrence & Holy Gale of a Divine Life & Power Opening

[1] Richard Baxter, *Reliquae Baxterianae*, London 1696. Vol. I, p. 77.

first & Principally in Mrs. Pordage wife of John Pordage Doctor of Physick: who married her for ye Excellent Gift of God he found in her; wch Gift he also became in a high Degree Partaker of. Mr. Pordage was particularly Acquainted with Oliver Hill a Great Mystick of St. John's College in Oxford, who was very familiar with Dr. Everard.

This last was the famous translator of the *Hermetica* and of the *Theologia Germanica*, as well as the mystic Tauler's works, and Oliver Hill was himself the author of a theological study.[1] Moreover, although Jane Lead herself, in her books, *Enochian Walks with God*, for instance, or *A Fountain of Gardens*, writes in a highly ecstatic vein of visions inspired by Boehme's symbolism,[2] one of her greatest admirers was the brilliant Oxford orientalist, Francis Lee, or 'Rabbi Lee' as he used to be called at St John's College. When he had relinquished his fellowship there as a Non-Juror, Lee was studying medicine at Leyden and came across a book of Mrs Lead's, translated into Dutch and German by a correspondent of hers, one Fischer; as a result he was so impressed that he set off back to London to meet the author. He became devoted to her, and acted as her secretary, for her sight was beginning to fail. In 1696, he married Mrs Lead's widowed daughter, Barbara, and it was Lee who edited the Philadelphian journal, *Theosophical Transactions*, which clearly reveals in its contents, Lee's own Cabalistical preoccupations. Jane Lead received loyal support from her son-in-law, and from others like him – Baron Knyphausen, for instance, who sent her an allowance from Germany – during the last year she spent in an almshouse at Stepney.

Since men like Edmund Brice, a Fellow of All Souls, his friend Thomas Bromley, a considerable Hebrew scholar, and Richard Roach himself, who made a successful ecclesiastical

---

[1] Oliver Hill, *Epistola ad Anglos. Being an Introduction Out of a Larger Treatise into the Mysteries of the True Christian Religion*, London 1689. Where Hill is then said to be an 'Exile for the Law and the Gospel at Lisbon'.

[2] Jane Lead, *Enochian Walks with God*, London 1694 (see for instance pp. 37–8); *Laws of Paradise*, London 1695; *Fountains of Gardens*, London 1696–1700, vols. I–II.

career for himself in London, mixed in Philadelphian circles, these were clearly not entirely composed of cranks. The Earl of Pembroke had been a frequenter of Pordage's conventicle and the Duke of Buckingham, who is said to have interested Charles II in Boehme's doctrines, employed Samuel Pordage, Dr Pordage's son, in his household.[1] In fact the admirers of the 'Great Theosopher', as Coleridge was later to call Jacob Boehme,[2] were often as not the learned and the cultivated. The theosophical tradition, as it has so far been traced, was not only the preoccupation of petty tradesmen. The intellectual world absorbed it, or challenged it, and no account of seventeenth century English thought can be complete without an examination of this subtle and complex network of symbolism.

[1] See *Jacob Boehme Quarterly*, New York, Vol. I, no. 5. 'The Behmenists and the Philadelphian Society', Serge Hutin, p. 9. Samuel Pordage published *Mundorum Explicatio, or the Explanation of a Hieroglyphical Figure*, London 1661, based on a diagram of his father's.

[2] Samuel Taylor Coleridge: Pencil notes to flyleaf of Vol. I of Boehme's *Works*. London 1764–81, British Museum copy, C,126,k,1 The paragraph runs as follows:

'The fault of the Great German Theosopher lies in the opposite extreme. But this ought not to excite thy scorn. For the attempt is dictated by Reason, nay even by Consistency . . . Jacob Behmen *the Philosopher*, surprizes us in proportion as Behmen the Visionary had astounded or perplexed us . . . Frequently does he mistake the dreams of his own over-excited Nerves, the phantoms and witcheries from the cauldron of his own seething Fancy, for part or symbols of a universal Process; but frequently likewise does he give incontestable proofs, that he possessed in very truth "the Vision and the Faculty divine!" '.

CHAPTER IV

The Men of Learning

*

What the French court circles had described as the 'Musical Philosophy', the concept of Universal Harmony stemming from the Florentine Platonists, took deep root in English intellectual life. Both the academics and the artists accepted it with enthusiasm, or else reacted against it with vigour. It satisfied a hunger for wholeness roused by the Renaissance, and in an age of extreme sectarianism the syncretic element appealed to that yearning for unity which has reawakened in our time. Such an essentially Jacobean figure as John Donne, whose adventurous mind instinctively strove to weave together into a harmonious pattern the odd fragments of new knowledge about the world that explorers, astronomers and natural philosophers were constantly uncovering, shows many signs of preoccupation with this symbolism. A particularly striking passage reveals Donne's instinct for reunion in faith. He is thinking of winning back the Jews, paradoxically by means of their own mystical tradition – a more optimistic point of view than that held by the Austrian scholar Widmanstadt who regarded the Kabalah, for all his interest in it, as a Trojan horse within the Christian church. Many of the Christian Cabalists had too much realism to accept the view Donne proposes. Speaking of the 'Torah', or the Old Testament books ascribed to Moses, the Pentateuch, Donne declares,

> The Author of these first five books is *Moses*. In which number, compos'd of the first even, and first odd, because Cabalistick learning seems to most *Occupatissima vanitas*, I will forbear the observations, both of *Picus* in his *Heptaplus*, and in the Harmony of *Francis George*, that Transcending Wit, whom therefore *Pererius*

charges to have *audax nimis, et ad devia et abruta opinionum praeceps ingenium*, though they have many delicacyes of honest and service-able curiosity, and harmless recreation and entertainment. For as Catechisers give us milk of the Religion, and positive Divines solid nutriment, so when our conscience is sick of scruples, or that the Church is wounded by schismes, which make *solutionem continui*, (as Chirurgians speak) though there be proper use of controverted Divinity for Medicine, yet there be some Cankers (as *Judaisme*) which cannot be cur'd without the *Cabal*; which is (especially for those diseases,) the *Paracelsian* Phisick of the under-standing, and is not unworthyily (if it be onely applyed where it is so medicinable) call'd *praeambulum Evangelii*.[1]

This is a passage that teaches us much. Donne knew enough of the Kabalah to understand the special significance for it of the Torah, of which it was an extension; the one being the written, the other the unwritten law. He was also aware of the special play on numbers often used in cabalistic symbolism. He had read Pico and Giorgio. Of the latter he rightly had a high opinion. He considered the chief use of the Kabalah was to heal the breach between the Jews and the Christians. Thus used it was a preparation for the gospel and a 'Paracelsian Phisick of the Understanding'. Paracelsus' doctrine of the 'Matrix' had long dominated Donne's mind[2] and he had the same sort of respect for the figure of Hermes Trismegistus, to whom the 'Hermetic' literature was attributed, as Ficino's circle; quoting a saying of his, '*Nequita anima Ignorantia*, Ignorance is not onely the drousinesse, the sillinesse, but the wickedness of the soule . . .' in his sermon on Ignorance.[3] Donne was fond of making such speculations as that 'the Pythagorean oath, by the number of four' was derived from the name of God, the Tetragrammaton, and he discusses the

[1] John Donne, *Essayes in Divinity*, edited by E. M. Simpson, Pt. I. 'Of Moses', p. 10.

[2] W. A. Murray, 'Donne and Paracelsus', *Review of English Studies*, XXV, 1949, pp. 115–23.

[3] John Donne, Sermon 29, *On Ignorance;* see *LXXX Sermons*, London 1640.

meaning of that other divine name used in Genesis, 'Elohim'.[1]
His poem, 'To Mr Tilman after He had Taken Orders' uses the
concept of the mystery cults that Spenser had employed, the
idea of Heavenly Beauty as an Hermaphrodite.

> These are thy titles and preheminances,
> In whom must meet Gods graces, mens offences,
> And so the heavens which beget all things here,
> And the earth our mother, which these things doth beare,
> Both these in thee, are in thy Calling knit,
> And make thee now a blest Hermaphrodite.

In all this Donne displayed that bent for curious learning
which appealed so much to James I, with his taste for Du
Bartas, and the favour he showed to such ingenious minds as
John Gordon's, a Scots scholar who had graced the French
court for many years after his royal mistress, the imprisoned
Queen of Scots, had been obliged to disband her household.
He was made Dean of Salisbury by James and was always ready
to delight him by approving the liturgical observances he
loved by passages 'out of Ezekiell and other places of the
prophets, and by certain hebrew characters and other cabalistical collections'. Gordon specialized in public disputations
with rabbis. He had held one much earlier in 1576, with the
chief rabbi, Benetrius, at Avignon. And the workings of his
imagination can be traced in his contribution to the exposition
of the Circe legend, as it was used for the *Ballet Comique de la
Reine*, performed in 1584 at the wedding of the Duc de Joyeuse
to the sister of Henry III's Queen. The ballet was designed to
demonstrate the belief that,

> The origin of the use of dance and music . . . comes from the
> opinion of the Pythagoreans who believed that God was a number
> and a harmony, and for that reason they honoured Him with
> measured cadences to show that they believed that He was.[2]

An interpretation of this legend on four different levels, together with a detailed description of the actual ballet, was pub-

[1] John Donne, *Essayes in Divinity*, Pt. II; 'Elohim', p. 25.
[2] F. A. Yates, *The Academies of the Sixteenth Century*, p. 270.

lished under the name of Balthasar Belgioso in Paris, 1582. Most of these explanations are rather stilted. On the physical level, for instance, Circe the daughter of the sun and of a sea nymph signifies mixture; the mixture of the elements which results from the movement of the sun, father and form and the mother and matter. But in the view of 'Sieur Gordon', Circe is desire, that desire which leads either to good or ill according to the dispositions of those who harbour it. For according to Gordon desire is inseparably linked with the underlying harmony of the universe and only fatal to base natures. He refuses to set reason and desire at odds, as do the other commentators, after the fashion Racine was to exemplify; and here one cannot help feeling Blake would have supported him.

But this quaint ingenuity, where strange oddments of learning are used to unfold deep truths, as in Sir Thomas Browne's works, was not without its opponents. The counter attack upon the 'Musical Philosophy' began early in the seventeenth century with Ben Jonson. Donne might draw upon the *Dialoghi d'Amore* for his poems *Aire and Angels* and *The Extasie*,[1] but to Ben Jonson the 'Musical Philosophy' was mostly pretentious nonsense. His quarrels with his colleague Inigo Jones, who had come back from Italy full of the theories of Barbari, Scamozzi and Palladio, may have intensified Jonson's irritation with this kind of symbolism.[2] Even Donne shows he is aware that 'Cabalistick learning seems to most *Occupatissima vanitas*', and one of Jonson's latest masques is entirely devoted to a satire upon the kind of outlook fostered by those who supported Francesco Giorgio's doctrines. *Love's Welcome at Bolsover*, performed in 1634, pokes fun at one 'Coronell Iniquo Vitruvius'. Still more at Vitruvius' clumsy workmen, consisting of a Carver, a Freemason, a Carpenter, a Plumber, a Glazier and a

---

[1] John Donne, *The Poems of John Donne*, edited by H. J. C. Grierson, pp. 21 & 47; Leone Ebreo (Judah Abarbanel), *Dialoghi d'Amore*, Rome 1535, pp. 333-4.

[2] D. J. Gordon, 'Poet and Architect', *Journal of the Warburg and Courtauld nstitutes*, Vol. XII, 1949, p. 152 ff.

Masterman, who all perform a dance, while he encourages them with such exclamations as

> *Time* and *Measure*, are the Father, and Mother of Musique, you know . . .
> Well done, my Musicall, Arithmeticall, Geometricall Gamesters! or rather my true Mathematicall Boyes! It is carried, in number, weight, and measure, as if the Aires were all Harmonie, and the figure a well-tim'd Proportion!

Moreover, a character called 'Philalethes' is brought in to describe,

> An Academie, or Court, where all the true lessons of Love are throughly read, and taught; the Reasons, the Proportions, and Harmonie, drawne forth in analytick Tables, and made demonstrable to the *Senses*.

Cornelius Agrippa is satirized in an earlier masque, *The Fortunate Isles*, where a Rosicrucian notary,[1] 'Mere-Foole' is shown in conversation with one 'Jophiel', 'Intelligence to the sphere of Jupiter'; one of the names taken from the same list in the *De Occulta Philisophia* as Blake used for 'Tiriel' and 'Zazel'. First Jophiel promises Merefoole that he shall be,

> Keeper of the Keyes
> Of the whole *Kaball*, with the Seales; you shall be
> Principall Secretarie to the Starres;
> Know all their signatures, and combinations . . .

and then he also promises to summon up whatever spirits from the past Merefoole wishes. The first demand is for 'King Zoroastres', then Hermes Trismegistus. Whereupon Jophiel remarks,

> Tis strange you should name him Of all the rest! there being *Iamblicus*, or *Porphyrie*, or *Proclus*, any name That is not busy.
> MEREFOOLE: Let me see Pythagoras.
> JOPHIEL: Good.
> MEREFOOLE: Or *Plato*.

[1] For the problems concerned with the rise of Rosicrucianism and Freemasonry, see Appendix A.

JOPHIEL: Plato, is framing some *Ideas*,
    Are now bespoken, at a groat a dozen,
    Three grosse at least: And, for *Pythagoras*,
    He's rashly run himselfe on an imployment,
    Of keeping *Asses* from a feild of beanes;
    And cannot be stau'd off.

Jophiel tries to fob him off with two English notables, Scogan and Skelton, but Merefoole wistfully says,

    I had rather see a *Brachman*,
    Or a *Gymnosophist*, yet.

Such passages show Jonson's wide acquaintance with the language of symbolism he satirized. Still, the fact that he could distil humour out of this material is evidence, not only for his interest in it, but also his audiences'. Although he is joking, Jonson is dealing with profoundly serious doctrines, ones with which he evidently expected his public to be familiar. What seems to emerge through his sallies at Inigo Jones is that Neo-classical architecture was being introduced into England together with Neo-Platonic principles, and even the mechanicals were drilled in these, as affecting the mystery of their trade. A certain amount of pomposity arose, therefore, offensive to men of real learning like Ben Jonson, who had a strong dislike of all secret societies and spurious occultism. This dislike of symbolism with any kind of esoteric associations was to mount throughout the century. But so was an equally passionate interest in it. For a true understanding of the situation both these developments must be kept in mind. Without the latter, many great achievements of the period could never have taken the shape they did. Without the former, the complete change of mental climate which so distressed Blake in the eighteenth century could never have come about.

Returning to the supporters of the movement called in France the 'Musical Philosophy', which had always been so distinguished for its syncretic enthusiasm, one cannot help noting that the French Ambassador to the court of James I was none other than Antoine Le Fèvre de la Boderie, the brother of Guy and Nicolas. And curiously enough, it was during the period of his embassy that a copy, dated 1607, was made by a learned Scot, James Hepburn, of a scroll entitled 'a Cabala of the Jewes', from the Royal Library in Paris, and later sent as a gift to Sir Thomas Bodley at Oxford for his newly-founded library, by a former Fellow of All Souls, Clement Edmonds.[1] But one of the most spectacular of these supporters was the English physician, Robert Fludd. Originally of a Welsh family, his father Thomas Fludd had been 'Treasurer of War' to Elizabeth I and had settled at Bearsted in Kent where Robert was born and where he expressed his wish to be buried. He had travelled widely in his youth studying medicine, in France, Spain, Italy and Germany, and throughout his life he poured out a stream of immensely complex treatises, employing an amanuensis, we are told, so that he could freely dictate his numerous works at odd moments.

Robert Fludd made such a great impact on his time for three reasons. First, he emerged as champion of the Rosicrucians,

[1] This is the MS. now classified as Huntington Addenda E. (2429) in the Bodleian Library. It was first brought to my attention by Rabbi Dr O. Lehman, who is at present engaged on an edition and translation of the text. The copy sent to Sir Thomas Bodley was accompanied by a Latin letter, MS. Adds. C.279, fol. 97, explaining how Casaubon, the librarian to Henry IV, caused James Hepburn, learned in oriental languages and well versed in rabbinical writings, to make a faithful copy of the original in the royal library. Hepburn afterwards became a Franciscan Minim Friar and was eventually appointed librarian to the Vatican.

MS. Huntington Addenda D. (1949), also a scroll of the sephiroth containing pictorial representation, is commented on by Moritz Steinschneider in a note in *Hebraeische Bibliographie*, Vol. XII (1812), pp. 111–12, as this is unusual for Jewish Kabalah. Such material, though rare, was apparently popular, for there are other copies in the British Museum, Mantua Municipal Library, Munich, Parma and the Jewish Theological Library, New York. The MS. is ascribed by Professor G. Scholem to Rabbi Reuben Sarphathi (the Frenchman), author of the commentary, with the title *perush ha – yerih ha-gedolah*, 'explanation of the big leaf' (page or sheet), which is sometimes with the text. (This is in the Bodleian collection as MS. Michael 35, No. 5, f. 90–148.) This text represents Italian Kabalah of the 14th or early 15th century and is purely Jewish.

addressing a manuscript, the *Declaratio Brevis*, to James I in 1617, clearing the society of accusations of heresy. Then he became involved in controversy with two figures of world-wide repute; the astronomer John Kepler who was interested in Fludd's cosmological speculations, and the Franciscan Minim Friar, Marin Mersenne, author of *Questiones in Genesium*, who was sponsoring a revival of Giorgio's doctrines, though in a form he hoped could be squared with the full rigour of Christian orthodoxy. John Kepler's attention was drawn to Fludd's work through the vast and miscellaneous study that came out in Oppenheim, in 1617, under the title of *Majoris scilicet et Metaphysica, Physica, Atque Technica Historia*. Kepler himself was basically Neo-Platonist in his thinking, believing firmly that 'inborn tendencies' existed, corresponding to the objective truth. In his *Harmonices Mundi* he quotes Proclus to support him on this point.

> . . . the mind itself, if it had never possessed an eye, would *demand* an eye in order to comprehend things outside itself and would prescribe the laws of its formation, having obtained them from itself. . . . Geometry is coeternal with the Mind of God before the creation of things; it is *God Himself* . . . and has supplied God with the models for the creation of the world. With the image of God it has passed into Man . . .[1]

Kepler accepted the Pythagorean-Platonic views of the universe as the creation of a mystical geometer, dependent upon the laws of cosmic harmony, so completely that it inspired one of his own most remarkable conceptions, the model of the universe to be found in his early work, the *Mysterium Cosmographicum*. Using the Platonic solids he constructed a figure in which these solids were imagined as fitting inside one another. His universe centres round the sun and he inscribed the orbits of the planets between each solid, and in this way dictated the distances between the orbits of the planets.

[1] John Kepler, *Harmonices Mundi*, Augsburg 1619, p. 222. (P. Silz's translation from W. Pauli.)

Into the orbit, or sphere, of Saturn he inscribed a cube; and into the cube, another sphere, which was that of Jupiter. Inscribed in that was the tetrahedron, and inscribed in it the sphere of Mars. Between the spheres of Mars and Earth came the dodecahedron; between Earth and Venus the icosahedron; between Venus and Mercury the octahedron. Eureka! The mystery of the universe was solved by young Kepler, teacher at the Protestant school in Gratz.[1]

Of course it had not been solved, but neither was Kepler talking nonsense. The theory which Kepler evolved and illustrated by a series of highly elaborate woodcuts has been intelligently commented on by Hermann Weyl in his modern study, *Symmetry*. Of Kepler's *Mysterium Cosmographicum* he remarks,

> A mighty hymn in which he proclaims . . . 'Credo spatioso numen in orbe' concludes his book. We still share his belief in a mathematical harmony of the universe. It has withstood the test of ever-widening experience. But we no longer seek this harmony in static forms like the regular solids, but in dynamic laws.[2]

In the same kind of way, the modern Modulor Society accepts the Vitruvian principles by which Renaissance architects like Palladio or Serlio built, according to the conception of it developed by Le Corbusier.

At any rate, it was natural for such a mind as Kepler's to be fascinated by Fludd's use of the theories of Giorgio in his *Utriusque Cosmi*. He was so impressed that his *Harmonices Mundi* contained an appendix, addressed to Fludd. Nevertheless there was bound to be a clash between these two unusual minds. Starting from the same premises they reach totally divergent conclusions. Partly by accident, as Arthur Koestler has shown, Kepler was impelled to accept the notion of natural laws and ceased to be able to see the universe as animated by a living soul and ruled by spiritual essences, angelic

[1] Arthur Koestler, *The Sleepwalkers*, London 1959, p. 251.
[2] Herman Weyl, *Symmetry*, Princeton 1952, p. 77.

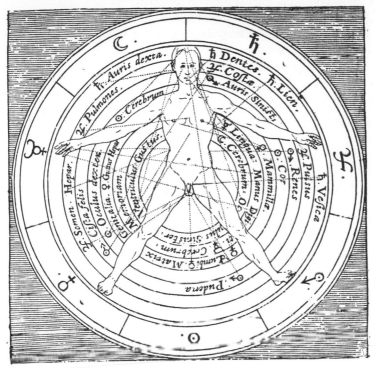

Fig. 7. Vitruvian figure under the planetary signs.

powers. His reading of Fludd's speculations forced him to clarify his own thought and state his disagreement.

> It is obvious that he (Fludd) derives his main pleasure from unintelligible charades about the real world, whereas my purpose is, on the contrary, to draw the obscure facts of nature into the bright light of knowledge. His method is the business of alchemists, hermeticists and Paracelsians, mine is the task of the mathematician.[1]

So Fludd and Kepler are driven their separate ways which may be said to represent the Ancient and the Modern outlook. They reflect, in fact, a crisis in European thought. On the one side the universe is viewed as supported by the Platonic World

[1] John Kepler, *Harmonices Mundi*, Appendix to Part V (Koestler's translation).

Soul, acting according to a harmony which has its source in spirit. On the other 'Science' is coming into being; nature is more and more divorced from super-nature. The natural laws seem dead, clockwork motions compared with the earlier insistence on living spirit informing all. It is ironical that Kepler includes this censure on Fludd in a book 'which is buzzing with astrological and Paracelsian ideas' but still the division is beginning to be clear; a division between an 'Appolonian' attitude and a 'Dionysiac', where the bright light of reason, shining with mathematical precision, confronts the dark mysteries of the unconscious mind working, perhaps, on a more profound level, but less satisfying and far more baffling. And there is no doubt where Blake stood in this conflict. He

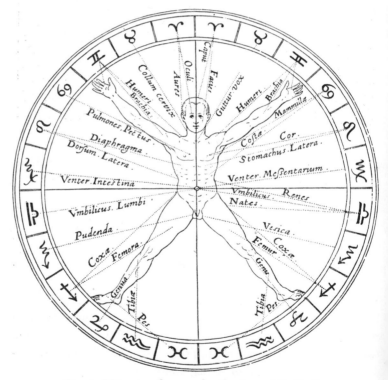

Fig. 8. Vitruvian figure under the signs of the Zodiac.

ranged himself on the side of Fludd, by whom he was clearly very much influenced. For Blake, Urizen, with his dead geometrical obsessions – so opposed to the mystical geometry of the spirit – was always the villain of his myth. And whereas Kepler objected to Fludd's geo-centric vision of the universe, Blake was such a conservative as to be positively a flat-earthist.[1] One of his chief grudges was against the astronomers of his day, who operated under the baneful influence of Urizen and were to be classed with Bacon, Newton and Locke in their materialism.

A curious sidelight on this fateful conflict has been cast by a recent study by W. Pauli, working in collaboration with the psychologist Jung, *The Interpretation of Nature and the Psyche*. Here Fludd's preoccupation with alchemical symbolism is underlined, for just as Kepler was delighted by the sheer mathematical beauty of Neo-Platonic symbols, Fludd had been deeply affected by the alchemist, Michael Maier. Pauli shows that all Fludd's arguments are based on the idea of the world soul being released from the primal matter in which it was originally dormant. Fludd's alchemy is a fairly simple, even primitive one, beginning with the universe divided into four spheres; the empyrean, the aethereal, the sublunary, and the terrestial (which is also the seat of the devil).

The world is a mirror image of the invisible Trinitarian God who reveals Himself in it. Just as God is symbolically represented by

[1] See for instance the following from *Milton*, Plate 29.
The Sky is an immortal Tent built by the Sons of Los . . .
And on its verge the Sun rises & sets, the Clouds bow
To meet the flat Earth & the Sea in such an order'd Space:
The Starry heavens reach no further, but here bend and set
On all sides & the two Poles turn on their valves of gold;
. . . As to that false appearance which appears to the reasoner
As of a Globe rolling thro' Voidness, it is a delusion of Ulro.
The Microscope knows not of this nor the Telescope: they alter
The ratio of the Spectator's Organs, but leave Objects untouch'd.
There seems to be something in this cosmic vision, with its 'valves of gold', close to the old Babylonian concept of the world as an oyster. See *The Sleepwalkers*, Chapter I.

an equilateral triangle so there is a second, reflected triangle below that represents the world. . . . The two polar fundamental principles of the universe are *form* as the light principle, coming down from above, and *matter* as the dark principle, dwelling in the earth. All beings from angels to minerals are differentiated only according to their greater or lesser light content. A constant struggle goes on between these polar opposites: from below, the material pyramid grows upward like a tree . . . the formal pyramid grows downward with its apex on the earth, exactly mirroring the material pyramid. Fludd never distinguishes clearly between a real, material process and a symbolical representation. Because of the analogy of the microcosm to the macrocosm the chemical process is indeed at the same time a reflection of the whole universe. The two movements, the downward and the other upward, are also termed sympathy and antipathy or, with reference to the cabala, *voluntas Dei* and *noluntas Dei*. After the withdrawal of the formal light principle matter remains behind as the dark principle, though it was latently present before as a part of God. In the middle, the sphere of the sun, where these opposing principles

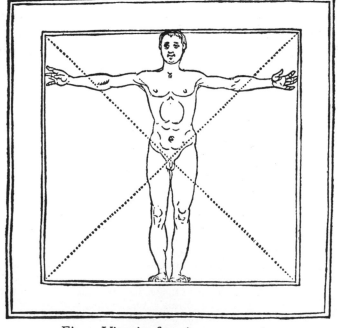

Fig. 9. Vitruvian figure in a square setting.

122

just counterbalance each other, there is engendered in the mystery of the chymic wedding, the *infans solaris*, which is at the same time the liberated world soul.[1]

In order to grasp Fludd's peculiar use of alchemical symbolism, and also because Blake, too, drew on such imagery now and then, the principles of this system must be briefly touched upon. Alchemy, in its European form, dates from about the time of the Neo-Platonists and the various Gnostic sects. It has been said to have arisen from a 'fusion of Egyptian metallurgical and other arts with the mystical philosophies of the Neo-Platonists and Gnostics'.[2] The reason why it took so long to develop into Chemistry proper is that both Neo-Platonists and Gnostics were biased against the material aspect of the universe. At its highest the impulse behind alchemy was idealist in the extreme. Its processes were considered as corresponding with the need to 'regenerate the human soul from its present sense-immersed state into the perfection and nobility in which it was originally created'.[3] In practice it depends on many of the factors we have already encountered. 'Sympathetic action, action at a distance, the distinction between occult and manifest properties, the influence of the stars and the mystical power of numbers.'[4]

The pattern of four elements, arranged in pairs and the idea of their convertibility, was taken from Aristotle; from Plato came the dialectical principle, 'One-two-three. Positive-Negative-Neutral.' And also the concept of a passive recipient upon which qualities could be impressed. But, of course, the basic document for all alchemy is the famous 'Emerald Table of Hermes' or 'Smaragdine Tablet', ascribed to the semi-mythical philosopher Hermes Trismegistus, sometimes identified with

[1] C. G. Jung & W. Pauli, *The Interpretation of Nature and the Psyche*, pp. 191-3.
[2] E. T. Holmyard, *Nature*, 1929. No. 123, p. 520; quoted by J. Read. *Prelude to Chemistry*, p. 8.
[3] M. A. Atwood, *Enquiry into the Hermetic Mystery*, London 1920, p.(26).
[4] E. T. Holmyard, *Nature*, 1929.

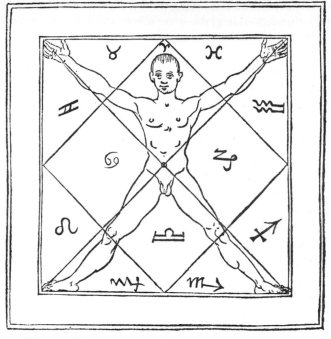

Fig. 10. *Vitruvian figure forming a St Andrew's Cross.*

the Egyptian scribe-god, Thoth. Its thirteen cryptic propositions were accepted as the key to the secret of the Philosopher's
Stone and the mystery of the universe itself. But the general
pattern of alchemic teaching never varies. It asserts the union
of spirit, symbolized by the eagle, or by mercury, with the
serpent or sulphur, matter. This union forms the dragon, or
winged serpent out of a conflict between opposites. The 'mortification', or death, of the dragon was necessary before that
resurrection could take place which alone produces the 'philosophers' stone. By Fludd's time the process was taken more
and more in a purely symbolic sense.

As the result of his controversy with the historian of the
sixteenth century French Academies, Marin Mersenne, by
which he stood for Giorgio's original unadulterated thought,
Fludd found himself adapting Giorgio's symbolism and com-

bining it with Alchemic imagery. It is notable that the learned orientalist, Jaques Gaffarel, who afterwards became librarian to Cardinal Richelieu, was entirely on Fludd's side. And one cannot help feeling that the unfortunate Mersenne set about his task with little enthusiasm. He was only forced to undertake it because in the more rigorous atmosphere of the seventeenth century Giorgio's works began to fall under suspicion. They had indeed been temporarily placed on the Index by the Council of Trent. But at any rate, Fludd obviously enjoyed taking passages of Mersenne's books, and tearing them to pieces, as in his *Clavis Philosophiae et Alchymiae Fluddanae in quo inanes Marini Objectiones . . . examinantur atque auferuntur*; a work which came out in 1633 in response to a defence of Mersenne by one 'Petrus Ganadus'. And when one looks at Fludd's diagrams and the illustrations scattered so lavishly throughout his books, the way in which he had wholeheartedly absorbed Giorgio's symbolism is apparent. Everything is based on three diagrams in Giorgio's *De Harmonia Mundi*. One is a triangle divided into measures from 1–27, which Giorgio ascribes to Adrastus and Calcidius, quoting also Porphyry and Proclus. The next is in the form of a pair of dividers, with the numerations 1–27 inside the figure, while the measurements on the outside continue up to 162. The last consists of interlinked brackets and demonstrates the Pythorgean scale. In other words, the Disdiapason or Double Octave representing the proportions 4 : 1; the Diapason or Octave with proportions 2 : 1; the Diapente or Fifth, proportions 3 : 2 and the Diatessaron or Fourth, proportions 4 : 3. These last two figures are further elaborated by bringing the numbers used up to 10368.[1]

In taking over these figures from Giorgio, Fludd commonly used the triangle to signify divinity, as Pauli has explained, making the 'mundane' triangle its reflection. The pyramid pattern which seems to be based on the dividers, is elaborated

[1] Francisco Giorgio, *De Harmonia Mundi*, Cantici Primi, gathering L. v–viii.

by Fludd by developing it into two interpenetrating pyramids, the 'material' and the 'formal'; again based on the idea of the divine and mundane triangles. While Giorgio's musical scale is quaintly illustrated by a primitive musical instrument with a single string, which Fludd calls the 'Monochordus Mundanus'. These themes appear over and over again, with variations. The monochord, for instance, is set within a celestial globe in one illustration,[1] while in another it stretches through a human figure, clearly based on one of Dürer's studies in proportion, or through a pillar used for the same purpose. Again, pairs of dividers are often used. One, stretched out sideways, appears in the second volume of the *Historia Utriusque Cosmi* and another, upright, on page 184 of the same book.[2] The sacred triangle often appears at the head of other illustrations, sometimes bearing within it the Tetragrammaton, the Divine Name. And the interpenetrating triangles are used to express everything from the heavenly spheres to rainfall. Perhaps Fludd's most faithful representation of Giorgio's figure showing the progression from 1–27 is in his *Mosaicall Philosophy*.[3] This, the only one of Fludd's books to have come out in an English translation (for the international nature of his reputation demanded that he write in Latin), contains the kernel of his teaching, and anyone reading it could come to a fair assessment of his system, provided the elaborate illustrations to the Latin works were also taken into account.

The *Mosaicall Philosophy* is interesting for the various figures contained in it demonstrating Giorgio's progression by means of a series of dots.[4]

---

[1] Robert Fludd, *Utriusque Cosmi Maioris scilicet et Minoris Metaphysica, Physica, Atque Technica Historia*, Oppenheim 1617, p. 90.

[2] Robert Fludd, *De Supernaturali, Naturali, Praeternaturali et Contranaturali Microcosmi historia*, Vol. I, p. 28; Vol. II, p. 184.

[3] Robert Fludd, *Mosaicall Philosophy: Grounded upon the Essential Truth or Eternall Sapience*, Written first in *Latin*, and afterwards thus rendered into *English*. By Robert Fludd, Esq., & Doctor of Physick, London 1659, p. 152.

[4] Robert Fludd, *Mosaicall Philosophy*, p. 152.

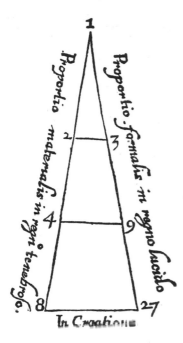

Fig. 11. *Fludd's version of the Triangular Progression from* 1–27.

To conclude, I will demonstrate the mystery of the worlds Creation, by way of an Arithmeticall progression, after this manner.

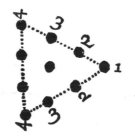

Fig. 12. *The Progression of Creation.*

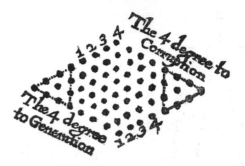

Where the four elements remain in their fimplicity, as they were created complicitely in one watry nature, or rather catholick element, called *Aire*, which is the root from whence generation arifeth unto the period of perfeet compofition, by four degrees or fteps of alteration, namely, from the 4 to the 8. and whither tendeth retrogradely corruption, namely, from 8 to 4.

Fig. 13. *The Four Degrees of Corruption and Generation.*

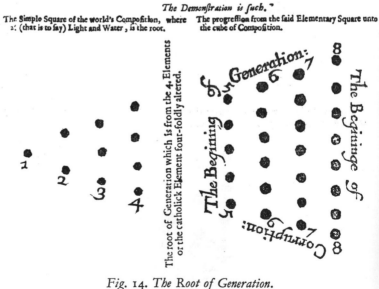

Fig. 14. *The Root of Generation.*

128

And full discussions of the process of creation viewed from an alchemic and cabalistical standpoint, abound. Using a manner of speaking not uncommon among the Christian cabalists, Fludd quotes 'Rabbi Zoar', for a discussion of the 'Catholick Unity', the primal matter from which all things were drawn by the Almighty.

> . . . All things are one in respect of God, but many in regard of us. *And* Plato, Not onely all things are in God, but also all things that exist, forasmuch as they are in God, and do proceed from him, they are but one Entity. *Moreover*, Hermes *in his Smaragdine Table*, As all things were by the mediation of one, so also all things sprung from this one thing by adaptation.[1]

One particular passage from the *Mosaicall Philosophy* seems to have made an impression upon Blake's mind, and as an expression of Fludd's distinctive outlook, deserves full quotation.

> Here you may see the two principles of concord and discord, of love and hatred, and consequently of sympathy and antipathy, of the effects whereof all the Scripture and each member of Philosophy, is full. The catholick matter which was originally extracted out of darkness, namely, the waters, which was made the materiall substance . . . was by the celestiall Alchimy, or spagerick vertue of the divine illuminating emanation, divided according to the contrary and discordant natures of the said two principles, into the upper waters, and the lower waters: whereof the first or higher waters were good, and obedient unto the bright Divinity, and were converted into a fiery nature, being thereupon tearmed the Emperiall nature, for their obedience unto the bright emanation, & were full of intellectuall fire and angelicall light. And therefore this portion of the waters was ordained for the seat of the good Angells. The lower waters contrariwise, as being fecall, gross, impure, and therefore rebellious unto light, and obedient by participation unto darknesse, were placed next unto their dark beginning, namely, the earth, and did possess all that space between the starry heaven and the earth, which is called Elementary, and for this cause is subject to all changes of generation and corruption: And this was ordained to be the seat of Satan and his angels, which is for that cause called the Prince of this world, the Prince of the aire. . . . Lo here the two extreams in the created

[1] Robert Fludd, *op. cit.*, p. 136.

nature! from the upper whereof, a generall sympathy and love, or a Symphoniacall consent of things, is made or effected in this world: by the other, namely the lower, an universall Antipathetical jar, is by turns effected, and intruded into the Symphoniacall accord of things in the lower world, namely when the severe Attributes of God, do rain down into the starry world, influences of a contrary nature, which afterward by their emissions unto the lower world, give liberty and power unto the bad Angells, to work their destructive and Antipatheticall effects, on certain creatures thereof.[1]

According to the pattern here sketched out, one of the two extremes or contraries, an 'Antipathetical jar', disrupts the balance and evokes divine influences from above, from the side of Rigour in the cabalistic scheme; these pour down, as it were from the crystalline sphere, into that of the stars, descending thence to the kingdom of the Prince of the Air, whose evil spirits can then hurt the earth. The source of this idea is in Reuchlin's *de Arte Cabbalistica*, which Fludd seems to have been reading. In a treatise, first published some years ago, of Fludd's *Truth's Golden Harrow*, there is evidence of names taken from Pistorius' collection, *Artis Cabalisticae*, which contains this book of Reuchlin's.[2] These names are from the dissertation upon the divine names of Jesus by Archangelus of Burgonovo, which was also included in this compilation. Certainly the passage is, in its turn, the source of some puzzling imagery in Blake's poetry. The fourth verse of the lyric, 'The Tyger' from *The Songs of Experience* is almost incomprehensible without it.

> When the stars threw down their spears,
> And water'd heaven with their tears,
> Did he smile his work to see?
> Did he who made the Lamb make thee?

And the theme reappears in the Preludium to *Europe: A Prophecy*, where the 'nameless shadowy female' who seems to

[1] Robert Fludd, *op. cit.*, pp. 192–3.
[2] C. H. Josten: '*Truth's Golden Harrow*, an Unpublished Treatise of Robert Fludd', *Ambix*, Vol. III, 1949, pp. 91 ff.

represent Nature, or Vala, complains how 'all the overflowing stars rain down prolific pains'. She uses also the figure of the tree with its roots in the heavens.

My roots are brandish'd in the heavens, my fruits in earth beneath
Surge, foam and labour into life . . .

This is lifted, of course, straight from the well-known illustration to Fludd's Treatise, the *De Theosophico, Cabalistico et Physiologico Utriusque Mundi discursu*, at the end of the first section; where the sephirotic tree is shown with its roots in 'Chether', the crown, and the other spheres as branches, spreading out in turn, rather like those of a date palm.[1] At its point, at 'Malcuth', the tree sprouts into the various orders of the angels, and each branch is labelled with the Latin name for the quality of its particular sphere.

Quite typically, this highly cabalistical treatise, quoting at every turn such authorities as Blaise de Vigenère, Azrael of Gerona, Reuchlin and Pico della Mirandola, is bound up with Fludd's theories about meteorites, and forms the second volume of his *Meterologica Cosmica*.[2] For one of Robert Fludd's characteristics was an outlook which regarded the whole universe as the divine laboratory and which refused to accept any dividing line between what we would call 'Science' and Religion. Thus speculation on Creation and the nature of Man is mixed with theories about thunderbolts and storms, disquisitions on anatomy and various crafts, including military strategy, in Fludd's voluminous Latin works. He absolutely refused to separate the natural from the supernatural, and here his attitude tallies with William Blake's impetuous affirmation, 'There is no Natural Religion'; his protest against eighteenth century Deism. Blake's borrowing from Fludd's Sephirotic Tree has long been as obvious as Fludd's own use of Vitruvian figures very close to Cornelius Agrippa's, in his *Historia Utriusque*

---

[1] Robert Fludd: *Meteorologica Cosmica*, Frankfurt 1626. Tom. II, Tractus Secundus, p. 157.
[2] Robert Fludd, *Meteorologica Cosmica*, pp. 2–156.

Cosmi.[1] What is not quite so obvious is the meaning of the cry
to Enitharmon, in the Preludium to *Europe*.

Ah mother Enitharmon!
Stamp not with solid form this vig'rous progeny of fires.

I bring forth from my teeming bosom myriads of flames,
And thou dost stamp them with a signet . . .

In the oldest books of the Kabalah the Sephiroth are called
'stamps', 'Hothamoth', and we have seen how Cornelius
Agrippa uses the idea, when speaking of the soul whose
'Character is the eternal word'. Very probably Blake took this
image directly from an eighteenth century reader of Fludd, a
Hebrew student of cabalistical leanings, Richard Clarke. In his
Spiritual Voice to the Christian Church and the Jews, Clarke goes
back to a Behmenistic idea, that all creation, or unfolding, in-
volves 'anguish'; the result of the 'deadly antagonism to each
other' of the first two principles, from which a frustration arises
that rolls back upon itself. As Martensen expresses it, 'a
symbolic expression which designates the unsolved dispute,
dissension and tension. . . . We call this Property *Rotation*'.[2]
Clarke explains,

> Wherever Light is, there must be *Fire*, which is its hidden Root
> and *rolling Wheel*, in all Worlds, which . . . the Jews mean, when
> they say that God set his Seal of Sephiroth so hard, that he
> printed it through the three Worlds.[3]

A more direct borrowing from Fludd appears in Blake's use
of visual imagery. The title page of Fludd's *Utriusque Cosmi*
shows a Vitruvian figure, which I have suggested is from
Agrippa, representing Man as the Microcosm. He is surrounded
by the image of the Universe as a coiled rope; temporal life
gradually unwinding itself in the history of the world with the

[1] Robert Fludd, *De Supernaturali . . . Microcosmi Historia*, Vol. II,
pp. 112–15 & p. 275.

[2] Hans Martensen, *Jacob Boehme*, p. 47.

[3] Richard Clarke, *The Spiritual Voice to the Christian Church and to the
Jews*, London 1760, p. 83.

figure of Time drawing it out. Here the cosmic man is juxta-posed against the elemental world, populated by humans, and ornamented with the arts they have developed, and against the world of the heavenly bodies. In one grand vision the prin-ciples of the spiritual and the natural orders are encompassed. While on plate 62 of Blake's epic, *Jerusalem*, an extraordinary and puzzling design shows a gigantic figure extending from top to bottom of the text, faced by a minute one,[1] standing at the base between two huge feet which give forth flames. The tortured head of the giant is formed of coiled rope, which is apparently uncoiling. A halo of peacock's feathers, symbol of worldliness for Boehme as we have noted, stretches out from the head. From the text, which seems inscribed upon a huge rock face the giant is peering over, it is clear that the smaller figure represents Los, confronted by 'the Divine Vision among the flames of the Furnaces', who is also described as pondering upon 'Death Eternal in fierce shudders upon the mountains of Albion'. Los, who stands for the creative imagination in Blake's system, is the symbolic figure with whom Blake usually iden tifies himself; the others among his 'Four Zoas' express roughly, Reason, the ever suspect Urizen, Passion, Luvah, and Tharmas, Instinct. Fallen Man can only regenerate himself through the Divine Vision, apprehended by the faculty of the Imagination and here this faculty confronts the world of generation, which is also the world of death and pain; of the 'devourers and the devoured'. The outlook is not wholly pessimistic, however, for the design seems to present also the vision of Christ made flesh, subject to death; who endures this ordeal to release us from bondage to material life, to 'Generation'. It was second nature for Blake to use, in this startling piece of page design, the layout of Fludd's frontispiece, perhaps very familiar to him, and to give the pattern of Man as the Microcosm his own distinctive twist.

Blake's borrowings were never uncritical. He seldom accepts without reserve the teachings and values of another man's

[1] William Blake, *Jerusalem*, Pl. 62. Keynes, pp. 695–6.

system, yet even those he castigates he has usually, conversely, been greatly influenced by. The *Song of Los*, a short prophetic poem, etched in 1795, already betrays Blake's awareness of the Pythagorean system which was to unfold into Platonism and into the Neo-Platonic movement of the early Christian era; a movement that, although partly a rearguard action against the rise of Christianity in the ancient world, was to have a great effect on the development of this new religion through such minds as Origen's and St Augustine's. But though Blake was aware of this system, and of the Hermetic literature associated with the name of Trismegistus, he was just as critical of it as he was of the negative religion of Sinai, with its tablets of the Law. Equally he was deeply affected by both.

> Moses beheld upon Mount Sinai forms of dark delusion.
> To Trismegistus, Palamabron gave an abstract Law:
> To Pythagoras, Socrates & Plato.
> > (The *Song of Los*, plate 3. Keynes, 245–6)

He is just as bold in his treatment of the basic Alchemic text, the Smaragdine Table of Hermes Trismegistus, which receives a sarcastic mention in his last great epic, where it is associated with the sterile operations of the limited reasoning power.

> The Spectre builded stupendous Works, taking the Starry
> > Heavens
> Like to a curtain & folding them according to his will,
> Repeating the Smaragdine Table of Hermes to draw Los down,
> Into the Indefinite, refusing to believe without demonstration.
> > (*Jerusalem*, IV, plate 91. Keynes, p. 738)

The words supposed to be the key to the mystery of the Universe are here seen as a sort of rationalist mumbo-jumbo, the incantation not of a witch-doctor, but of his modern equivalent, the scientist. Nevertheless, with typical ambivalence, Blake shows many signs of having adapted the alchemic vocabulary of Robert Fludd to his own uses. *The Marriage of Heaven and Hell*, for example, is a highly alchemic book. The images employed, the Eagle, the Lion, Dragon and Viper, are all basic to the language of Alchemy and plate 15 actually shows as a motif an eagle bearing a serpent in its claws, symbol of the union of sulphur and mercury, matter and spirit. The four plates on the elements in *The Gates of Paradise*, on Water; 'Thou Waterest him with Tears'; Earth, 'He struggles into Life'; Air, 'On Cloudy Doubts and Reasoning Cares'; and Fire, 'That end in endless strife' seem to point in this direction. While throughout *America, A Prophecy*, etched like *The Gates of Paradise* in 1793, the action of the poem depends on the struggle between Orc, who is all fire, and Urizen, who fights back against 'the Demon red, with clouds and cold mists from the earth'. David Erdman has likewise drawn attention to the very alchemical manner in which the four sons of Urizen are born in *The First Book of Urizen*, also etched in 1793.

> . . . First Thiriel appear'd,
> Astonish'd at his own existence,
> Like a man from a cloud born; & Utha,
> From the waters emerging, laments:
> Grodna rent from the deep earth, howling
> Amaz'd; the heavens immense cracku
> Like the ground parch'd with heat, then Fuzon
> Flam'd out, first begotten, last born;
> (*First Book of Urizen*, Plate 23. Keynes, 234)

Robert Fludd's special use of a number of technical terms peculiar to this kind of Neo-Platonic, cabalistic speculation may also have influenced Blake; although he would have come across these expressions in the same type of literature elsewhere. When speaking of the primal matter, or *Chaos* from which creation came, Fludd often makes use of the Greek term 'Hyle', which has roughly this meaning. The 'lively presence of the . . . all-informing Spirit,' says Fludd, has to act upon a passive principle 'that . . . is no way enclined of its own nature unto motion or life. . . . Wherefore of its selfe it endueth its mother *Chaos*, or *Hyles* her condition, and is enclined to rest, immobility, darknesse, cold. . . .'[1] As is well known, this word is often

[1] Robert Fludd, *Mosaicall Philosophy*, p. 191.

used by Blake, especially in the epic *Jerusalem*, and has caused much bewilderment. I cannot help feeling, however, that the symbolic figure 'Hyle' who appears in this poem may at the same time represent Blake's worldly and materialistic patron, Hayley. For Blake seems given to play on words, almost as much as James Joyce later; an author who now turns out to have been steeped in Blake's poetry. And a cockney pronunciation of this gentleman's name produces the same sound as the Greek word. However this may be, the expression 'emanation', current coin in Blake's system, is sometimes used by Fludd in a personal, particular sense, not just a general one; and from that Blake may, perhaps, have borrowed. Though the word often simply conveys the sense of a manifestation of life in Fludd's usage; 'that vivifying flame, issuing from the eternal emanation of life', equally it sometimes refers to distinct personal beings.

> Hermes saith: *The gods were discerned in the ideas of the stars.*
> . . . Where, by gods he meaneth, the variety of angelicall emanations.[1]

More important than specific points of contact there is the mental climate of Fludd's system, the feeling after the obscure sources of mysterious truths, inevitably congenial to other thinkers and artists of a prophetic bent. This remarkable man, endowed with a lively curiosity about the world yet working within a framework of thought derived from the Syrian monk 'Dionysius the Areopagite', from Plato himself and the Neo-Platonists, stood by a vision of the world that asserts 'the qualitative indivisibility of the whole' in contradistinction to the passion for 'the quantitative relations of the *parts*' that moved John Kepler, his opponent. As Pauli has emphasized, he held Plotinus' definition of beauty as the eternal radiance of the 'One' shining through material phenomena, rather than the concept which sees it as the correspondence of the parts to the whole. 'Goethe and Fludd,' Pauli says, 'represent the feeling type and the intuitive approach, Newton and Kepler the think-

---

[1] Robert Fludd, *op. cit.*, p. 187.

ing type.'[1] We may bracket Blake with the first pair.

Well within the tradition of Robert Fludd comes the work, later in the century, of the alchemist Thomas Vaughan, the poet Henry Vaughan's brother, and of the theologian John Everard. Vaughan was actually the translator of Pistorius' *Artis Cabalisticae* which Fludd had, as we have seen, drawn upon, and Everard of these mystical classics, The *Theologia Germania*, and The *Mystical Divinity of Dionysius the Areopagite*, of Tauler's works, and above all of The *Divine Pymander of Hermes Mercurius Trismegistus*, which ever since Ficino had published his translation of the *Corpus Hermeticum* in 1462, had been a key text for this whole way of thought. In fact only Book II of Everard's translation can really be called The *Pymander*, the other books being given different names in the 1650 edition of the volume, such as *The Holy Sermon, The Key, His secret Sermon in the Mount of Regeneration*, and representing a group of allied writings all ascribed to the sage Hermes, but of varying dates; some definitely Post-Christian, some apparently Pre-Christian. The tone of Everard's translation is Neo Platonic, to the point almost of Gnosticism, and it is not surprising that for part of his life Everard was under suspicion for heresy. Though he made a brilliant start to his career, taking his doctrate of theology at Clare College, Cambridge, in 1619 and then gaining fame as a preacher at St Martin's-in-the-Fields, John Everard was seldom out of trouble with the authorities, not only on doctrinal issues but also for his boldness in denouncing the 'Spanish Marriage' proposed by James I for his son. It is perhaps providential, however, that Everard was so many years in prison, either awaiting or actually standing trial, for they were the years that he devoted to these important translations. His *Pymander* is notable especially for its discussion of Time and Space and how they came to be. After Man has been made in God's image he falls in love with Nature, or rather with his own shadow reflected in her. It is only after this that Man is embodied and falls into bondage to

[1] W. Pauli, *The Interpretation of Nature and the Psyche*, pp. 205-6.

Time. For, 'Time is the Corruption of Man'; and, 'The Generation of Man is Corruption, the Corruption of Man is the beginning of Generation'. These statements are prefaced by the very Blakean proposition, 'Dissolveable matter is altered into contraries; to wit Corruption and Generation, but Eternal into its self, and its like'.[1] The theory of emanation and of the archetypal man are both prominent in this early text and as in Boehme, the original man first dwelt with God,

> But he, seeing and understanding the *Creation* of the Workman in the whole, would needs also himself *fall to work*, and so was separated from the Father, being in the sphere of Generation or Operation.

In considering such an influential work as the *Pymander* it is not surprising to find that Paracelsus' conception of the Archeus and of the Vulcan, the individualizing principle, is close to that of the 'Workman' operating in Nature and that Blake represents his fallen Man, under the figure of Los, as a workman, a smith. In all the Hermetic literature there is an emphasis on spirituality and a contempt for the body, especially for sexuality, and in paragraph 37 of the second book of *The Pymander*, this is expressed in a curious parody of Scripture.

> . . . the bond of all things was loosed and untied by the Will of God; for all living *Creatures* being *Hermaphrodical*, or *Male* and *Female*, were loosed and untied together with Man; and so the Males were apart by themselves and the Females likewise.
>
> And straightways God said to the Holy Word, *Encrease in encreasing, and multiply in multitude all you my Creatures and Workmanships. And let him that is endued with Minde, know himself to be immortal; and that the cause of death is the love of the body, and let him learn all things that are.*

Here we have set out exactly the formula accepted by Boehme and adopted also by Blake, for the origin of the present creation and particularly for the distinction of sexes.

The Neo-Platonism of Thomas Vaughan, whose prose style has been almost as much admired as his twin brother's poetry,

[1] John Everard, *The Divine Pymander*, London 1650, pp. 7–9.

takes a rather different form. He is much absorbed by the concept of the *Pratum* or meadow of ideas, which he equates with certain symbols used by the Alchemist Flammel and with cabalistic ones. He speaks, too, of the 'Original *Leprosie* of Matter' and shows a picture of the descent of spiritual essences very like Spenser's in his *Mutabilite Cantos*.

> They are shower'd down from the Father of *Light*, through the holy *Intelligence* and the *Heavens*, untill they come to the Moone; Their influence is *good*, as in the first degree, But when it is received in a *corrupt Subject* the influence is also corrupted.

In his book *Magia Adamica*, Thomas Vaughan makes great play with legendary material from the *Zohar*, like the story of the dimunition of the moon's light after the Fall, and the state called the *Nox Corpori* or 'Rendezvous of all Spirits'. This last seems to be what Henry Vaughan is referring to in his poem, 'The Night'.

> . . . His still soft call;
> His knocking time; The souls dumb watch,
> When Spirits their fair kindred catch

And strangely, but typically, side by side with Neo-Platonic images in Thomas Vaughan's work come criticisms of the Greeks for their frivolity and superficiality. For instance his preface to his translation of *The Fame and Confession of the Fraternity of the Rosie Cross*, quotes Philostratus in his *Life of Apollonius* in praise of the 'Brachmans, *with the Excellent and wholesome Severity of their* Discipline', and for a black picture of the minds and manners of the Greeks in contrast with the sound values of the Indian Prince Phraotes. Upon Apollonius asking the prince 'Where he had learnt his Philosophy, and the Greek Tongue, for amongst the Indians . . . there are no Philosophers',

> *To this simple* Quaere *the* Prince, *replies . . . and with a notable* Sarcasm. . . . Our Forefathers (*said he*) did ask all those who came hither in ships, if they were not Pirates; for they conceived all the World (but themselves) addicted to that vice, though a great one:

But you Grecians ask not those strangers who come to you if they be Philosophers. *To this he adds a very dissolute* Opinion *of the same,* Grecians, *namely*, that Philosophy, which of all Donatives is . . . the Divinest, should be esteemed amongst them as a thing indifferent, and proportionate to all Capacities. . . .[1]

Finally, it is important to remember that Thomas Vaughan was the translator of the famous collection of Pistorius, the *Artis Cabalisticae*, which contains Reuchlin's study, the *de Arte Cabalistica*.

An even more extreme position than that adopted by Fludd, Vaughan or Everard is boldly asserted by another seventeenth century writer, Joseph Glanvill; notable for his early use of the Cartesian term 'Vortex', which Blake employs for symbolic purposes, and as collaborator with Bishop Rust of Dromore. Also for the interest this work provoked in Henry More, the Cambridge Platonist. In his *Lux Orientalis* of 1662, Joseph Glanvill gives a Cartesian version of what can only be described as 'the end of the world'.

> At length . . . that great *orb* of *fire* that the *Cartesian Philosophy* supposeth to constitute the *centre* of this *Globe*, shall perfectly have recovered its pristine *nature*, and so following the Laws of its *proper motion*, shall fly out of this *vortex*, and become a *wandering comet*, till it settle in some other.[2]

While in the edition of 1682, where this work is bound up with Bishop Rust's *Discourse of Truth*, it is accompanied by some anonymous notes, actually by Henry More himself. On this passage More remarks that the idea

> . . . looks like an heedless mistake of this ingenious Writer, who though he speak the language of *Cartesius*, seems here not to have recalled to mind his *Principles*.

More, however, substitutes a conception of even greater daring.

[1] Thomas Vaughan, *The Fame and Confession of the Fraternity of the Rosie Cross*, published by Giles Calvert, London 1652. Preface. (Although Vaughan defended the Rosicrucians there is no evidence that he belonged to this movement.)

[2] Joseph Glanvill, *Lux Orientalis*, London 1662, pp. 179–80.

Nor if the Earth become a Sun again, is it like to leave our *Vortex* according to the *Cartesian* principles, but rather be swallowed into the Sun of our *Vortex*, and increase his magnitude. . . . This seems most likely especially if we consider this *Sol Redivivus* or the Earth turned all into the *Materia subtilissima* in itself.[1]

The same kind of imaginative fertility can be found in an earlier book of Glanvill's, *The Vanity of Dogmatizing*, where he is speaking of the great souls that visit the earth from time to time.

. . . those *Mercurial* souls, which were only lent the Earth to shew the world their folly in admiring it; possess delights, which as it were antedate Immortality. . . . The Sun and Stars, are not the worlds *Eyes*, but these. . . These out-travel theirs, and . . . skipping into *Vortexes* beyond their light and Influence . . . with an easie twinkle of an Intellectual Eye look into the Centre, which is obscur'd from the upper Luminaries. This is somewhat like the Image of *Omnipresence*: And what the *Hermetical Philosophy* saith of *God*, is in a sense verifiable of the thus *ennobled soul*, That *its Centre is every where, but its circumference no where*.[2]

Glanvill taught the doctrine of Reincarnation under the title of the *Pre-existence of Souls*, and supported it with what he called 'the Origenian Cabbala' and with arguments not only from Origen as a father of the church, but from the Neo-platonists in general. This belief he regards as 'a Key to unlock the Grand Mysteries of Providence' and the usual majestic train of sages is invoked to sanctify it.

Therefore it was the opinion of the *Indian Brachmans*, the *Persian Magi*, the *Aegyptian Gymnosophists*, the *Jewish Rabbins*, some of the *Grecian Philosophers*, and *Christian Fathers*, that the souls of men were created all at first; and at several times and occasions upon forfeiture of their better life and condition, drop't down into these *terrestial* bodies. This the learned among the *Jews* made a part

[1] Henry More, *Annotations upon* . . . *Lux Orientalis*, London 1682, pp. 141–2. [Followers of Eliphaz Levi in the nineteenth century also used the symbol, in a rather Blakean sense.]

[2] Joseph Glanvill, *The Vanity of Dogmatizing*, London 1661, p. 241.

of their *Cabbala*, and pretend to have received it from their great *Law-giver*, Moses.[1]

Quoting an authority who had gained some respect among interested Gentiles of that period, Glanvill cites Menasseh Ben Israel for the assurance that 'Pre-existence was the common belief of all wise men among the *Jews*, without exception'.[2]

Material of the same nature as Thomas Vaughan used for his translations and Joseph Glanvill for his speculations forms the substance of the Rosicrucian, John Heyden's, work. He was the author of a study called *The Harmony of the World*; almost a compendium of such knowledge, since it begins with a definition of the emanative system and continues with surveys of astrology, alchemy, platonic geometry and spirit lore. Some of Heyden's definitions, are in fact admirable, being both subtle and clear. Here is his presentation of the Cabalistic sephiroth.

> God is a Spirit Eternal, Infinite in Essence and Goodnesse, Omniscient, Omnipotent and of himself necessarily existent; He is a Globe of Light, whose Centre is everywhere and Circumference no where. . . . There are some Properties, Powers and Operations immediately appertaining to him, of which no Reason can be given nor ought to be demanded; nor the way or manner of the Cohaesion of the Attribute with the subject can by any means be fancied or imagined.
>
> In the second Region stand *ten spirits*, which are substances *penetrable* and *indiscernable*, they are the principal names of *God*, or as it were his members, that have *Divine powers*, by *Instruments*, *Vestments*, or *Exemplars* of the *Archetype*. . . .

These influences, Heyden explains, penetrate first to the angelic world and its hierarchies, then to the 'quire of blessed

[1] Joseph Glanvill, *Lux Orientalis*, p. 34.

[2] Joseph Glanvill, *Lux Orientalis*, pp. 2–3. [Menasseh ben Israel engineered a campaign on behalf of his people which has been ably documented in Lucien Wolf's *Menasseh Ben Israel's Mission to Oliver Cromwell*, London 1901. As part of the current effort to enlist sympathy for the Jewish people, a rabbi, Jacob Jehudah Leon, constructed a model of Solomon's temple for the States of Holland, which was exhibited in Paris, Vienna and London.]

souls', then into the heavens and finally the 'planets and men'. A highly Christianized version of the Sephiroth follows, where the first three spheres are thus described.

> The first of these Lights is called *Eheie*, and he is attributed to God the Father and Rules *Cether* . . . the second light is called *Jod Tetragrammaton*, and he is attributed to the second person, *Jesus Christ*, and at his command *Hochma* . . . The third spirit is called *Elohim Jehovah*, and is attributed to the *Holy Ghost*, he commands *Binah* . . .

He then lays down a definition of the emanative principle itself.

> An Emanative cause is the Notion of a thing possible, an Emanative effect is Co-existent with the very substance of that which is said to be the cause thereof.[1]

By mid seventeenth century, then, a number of distinguished and powerful minds had explored the traditional symbolism that had found its way into England from Italy, France and Germany and had made it their own, handling it with skill and defining it with perspicacity. Although already under challenge from the more sceptical and materialist view beginning to develop, this traditional imagery permeated the thought of the age to a remarkable extent.

[1] John Heyden, *The Harmony of the World*, London 1662, pp. 1–9.

CHAPTER V

The Cambridge Scholars

*

The traditional symbolism with which we have been concerned
was far from being the preserve of the learned, yet we have
seen how great a part such men in fact did play. Of them all,
however, out of all the scholars of that age, John Milton, and
the group who followed him at Cambridge University and are
usually known as the Cambridge Platonists, must be considered
key figures for our purpose. Milton, one of the most massively
erudite men of his day, exercised an enormous influence over
Blake, among many others, as a thinker as well as a poet. And
the Cambridge Platonists affected the eighteenth century
through William Law and his disciples, for instance, almost as
much as the seventeenth.

What was the reason for the extraordinary hold which
Milton's life and personality had over Blake? For he made him
the subject of one of his own epics. Milton was, of all English
poets, the one most filled with a high sense of vocation, of
religious dedication in the exercise of his art; and from an early
age. His republican sympathies would have appealed to Blake,
who lived, after all, in a very similar situation in history. The
sense of excitement and exultation which Wordsworth felt
during the early days of the French Revolution came through
many of Milton's political writings at the beginning of the
English Civil War. And the conviction of the high spiritual
destiny of England among the nations, which made Blake name
his archetypal man 'Albion', comes through Milton's writings
again and again. Also, since Blake belonged to the intellectual
climate of the seventeenth century in so many ways, and inherited the tradition of those times, he must have found Milton's

outlook congenial. Then, during his middle years Milton lived in a certain obscurity, because of his blindness and the turn of political events. So did Blake during the Napoleonic wars. Both men possessed an ingrained native obstinacy and their psychological make-up could be said to be complementary. Blake has been described as an Introverted Intuitive in W. P. Witcutt's study,[1] and it may well be that he was fascinated by a temperament in which emotion and instinct struggled against the domination of reason.

There are signs of a genuine tension, also, in Blake's feelings for the earlier poet. For in spite of Milton's concern for spiritual things, and his powerful imagination, his mind was too matter of fact to hold the genuine prophetic quality. He remained precise and concretely materialistic even when speaking of heavenly matters, so much the scholar that his respect for abstract reasoning limited his vision and made him produce a very prosy deity, for example. Above all, he had 'single vision or Newton's sleep', and had it very badly. His mind could never accept paradox and it was this defect which drove him to the Unitarian position he finally adopted. Blake saw all this, and indeed the essence of Milton's attraction for Blake lay in the fact that he felt bound to stand out against him. For to Blake 'Opposition is True Friendship'.

On one subject Blake's prejudice and Milton's coincided. Traces of Milton's conception of Woman as a purely secondary and derivative being, combined with Boehme's picture of Eve as a degraded substitute for the Virgin Sophia, appear in scattered passages throughout Blake's work. An example is the opening of the second book of *Milton*.[2] In Blake's case the bias

---

[1] W. P. Witcutt, *Blake – A Psychological Study.*

[2] William Blake, *Milton*: Book the Second, plate 30:

But the Emanations trembled exceedingly, nor could they
Live, because the life of Man was too exceeding unbounded.
His joy became terrible to them; they trembled and wept,
Crying with one voice: 'Give us a habitation and a place
In which we may be hidden under the shadow of wings:
For if we, who are but for a time and who pass away in winter,

of the tradition he took over helped to push him in this direction, though there are signs of tension with his wife. In Milton's case the shock of the desertion by his first wife that reverberates through his pamphlet, *The Doctrine and Discipline of Divorce*, might be expected to account for his bitterness. It was a bitterness that Blake felt uneasy over both as it appeared in Milton and as he detected it in himself.

There is, however another question to be considered. One which would need a very detailed analysis for a full and accurate conclusion to be arrived at. Did Milton have an acquaintance with the system of the academies and the theosophy represented by such doctrines as Jacob Boehme's? Did it colour his outlook at all thoroughly? The studies of Dennis Saurat on this matter which championed Milton's dependence as this tradition have been to a great extent discredited and it is very difficult to prove from Milton's own writings that he must have had such interests.[1] The most that can be done is to look at his background, his circle of friends and at the sources available to him, and to put forward a few suggestions. To begin at the beginning, John Milton's mind had been moulded in his youth by two remarkable schoolmasters of St Paul's, the elder and the younger Gill. They shared the outlook of men like Gabriel Harvey and the circle of Sir Philip Sidney and apart from being sensitive to the achievements of the academies in reviving the thought and literature of the ancient world, they were well aware of the Jewish mystical tradition also. Alexander Gill, the senior, who taught Milton Hebrew, mentions the *Sepher Yetzirah*, the earliest cabalistic text, in the *Treatise on the Trinitie*, while his later book, *Sacred Philosophy of Scripture*,

---

Behold these wonder of Eternity we shall consume:
But you, O our Fathers & Brothers, remain in Eternity.
But grant us a Temporal Habitation, do you speak
To us; we will obey your words as you obey Jesus
The Eternal who is blessed for ever & ever. Amen.'

[1] Dennis Saurat, *Milton: Man and Thinker; Blake and Modern Thought; Blake and Milton.*

shows clear signs of his reading Pico della Mirandola, Archangelus and Reuchlin, whose works would have been available in Pistorius' collection.[1] Gill also used Jacob Brocard's *Mystica et Prophetica Libris Genesis interpretatio.*

Again when Milton went up to Christ's College, Cambridge, he may very well have heard about a remarkable former fellow of that College, the Hebrew scholar Hugh Broughton. He had long since created a considerable sensation in wider circles, being very aggrieved that he was not allowed to translate the whole Bible single-handed. Though he was not included among the scholars who worked on the Authorized version, for his Puritan leanings were disapproved of, some old copies of this version do have genealogical tables which are the work of Broughton. Since 'the bishops would not endure to have Mr Broughton's name' attached to these, they were marked with the Broughton owl; (the family came from Owlbury in Shropshire). The translations of some of the Old Testament prophets Broughton did make give us an idea of why his style was described as 'curt, and something harsh and obscure', yet they 'do carry in them a kind of holy and happy fascination'. Like John Gordon he had a leaning towards public disputations with rabbis. A dispute which took place at Frankfurt with Rabbi Elias, in 1590, for example, occasioned a long letter from Rabbi Abraham Reuben at Constantinople. His encounters with rabbis gave him a feeling for the predicament of the Jews and he reveals the way in which his conscience had been touched, after his puritan fashion, and also his considerable knowledge of Hebrew, in a work entitled *A Require of consent to agreement against Jews, who by us are hardened, and perish.* From his experiences in disputations Broughton had learnt how Jews reacted to the Christian attitude towards them and had discovered, too, that they were much impressed by arguments in favour of Christ as the Messiah, based on the Kabalah. He quotes Rabbi Elias as exclaiming,

[1] H. F. Fletcher, *The Intellectual Development of John Milton*, Vol. I, University of Illinois Press, 1956, pp. 276–83.

Oh that you would translate the New Testament in such Hebrew as now you speak to me, ye should turn all our Nation.[1]

Broughton continually quotes Abarbanel, the Talmud, the Mishnah, and especially the *Zohar*. He delights in legendary material, drawing on the Babylonian Talmud for the belief left by the prophet Elias that

> . . . 6000. years the world stands 2000. years *Tohu* (or before the Law) 2000. in the Law. 2000. *in the dayes of Messias*: which is by interpretation *Christ*.[2]

We know how much play Blake continually made with the figure of 6,000 years throughout his symbolism.

A young scholar well versed in Hebrew, at Broughton's Cambridge college might easily become interested in his curious works, especially if he shared his Puritan leanings. Just as he might have noted the biblical commentaries of Henry Ainsworth, a member of the sect of Brownists, whose interpretations are all of a highly cabalistic sort.[3] Or again as a poet he could have followed the mystical speculations of William Alabaster, another man learned in Hebrew traditional symbolism and with strongly syncretic leanings.[4] As a convert to Catholicism Alabaster was in trouble with the Inquisition for the daring nature of his cabalistical treatise, *Apparatus in Revelationem Jesu Christi*. After returning to the Anglican communion he produced a commentary upon the four living creatures of the Apocalypse in 1621 and his *Ecce Sponsus Venit* and *Spiraculum Tubarum* appeared in 1633, while a Hebrew Lexicon came out in 1637. Milton could have found much to attract him in the workings of such a visionary and original mind as Ala-

---

[1] Hugh Broughton, *A Require of Consent*, p. 617f. of John Lightfoot's edition of Broughton's *Works*, London 1662.

[2] Hugh Broughton, *A Treatise of Melchisedek*, *Works*, p. 244.

[3] Henry Ainsworth, *Two Treatises*, London, 1789. See Introduction, 'Some Account of the Author', LX.

[4] William Alabaster, best known as a poet, included many speculations on the reunion of Christians and the basic 'True Religion' in the two books he published in 1633, the *Ecce Sponsus Venit* and *Spiraculum Tubarum, seu Fons Spiritualium Expositionum*.

baster's. And the publication of the English translation of Blaise de Vigenère's Treatise *of Fire and Salt* in 1647 would have provided Milton with a very convenient handbook, if he had cared to use it, as a guide to the Jewish Mystical Tradition. Again Milton's debt to Du Bartas's poem on the Creation, the *Devine Weekes*, has long been acknowledged. Much of this poem is meaningless without an appreciation of the traditional symbolism, including Kabalah, employed in it. And while Milton's use of Walton's Polyglot Bible has been stressed, the way that Walton looked back to the great Antwerp Polyglot in compiling his book is often forgotten. And that bears the strong influence of the brothers Boderie,[1] whose cabalistic preoccupations left many traces in the sections of the Polyglot each was responsible for. On his Italian tour we know that Milton deliberately frequented the academies there, which still kept up the Renaissance tradition.

Finally his friendship with Samuel Hartlib has to be taken into account. This Prussian merchant kept up a correspondence with many of the great continental figures still concerned with the tradition while he was living in England. One key letter of his to Boehme's friend, the Silesian nobleman Abraham von Frankenberg, has already been published in Margaret Lewis Bailey's *Milton and Jakob Boehme*,[2] but its full implications seem to have been passed over. Frankenberg was friendly with the famous Menasseh ben Israel, who was able to arrange for the readmission of the Jews into England during Cromwell's rule. And he knew the great Bohemian scholar, Comenius, another figure well versed in Kabalah. Hartlib's letter to Frankenberg, dated 1646, speaks of the latter's 'pamphlet with the fourfold and geometrical figures', touches upon Alchemic, Neo-Platonic and Cabalistic symbolism and especially, apparently, the

---

[1] See the Preface by Arias Montanus in Vol. I of the Antwerp Polyglot (1569–72), where he pays tribute to the work of Nicolas Le Fèvre de la Boderie; the Syriac Grammar and Dictionary in Vol. VI and the preface to Vol. V by Guy Le Fèvre de la Boderie.

[2] Margaret Lewis Bailey, *Milton and Jakob Boehme*, New York 1914, pp. 84–9.

Lurianic Kabalah. Allusions are made to Athanasius Kircher, Benedict Figulus, a Rosicrucian scholar, to the 'Tabula Smaragdina of the chronology of the Cherubims', to a 'Table of Hebrew Philosophy'; and Frankenberg is also required to procure for him the works of Gaffarel, Giorgio's French supporter; *Codicus Caballistarum*, *Avis sur les Langues* and the *Abdta Divinae Kabala Mysterium*. A reply is sought through 'Dr Comenius or kinsman George'. If Hartlib shared his interests at all with him Milton must have known his way round this kind of symbolism, at least to some degree. The thought of Commenius, of Hartlib, and of their friend John Dury, the Scottish minister from Hugenot France, has lately been shown to be the moving force behind the English Civil War. Their influence in the circles Milton frequented at the time cannot be overestimated. Hugh Trevor Roper proves that Cromwell's supporters were fired by a vision of society

> made vivid to them by three philosophers, none of whom was English but who may be called, both in their limited practical aims and their wild bloodshot mysticism, the real philosophers and the only philosophers, of the English Revolution.[1]

Like the idealism of the French academies, the absorption in the traditional symbolism stemming from the Renaissance that moved their thinkers, whether one considers it 'bloodshot mysticism' or no, affected the course of history, not simply the private studies of scholars. For a man in Milton's position, then, to have been ignorant of the Kabalah and the Neo-platonism associated with it, would be extraordinary indeed.

Milton had not long left Christ's College, Cambridge, when Henry More arrived there from Eton, in 1631. This was the youth who was to become the most famous among the 'Cambridge Platonists'. The long tradition of Greek studies in Cambridge made it a likely centre for such a development, and the young Henry More was immediately impressed by the then Mildmay lecturer in Greek studies, Joseph Mede, whose

[1] Hugh Trevor Roper, 'Three Foreigners and the Philosophy of the English Revolution', *Encounter*, February, 1960.

Clavis Apocalyptica turned More's mind to the allegorical interpretation of Scripture; a subject in which he became increas-
ingly engrossed.[1] Robert Gell, More's college tutor, after
being Wentworth Hebrew lecturer, succeeded Joseph Mede as
Mildmay lecturer in 1638. His published sermons show a preoccupation with cabalistical symbolism which may have formed
More's tastes in this direction also. He freely quotes in them
'*Georgius Venetus* . . . his *Harmonia Mundi*', Joachim of Flora,
Paracelsus, Dionysius the Areopagite and Origen. Speaking
of the biblical Wisdom, he defines the Sophia as

> . . . the emanation of the power of God, a pure influence flowing
> from the Almighty: from whom, as from a living fountain, all
> forms flow; who is the great President of the Universe, For the
> emanation of this Angel, is that which the *Platonists* call, *The soul
> of the world*; who *beareth all things by the word of his power, Hebr.* 1.3.
> the same whom the *Cabalists* call the greatest and supreme Angel,
> Metatron.[2]

The other major influence upon the young Henry More was
Benjamin Whichcote, the Vice-Chancellor, who formed the
minds of men like Cudworth, Smith and Tillotson; as well as
Henry More's, from the time when he became fellow of
Emmanuel College. Whichcote adopted a position which broke
down the barriers between Philosophy and Theology and is
close to that of Plotinus among the Neo-Platonists and Ficino
among the Renaissance scholars. Following Whichcote, Henry
More soon became a devotee of that collection of ancient
authors so continually cited from the time of Ficino onwards:
Pythagoras, Plato, Philo, Hermes Trismegistus, Plotinus,
Clement of Alexandria, Origen and Dionysius the Areopagite.
Plotinus' *Enneads*, the *Theologia Germanica* are the main sources
for More's 'Philosophical Poem', the *Psychozoia*, written in
Spenserian style and continuing the tradition of Spenser's

---

[1] Joseph Mede, *Clavis Apocalyptica*, London 1627.
[2] Robert Gell, *A Sermon Touching God's Government of the World by
Angels*, London 1650, p. 12.

Platonism. In the introduction to his edition of this remarkable poem Geoffrey Bullough has defined its aims.

> The purpose of the *Psychodia Platonica* is to combat materialism by showing the spiritual nature of all existence, the modes of spirit in the world of human experience, the religious implications of the theory of immanence. In *Psychozoia* he takes as his central figure the Soul of the World, Psyche, and arranges his poem systematically to display the phases of this third Hypostatis of the Plotinian Triad. Representing Psyche as the daughter of the Absolute, he embarks on an account of her 'Parentage, Marriage, Clothing and Offspring'.[1]

Two figures from among the varied characters of the poem particularly concern us; the abominable *Hyle*, representative of materialism, and *Physis*, embodying the concept of the 'veil', the principle of 'nature vegetative', and of 'Arachnea, the web of sense-perception'. Inevitably Hyle is the villain.

> Foul *Hyle* mistress of the miry stroud,
> Oft her withstands and taketh great delight
> To hinder *Physis* work, and work her all despight.[2]

But though More uses Plotinian concepts he does so in the service of Christian theology. When speaking of the Plotinian triad, *Ahad*, *Aeon* and *Psyche* he quickly points out the parallel with the Christian Trinity.

> This is the famous Platonicall Triad: which though some that slight the Christian Trinity do take for a figment; yet I do think it is no contemptible argument that the platonists, the best and divinest of Philosophers, and the Christians, the best of all that do professe religions do both concur that there is a Trinity.[3]

A similar position was taken up by Ralph Cudworth, the celebrated master of Christ's College, in his great *True Intellectual System of the Universe, wherein all the reason and philosophy of Atheism is confuted and its impossibility demonstrated*, written in opposition to the philosophy of Hobbes. Both More and Cud-

---

[1] Geoffrey Bullough, *Philosophical Poems of Henry More*, p. xli.
[2] Henry More, *Psychozoia*, Canto 1, verse 44.
[3] Henry More, Preface to the *Psychozoia*, 'To the Reader'.

worth were frequent targets of the Neo-Pagan Platonist of the eighteenth century, Thomas Taylor, precisely because of their devotion to Christian doctrine.[1] A religious impulse, likewise, moved another important member of More's circle, his 'heroine pupil' Anne Finch, who became Viscountess Conway. Sister of one of More's favourite students, John Finch, Lady Conway made her house at Ragley a centre for Henry More's circle and had a share in guiding the enthusiasms and speculations of this circle. Already as a young bride she had exchanged letters with her father-in-law championing the Egyptians as the source of Greek learning, alluding to the prophet Enoch and attributing to him the 'two pillars' of the 'Craft Legend', 'the one of stone against the inundations of water, the other of brick against the fury of fire'.[2] This might seem an odd subject for a letter from a daughter-in-law, but Lord Conway evidently considered it quite natural that Anne should correspond with him in these terms. Only we find him taking her somewhat severely to task.

> Daughter
> You seeme to thinke that Philosophy was fitted for the Religion of the Heathen, and that it cannot agree with Christian Religion, and also you seeme to think the Aegiptians had better learning then the Graecians. . . .[3]

Into the calm life of happy friendships, devoted family relationships and study Lady Conway led, there entered early the tragic element that was to bind her closer to her brother's tutor. At the age of twelve she had suffered from a violent fever and since that time had been subject to severe migraine. This terrible disease grew worse and worse, in spite of the attentions of William Harvey, then the most famous physician in England, until eventually she lived in almost continual agony. Her relatives were naturally quick to blame her ailment upon her

[1] Thomas Taylor, *The Cratylus, Phaedo, Parmenides and Timaeus of Plato*, London 1793. See for instance p. 260 following, and the passage quoting Damascius in the Preface to Plato's *Parmenides*, pp. 286 ff.

[2] Marjorie Nicolson, *The Conway Letters*, p. 37.

[3] Marjorie Nicolson, *op. cit.*, p. 34.

studious habits. In fact these intellectual interests must have helped to keep her sane, but this did not prevent her brother writing to her in such terms as the following.

> Wherefore Madam, walk into the cool fresh ayr, mornings and evenings, play at any trifling and easy games, pass away the time merrily with your Associates and Companions, and give your minde abundance of ease from curious mediations. For besyde that you shall releive nature, you also do an act of reall vertue and Christianity. For assuredly the main end that Christ came into the world for, was to sett us free from the slavery and drudgery of our naturall complexions, be this complexion, wordly, sensuall, or Intellectuall.[1]

With these subtleties did Anne's brother John try to temper the ardour of her intellectual pursuits; but without success. For at this very time Anne was instrumental through her correspondence, both with Henry More himself, and with his former tutor Robert Gell, in setting More to work on his first cabalistical book, the *Conjectura Cabbalistica*. On 28th March 1653 More writes to her from Christ's College, Cambridge, with this admission.

> Now to your Ladiships long and learned letter, I will say onely thus much to it, that it is penn'd with very good judgement, but I take it not to be fitt to trouble your Ladiship, now in course of Physick, with any answer to the particular passages thereof. Onely I tell you, if you intimated, which I suspected before, that you looked for an Allegory of Adam and Eve, it has injected such a peremptory purpose in me of interpreting the 3 first Chapters of Genesis with a continuall paraphrase verse by verse according to a triple sense, Literall, Philosophicall, and Morall, that I can not for my life sett my self about any thing but this till it be done . . .[2]

Henry More was responsible for interesting the physician François Mercure Van Helmont, son of the great scientist Jean Baptiste of that name, in Lady Conway's malady, and for years at a time Van Helmont made his home with her at Ragley. From the first, too, he communicated to them both his caba-

---

[1] Marjorie Nicolson, *op. cit.*, p. 76.
[2] Marjorie Nicolson, *op. cit.*, pp. 74–5.

listical enthusiasms, as More's letter describing their first meeting shows clearly enough.

He brought me recommendations from the Princess Elizabeth, and a large letter from a learned person in Germania . . .[1]

This person showed that he had the intention 'to bring into view again the old Judaicall philosophy out of their own writings, which is a noble designe' . . . and he was, of course, the famous Knorr von Rosenroth, compiler of the *Cabbala Denudata*, which appeared in two volumes; the first in Sulzbach in 1677 and the last in Frankfurt, 1684. His contacts with Van Helmont and his correspondence with Rosenroth, which is printed in the *Cabbala Denudata*, brought Henry More's knowledge of Jewish mystical symbolism up to a higher standard. His earlier work, the *Conjectura Cabalistica*, shows a defective understanding of this system, as a Jewish critic, Zwi Wereblowsky, has been quick to point out.[2] The last part of the compilation, the section on the Christian cabala, is now thought to have been the work of Henry More and Van Helmont. But the work is valuable chiefly because a Latin translation has been given in full of the oldest books of the *Zohar*, the *Sifra di Tseniutha*, or *Book of Concealed Mystery*, the *Idra Rabba* or *Greater Holy Assembly* and the *Idra Zutta* or *Lesser Holy Assembly*, together with a very full, Luranic commentary on these three books.[3]

[1] Marjorie Nicolson, *op. cit.*, p. 323.

[2] Zwi Wereblowsky, 'Milton and the Conjectura Cabbalistica', Vol. XVIII, *The Journal of the Warburg and Courtauld Institutes*, 1955, pp. 90–113.

[3] Among the contents of the *Cabbalah Denudata* may be listed: the *Porta Coelarum* of Abraham Hereira; the *Valley of the Kings* by Naphtali Hirtz, a key to Lurianic Kabalah; the first tract 'on souls' by Moses Cordovero; a 'key to the Kabalah' based on Cordovero's *Pardes Rimmonim* and on Joseph Gikatilia's *Sha'Are Orah*; the three oldest books of the Zohar; extracts from a work called *Precious Moon* by Chagim Vital and two Lurianic tracts on the transmigration of souls. Henry More's contributions were as follows: in volume I, part 2, *Quaestiones & Considerationes paucae brevesque Tractatum primum libri Druschim*. Then, following Von Rosenroth's *Amica Responsio ad D. Henricum Morum*, comes a letter in English addressed from Ragley. There is also the *Visionis Ezechielticae sive Mercavae Expositio*, and

It is, of course, impossible to tell if Blake ever had any access to the *Kabbala Denudata*, a book which was to dominate the Christian approach to the Kabalah from that time on. But the number of concepts, which are prominent in these three Zoharic books and which reappear within Blake's own system is extraordinary, whatever the reason for it. For instance, great play is made with the idea that Man being made in the image of God means that the divine must bear a family resemblance to the human.

> And in that formation appeareth the true perfection of all things which existeth above the Throne. Like as it is written 'And the appearance as the likeness of Adam upon it from above' Ezekiel i. 20 . . .[1]

Blake expressed this in his defiant line from *The Everlasting Gospel*.

> Thou art a Man, God is no more . . .

And the doctrine of original androgyny is unmistakably asserted in the *Idra Rabba*, also. The creative activity is seen as the work of a cosmic smith; a 'workman', like the workman of the *Pymander*. From his anvil sparks fly forth.

> And those sparks which fly forth flame and scintillate, but shortly they are extinguished. And these are called Prior Worlds.
> And therefore they have been destroyed, and persist not, until the Holy Ancient One can be conformed, and the workman can proceed unto his work.
> . . . Then proceeded the workman unto His work, and was conformed, namely as Male and Female.[2]

Blake's Los in his 'binding of Urizen', works in the same way. Seizing 'the Light that flow'd down on the winds', he beat the 'subtil particles', 'condensing' them into an orb.

---

finally the *Fundamenta Philosophiae Sive Cabbalae Aeto-Paedo-Melissae*, a highly Platonic work on matter and spirit. The section entitled *Adumbratio Kabbalae Christinae* and the end of volume II, is now attributed to Van Helmont.

[1] S. L. MacGregor Mathers, *The Kabbalah Unveiled*, the *Idra Rabba*, chapter 43, p. 251.

[2] S. L. MacGregor Mathers, *The Kabbalah Unveiled*, p. 301.

> Roaring indignant, the bright sparks
> Endur'd the vast Hammer; but unwearied
> Los beat on the Anvil, till glorious
> An immense Orb of fire he fram'd.
>> (*The Book of Los*, chapter IV. Keynes, p. 260)

The notion of the 'shrinking' of Adam after the Fall which is part of Lurianic Kabalah,

> When Adam Protoplastes sinned his stature is said to have diminished, his members are said to have dropped off . . .

is a constant theme of Blake's prophecies.

> . . . till weaken'd
> The Senses inward rush'd, shrinking
> Beneath the dark net of infection.
>> (*The First Book of Urizen*, chapter II. Keynes, p. 236)

And so is the belief in early giants which the *Zohar* derives from Genesis and from the *Book of Baruch*, and who are called 'the sons of the Elohim'. Blake conceived of Nature, again, as a veil before eternal reality and in the *Idra Rabba* a veil is stretched out before the Ancient of Ancient Ones which becomes eventually conformed into a feminine personification of light.[1] The fourfold division, so important in Blake's vision, is evident; based on the four rivers of Paradise. The ultimate heaven is seen as Eden, too, as distinct from 'the Garden', which is already in the created world, and a distinction is continually made between the Upper and Lower Mothers; between Enitharmon and Vala in Blakean terms. And Blake is highly conscious also, of the Hebrew attitude to the Divine Name which out of respect must not even be enunciated. The ultimate blasphemy for him is the picture of

> . . . the Spectres of the Dead, (who) calling themselves Sons of God
> In his Synagogue worship Satan under the Unutterable Name.
>> (*Milton*, plate 11. Keynes, p. 491)

And the elaborate balance struck within the system of the

---

[1] S. L. MacGregor Mathers, *op. cit.*, pp. 113–15.

Kabalah, the balance between opposites; the column of rigour
set against that of mercy, is fundamental to Blake, who even
speaks of the 'Equilibrium' as a state in *The Four Zoas*.[1] The
Lurianic image of the 'Kelipot', the 'Shells', the spiritual
dregs which become attached to matter may possibly be echoed,
too, by Blake's Tharmas in his lament,

> I sit in the place of shells and mourn, & thou art clos'd in clouds...
> (*Four Zoas*, Night the Ninth, Keynes, p. 370)

An American critic has seen Blake's symbol of the 'False
Tongue' as a cabalistic allusion likewise,[2] and his addiction to
pictorial patterns arranged in threefold columns is well known.
A few examples are the illustration of James Hervey's *Meditation among the Tombs*, the *Last Judgment* and the tempera painting
now in the Fitzwilliam Museum called *The Spiritual Condition
of Man*. This last comes closest to the pattern of the Sephirotic
Tree, although there are departures from the strict pattern even
here, and the picture shows traces of Far Eastern symbolism in
addition.[3]

[1] William Blake, *The Four Zoas*, Night the Sixth, Keynes, p. 316.

[2] Laura De Witt James: *William Blake: The Finger on the Furnace*, pp.
59–104.

[3] Although *The Spiritual Condition of Man* is a tempera painting composed of three columns of figures arranged in Trinities, with the one
column headed by a male figure, the opposite by a female and the central
by the symbol of a dove, from which rays of light shine down upon the
lower figures, at the same time the masculine column contains female
figures and *vice versa*. Likewise the central figure in the middle column
which should represent Tiphereth in an accurate transposition of the
Sephirotic Tree, is in the fourth and not the sixth position. (Such a position
for Tiphereth is not unknown, however, as in the *Zohar*, folio 246. It is
rather natural too, in Christian versions of the Kabalah, where Tiphereth
stands for Christ, that this sphere should be raised into the upper Trinity.)
Then a feminine, madonna figure appears in the position of Yesod, normally
a phallic symbol of generation. The movement of the painting seems to be
upward, tracing the ascent of the soul, rather than the downward descent
of the Sephiroth. Of the three figures at the base of the painting, who
obviously stand for Faith, Hope and Charity. Faith wears a 'jatta' or top
knot on his head peculiar to Hindu and Buddhist sagas and with a halo in
Buddhist style; (also the female figure at the top of the left hand column
carries a lotus flower). Hope has her anchor and Charity is a Queen whose

In considering the type of symbolism drawn upon so freely by Robert Fludd for example, or Henry More, to illustrate their mental systems, it is scarcely surprising to see that Blake gives the creator a pair of dividers, which he holds in his left hand (the side of rigour and of materialization, cabalistically speaking), in the famous colour-print often called *The Ancient of Days*. Nor is it surprising to find Blake using the term 'Vortex' in a special sense of material creation coming out of the void.

Creating many a Vortex, fixing many a Science in the deep,
(*Four Zoas*, Night the Sixth, Keynes, p. 316)

For this is one of the Cartesian theories which Henry More, like Glanvill, as we have seen, had adapted to his Neo-Platonic vision, quoting Pythagoras and Democritus for the basis of finite creation as a Vortex of particles of fire,

... *this* Vorticall *Motion being the cause of the generation of all things* ... and it may be for this cause also the *Pythagoreans* called the *Decad*, that is the World, Generation.[1]

Again, some light may possibly be cast on Blake's use of the symbol, 'the Lilly of Havilah' (as, for example, in *Jerusalem*, Plate 19), by Henry More's speculations on Genesis in his *Philosophick Cabbala* and *Defence of the Philosophick Cabbala*. In chapter two, speaking of Wisdom, he explains,

And this is that *wisdome* which God himself doth shew to the Soul by communication of the divine Light; for it is said to compass the land of *Havilah*!

crown is the focus of the rays spreading out from the Dove. Her left foot is forward, the side of materiality and this is quite appropriate if she is Malkhuth, in whom the emanations descend down to the material world. The entire picture is surrounded by a series of vignettes, telling the Bible story, from creation to the Last Judgment. For a full explication of this tempera, the largest of Blake's paintings, see Kerrison Preston, *Notes on Blake's Large Painting in Tempera*, Bournemouth 1949, and Sir Geoffrey Keynes's critical catalogue, *The Tempera Paintings of William Blake*, the Arts Council, London 1951.

[1] Henry More, *A Collection of Several Philosophical Writings*, London 1662, p. 103.

In the *Defence* he comments on the word 'Havilah',

From . . . *Deus indicavit, God hath shown it.*

And More likewise is careful to comment upon his description of '*The Region of mortality and death*' which Man entered into upon his eating of the forbidden fruit; and that in a Platonic and Cabalistic sense.

> Nothing is more frequent with the *Platonists* than the calling of the *Body* a *Sepulchre* and this life we live here upon Earth, either *sleep* or *death*. Which expressions are so sutable with this Cabbala with the Text of *Moses*, that mentions the *death* and *sleep* of *Adam*, that it is a shrewd presumption that these Phrases and Notions came first from thence. And *Philo* acknowledges that *Heraclitus*, that mysterious and abstruse Philosopher, (whom *Porphyrius* also has cited to the same purpose, in his *De antro Nympharum*) has even hit upon the very meaning that *Moses* intends in this *death* of *Adam* . . .

And if Blake had already been struck by Porphyry's myth of the Naiades, the Water Nymphs who are the instruments of this process of 'generation', he would have been reminded of them once more by More's treatment of the myth in his *Defence of the Philosophick Cabbala*. These nymphs are shown as drawing the '*Seminal Form* of things' into 'Outward Creation'. He quaintly identifies them with the 'Upper Waters' of Genesis and cites 'that excellent Platonist Virgil' who treats of the Water nymphs in the River Peneus.

> By which passages certainly that knowing Poet understands nothing else but this, That the spinning and weaving of the first contexture of things is in a certain *primordial* or *genital* moisture, in which these Spiritual Powers, the *Water Nymphs* work; whom therefore he brings in teasing and spinning and singing of Love-songs, and the hidden and stollen Venery of the Gods, (that is, of those parts of the celestial Creation that descend . . .) under the waters of the River *Peneus*.[1]

This is just the kind of imagery which Blake in his capacity

[1] Henry More, *Defence of the Philosophick Cabbala*, London 1662, Chapter I, p. 77.

of poet and painter used with mastery.[1] His prophetic poems echo to the sound of the looms of the Daughters of Enitharmon. Sensitive as he was to so much in the achievement of the master minds of the seventeenth century Blake might well have agreed with Coleridge's verdict on Henry More.

> ... Henry More's theological writings ... contain more original, enlarged and elevating views of the Christian Dispensation, than I have met with in any other single volume. For More had both the philosophic and the poetic Genius, supported by immense erudition . . .[2]

And it was an erudition used to noble effect as a genius of Blake's calibre could well appreciate.

---

[1] The most striking example of Blake's preoccupation with this myth of the Water Nymphs, is of course the Arlington Court tempera painting, now usually called *The Sea of Time and Space*. Miss Raine has commented exhaustively on this picture as an illustration to certain passages of Homer's *Odyssey*, given a symbolic significance by Porphyry. (See her article, 'The Sea of Time and Space', *Journal of the Warburg and Courtauld Institutes*, Vol. XX, 1957.)

[2] Samuel Taylor Coleridge, Notes on the fly leaf to Henry More's *Theological Works*, London 1708, British Museum copy, Ashley 5176.

CHAPTER VI

The Turn of the Century

*

Having surveyed the development of a line of thought and a language of symbolism that had been applied in England to philosophy, science and many of the arts for more than a century after its influence had first begun to be felt, how can we fairly assess the situation at the turn of the eighteenth century? Are we dealing with something on the point of decline, or still active and vigorous when the eighteenth century opens? There is no doubt that the climate of thought was changing, and the tradition which derives from the Italian academies and was modified by the powerful influences of geniuses like Paracelsus and Boehme, survived on into the eighteenth century as a kind of undercurrent running against the tide. That it was still a very strong undercurrent can be demonstrated. The period of real decline did not come until the early nineteenth century. And it is an interesting as well as a curious fact that some of the most forthright and challenging expressions of support for it were published in the final decades of the seventeenth century. A sort of crescendo was reached with a work like Anne, Viscountess Conway's, short but penetrating study, brought out in 1692 under the momentous title of, *The Principles of the Most Ancient and Modern Philosophy, Concerning God, Christ, and the Creatures, viz. of Spirit and Matter in general: whereby may be resolved all those Problems or Difficulties, which neither by the School nor Common Modern Philosophy, nor by Cartesian, Hobbesian or Spinosian, could be discussed.*[1] This was actually a translation from the Dutch undertaken at the instigation of the Viscountess's friend, Van Helmont, by a certain 'J. C. Medicinae'. This

[1] Published in London 1692.

162

gentleman had asked Van Helmont if any worthwhile writings of his own or anyone else's remained to be published and had his attention directed to the works of an English Countess which, he says,

> after a brief perusal, I have endeavoured to render into an *English* style, as familiar as the Language would conveniently admit, without some abuse to the Author.[1]

This little book shows a mind steeped in the Kabalah and reveals, too, the great interest taken by Lady Conway in Jacob Boehme's philosophy. Since she gave shelter during her later years to the much persecuted sect of Quakers, their teachings also left a mark on her mind. Above all she was dominated by considerations of a syncretist kind, such as had inspired Ficino and his followers. But in the course of this enthusiasm, she had clearly moved over to a far more unorthodox position from the strictly Christian standpoint, than they would ever have sanctioned; for instance Chapter One discusses,

> How a Trinity may be conceived to be in God, according to the Scriptures; and yet without offence to *Turks, Jews*, or any other People; although we should omit the Terms of Three distinct Persons, which are neither built upon Scripture or sound Reason.

In a note to this chapter Lady Conway draws upon a doctrine developed by Isaac Luria, in his version of the Kabalah; the doctrine of 'Tsimtsum'; the retreat of God into Himself.

> '*God dwelleth in an inapproachable Light. No Man hath seen God at any time.*'
> He diminished therefore (for the sake of his Creatures) the highest Degree of his most intense Light, that there might be room for his Creatures, from whence Place immediately arose, as it were a Circular Vacuity or Space of Worlds.
> This Vacuum was not a mere Privation or *Non ens*, but a certain real Position of Light, diminutively, which was the Soul

[1] *Op. cit.*, Preface.

163

of the *Messias* called by the *Hebrews, Adam Kadmon,* which filleth all that whole Space.[1]

There follows a long discussion of time and space and the problem of how God exists outside them both, yet operates within them. Later, at the end of Chapter Three, there is a long passage on the concept of Emanation.

> . . . all Creatures from the highest to the lowest are inseparably united one with another, by means of Subtiler Parts interoeding or coming in between, which are the Emanations of one Creature into another, by which also they act one upon another at the greatest distance; and this is the Foundation of all Sympathy and Antipathy which happens in Creatures: And if these things be well understood of any one, he may easily see into the most secret and hidden Causes of Things, which ignorant Men call occult Qualities.

This is an interesting use of the idea of emanation since it is considered particularly in the world of creation, as in Blake's system, not simply as existing in God. Lady Conway handles very difficult themes ably and reveals how much preoccupations with a traditional symbolism moulded the thought of the aristocratic and intellectual group to which she belonged.

The pattern of emanation and its mode of working had already been deeply explored by François Mercure Van Helmont, Lady Conway's friend and physician. A remarkable man if only for his life and adventures – there is little doubt that he was the original of the 'Scholar Gypsy' described by Joseph Glanvill in the first edition of his *Vanity of Dogmatizing,* later immortalized by Matthew Arnold[2] – he bequeathed to English readers clear expositions of the way of thought he and his circle accepted; ones that could have been of great use to curious readers of a later date. His book *A Cabbalistical Dialogue* presents the relationship of the emanation to its source,

> . . . No otherwise, than as a beam or light is said to be co-existent with the Sun . . .[3]

[1] *Op. cit.,* pp. 5–6.
[2] Marjorie Nicolson, *The Conway Letters,* p. 309.
[3] F. M. Van Helmont, *A Cabbalistical Dialogue,* London 1682, p. 5.

His *Seder Olam* strongly emphasizes the idea of the 'Spiritual Body', taking up the same position as Blake when he laid down in *The Marriage of Heaven and Hell*, Plate 4.

> . . . Man has no Body distinct from his Soul . . .

Van Helmont insists,

> . . . Spirit and Body are not contrary Essences, as many do vainly and falsely affirm; for every created Spirit is corporeal, having in it the true essence and nature of a Body, *viz*. it is an extended Being, bounded, circumscrib'd with place, moveable, *&c.*
>
> And therefore a humane Soul (which is also a Spirit) is corporeal, and comprehends in it the true Nature and Essence of a Body. The most pure and Spiritual Angels also are corporeal, and as it were Spiritual Bodies.[1]

Though Van Helmont was at pains to dissociate himself from the doctrine of Reincarnation, so positively asserted by Joseph Glanvill in his *Lux Orientalis* where Origen is continually cited as authority for this, amongst other teachings of the 'Origenian Cabala',[2] he gives at the same time much space to the theories of the Lurianic Kabalah on the 'revolution of souls' and particularly on 'world ages'. He links up these with the Vision of Ezekiel of the four 'living creatures', with that in the Apocalypse of the same beings, and these in their turn with the four worlds or States of the Kabalah. The seven Spirits of the Apocalypse he connects too, with the last seven Cabalistic Sephiroth. So it can be said that the main principles of Lady Conway's 'Ancient and Modern Philosophy' are all sketched out in those books of Van Helmont that came out in England during the last decades of the seventeenth century.

A mine of information, likewise, for anyone interested in such matters, was to be found in the journal of the Philadelphian society, *Theosophical Transactions*, edited by Francis Lee. A feature of this periodical was a series of letters supposed to pass between 'Altheus' and 'Crito'. The first correspondent is

[1] F. M. Van Helmont, *Seder Olam* and *Some Questions upon the Revelations*, London 1694, p. 11.

[2] Joseph Glanvill, *Lux Orientalis*, London 1682, Preface. C.2.

much pre-occupied with such cabalistic matters as number symbolism, the use of Hebrew letters, the significance of the arrangement of the High Priest's breast plate and of the imagery of the Apocalypse. The other takes a more down to earth point of view.

> . . . If true, [Crito protests] yet such sublime Notions are of no concern to Religion. The Christian Religion is very simple and plain, fitted for all Capacities. . . . Such Cabalistick and Pythagorean Notions will not be relish't in this Age . . . Divine Emanations are things not to be understood by the common sense of Mankind. And if Intelligible and Orthodox, yet may be of ill consequence to Phantastick and Imaginative Persons. The Ancient Hereticks, *Gnosticks*, *Valentinians*, and others broach'd their Heresies from such kind of strain'd Speculations. There ought to be such a Reverence for God, as to be in some things even afraid to speak the Truth concerning Him.[1]

For the rest the *Transactions* are a mixture of hymns composed for use at the meetings, accounts of visionaries, like the 'Berger Illumé', held up for admiration in the second issue, alchemical disquisitions, discussions on the nature of prophecy, allusions to Jane Lead's own work and a certain amount of serious consideration of mysticism as such. The Catholic mystics are given a respectful place here, though perhaps the bias is Neo-Platonic, being concerned with the handing down of Spiritual powers.

> . . . The Tradition and Succession hereof through the Colleges of the Prophets among the *Jews*; through the Priestly Colleges of the Eastern Magi, among the *Egyptians*, *Chaldeans*, and *Arabians*; and through the Pythagorean and Platonick Schools . . .

It is justly remarked that the tracing out of this tradition in full line of descent, 'were it Accurately and Judiciously done, would be a considerable work'. The discussion of such topics provoked a 'Theosophical Epistle', from 'a learned Gentleman living very remote from London', full of the technical language of the Kabalah.

[1] *Theosophical Transactions of the Philadelphian Society*, London 1697, pp. 80–1.

... From those first Transactions of your Illuminated Fraternity, I
see your Design proceeds from no ordinary influence ... of the
Sidereal Firmament: but from that *Star of Jacob* on high, in the
East of Tiphereth which now appears in the *Aziluthick* World, to
conduct the Wise men to the New *Jerusalem*.[1]

Tiphereth is of course the central sphere of the cabalistic
system of descending emanations, or sephiroth, and the Aziluthick world is the highest, the archetypal world, of the four
worlds of the Kabalah. (The other three are the world of
'Briah' or Creation, the world of 'Yetzirah' or Formation and
the world of 'Asiah' or matter, respectively.) This, then, was the
tenor of the organ of the Philadelphian Society. The warning
voice of Crito could be said to represent the spirit of the approaching age, but the bulk of the contents belong to the
earlier tradition. The *Theosophical Transactions*, among other
things, give a very revealing insight into the mind of their
editor. Francis Lee was torn all his life between the Aletheus
and the Crito in himself; between his predilection for hidden
truths and his straightforward piety as a Christian. There are
signs that in the end Crito won.

But Francis Lee was only one of the scholars preoccupied
with the Philadelphian Society. There was Richard Roach, the
historian of the Society, a schoolfellow of Lee's at Merchant
Taylors', who afterwards also went up to St John's College,
Oxford. Roach was the author of an apocalyptic work, *The
Imperial Standard of Messiah Triumphant*, dealing with the ages
that lead up to the end of the world from a Behemenist point
of view, and also of *The Great Crisis*.[2] Though he was mainly
absorbed in thoughts about the approaching Last Days, Roach
did outline, in the glossary to *The Imperial Standard*, a definition
of the common characteristics of mystics of all ages and faiths.

... in their Process towards Perfection. It is as to the Substance of
it the *Same* in the Writers of all Ages, however differing in External
Profession or Denomination.

[1] *Theosophical Transactions*, 'A Theosophicall *Epistle*', p. 270.
[2] Richard Roach, *The Great Crisis*, London 1727; *The Imperial Standard of
Messiah Triumphant*, London 1727.

And this must be a very early example of an observation which has since become a commonplace. Although it is only fair to point out that Roach's idea of mysticism, as a modern critic has discerned, is closer to Theosophy or even Gnosticism than to the more orthodox conception.[1] Edmund Brice, the Fellow of All Souls who figures in Roach's history of the Philadelphian Movement, also left through his translations moving observations on the interior life, like this one.

> ... The highest wisdom consists in this, for Man to know himself, because in him God has placed his Eternal Word, by which all things were made ... This is that precious thing which *Adam* and *Eve* brought out of Paradise with them for their consolation and refreshment, and left it through their Offspring to posterity.[2]

And Thomas Bromley's works, inspired by his Hebrew studies, show the same preoccupation. *The Way to the Sabbath of Rest* was popular and had several editions, but he also wrote *The Journeys of the Children of Israel* and *An account of the various ways of God's manifesting Himself to Man*.[3]

At the same time, there is no doubt that the very heart of the Behmenist movement in England was the influence of John Pordage, and originally of his wife. Pordage was a controversial figure and even Francis Lee found it necessary to defend him in response to criticism of the Behmenists from his Non-Juror friend Henry Dodwell. Whatever was the truth behind the commotion of his indictment before the *Commission for the ejecting of Scandalous, Ignorant And Insufficient Ministers and Schoolmasters* during his tenure of the living at Bradfield, Lee felt that

> whatever he might have been in 1654, and before that, it is possible that in the space of twenty years, and those two under the

---

[1] Serge Hutin, *Les disciples anglais de Jacob Boehme*, Paris 1960, p. 99.

[2] Edmund Brice, Translation of Ali Pili's *Centrum Naturae Concentratum*, London 1696. Preface, pp. 3–4.

[3] Thomas Bromley, *The Way to the Sabbath of Rest*, London 1650. (Also 1692, 1710, 1802); *The Journeys of the Children of Israel*, London 1710; *An Account of the various ways of God's manifesting Himself to Man*, London 1710.

Cross, that he might become a new man. For it is not till about that time, . . . that his familiar friendship began with my mother.[1]

However one may assess the extraordinary and in some ways contradictory character of John Pordage, his books are extremely able and he shows remarkable theological skill, for instance, in the treatment of the doctrine of the Trinity which opens his *Theologia Mystica*. He then explores the 'Aeternal Invisibles', explaining how Boehme's Eternal Nature emanates from the Godhead. He is particularly absorbed in the image of the Single Eye of God, which we have already noted in Paracelsus, in Agrippa and originally in Suso,

> . . . *which essential Eye of God, looking into it self, and finding nothing besides it self, gives a beginning and end to it self; which beginning and end entring into, and joyning with one another, do constitute and form the Globe of Eternity. So that the Globe of Eternity is nothing else, but the dilatation of the Eye of Eternity, from the Center to the Circumference.*[2]

Another description of this 'Archetypous Globe' appears in his earlier book *Treatise of Eternal Nature*.

> . . . you see the *form* or *figure* that God's Eternal Will formed this Abyss into, *even into a Circle or Globe, and the manner how, viz.* that the desiring Will looking into it self, and finding nothing but himself doth put an end to himself; and so the *beginning, closing with the end there is formed a Round or Globe.*[3]

Here Pordage is drawing out an aspect of Boehme's symbolism, probably borrowed in its turn from the Christian cabalist Reuchlin, which seems to have almost obsessed Blake. The prophetic poems are full of instances of this 'conglobing'. Fuzon is shown

> Moulding into a vast Globe his wrath,
> As the thunder-stone is moulded.
> (*The Book of Ahania*, Chapter I, Keynes, p. 249)

[1] Francis Lee, Letter to Henry Dodwell, 9th April 1699. In Christopher Walton's *Notes and Materials for an Adequate Biography of William Law*, London 1856, pp. 194–221.

[2] John Pordage, M.D., *Theologia Mystica*, London 1683, p. 17.

[3] John Pordage, M.D., *Treatise of Eternal Nature*, London 1681, p. 111.

And during the binding of Urizen,

> Down sunk with fright a red
> Round Globe, hot burning, deep,
> Deep down into the Abyss;
> Panting, Conglobing, Trembling . . .
> (*The First Book of Urizen*, Plate 11, Keynes, p. 228)

These passages show, however, that as with his handling of Swedenborgian imagery in *The Marriage of Heaven and Hell*, Blake was perfectly capable of turning Behmenistic imagery upside down.

No serious study of Pordage's thought can really be made without recourse to the complete edition of his writings in German, published at Amsterdam, 1698–1704. But from the two books that come out in English one draws out an exposition of Boehme's system that is strikingly forceful, showing a well ordered mind with a capacity to mould difficult material. The estimation of him jotted on the fly leaf of a copy of the *Theologia Mystica* belonging to John Byrom, William Law's disciple, and apparently in his handwriting, may not be far wrong.

> I have seen all those treatises, nor without admiration of the most divine and deep mysteries, which . . . can come into the mind of man. They snatch the mind beyond itself – above heavenly things. They are described in a common & perspicuous elocution. To the more obscure writings of Behmen they bright light necessary to understand them. It appears that the Author was taught by God in those mysteries most singularly.[1]

Certainly it is difficult to believe that the author of these books could be the same man as the eccentric of Bradfield but these contrasts are part of the baffling phenomenon that came to be called 'Enthusiasm'. At any rate the Pordages were never long out of the public eye, for one finds Samuel Pordage publishing a poem entitled *Azaria & Hushai* in reply to the first part of

---

[1] John Byrom (?), MS. notes on the fly leaf to a copy of John Pordage's *Theologia Mystica*, (no. 1980, L.B. – 2. 1. 3. 74 of John Byrom's library). Chetham's Library, Manchester.

Dryden's *Absalom & Achitophel,* and another, directed at Dryden's *Medal,* called *The Medal Revers'd, a Satire against Persecution.* As a result he found himself referred to as 'Lame Mephibsheth the Wizard's son' in the second part of *Absalom & Achitophel.* Clearly Dryden was inclined to the same rather sarcastic view of the members of enthusiastic sects as Butler in his *Hudibras.*

Equally, Jane Lead, Pordage's second 'Prophetess', excited a good deal of criticism; indeed she was the object of some persecution from the German Behmenist Gichtel and his followers. Again, her son-in-law Francis Lee defended her hotly. Speaking of her source of inspiration, Lee remarks,

> . . . it is true she pretends not to any visible Schechinah, such as was accommodated to the infant state of the Jews; but she pretends to . . . a Schechinah that is substantial and permanent, even to the real inhabitation of the Holy Ghost as in his Temple . . . I cannot see why she may not depend safely upon the Divine authority of what is thus revealed . . .[1]

Jane Lead was very conscious of her role as a woman, who, because of her sex, had special qualities as a spiritual leader, and this accounts for the considerable literature produced by herself and her followers, in defence of prophetesses. In her vision of the Tree of Life, for example, she conceives the Tree with an Eagle's nest in its branches; the nest of Eve, for, as of old '*Eve* will now come forth as a mighty, strong, terrible Eagle. And henceforth will more wisely build her Nest, than at first she did, through the Lord's permission.'[2]

Her visionary glimpses into certain states of the soul obviously take over something from Dante but in other ways seem to anticipate Swedenborg's pictures of the spiritual world. Here is a typical example from *Enochian Walks with God.*

> . . . the first Circle, was a Pure white Glass of Light; in which, there appeared the Personal Prince of Glory, with a numberless Number of bright Bodily-Figures, with whom the Elders were . . . Then

---

[1] Francis Lee, Letter to Henry Dodwell, above.
[2] Jane Lead, *Fountains of Gardens,* London 1700, Vol. II, p. 106.

next to this was an Azure-Blue-Circle; and here appeared the Faces only of numerous Persons, that are yet living in Bodily Figure in this World (who are some known, and others unknown to me) and the Motto that was written on their Fore-Heads was, *These are Those who are waiting for to break through into Mount Sion.* . . . Then in the third Circle, which appeared like Pale-Lighting, there open'd Seraphims and Cherubims, bright Angels, very numerous that ascended; and were appointed as a Guard, always Ministering to Those . . . The fourth Circle was a more Dark-Dusky-Colour; and here were those who were yet to be gathered in, and born again; Some among them were known by Face to me; they were yet but moving in the Dark Principle . . .[1]

As long as Jane Lead remained alive she was the moving principle of the Philadelphian Society. But even after her death in 1704 a small group of Behmenists, some English some German, used to meet together at Bow Lane Church and their activities have been described by Donovan Dawe in his study of a City firm of which some were members, *Skylbecks: Dysalters, 1650–1950.* Nevertheless as the eighteenth century progressed, interest in Boehme's doctrines took on a rather different character. It is crystallized round the figure of the theologian William Law and it is his inspiration, and that of the men whose writings he drew upon, that was its moving force.

The traditional symbolism, the way of thought, of which Behmenism is one important expression, has now been traced throughout two centuries. It entered the eighteenth century and, as I have said, was more influential at that time than has been realized. But by then its nature had somewhat changed. What were these changes, and how did they come about? And how are we to weigh the value of the tradition itself? The time has come to consider these questions in detail. My own answers to them are bound to seem partial and coloured by personal views. But I can only give what solutions to the problems they raise as occur to my own mind. To sum up: the tradition was the outcome of a genuine religious aspiration; a desire to

[1] Jane Lead, *Enochian Walks with God*, London 1694, p. 37.

create a unity between past and present, between the Christian and the non-Christian past, between the two opposites of an enduring dialectic in the world. The vision of creation as a shadow of the uncreate, bearing divine marks, of man as the microcosm of the universe, of the interaction of various forces to make a tension which alone is fruitful, all this is the result of a real piety and it had effects in every branch of life. The art, architecture, poetry, medicine, music and theology which have come down to us from that time and are part of our common European heritage, all bear its traces. They can be seen in the moulding of our porches, the design of gateposts, the theory of the sexes which we use in our imaginations, the steps of the ballet, the most common poetical allusions. How many literary critics, for instance, fully understand Dryden's meaning in the line from 'The Ode for St Cecilia's Day'?

The diapason closing full in man.

But what happened to the tradition at a later stage? How is it that we have lost track of it, so that we do not even realize it was ever there? Publications, as we have observed, were quite numerous. There seems to have been less attempt at secrecy than might be imagined. The answer to these questions can partly be found in changes taking place in the European outlook as a whole; partly, I feel sure, in certain defects already present within the tradition itself. Founded on Neo-Platonism and therefore lacking the element provided by Aristotle's reverence for natural things in their own right and united with a Jewish attempt to show the descent of the divine without incarnation, it contained within it a profound unbalance which gradually became clear to thoughtful people, and was bound to be especially noticeable to the ecclesiastical authorities. Those who gave their allegiance to this tradition were at first quite unaware of anything within it which might threaten the central Christian doctrines. They did not grasp the dangers of the Neo-Platonic position; the way it could, under cover of 'Spirituality', undermine belief in Man as a 'bridge-being', deliberately created by God as an animal endowed with an immortal soul, belonging at once to nature and to the supernatural world. Unlike the various Gnostic systems which developed in the Middle East during the early Christian centuries, under the inspiration of Montanus, Valentinus, Ammonious or Marcion, for instance,[1] Christian orthodoxy has never accepted a view of Man which regarded him as a dwindled angel, a pure spirit caged in a prison of flesh through some original disaster. For why should God create Man so when He had already hosts of angels? Those thinkers who accepted a philosophy with such Gnostic overtones did not always understand either, that the division into sexes was a God-given ordinance, designed to reveal to each sex its own limitations and necessary dependence on the other. For it was through a desire for self-sufficiency that the angels fell, and in Man God was working out a new and different plan. Then too, Man being made in God's image, this is reflected in the qualities of the sexes. Maybe there is no sex in God, yet if there is Fatherhood there is also Motherhood. This fact was well grasped by the medieval mystic, Julian of Norwich.

In the same way the devotees of the Jewish Kabalah could not grasp the truth that God's immanence does not at all threaten His transcendence. Objectively speaking there is simply no need for any gradual descent into the universe, an approach to the human mind, in which the Divine Essence, is, as it were, progressively diluted. God did not even need Creation in order to love; although Creation is the fruit of Love. The 'Limitless Light', the 'Ain Soph Aur' of the Kabalah, may indeed exist in lonely splendour. But not the Christian Trinity which is itself a community of Love containing the Lover, the Beloved and Love itself; One God. So, after the same pattern, while sexes exist, there is no excuse for

---

[1] These various Gnostic teachers and their doctrines were efficiently described by the scholar J. L. Mosheim in his *Ecclesiastical History*, London 1774, translated by Archibald Maclaine; and *Commentaries on the Affairs of the Christians*, London 1813, translated by R. S. Vidall.

self-love among men. A certain unselfishness is, in fact, demanded.

Yet this is not to say that the system devotedly followed by so many brilliant minds is worthless. It contains deep psychological truth. The pattern which it traces seems to correspond with the way the human mind apprehends certain realities and with the structure of the human imagination itself. There is then considerable subjective validity within this system though it is an unreliable guide to objective truth. Undoubtedly it conforms to archetypal patterns which have great force. The images used alone show that. The Tree of Life, the Cosmic Man, the Balance; these have a profound effect on the deeper levels of consciousness. And after all, we have to consider the Friar Giorgio had dedicated his work to the reigning Popes in complete sincerity. The same spirit of Catholic piety we have seen displayed by men like Blaise de Vigenère when he used the Kabalah in his treatise on Penitence, and Guy le Fèvre de la Boderie, inspired as he was with Counter-Reformation fervour. And there is another aspect to be taken into account. The attraction which the system exercised cannot be fully understood without allowing for the aesthetic sense of Renaissance minds. There is no doubt, to those who have seriously studied it, the *Zohar* is one of the greatest, and most poetic expressions of the human spirit. Their feeling for beauty and fitness was partly responsible for the devotion of the men of that time to the tradition.

Perhaps the most penetrating criticism of this outlook, especially in its Greek aspect, comes in J. Maritain's metaphysical work, *The Degrees of Knowledge*.[1] Speaking of the Alexandrian school he says,

> . . . they desired an intellectual knowledge of God of which the very mode should be divine, . . . and wished at the same time that this supreme . . . knowledge should remain in the intellectual mode, should be a philosophy. And it is impossible to have at one and the same time a philosophy which to be true must enunciate,

[1] Jacques Maritain, *The Degrees of Knowledge*, p. 296.

and a philosophy which in being destroys enunciation; the one cancels out the other.

Maritain goes on to point out the weakness in a system,

which claimed to be mystical, and at the same time remained metaphysical, a dialectic ascension to ecstacy. The same ambiguity reappears in history with every return to neo-platonism. Nicholas of Cusa extended one hand to pseudo-Dionysius and the great mystics of the Middle Ages, but the other to Boehme and Hegel. The phrase apophatic theology then describes an intellectual super-knowledge raised above yes and no, where contraries are identified, in place of the reality of apophatic theology which is 'mystical theology' itself, the contemplation in charity of the saints.

This is the dilemma in which any kind of 'theosophy' stands. The mistakes Maritain describes above, which are the mistakes of minds determined to reach God through the masculine path of power and wisdom rather than through the feminine one of love, were made by most of the figures which have been under discussion, and indeed were made by Blake himself. (It is strange how Maritain's 'intellectual super-knowledge raised above Yes and No', reads like a description of Blake's state, 'Beulah', where 'contraries are equally true'.) Historically speaking, also, one can see that despite the aspiration of the Christian Cabalists, their desire to find a layer of Truth in all religious systems and their wish to convert the Jews, in reality the pursuit of the Kabalah, often had the unintended effect of Judaizing men's minds. And this has rightly been insisted upon by Leon Blau in his study of the subject. The original drive behind the whole intellectual movement we have been following from the time of the Renaissance onwards, was a profoundly Christian one. The power of this driving force became in different ways, weakened, and this was the real reason for its eventual decline. Too great an influence from the Jewish and Greek elements used in the syncretic process itself was one cause of this weakening. But there were others, of a wider sort, which must now be examined.

Vidit cuncta quæ fecerat הוה et erant valde bona gen.1.31

D. IACOBO MAGNÆ BRITANIÆ FR. ET HIBERNIÆ. REGI, SACRVM

BARTAS
HIS
Deuine WEEKES & Workes
Tranſlated:
&
Dedicated
To the KINGS moſt excellent
MAIESTIE
by
IOSVAH SYLVESTER.

ACCEPTAM REFERO LVCEM SVB LVCE SILEBO

. Title page to Josuah Sylvester's *Bartas, His Devine Weekes & Workes*, London, 1605

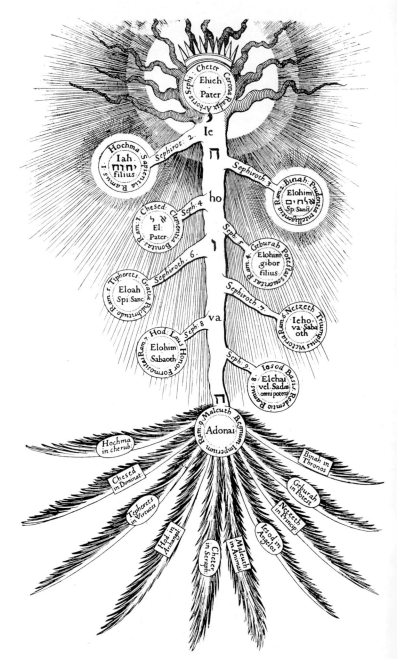

6. The Sephirotic Tree
From Robert Fludd's *Philosophia Sacra*, Frankfurt, 1626

During the seventeenth century, when the long-term effects of the Reformation were working themselves out, a fragmentation into numberless sects and religious groups began to take place. This made for extremes of behaviour and a certain eccentricity, which was later stigmatized under the name of 'Enthusiasm'. It also made for a degree of pettiness and narrowness. The scope of the movement was definitely reduced. There is plenty of evidence for this development in the story of the English Behmenists we have just been tracing out. Then again, there came the gradual growth of that sceptical materialism which was to be the prevailing temper of the eighteenth century; a temper not at all favourable to the values affirmed by the earlier intellectual movement stemming from the Renaissance. Once more, there are various reasons for this change of atmosphere. A disgust with the excesses of religious fanaticism, and particularly the tolerance which grew up as a natural reaction from the horrors of the Thirty Years War, had the effect of lowering, as it were, the spiritual temperature of the age and encouraging a more easy-going approach. This attitude, in its turn, had its own weaknesses. The greater scientific knowledge which grew up with the rise of the Royal Society in England, produced a complacent approval of 'progress'. The 'Enlightenment' had arrived; an outlook in many ways far more superficial and cynical than the one which preceded it. The mechanistic, clockwork view of the universe prevailed which was to provoke William Blake's bitter outbursts, and the beginnings of Western Materialism in its more degraded forms began to be apparent. Although the men of the Enlightenment looked with contempt upon their superstitious ancestors, their mentality was in many ways more childish and much shallower.

When all allowances are made, however, for these external changes, a great deal has to be explained by the degeneration of the tradition from within. It is not surprising, for example, that Samuel Butler in his *Hudibras* should have done his best to make the queer fish of the Commonwealth era appear as absurd as possible. The piety of its earlier followers linked the tradition to the mainstream of Christian thought and devotion. This had a strengthening and vivifying effect and to some extent balanced off the Neo-Platonic extreme. As long as the link held the symbolism we have been examining influenced every aspect of life. Neither the arts, the politics of the time nor the beginnings of science in that age can be justly estimated without taking it into account. There was nothing narrowly esoteric about the movement then. Speaking from such a standpoint Lady Conway was entitled to say that only 'ignorant Men' were concerned with what they called 'occult Qualities'. As long as there remained a close relationship with the Christian culture that distinguished the West, this tradition could never simply be dismissed as 'occult'. Its references were far too wide for that. But the situation changed. The tie with the Church was broken. 'Theosophy' set up as a religion of its own and a certain vulgarization was the result, one naturally repulsive to many sensitive and spiritually-minded people. An immature delight in secrecy for its own sake replaced the earlier discretion. Various secret societies appealed to an appetite for sensationalism. And gradually this provoked a hostile reaction from the public. In Jewish circles the same revulsion took place. Many scholars regarded the Kabalah as a dangerous superstition and the rabbis perceived how by its doctrines the unity of the Godhead might be threatened and also the direct personal contact between the Most High and the individual soul. Only in our own century has this Jewish tradition once more come to be valued among Jews. The same might be said of the reputation of Christian mysticism, which fell under a cloud for a while because of the general disgust with religious enthusiasm. But in making these remarks I am anticipating. Some of them hold good more for the nineteenth than for the eighteenth century. Many traces of an earlier age survived on into Blake's lifetime, as we shall see. The original climate of thought was in some degree preserved. But Blake's own system must be judged as containing certain weaknesses, inherent from the start, in the traditional symbolism he used. Within his system, however, the splendours of its strength were likewise manifested, the more so because Blake had such a firm hold on basic Christian truth. His creation gives a vital, one might almost say a final, expression to a mode of thought long venerated in Europe; the inspiration of numerous masterpieces of the past.

CHAPTER VII

William Law and Eighteenth-Century England

*

By the opening of the eighteenth century the tide of thought had set heavily against mystical fervour of every kind, and the symbolism used in that Renaissance tradition developed by Agrippa, Paracelsus and Boehme among others, was either ridiculed or ignored. Most of those who gave their attention to such things at all would share the view expressed earlier by Samuel Butler, in Canto III of his satirical poem *Hudibras*, where one of the characters maintains,

> Agrippa kept a *Stygian-pug*,
> I' th' garb and habit of a *Dog*,
> That was his Tutor, and the *Curr*
> Read to th' occult *Philosopher*,
> And taught him subtly to maintain
> All other Sciences are in *vain*.
>   To this, quoth *Sidraphello*, Sir,
> Agrippa was no *Conjurer*,
> Nor *Paracelsus*, no nor *Behmen*;
> Nor was the Dog a Cacodaemon
> But a true Dog . . .
> As for the Rosie cross *Philosophers*,
> Whom you will have to be but Sorcerers
> What they pretend to, is no more,
> Than Trismegistus did before,
> *Pythagoras*, old Zoroaster,
> And Appolonius their Master;
> To whom they do confess t'ow
> All that they do, and all they know.

Yet there were undercurrents running through this century, as through the seventeenth. And the central point of these eddies was the figure of the great Non-Juror William

Law, whose friend and disciple John Byrom we have noted for the respect in which he held Dr Pordage's theology. Law gathered round him a comparatively wide circle of followers in his lifetime and exerted a powerful influence even after his death. We have seen from the beginning how those men whose minds were uneasy about the state of religion in the eighteenth century turned naturally to Law as their support.[1] Jacob Duché gives testimony of the profound impact of Law's teaching on his own spiritual development. And I have also stressed its impact upon John Wesley in his youth, and on Samuel Johnson. But the other side of that picture shows the extent to which he was influenced in his turn, by earlier minds, and the way in which he incorporated other men's writings into his own system, wholesale. In some ways William Law's own influence was more a question of the preservation of his predecessors' work than of any new vision being brought to the tradition. Though to understand Law's later writings without some grasp of that tradition is far from easy. It took some time, however, before material published under Law's name was recognized to be really the work of Dionysius Freher or Francis Lee. And since these two exponents of Jacob Boehme's philosophy had great originality and a formidable grasp of the difficult ideas present within it, they deserve further attention.

Dionysius Andreas Freher was a German immigrant, from a distinguished Nuremberg family, who seems to have settled in England, like many other Germans, during the reign of William and Mary. Once in London, he drew around him a group of English and German Boehme enthusiasts, among the most memorable being the artist J. D. Leuchter, the illustrator of Freher's own systematization of Boehme's thought. It is Leuchter who tells us that Freher was born in Nuremberg on 12th September 1649, and died in London on 24th November 1728. One of his uncles, Paul Freher, was the author of a famous biographical collection, the *Theatrum Virorum Erudi-*

[1] See introduction.

tione, Nuremberg, 1688, and a work published in London, in 1646, *A Treatise Touching the Peace of the Church*, by a Philip Freher may well be by another uncle of that name.[1] Freher himself insists that his study of Boehme had begun before he settled in England. Certainly once there, his disciples helped to copy out the large mass of writing he produced on the subject. We have it from a note contributed by Christopher Walton to *Notes and Queries*, 21st November 1863, that Freher had spent some years in Holland with Gichtel and Poiret before being attracted, like Francis Lee, to London by the fame of Jane Lead and the Philadelphian Society. But Freher was not long in gathering a circle of his own around him. Besides his German followers, Leuchter, Lorentz and Carlsshoff, two Englishmen were greatly devoted to him, Allen Leppington and John Berry. John Berry was a clockmaker, indeed master of the Clockmakers' Company in 1723, while his friend Allen Leppington was a drysalter in Bread Street, in the City. He seems to have been a leading spirit in the group which met at the Bow Lane Chapel, not far from Bread Street, where the tradition of the Philadelphian Society was carried on after that Society's dissolution. We have seen that Freher and those attached to him visited this group, and a number of letters from Freher exist in which he exhorts them to practise the spirit of Behmenism as well as studying its doctrines.[2]

Of Freher's own circle we know, from Donovan Dawe's study (*Skilbeck's: Drysalters 1650–1950*, pages 45–50), that Lorenz was a tailor, living at Cross Lane near Long Acre; and we also have some information about a Charles Hayes, of Hatton Garden, who was later associated with the great interest Allen Leppington showed at the end of his life in William Law's own writings. In fact Charles Hayes, a mathematician and chronologist and a prominent member of the Royal African Company, is mentioned for a legacy of £50 in

[1] Charles A. Muses, *Illumination on Jacob Boehme*, The Work of Dionysius Andreas Freher, New York 1951, pp. 1–6.
[2] Charles A. Muses, *op. cit.*, pp. 16–19.

Allen Leppington's 1743 will, and William Law's name is also quoted for a legacy of the same amount. Apart from Boehme's system, which preoccupied him greatly, Hayes was interested in Biblical scholarship and published *A dissertation on the chronology of the Septuagint* in 1751. It is interesting to note that a further bequest of £50 appears in the same Leppington will to Dr John Heylin, a saddler's son, who was Rector of St Mary-le-Strand from 1724 to 1759. Though this has never been proved, it was suggested that William Law was once curate to John Heylin for a while, and certainly the rector was another strong Behmenist. So the picture we are given is of an active group of intelligent men, some men of learning indeed, others prosperous and serious minded citizens, centred in London, who studied the mystics in general and Jacob Boehme in particular, and attempted to guide their lives by their beliefs. They still suffered from that fatal sectarian tendency towards fragmentation, however, and Freher was very conscious of this weakness in the congregation of the Bow Lane chapel, whose 'frequent fallings out, continual discords, heats and animosities' he describes in the first of his *Three Tables with Their Explanations*.

Apart from the Bow Lane group and his own immediate circle, Freher had other important contacts in England. He lived for many years, for instance, at the house of a clergyman, the Rev. Edward Waple, of St Sepulchre's, Skinner Street, London, who had long pursued the study of Boehme's thought. It was to meet his difficulties that one book, the eighth, of Freher's large *Serial Elucidations of the Principles of Philosophy and Theology of Bohemius*, was written. Also a treatise called *Three Conferences between a German Theosophist and an English Divine*.[1] And for a friend of Waple's, a Mr Pierce, Freher composed another, very important, section of the *Serial Elucidations*, entitled 'Nothing and Something'. Dr Charles Muses has explained in his study of Freher, *Illuminations on Jacob Boehme*, that all Freher's early works were written in response to

---

[1] Charles A. Muses, *op. cit.*, pp. 19–20.

requests from friends.[1] And among the friends he must have met regularly while living with the Rev. Waple, and later when he removed to Eagle Court, St John's Lane, Smithfield, after Waple's death in 1712, was Francis Lee, the earlier Non-Juror, whom we have seen make the sacrifice of his Oxford Fellowship, as William Law was later to sacrifice his, and become Jane Lead's devoted son-in-law. Dr Muses quotes the same letter where Lee defends Mrs Lead against the attacks of his fellow Non-Juror, Henry Dodwell, for a pointed reference to Freher's vast expository enterprise.

> ... I know a person of great accuracy of thought, and coolness of mind, as well as of a most holy and primitive life, who is undertaking to render him (Boehme) intelligible by a true and genuine representation of his Principles, both of Divinity and Philosophy, after having read all his books in the original more than ten times, though not without the greatest disgust imaginable in the beginning.

It would be impossible to summarize Freher's achievement, which has been as unjustly judged as he himself first judged Boehme. Hopkinson, one of Law's biographers, makes this sweeping statement on pages 119–20 of his book, *About William Law*, published in 1948.

> Freher can be dismissed in a few words: he wrote pestilential gibberish, and it is a mystery how a man who could rise to such heights as Law did could ever have attached any value to what is nothing more than unspiritual, muddled (and sometimes immoral) occultism.

But there are some points of special interest in Freher's work that can be seized upon. One is his respect for the pagan past which expresses just that sense of a 'True Religion' in existence before Christianity so characteristic of the Renaissance. Like the members of the Italian Academies, Freher turns towards Plato rather than Aristotle. In a dialogue he wrote (*Some Conferences between Adam, Blessed and Constantine*, dated at 1716), he makes Adam deplore those who, 'Forsake the interiour recol-

[1] Charles A. Muses, *op. cit.*, pp. 164, n.40.

lection of the heart, by a vain curiosity of contemplating but the works of God, and sometimes mere chimeras, as the blind Aristotle' and praise the opposite approach of those minds who 'applied themselves to consider God in their interiour . . .' Of these latter Freher feels there were many pagans who came to a real understanding of God, 'of his power, his goodness, wisdome, mercy, providence, holiness, unity, and even of the Mystery of the Holy Trinity'. He quotes examples of such figures, but the more discerning scholarship of his day causes him to show greater restraint in his choice than his Renaissance predecessors.

> If ye are curious to be informed in these matters, ye need only to read the Discourses of Epictetus collected by Arrian, or Simplicius' Comment upon his Manual, – books that are not suspected of pious frauds as are the Sybil Verses and the Paemander of Trismegistus. To these ye may add the writings of some Platonists and of Plato.[1]

Another, very vital characteristic of Freher's teaching, is his refusal to accept a dualist position. When he considers the Light and Dark Worlds of Boehme, he will not identify these with good and evil.

> Darkness could not have been evil . . . unto the light, for it was its helpful root and ground . . . What reason can there be to call it evil? . . . Certainly no reason at all can be given *a priori*, why the darkness should be called evil, and the light alone good; but all that we may find and say will prove to be fetched only *a posteriori* from an outward consideration of their present state, divided by the fall of creatures . . . The same which is here called an eternal opposition shall, without any contradiction, be called an eternal friendship and harmony.[2]

It is, I believe, in the light of such a vision that Blake's great lyric, *The Tyger*, must be read. And have we not in this passage an inspiration for Blake's famous saying, 'Opposition is true Friendship', from *The Marriage of Heaven and Hell*? It is possible

[1] Charles A. Muses, *op. cit.*, p. 15.
[2] Charles A. Muses, *op. cit.*, p. 147.

too, that some of the 'mystical geometry' which Blake uses in the imagery of his prophetic poems, owes much to the language of Freher's *Paradoxes Emblemata*. This work is much preoccupied with the spiritual significance of the 'centre' and the 'circumference'. Freher insists,

> The circumference consists of innumerable little points, answering fitly unto so many particular somethings, all distinguished and discernible from, and placed in number and order beside each other. But the center is only one individual point; as to its quantity not bigger than any of the rest, but as to qualities the most considerable of all, and in a sense so big as all the circumferential points taken all together; nay upon another account even infinitely bigger. For upon this only all the circumferential points do depend, being and having from that one all that they are and have . . .

On Plate 71 of his epic *Jerusalem*, Blake seems to be reversing this scale of values, after his customary fashion.

> What is Above is Within, for every-thing in Eternity is translucent:
> The Circumference is Within, Without is formed the Selfish Center,
> And the Circumference still expands going forward to Eternity,
> And the Center has Eternal States; these States we now explore.
> (Keynes, p. 709)

In the same way the images are applied to the figure Albion, on Plate 19. 'Albion's Circumference was clos'd: his Center began dark'ning. . . .' Although Freher's writings remained in manuscript these had considerable circulation during Blake's lifetime. Two almost complete sets, for instance, were bought in Islington by the bookseller John Dennis in 1782, and remained at New Bridge Street, Blackfriars, until Edward Fisher, who eventually gave them to the British Museum, bought them. Another manuscript, of *Serial Elucidations*, belonged to Blake's portrait painter friend Richard Cosway.[1] There is no reason why Blake should not have had access to Freher's works.

[1] For Richard Cosway's relations with Blake see Mona Wilson's *Life of William Blake*, London 1948, pp. 361–2.

Apart from the commentaries of Freher, which passed into Law's hands and from which he made extracts in his own handwriting, there is also to be considered the collection of Francis Lee's writings given over to him by Lee's daughter, Deborah Fontaine. (Or rather, they came into Law's possession through a third party, Lee's friend from St John's College, the Rev. Dr Thomas Haywood.) There is a provoking reference in Deborah Fontaine's 'Short Account of the Author' prefacing the 1752 edition of her father's *Dissertations, Theological, Mathematical, and Physical*, to a life of Lee written by Dr Haywood.

> And as there has been some Inquiry made after the *Exposition of the Seven Visions of Esdras;* they are with all the Papers that I entrusted the late Rev. Dr. *Thomas Haywood* with at the Death of Dr. *Lee*, are in the hands of the Rev. Mr. *William Law* . . . together with his life written by Dr. *Haywood*; in which there being many Mistakes, I never would suffer it to be made public.[1]

In spite of the imperfect nature of Dr Haywood's life it would be very useful for us to have it. The last part of Francis Lee's career holds several difficult puzzles. There is, for example, the problem of his book, *An Historical Account of Montanism*, which came out anonymously in 1709 as part of George Hickes's *The Spirit of Enthusiasm Exorcised*. It is certain that many of his friends exerted all their influence against Lee's Behmenist tendencies and it has been suggested that Dodwell's arguments, and those of Edward Stephens, unsettled Lee's allegiance and caused the break-up of the Philadelphian Society in 1703. In his later years Lee occupied himself more with his medical work and with projects for charity schools, like the one which engaged William Law later in the century, and which Lee brought to the attention of his distinguished fellow Non-Juror, Robert Nelson. At any rate the *History of Montanism* reads like an exposure of the excesses of religious enthusiasm and has been taken as Lee's recantation. But although it powerfully attacks the follies and heresies of Montanus and his asso-

[1] Deborah Fontaine, 'Short Account of the Author', p. xviii of *Dissertations, Theological, Mathematical, and Physical*, London 1752.

ciate Maximilla, leaders of one of the earliest Gnostic movements, Lee shows in the process his sound grasp of the Kabalah
and Jewish studies generally. And his knowledge of Eastern
doctrines also. Lee seizes on the doctrine of the *'Consubstantiality of Spirit with matter'* to mark the Montanist's essential
beliefs, as it did those of the Cabalists; 'carving out to themselves,' he says, such an Image of the Deity, according to the
First Principle of *Manes,* on either *Xin* of the *Chinese* or the
Parabrama of the Indian Brahmins'.[1] This presentation of what
is a basically Pantheistic, or rather Monistic view of God, is
very perceptive.

Then there remains the question of quite why Francis Lee
made the curious declaration of his right to 'catholic' communion in his brother's private chapel during the year 1718,
which is recorded in a Bodleian manuscript.[2] And finally the
controversy about his death at Gravelines. The record of his
old school, Merchant Taylors' Register, simply states, 'joined
the R.C. Church; d. 23.8.1719; Gravelines, France; buried in
the Abbey precincts there.'

He was certainly so buried by the special arrangement of the
abbess, but his conversion was hotly denied in a later letter by
the Hon. Archibald Campbell. In the Bodleian record this
account of him is given,

> A very learned man, if not (a little) too curious in things sacred.
> He followed the (doctrines) of the Philadelphians and of the
> Bourigonists. Eventually, however, the prejudices of the true
> Anglican Church were overcome and he then died at Guada or at
> Bruges in Flanders.[3]

Whatever the truth about the confession he died in, it was
precisely because Francis Lee was 'curious in things sacred'
that his writings were of interest to William Law.

Besides his very beautiful translation of Jacob Boehme's

---

[1] Francis Lee, *An Historical Account of Montanism,* pp. 312–3, Part II of
George Hickes's *The Spirit of Enthusiasm Exorcised,* London 1709.

[2] Bodleian Manuscript, Rawlinson J., 335.

[3] *Op. cit.,* 196, (in Latin).

Supersensual Life, which was included in some copies of the four volume edition brought out by Langcake and Ward, other papers of Francis Lee's were clearly in William Law's possession. The most curious of these is surely that in the Dr Williams Library, which Law must have copied out himself, entitled *An Hundred Queries upon the Mosaick Cabala*. At the end it bears the inscription,

> This original Manuscript is the Hand-Writing of the Revd William Law, A.M. Witness my Hand December 22nd, 1781. Thomas Langcake.

The questions concern various problems arising out of the account of Creation in the Book of Genesis, all viewed with a mind steeped in the Kabalah and raising points which had been pre-occupying Cabalists for centuries; how creation arose out of the void, for instance, the *tohu va bohu*. Here are just a few of these questions.

> 1. Wherefore is this Word Elohim used in this first chapter of Genesis, & how shall it be properly interpreted? Because it is set in ye plural number, why is it constructed with a singular? What also is the Reason, that these two Names Jehovah and Elohim are found together in the 2nd chapt: after the accomplishing of ye seventh day and not before?

> 2. Wherefore was the Earth created before the sun? And why doth it now (with all its Creatures) desire & thirst after ye Suns Power or Virtue, notwithstanding it could at that time, as ye sun was not existing, bring forth all its growths, with its seeds, which it can do now no more?

> . . . 7. Wherefore is here, in the First chapter the Earth called Aaretz? When in ye second, after the finishing of the Seventh day, the Earth is called Haadamah, whereof is no mention made in the First chapter. What is the Reason thereof? Is Haadamah created wth Ha-aretz together, or was it created before Haaretz?

> 8. What is tohu? What is bohu? How far doth this tohu extend itself? And where-fore is this tohu not attributed to ye Heavens also? Were the Heavens full or replenished? Did not this tohu extend itself even so far as the Heavens did extend themselves?

And how may it then be said the Heavens were Created? If now everything was tohu, where ye Earth was, where was ye place of ye Earth?

9. But if the Heavens were not void or Tohu, where have they been before they were created visibly? Were they in ye same place, whereunto they came thereafter as they became created & manifested? Did they not fill this place full wherein it before was as Nothing? . . . How far did reach this fullfilling, or this Plenitude of the Heavens & the Earth, in opposition to Vacuity & Nothing? . . .[1]

No-one but an author deeply versed in the symbolism of the Kabalah in general and in the *Zohar* in particular would ever think of asking such questions as these. Though, of course, the reference to an invisible nature which preceded the 'created & manifested' one, is very Behmenist.

Christopher Walton, who published some extracts from this manuscript in his *Notes and Materials for a Biography of . . . William Law*, has also preserved for us another one of Lee's, entitled *Concerning Wisdom*.[2] This begins by putting a Cabalistic interpretation of the verse from *Exodus* xiii, 2: 'Sanctify unto me all the first-born, whatsoever openeth the womb.' Which signifies, apparently,

That all the first-born do appertain to *Cochmah*, that is, the Wisdom of God; as being the first emanation from the Divine Being, through which the Supreme Unity (which they call the Crown) descends down into nature and creature, for manifesting the heavenly kingdom of Messias throughout, by and in all the archetypal numbers and modes of being: and moreover that to the kingdom itself . . . is given the name of the *firstborn*.

Lee goes on to an interesting identification of the mysterious biblical figure *Melchisedech* with *Malcuth*, the Kingdom, and also with the oracle of the Lord mentioned in Psalm 110. Then follows a comparison of the Sephiroth Tiphereth and Malkhuth

---

[1] *An Hundred Queries upon the Mosaick Cabala*, Dr Williams' Library, Walton Room. MS.186.17.(18.)

[2] Christopher Walton, *Notes and Materials For An Adequate Biography of the Celebrated Divine and Theosopher, William Law*, London 1854, pp. 513–14.

and their respective significances, which is full of meaning. This is Lee's tabulation.

TIPHERETH	MALCUTH
1. The Supernal Man, or Heavenly Adam.	1. The Virgin of Israel, or Heavenly Eve.
2. The Bridegroom.	2. The Bride.
3. The Husband of the Church.	3. The Church and Congregation of Israel.
4. The King.	4. The Queen of Heaven.
5. The Great Priest.	5. The Sanctuary.
6. The Sun.	6. The Moon.
7. The Glass of Illumination.	7. The Glass Illuminated.
8. The Law.	8. The Tables of the Law.
9. The Covenant.	9. The Ark of the Covenant.
10. The World to come.	10. The Ark of Noah.
11. The Tree of Life.	11. The Earth of Life.
12. The Root of the Tree.	12. The Branches.
13. Heaven.	13. Earth.
14. Spirit.	14. Body.
15. The Throne of Judgment.	15. The Tabernacle of Judgment.
16. David.	16. The House of David.
17. Metatron.	17. The Schecina, or Glory of God.
18. Melchisedech.	18. The Temple of Peace.
19. Jacob.	19. Leah, or the Mother of Seven Children.
20. Israel.	20. Rachel.
21. Solomon.	21. The Shulamite.
22. The Voice.	22. The Echo.
23. The WORD.	23. The Speech.
24. JEHOVAH.	24. ELOHIM, the Angels, or Souls. . . .

Such was the mental world in which Francis Lee was most at home. The vicissitudes of his exterior life were not what mattered to him.

The most important events in William Law's life, too, are all mental ones. Outwardly it was a placid, rather retired existence. He was born in the quiet Northamptonshire town of Kings Cliffe in 1686, the fourth son of Thomas Law, a grocer, and his wife Margaret Farmesy. From the time when he entered Emmanuel College, Cambridge, as a sizor, in 1705, to the accession of King George I, he pursued a successful academic career, studying not only classics, philosophy and mathematics, but Hebrew too, and becoming a fellow of the College in 1708. Law took orders in 1711. It was in 1714, that he was forced to make the most notable decision of his life and refuse to take the oath of allegiance to the new Hanoverian king. He found he could not accept a king chosen for motives of expediency without any firm right to the throne. As Arthur Hopkinson has put it, quoting Sir Charles Petrie,

'Whoever may have gained by the accession of the House of Hanover, the Church of England lost its soul.' The Non-jurors might be called the lost soul of the Church of England.[1]

The next ten years of Law's life could be called, in their turn, the lost years. There are rumours, we have noted, that after surrendering his Cambridge Fellowship, he began again as Dr Heylin's curate.[2] Yet this is uncertain. All we know is that Law finally became attached to the household of a London merchant at Putney where he was tutor to Edward Gibbon, who was to be the father of the historian. Edward Gibbon entered William Law's old college, and Law seems to have alternated between Cambridge and Putney during these years. He met his future disciple, John Byrom, in March 1729. Byrom was a gifted young man who had been drawn to Law through his book, *A Serious Call to a Devout and Holy Life*, which like the *Practical Treatise upon Christian Perfection*, belongs to this period. And both Charles and John Wesley also visited Law at Putney.

Particularly vital contacts for Law were Dr George Cheyne, who is said to have introduced Law to Boehme's works, according to John Byrom; and a member of Parliament, Archibald Hutcheson. This gentleman was so impressed by Law's

[1] Arthur Hopkinson, *About William Law*, London 1948, p. 11.
[2] Arthur Hopkinson, *op. cit.*, p. 115.

7a. Jacob Boehme
From Edward
Taylor's and Jacob
Boehme's *Theoso-
phick Philosophy
Unfolded*, London,
1691

7b. John Pordage
From *Gottliche und
Wahre Metaphysica*,
Frankfurt and
Leipzig, 1715

8. The Fall by William Blake
'As the stars are apart from the earth', Plate 6, *The First Book of Urizen*
(F. T. Palgrave copy, British Museum)

qualities as a spiritual director that he wished him to take over the care of his wife after his own death. And indeed when Law finally moved from Putney back to his native town of Kings Cliffe, it was with Mrs Hutcheson and a sister of his former pupil, Hester Gibbon. They formed a little community, devoted to the support of the Charity schools which Law had founded and to the alms-giving he also instituted. The combined incomes of Miss Gibbon and Mrs Hutcheson amounted to a considerable sum for those days, and this could be supplemented by Law's earnings from his books. With his increased leisure he was in a position to write more seriously than ever before. A stream of books came out of Kings Cliffe, of which *The Spirit of Prayer* and *The Spirit of Love* are perhaps the best known. After Law's death, in 1761, Thomas Langcake and George Ward evidently had some support from the ladies of the Kings Cliffe community, in their venture of producing a complete English translation of Boehme's works; but after Mrs Hutcheson's death in 1781 Miss Gibbon withdrew her financial help and so the work remains at four volumes instead of the six projected. Though, as we have seen, a further volume was assembled independently by Holcroft in Dublin, and published in 1820.

Such was the background to Law's real life, one of intense intellectual activity. It began with his heated controversies against Bishop Hoadly of Bangor in defence of true independence for the Church, and ended with the serious effort to explore those mystical riches of the Christian past, for which he is now best remembered, and with the particular study he made of Jacob Boehme, the only Protestant figure he could acclaim as a major mystic.

Law was not allowed to pass unchallenged in his devotion to the great Lutheran he took as his spiritual guide. John Wesley later parted company with him on just this issue. Wesley admits that after Law's books, *Christian Perfection* and *A Serious Call*, were first put into his hands, 'these convinced me, more than ever, of the absolute impossibility of being half a Christian . . .'

His ethical teaching always met with Wesley's approval, but he became more and more suspicious of Law's theology and especially after returning from his first evangelical mission to America Wesley began to feel that Law 'does not see any meaning in the actual business of life . . . "Christianity is a Calling that puts an end to all other Callings" . . .' This reaction is, of course, partly the natural one of an active evangelist towards a contemplative mind. But the uneasiness is also partly due to Wesley's understanding of how the sinner depended upon all possible means of grace. Too much scorn of outward expression was dangerous here. It partly springs from his sense of Law's leanings in a Quietist, not to say Gnostic, direction. This sense grew until after the publication of Law's *The Spirit of Prayer* and *The Spirit of Love*, when Wesley felt constrained to publish his *Open Letter to William Law* (6th January 1756).

> Law: All that can be conceived is God, or *Nature*, or *Creature*. Wesley: Is *Nature* created, or not created? It must be one or the other; for there is no Medium. If not created, is it not God? If created, is it not a creature? How then can there be three, God, *Nature*, and *Creature*? Since nature must coincide either with God or Creature? . . .
> Law: There is an *Eternal Nature*, as universal and *unlimited* as God.

It is quite clear, for instance, that Law accepted the idea of creation as emanation which is so characteristic of Boehme's system, and of the Kabalah. He insists upon it in an important work, *An Appeal to all that Doubt or Disbelieve the Truth of the Gospel*.

> Herein also appears the high dignity and never-ceasing perpetuity of our nature. The essences of our souls can never cease to be because they never began to be, and nothing can live eternally but that which hath lived from all Eternity.
> The essences of our soul were a breath in God before they . . . lived in the created soul, and therefore the soul is a partaker of the eternity of God and can never cease to be.[1]

[1] William Law, *An Appeal to all that Doubt or Disbelieve the Truths of the Gospel*, London 1742, p. 10; (pp. 74–5 in *The Pocket William Law*, edited by Arthur Hopkinson, London, 1950. Used for subsequent quotations from Law, but with references to the original edition).

The same position is revealed, still more uncompromisingly unorthodox, in *The Spirit of Prayer*, where Man's original creation is seen as a spiritual one. He was, in fact, an angel.

> He was created an Angel, both as to Body and Spirit; and this Angel stood in an outward Body, of the Nature of the outward World; and therefore, by the nature of his State he had his Trial, or *Power* of choosing whether he would live as an Angel, using only his outward Body as a means of opening the wonders of the outward World to the Glory of his Creator; or whether he would turn his Desire to the opening of the bestial Life of the outward World in himself, for the Sake of *knowing the Good and Evil* that was in it . . .
>
> Our *Fall* is nothing else, but the falling of our Soul from this celestial Body and spirit into a *bestial* Body and Spirit of this World.[1]

Not only does Law make the mistake of concluding that good and evil can exist only in the world of nature, whereas they have their true source in the spirit, but he has the same attitude towards the sexes as Boehme had, and as William Blake was later to show.

> Marvel not therefore, my Friend, that Adam, standing in the power of his first Birth, should have a divine power of bringing forth his own Likeness, . . . For I will shew you that all the Gospel bears Witness to that heavenly Birth which we should have had from *Adam* alone. – This birth from *Adam* is still the one Purpose of God, and must be the *One Way* of all those that are to rise with Christ to an equality with the Angels of God. All must be children of *Adam*, for all that are born of Man and Woman, must lay aside this polluted Birth and be born again of a second *Adam*, in that same Perfection of an holy angelic Nature, which they should have had from the first *Adam*, before his *Eve* was separated from him.[2]

Though there is a certain symbolic truth in what Law says here, as it stands it represents a thoroughly Gnostic position, with few grounds either in scripture or the tradition of the Church.

---

[1] William Law, *The Spirit of Prayer; Or The Soul Rising out of the Vanity of Time, Into the Riches of Eternity*, London 1750, pp. 8–10.

[2] *Op. cit.*, Part the Second, pp. 82–3.

And one cannot blame Wesley for taking a critical attitude towards a theologian of great influence who taught such ideas as Christian doctrine.

At the same time one has to remember Law's motives for his enthusiasm for Boehme. Law's interests were primarily mystical and Boehme stands out from among the generally rather anti-mystical Protestant spiritual writers as one of those few who can compare with the great Catholic mystics. That Law admitted this appears from a letter of Langcake's to Henry Brooke, dated 30th November 1782.

> Mr. Law said to me (of the . . . Protestant Mystics) that Jac^b: Behmen was the first in Excellency, Hiel the next, and in the third place the Quakers . . . tho' the deep mystic writers of the Romish Church surpassed them in their exceeding Love of God and Divine Wisdom.

Law's efforts were really directed towards finding his way back to the main stream of Christian spirituality. And where he is most in union with this his own work is finest. The admirable treatment of humility, towards the end of *The Spirit of Prayer*, is an example. He exhorts the reader to approach God as the publican of Christ's parable did.

> This, my Friend, is a Secret or Secrets, it . . . will not only help you to receive Good from those Prayers, which seem too good for the State of your Heart, but will help you to find Good from every Thing else. For every thing that inwardly stirs you in or, outwardly happens to you, becomes a real Good to you, if it either finds, or excites in you this humble Form of Mind . . .
>
> Shut up yourself therefore in this *Form* of Humility, all Good is inclos'd in it, it is a Water of Heaven, that turns the Fire of the fallen Soul into the meekness of the divine Life, and creates that Oil, out of which the love to God and Man gets its Flame . . .
>
> The *painful* sense and Feeling of what you are, kindled into a . . . State of Sensibility by the Light of God within you, is the *Fire* and *Light* from whence your Spirit of Prayer proceeds. In its first kindling nothing is found, or felt but Pain, Wrath and Darkness, as is to be seen in the first kindling of every Heat or Fire. And therefore its first Prayer is nothing else but a Sense of Penitence, Self condemnation, Confession and Humility. This Prayer

of Humility is met by the divine Love, the Mercifulness of God embraces it, and then its Prayer is chang'd into Hymns and Songs and Thanksgivings. When this State of Fervour has done its Work, has melted away all earthly Passions and Affections, and left no Inclination in the Soul but to delight in God alone, then its Prayer changes again. It is now come so near to God, has found such Union with Him, that it does not so much pray as live in God . . .[1]

There could be no more accurate description of spiritual growth than this one, and the lyricism with which it is expressed helps to explain the impact Law made on his contemporaries and the claims that have been put forward for his prose as among the glories of English literature.[2]

Perhaps the range of William Law's interests can best be demonstrated from the catalogue of his disciple John Byrom's library; this collection is now housed in the Chetham Library at Manchester. Byrom was a lively-minded man, the author of some hymns still in use and of a system of shorthand. He was extremely sociable and his diary shows how he chatted about his book purchases and his intellectual preoccupations to a wide range of friends throughout the country.[3] But he did not have a particularly original mind; representing William Law's enthusiasms more than his own in the library he built up. The contents range from Cornelius Agrippa's works and Elias Ashmole's, to St Peter of Alcantara, Albertus Magnus, Athenagoras, St Teresa of Avila, Father Augustine Baker, and of course the whole of Boehme's works. In the same way, John Dee the astrologer, and Joseph Glanvill are in the list with Dionysius the Areopagite, St Bernard, Catherine of Sienna and St Bonaventure. Antoinette Bourignon the Quietist, figures with Buxtorf the Hebrew specialist and the Neo-Platonists, Ficino and Ralph Cudworth. John Everard and the Van Helmonts are to be found with St Francis de Sales, Mme Guion, Ignatius Loyola, Athanasius Kircher, the orientalist, and

---

[1] *Op. cit.*, Part the Second, pp. 157–172.
[2] Henri Talon, *William Law. A Study in Literary Craftsmanship.*
[3] Henri Talon, *Selections from the Journals & Papers of John Byrom*, pp. 81–3; 149; 155–8; 191; 198.

William Langland. Michael Maier, the Rosicrucian, comes close to Menasseh ben Israel, and Molinos, Paracelsus and Pico della Mirandola appear with Pascal, Pordage and Thomas Aquinas and there is a considerable space devoted to Thomas à Kempis, as to the works of Henry More and Thomas Vaughan. While this is a strange mixture, it is easy to see that Byrom has really been drawing on the tradition we have traced from the Renaissance, with an especially strong emphasis also, upon mystical literature, in William Law's style. Both Byrom and Law were rather more friendly to the Quietist school of mysticism than most authorities on the subject have been, and this we shall find to be true of Law's followers later in the century. But Law himself was not without a consciousness of their defects. Again, Langcake reports to Henry Brooke,

> As Mr. Law had read the Mystic writers through every age of the Church, so Madame Bourignon could not have escaped his notice. He consider'd her, nay, said she was, an Illuminated Woman, but petulant . . .

However, there was much enthusiasm stirred up in England over Archbishop Fénelon's championship of Mme Guion, whom Bousset accused of Quietism; and the author of a preface to an edition of Fénelon's letters, published in London, in 1738, praises him by exactly those standards that Law and Byrom upheld. He explains that,

> Besides the Archbishop of *Cambray*'s Dissertation on PURE LOVE . . . we have given his Meditation on the Inward Operation of God's Spirit, which was inserted in the *White-Hall* Evening Post, Feb. 19. 1733–4. 'Tis an Illustration of several sublime and spiritual Passages in the *BIBLE*, and contains the Quintessence of the Pythagorean and Socratic Philosophy, as well as the Sum and Substance of Divinity . . . 'Tis what *Solomon* most emphatically calls the CANDLE of the Lord: *The Spirit of a Man is the Candle of the Lord* . . . And, according to HOMER, one of the ancientest Greek Poets and Writers, 'tis *Hermes* or *Mercury* whom JUPITER sends to warn Mankind. 'That is, says an ingenious Expositer of *Homer*, the LIGHT of Nature which Heaven implants in the Breast of every Man . . .'

We are back here in the atmosphere in which Botticelli painted and Ficino wrote. William Law was never very distant from it.

Like the Cambridge Platonists, however, Law upheld formal Christianity. As a Non-Juror he may have been in disagreement with the Anglican Church of his time but he was quite out of sympathy with the radical attitude stemming from the seventeenth century Levellers and their fellows. When he was given the works of Langcake's friend, Richard Clarke, a late representative of the radical tradition, he was nonplussed by them and apparently rather repelled. Law's instinct had been to associate himself with the mind of the Church, as it was expressed in all ages, but especially with Christian mystical theology. Yet Richard Clarke was a most sincere devotee of Law's teaching. It was around the figure of William Law while he was alive, and round his work when he was dead, that those who clung to an earlier and more spiritual way of thought in reaction to eighteenth century materialism, grouped themselves. So we have the strange paradox that William Law was to be invoked as the patron of many positions which he could not have approved. While on the other hand, because of his great enthusiasm for the system of Jacob Boehme, we find the Church of England represented in the eighteenth century by a theologian, far more profound and impressive than any other Anglican mind of that age, and yet in some directions curiously heterodox. Perhaps, then, it is not so surprising that the age which produced William Law should later have given us William Blake.

CHAPTER VIII

The Swedenborgian Movement

*

Apart from the spirituality of William Law, and the great evangelical movement launched by the Wesleys, there is another important religious development in the late eighteenth century which cannot be ignored. Out of the teaching of Emanuel Swedenborg there arose the 'New Church', and many restless minds turned in this direction, at least for a time. One of these was Blake. The 'New Church' can be said to have begun with three members; Stephen Penny, 'a prominent citizen of Dartmouth', a Quaker friend of his, 'a well-to-do chemist from Plymouth', Thomas Cookworthy, and the Rev Thomas Hartley, an Anglican minister who had been impressed by Swedenborg's work from the time when the book *Arcana Coelestia* was first advertised in the London newspapers by Swedenborg's publisher, John Lewis.[1] Cookworthy and Hartley visited Swedenborg in London in 1769, where they found that the distinguished Swedish scientist and theologian was generally known as 'the New Jerusalem gentleman'. Their visit inspired them to set about the task of translating Swedenborg's books into English. During the next decade two other clergymen were also attracted to the Swedenborgian doctrines; the Rev. Jacob Duché whom we have already met as an enthusiast for William Law, and the Rev John Clowes of Manchester. All these gentlemen, however, held by Swedenborg's own position; that these doctrines should gradually regenerate the existing churches. They had no intention of setting up a separate organization.

[1] Marguerite Beck Block, *The New Church in the New World*, New York 1932, p. 61.

Such an organization did, in fact, come into being during the '80s under the influence of a further group headed by Robert Hindmarsh, a dynamic young man, the son of a Methodist minister, who had been so inspired by the copy of Swedenborg's *Heaven and Hell* lent him by a Quaker friend, as to institute a reading circle. At first this was attended by a surgeon, Peter Provo, William Bonington, a clock-case maker, and the Hon. Augustus Tulk. They advertised a public meeting at the Queens Arms, a coffee house at Ludgate Hill, on 5th December 1783. There they were joined by the surgeon William Spence. From this nucleus arose the 'Theosophical Society, instituted for the purpose of promoting the Heavenly Doctrines of the New Jerusalem, by translating and publishing the Theological Writings of the Hon Emanuel Swedenborg'. And during this period it flourished, meeting regularly at Jacob Duché's house; just as Robert Hindmarsh himself flourished, becoming Printer Extraordinary to the Prince of Wales. The members of the society had worshipped together at the Rev. Duché's chapel at the Female Orphan Asylum at Lambeth. But in November 1787 a chapel was rented in Great East Cheap and a liturgy devised by Hindmarsh entitled *The Order of Worship for the New Church signified by the New Jerusalem in the Revelation*.[1] A strong effort followed, from the Rev. John Clowes, to avert this separation into a 'New Church', but it was an unsuccessful one. The first independent service was held at Great East Cheap on 27th January 1788, while in Easter week, 1789, the first General Conference took place, also at Great East Cheap. Among the names of those who attended are listed William and Catherine Blake. They both signed the resolutions drawn up at the end of the conference. Every day, from Monday to Friday, the sixty or seventy men and women present dined together at an inn nearby, in Abchurch Lane.

What did these people meet to discuss? Indeed who was Swedenborg and why were his doctrines so important and attractive at this particular time in the eighteenth century?

[1] *Op. cit.*, pp. 65–6.

Emanuel Swedenborg was in a strange way a link between two worlds. No-one could have been more a child of the 'Enlightenment'. Yet this very considerable scientist became in the end a religious visionary influenced by the metaphysical and mystical literature he had formerly despised. Still, he never lost a certain matter-of-factness, even a materialism that he carried over from his former way of thinking and that can be compared to the absurdity in much spiritualistic writing, where the next world appears even more trivial and petty than this! The riddle is to some extent explained by his parentage. Signe Toksvig in her biography *Emanuel Swedenborg, Scientist and Mystic*,[1] gives very interesting portraits of his parents. His father, Jasper Swedenborg, Professor of Theology at Uppsala University and later made Bishop of Skara in Sweden by Charles XII, was a prize prig. This is proved by the life of himself which he wrote and which, as Miss Toksvig relates, he dedicated to his 'children and posterity for needed instruction in how to pass well through this world'. One copy was placed in the library of Uppsala University so that the 'less envious' might profit from it. In this book Jasper Swedenborg described how he himself had a 'fine' mind and beautiful character; how since his youth he had always sought good and hated evil; though to begin with he had some faults, yet he loved to be told of them; how he hated quarrels and enmities; how he took special joy in forgiving his enemies and doing good to them. He admits to a quick temper, but stresses his gentle and forgiving heart. He was always sober. But always merry and bright. He loved work! There is a portrait of this paragon in Gripsholm Castle which shows him to be a dour ecclesiastic with a very smug expression, looking rather like the sort of minister Ibsen might have satirized in one of his plays. Emanuel's mother, on the other hand, had a face which shows humour and deep thought. She was originally Sara Behm, an heiress, daughter of an official of the Board of Mines, and she

[1] Signe Toksvig, *Emanuel Swedenborg, Scientist and Mystic*, London 1949, pp. 14f.

died when Emanuel was eight, having borne nine children. Miss Toksvig thinks that Swedenborg must have inherited his genius from her, and most probably she is right.

As a young man Swedenborg was attached by Charles XII to the Board of Mines. By that time he had already published an article on how to get salt from the sea and was soon set to establish a salt works. He was interested in canal transport and then became absorbed in geology. In 1719 he published a work proving that most of Sweden had once been under water. His next substantial book was the *Opera Philosophica et Mineralia* which came out in 1734. In the cosmological section he anticipated many later theories, insisting for instance that the milky way was but one of many galaxies. Next he studied medicine and became particularly preoccupied with anatomy. His explanation of the brain was of outstanding quality; he demonstrated the use of the cerebral cortex, the relation of the parts of the brain to the muscles controlling different parts of the body, the connections of the nerve fibres in the brain and the existence of nerve cells. From an interest in the body Swedenborg passed over to one in the soul. After a number of extraordinary psychic experiences he became convinced of a connection between the Infinite and the Finite, an unbroken chain of being. His gift for second sight was so remarkable that it was specially investigated by the philosopher Immanuel Kant who became completely convinced of its authenticity. Next he undertook a long series of biblical commentaries, beginning with *The Word Explained* and proceeding to the *Arcana Coelestia* which was published in London, though in Latin, between the years 1749–56. From this time onwards Swedenborg devoted most of his energies to religious writing and while living an active social life either in his own country, or in Amsterdam or London, for which he had much fondness, he carried on another life simultaneously in which he met and conversed with many persons from the spiritual world – some recently dead and others famous men from the past – and experienced many visions. The books which most deeply influenced Blake among those which Swedenborg produced at this time were *The Wisdom of Angels concerning Divine Love and Wisdom*, *The Wisdom of Angels concerning Divine Providence* and his last work, *True Christian Religion*. In spite of what might have seemed to have been considerable eccentricity Swedenborg was always received with respect and deference and his opinions still carried much weight in Sweden, where as head of the house of Swedenborg, he was a member of the House of Nobles. He continued to take an interest in political affairs and often sent memorials to the Diet on different matters. When he died in London in 1775 he left behind him a circle of followers who carried on his work, as we have seen, and his books continued to be published. Indeed a printing society was founded in Manchester in 1782 solely devoted to this task.

Perhaps the turning-point in Swedenborg's career came with the writing of his book, *The Economy of the Animal Kingdom*, which Signe Toksvig explains was finished at Amsterdam in December 1739, after Swedenborg had been studying the anatomy of the brain in Venice. It was this study which brought him up against the mysteries of psychology and there are to be found references in his book to such unlikely figures as Dionysius the Areopagite, the French Platonist Malebranche and his English interpreter John Norris and Henry More himself. Spinoza is much drawn on, and indeed Signe Toksvig insists that the whole book is so Plotinian as to repeat many of Plotinus' similes.[1] Then, although Swedenborg always denied having read Jacob Boehme, there are signs that he borrowed the doctrine of the 'Grand Man'; Gichtel's name for the figure he had developed out of Boehme's Heavenly Adam and the Adam Kadmon of the Kabalah.[2] So that a typical eighteenth century scientist, not previously much interested in such matters, found himself adopting what was in some ways a Neo-Platonic position and certainly inheriting much from the vital ideas of the

[1] *Op. cit.*, p. 112.
[2] *Op. cit.*, p. 234.

tradition we have been following. It is clear from Swedenborg's notebook, for instance, that he was acquainted with cabalistic symbolism.[1] Therefore his picture of 'the Lord . . . as one Man', or the 'Heavenly Man', has nothing very surprising in it.

> This Divine Man is in every particular of his form a Man, not only as to the external members and organs but also as to the internal members and organs which are more in number; and also as to the skins, membranes, cartilages and bones; but in that Man all these, both external and internal, are not material but spiritual.

This passage from *The Wisdom of Angels Concerning Divine Providence*, section 254, illustrates very well the curiously prosaic nature of Swedenborg's approach. It is the vision of an anatomist as well as a spiritualist. And one of its features is the inclusion within the heavenly body of souls who did not know Christ during life. These are not to be excluded through no fault of their own but in fact form the 'skins, membranes, cartilages and bones' of the Divine Man. No soul can bear more than its due measure of heavenly joy, for it would only be suffocated by this. But the hierarchy is not absolutely rigid, for all are merely men. Even angels and demons are simply good and bad human spirits and a soul after death may pass through a number of different angelic societies until the highest level of which it is capable is arrived at. The descriptions Swedenborg gives, in books like the *True Christian Religion* and the *Apocalypse Revealed*, of these various spiritual societies strangely echo passages in Jane Lead's works. Her vision seems to have paralleled his in some ways, as I have suggested. And whether he agreed, or not, over the details of Swedenborg's angelic societies, Blake most certainly affirmed the concept of the 'Heavenly Man'. Here is a picture which might be a literal presentation of this doctrine, from *The Four Zoas*, Night the First.

> Then those in Great Eternity met in the Council of God
> As one Man, for contracting their Exalted Senses

[1] *A Philosopher's Notebook*, translated and edited by Alfred Acton, p. 169.

They behold Multitude, or Expanding they behold as one,
As One Man all the Universal family; & that One Man
They call Jesus the Christ, & they in him & he in them
Live in Perfect harmony, in Eden the land of life . . .

(Keynes, p. 277, lines 469–74)

What was it in the doctrines of Swedenborg that attracted
so much enthusiasm in late eighteenth century England?
Possibly a combination of symbolism belonging to the earlier
tradition, still familiar to some minds, with certain limitations
that made it more acceptable to the age. Swedenborg, for
instance, took over the concept of the 'Equilibrium', the
balance, which is so vital to Jacob Boehme's system and to the
Kabalah, and which we had seen Blake used. In the *Treatise
Concerning Heaven and Hell* it is set out in this way.

> . . . as heaven and hell are to each other as two contraries in mutual
> opposition, from the action and reaction of which results that
> equilibrium by which all things subsist, therefore, in order to the
> preservation of such equilibrium, it necessarily follows, that he
> who governs the one must govern the other; for unless the same
> Lord was to restrain the fury and madness of hell, the equilibrium
> would be lost, and all would be destroyed.[1]

He believed, too, in the original androgyny of Man; but such
was his respect for marriage that he considered Heaven as a
state of perfect matrimony. In the same way Swedenborg's
doctrine of Hell asserts exactly that refusal to admit any
essential difference between the body and soul which we have
noticed so often before. Yet with him this concept springs
much more out of a certain materialism than from Gnosticism.
It is connected with that anthropomorphic attitude which is so
characteristic of his whole system. His statement,

> God is very Man. In all the Heavens there is no other Idea of
> God, than that of a Man . . .

was endorsed by Blake in these terms,

[1] Emanuel Swedenborg, *Treatise Concerning Heaven and Hell*, London
1778, No. 536.

Man can have no idea of anything greater than Man, as a cup cannot contain more than its capaciousness. But God is a man, not because he is so perceiv'd by man, but because he is the creator of man . . .[1]

However one may criticize this attitude it was certainly attractive to the eighteenth century mind.

For just this reason it is as well to look more closely at the personalities who were drawn to these doctrines and to follow the course of the Swedenborgian movement rather further ahead, returning first for a moment to the Rev. Jacob Duché. An article in *The Monthly Observer* for 1857 (Vol. I, page 79), provides a good deal of background material about him, and he is described as,

> personally acquainted with the Rev. Mr. Hartley and the Rev. Clowes. His connexion with the Church was not of a public or striking nature, but had a quiet and private influence on its earlier states.

There may be a special significance in his Huguenot descent, but he was born in Philadelphia and after taking orders in England became rector of the Episcopalian Church there. The most dramatic incidents of his career are associated with the American War of Independence. Duché was chosen to pronounce the opening prayers at the old Continental Congress of 1774 and he became chaplain to the Congress of 1776. The effect of some of his sermons was described by John Adams, later President of the United States, as sensational. But, as may be imagined, a letter which he wrote to George Washington, on 8th October 1777, 'urging him to abandon the cause of independence' was not well received, and Duché fled to England. This is how he was to be found chaplain to the Female Orphans' Asylum, St George's Fields, Lambeth. While there, his interest in Swedenborgianism developed. We are told that when he was in England before, he had heard of Swedenborg and had in his library in America 'a complete set of the Writings in the

[1] William Blake, Annotations to Swedenborg's *Wisdom of Angels Concerning Divine Love and Divine Wisdom*, London 1788, p. 11.

original . . . but at that time was quite ignorant of the nature of them and the treasures they contained, till his attention was drawn to them by Mr Hartley and Mr Clowes, when he became a most cordial receiver, as did his wife and family'. Duché distinguished himself by writing a preface to Swedenborg's newly translated *The Doctrine of Life*, which was much admired by Hindmarsh; and his son-in-law, a Mr Hill who married Duché's eldest daughter Esther, was responsible for translating the *Apocalypse Explained*. While Duché had begun by being as famous for his sermons in England as he had been in America, partly because of ill-health and partly 'from a repugnance to continue a preacher in a church with whose opinions he could not coincide', he left off preaching and contented himself with gathering fellow 'receivers' of the Swedenborgian doctrines at his Sunday services and encouraging them to frequent his house on Sunday evenings. When the peace was arranged at the end of the American War of Independence, Duché decided to return to his native country, and was back in Philadelphia in 1790.

By that time, of course, the Swedenborgian movement had taken a completely new direction. This was undoubtedly the doing of Robert Hindmarsh and his reading circle. But there is more to the change than appears on the surface. After their first public meeting at the Queens Arms the reading circle took a room in the Inner Temple, where a new member appeared, a sugar planter from Demarara called James Glen, who had been educated at Glasgow University, with an amazing flair for languages, both ancient and modern. He was to be the first active propagandist for the New Church in America.[1] More permanent headquarters were found at New Court in the Middle Temple and from there a stream of literature was issued by the 'Theosophical Society', including an *Address to the Christian World at large, but especially to the Clergy*. The name of the society was changed in 1785 to 'The British Society for the Propagation of the Doctrines of the New Church' and a sub-

[1] Marguerite Beck Block, *The New Church in the New World*, p. 63.

scription of six pounds yearly was demanded; a pretty stiff fee for those times. But already more open evangelism was being undertaken. Two men, whose names are important, Joseph Salmon and Ralph Mather, began preaching in the open air, both in London and in the West Country, around Bristol and Salisbury. They set up local societies in these areas.

But it was not simply that this propaganda work helped to make the followers of Swedenborg stand out from among their fellow Christians. The type of people being attracted into the society began to change. Besides the prosperous citizens and clergy of the Established Church, numbers of dissenting ministers began to be drawn in. And just as John Wesley had been impressed with Law's teaching at first sight and then turned away from it, so he repeated the pattern in regard to Swedenborg's writings. And he was particularly irritated when he found that six of his own ministers had become 'receivers' of the Swedenborgian doctrines. One of them was Robert Hindmarsh's father, the Rev. James Hindmarsh. A friend of his, the Rev. Isaac Hawkins, held study meetings in his house and when Wesley heard this he expelled him. It was about the same time that the Rev. Aaron Mathesius began to spread abroad accounts of Swedenborg's supposed insanity, which he based on stories supplied by the Baron's landlord in East London, Brockner. As the result of such pressure the position of dissenting ministers who came to hold Swedenborgian doctrines grew more and more impossible. A man like the Rev. John Clowes at St John's Manchester was actually defended by his bishop, Dr Beilby Porteus, when he preached Swedenborg's teachings, and held in such respect that De Quincey, for instance, described him as 'the holiest of men whom it has been my lot to meet'. But the Non-Conformists could not afford to emulate the tolerance, or possibly the indifference, of the Establishment. And the only hope of a livelihood for ex-ministers of these sects was to become ministers of a Swedenborgian 'New Church'. That, indeed, is clearly the chief reason why one came into being. In 1788, as has been noted, the first

P

service was held according to the liturgy supplied by Hind-marsh. But there were still many doctrinal points at issue; which explains the need for the General Conference of 1789, at Great East Cheap.

An upheaval earlier in the same year, within the Great East Cheap society, reveals the kind of dissensions that could take place and also throws some very interesting light on Blake's own attitudes. This disturbance sprang from,

> a perverted view of Swedenborg's doctrine of concubinage in his work on Conjugal Love, then just published; whereby some held that if a husband and wife did not agree, they might separate, and the man take a concubine; I forget whether or not the wife was to have the same privilege . . .[1]

The matter is explained more fully in a book by Augustus Norderskjold, who was involved in the Great East Cheap episode, called *The Form of Organization in the New Jerusalem*. According to this account concubinage was to be regulated.

> No one is permitted to live thus in our Church who does not report it to the Bishop or the Marriage Priest. These are to examine according to Swedenborg's rules *De Fornicatione et Concubinatu* – if his case is truly such as he presents it. After this he is to receive their written permission, in which the conditions are to be carefully stated, and he may then live with his mistress or concubine.

We have all heard the story of how Blake proposed to take a concubine, but when Mrs Blake cried, gave up the plan. It is not surprising that such an idea should have passed through his head when there was so much talk of concubines within the New Church. Though of course Blake's own ideas were in some ways much more daring than ever Swedenborg's had been. Crabb Robinson reports, in his diary for 13th June 1826, that he held Plato's belief in Community of Women, and in an outburst of protest against Jealousy,

> Can that be Love that drinks another as a sponge drinks water,
> That clouds with jealousy his nights, with weepings all the day . . .

[1] *Op. cit.*, p. 68.

Oothoon, Blake's heroine of the *Visions of the Daughters of Albion*, Plate 7, paints a passionate picture of ideal Free Love.

> But silken nets and traps of adamant will Oothoon spread,
> And catch for thee girls of mild silver, or of furious gold.
> I'll lie beside thee on a bank & view their wanton play
> In lovely copulation, bliss on bliss, with Theotormon:
> Red as the rosy morning, lustful as the first born beam,
> Oothoon shall view his dear delight, nor e'er with jealous cloud
> Come in the heaven of generous love, nor selfish blightings
> bring . . .
> (Keynes, pp. 194–5)

These extremes would probably have shocked even such ardent Swedenborgians as Blake's friends John Flaxman and Thomas Butts, had they been aware of them.

There were other, and perhaps rather more serious points of dissension within the New Church, however. The question of relative power amongst clergy and laity arose. Robert Hindmarsh was all for strengthening the position of the clergy and even instituting an episcopacy. To other elements within the Church the idea of bishops was horrifying, and as a result a schism came about which was not mended until the General Conference of 1807. Another problem was the rise of spiritualistic practices which were much stimulated by the presence of a certain Count Grabianka in London. Of course, Swedenborg himself had described many amazing psychical experiences and his followers were not slow to make the same claims. The James Glen who has been mentioned as spreading Swedenborgian doctrines in America – the same work was later carried out by Ralph Mather – makes this statement,

> . . . several persons in Manchester are having open communication with the spiritual world and receive ocular and auricular proofs of the statements of Swedenborg.[1]

The Rev. John Clowes there, always claimed that some of the books he wrote were actually dictated by angels. In this context Blake's 'Visionary Heads' of characters from the past, and the

[1] *Op. cit.*, p. 70.

dictation of his poems by the 'Eternals', is not so surprising. Indeed the whole picture of Blake's work needs to be seen against a Swedenborgian background, even when he was revolting away from that very background.

What exactly was Swedenborg's influence on Blake and how is it to be estimated? There is a possibility that this influence began from a very early time in Blake's life. Building on Alexander Gilchrist's description of Blake's father as a dissenter, Edwin Ellis and H. N. Morris went on to maintain that he was a Swedenborgian. The whole question has been discussed by the Rev. J. G. Davies in his *The Theology of William Blake*, and he rightly insists that as the elder Blake died in 1784 he could not have been a member of the 'New Church', which had not been formed by then.[1] But of course he might possibly have been in contact with Jacob Duché after he fled to London in 1777, and with some of the very early 'receivers' who gathered at the Orphan Asylum chapel and at Duché's house. Jacob Duché only held the post of Chaplain to the Female Orphans Asylum in Lambeth from 1782–9. But it has been pointed out[2] that he was succeeded in the office by men who were also Swedenborgians, and like Duché himself anxious that the Church of England should be reformed from within. Even before his appointment there are signs that Blake showed interest in Duché's outlook, for the subscription list for his *Discourses on Various Subjects*, London 1779, contains the names of 'William Sharp, Esq., Jacob Bryant Esq.,' and 'Mr. William Blake'. David Erdman has suggested[3] that it was the engraver Sharp who first interested Blake in the movement; although of course there is always the possibility that the name on the subscription list referred to another Blake.

And as Duché had gathered round him a group of sympathizers with Swedenborg's doctrine while he was at Lambeth

[1] J. G. Davies, *The Theology of William Blake*, Oxford 1948, p. 32.

[2] Charles Higham, Article on Duché in *The New Church Review*, XXII, July 1915, pp. 408–9.

[3] David V. Erdman, 'Blake's Early Swedenborgianism', *Comparative Literature*, V, p. 3.

it is possible that Blake's move to Lambeth may have been influenced by these associations. We now know that it took place in March 1791, as Paul Miner has proved in his article 'William Blake's London Residences'.[1] Although Blake's enthusiasm for Swedenborg was short lived, he did, as we have seen, absorb a great deal from his system. And he managed to keep on very friendly terms with Thomas Butts and John Flaxman, both earnest Swedenborgians. Flaxman's contact with the movement also seems to have been fairly early, for Erdman has noted that his name and address are listed in Robert Hindmarsh's *Rise and Progress of the New Jerusalem Church*, London 1861, amongst those of 'Gentlemen of respectability . . . who found their way to our meetings' and that the Wardour Street address given there was out of date after 1787.

Still, this is all conjecture. What we do know definitely is that the results of the 1789 Swedenborgian Conference at Great East Cheap were set out in a list of resolutions, and it was to these that a 'William' and 'Catherine Blake' added their signatures. So it is pretty certain Blake then believed, for instance, that

on the Death of the material body (which will never be re-assumed,) man rises again as to his spiritual or substantial body, wherein he existed in perfect human form.

And he never seems to have rejected this particular belief, which forms the basis of the lyric 'To Tirzah', added to *The Songs of Experience*, as well as of numerous passages in the prophetic poems. In the same way Blake apparently accepted the thirty-eighth resolution,

That the Last Judgment was accomplished in the Spiritual World in the year 1757.

Indeed he found the idea flattering, as this was the year of his own birth. Then Blake always affirmed the emphasis upon the

[1] Paul Miner, 'William Blake's London Residences', *Bulletin of the New York Public Library*, November 1958.

'Divine Humanity' of Christ which appears in the eighth resolution and at this stage he evidently agreed with the rejection of the Trinity as a Christian doctrine, figured in the third and twenty-sixth resolution.

It is typical of Swedenborg's limitations of mind that he happily challenged the basic Christian tenet of the Trinity and maintained that this really amounted to asserting the existence of three gods! He would have done better to have studied the works of the more reputable medieval theologians whose minds were very much clearer and keener than his own. Thomas Aquinas or Duns Scotus would have made short work of his mental confusion. But with the complacency of his own age Swedenborg took it for granted that his predecessors must have been deluded fools. The world had to wait for the eighteenth century before the real fallaciousness of such doctrines could be revealed. That the most acute minds of every generation had meanwhile been brought to bear on them did not concern Swedenborg at all.[1] And Blake began to be more and more aware himself of Swedenborg's defects. Even in his annotations to Swedenborg's book, *Wisdom of Angels Concerning Divine Love and Divine Wisdom*, which are to be dated about 1788 and are mostly complimentary, he begins to doubt the Master's reliance upon 'Sciences' and rationality. Against a passage on pages 195–6, dealing with the levels of human nature,

> These three Degrees of Altitude are named Natural, Spiritual and Celestial ... Man, at his Birth, first comes into the natural Degree, and this increases in him by Continuity according to the Sciences, and according to the Understanding acquired by them, to the Summit of Understanding which is called Rational ...

Blake indignantly notes,

> Study Sciences till you are blind, Study intellectuals till you are cold, Yet science cannot teach intellect. Much less intellect teach Affection.

[1] Nevertheless see Augustus Alstromer's letter, March 17, 1770: 'Neither Beyer nor Swedenborg denies the Trinity, but they say that the term "three persons" confuses the thought.' Cyriel Odhner Sigstedt, *The Swedenborg Epic*, New York 1952, p. 403.

And when one looks at the annotations to *The Wisdom of Angels Concerning Divine Providence*, dating from about 1790, they are entirely unfavourable. To Swedenborg's assertion 'that all the grandest and purest Truths of Heaven must needs seem obscure and perplexing to the natural Man at first View' – Blake reacts with, 'Lies & Priestcraft. Truth is Nature.' For the rest he exclaims against Swedenborg's tendencies towards Predestination.

> Predestination after this life is more Abominable than Calvin's, & Swedenborg is such a Spiritual Predestinarian –

Nevertheless there are aspects of the Swedenborgian system which sunk deeply into Blake's consciousness. He was never happy about the orthodox doctrine of Atonement, which Swedenborg rejected, and even towards the end of his life he told Crabb Robinson,

> . . . it is a horrible doctrine. If another man pay your debt, I do not forgive it.

And no doubt Blake was affected by the Swedenborgian theory of 'Influx', derived really from the emanative system of the Kabalah. Interestingly enough, the influx of divine life is passed on to mankind through two channels – Love and Wisdom, in Swedenborg's system; and this bears a resemblance to the two columns of the Sephiroth. Again, the belief that every natural phenomenon 'corresponds' with a spiritual force was taken by Blake to form what he called 'Divine Analogy' and J. G. Davies sees this as the meaning behind a passage in his epic *Milton*.

> . . . every Natural Effect has a Spiritual Cause, and Not
> A Natural; for a Natural Cause only seems; it is a Delusion
> Of Ulro & a ratio of the perishing Vegetable Memory.
> *Milton*, Pl. 26. (Keynes, p. 513)

He must surely be right, too, in suggesting references to Swedenborg's doctrine of 'Uses' in *The Book of Thel*. For Swedenborg declared quite categorically,

> Love and Wisdom are mere Nothings, and only ideal Entities, without Reality, until they are applied to Uses; for Love, Wisdom

and Use, are three things which cannot be separated ... for Love
is Nothing without Wisdom, but being in Wisdom it is formed to
a Something, which Something is Use; wherefore when Love by
Wisdom is in Use it then becometh a Reality, because it actually
existeth. . . .[1]

And the heroine of *The Book of Thel* questions the value of her
existence on plate 3 of the poem.

For I walk thro' the vales of Har, and smell the sweetest flowers,
But I feed not the little flowers; I hear the warbling birds,
But I feed not the warbling birds; they fly and seek their food:
But Thel delights in these no more, because I fade away;
And all shall say, 'Without a use this shining woman liv'd,
Or did she only live to be at death the food of worms?'

The Cloud reclin'd upon his airy throne and answer'd thus:

Then if thou art the food of worms, O virgin of the skies,
How great thy use, how great thy blessing! Everything that lives
Lives not alone nor for itself . . .

(Keynes, p. 129)

The particular emphasis on self-love as the root of all evil,
which forms Swedenborg's doctrine of the 'proprium',
signifying the worldliness that springs from this selfishness,
seems also to have impressed Blake. And there are several
concrete images which Blake may have taken over. Swedenborg
believed in the existence of two quite separate suns.

. . . without two Suns, the one living and the other dead, there
can be no Creation.[2]

And there are two different suns which figure in Blake's
mythology. He accepted the idea of the natural world, which,
without the spirit is really dead and a spiritual one that is truly
alive. In *Milton*, plate 23, he speaks of the 'Sun of Salah' or
the body of error, and on plate 21 the sun is 'the sulphur Sun',
'the unwilling Orb', while in the *Vision of the Last Judgment*
Blake sees it, rather, as a spiritual symbol.

[1] Emanuel Swedenborg, *True Christian Religion*, London 1781, no. 387.
[2] Emanuel Swedenborg, *Wisdom of Angels Concerning Divine Love and
Divine Wisdom*, London 1788, no. 163.

'What,' it will be Question'd, 'When the Sun rises, do you not see a round disk of fire somewhat like a Guinea?' O no, no, I see an Innumerable company of the Heavenly host crying, 'Holy, Holy, Holy is the Lord God Almighty'.

The symbolism of the points of the compass, too, was used in Swedenborg's *Treatise Concerning Heaven and Hell*, where the various types of temperaments are assigned to different quarters.[1] This is a very old pattern, of course, and Blake's use of it in his treatment of the Four Zoas is well known.

Even more striking is the effect on Blake's mind of the Swedenborgian conception of 'States'. In keeping with that attitude towards material creation which is so common among all those who reject the resurrection of the body, Swedenborg's view of our first state is an even more depressing one than the doctrine of Original Sin would warrant.

> *The first State of Man, which is a State of Damnation*, every Man hath by an hereditary Principle from his Parents, for Man is born thence to the Love of Self and the Love of the World, and from these Love as Fountains, to Evils of all Kinds. . . .[2]

The second state is the 'reformed' one, when a man recognizes the need for reformation. And the third is one of 'regeneration'. Besides those, there are certain states 'that are not of Rationality and Liberty', such as fear, misfortune, mental or physical disease, ignorance and mental blindness, within which Swedenborg believed a man could not be 'reformed'. The discussion of the whole question of states, in Swedenborg's *Wisdom of Angels Concerning the Divine Providence*[3] must have focused Blake's attention on this subject. But as so often, he did not entirely accept Swedenborg's ideas. Rather, he challenged them.

The challenge comes in Book the Second of Blake's poem *Milton*. He has already paid tribute to Swedenborg in Book the First, plate 22,

[1] Emanuel Swedenborg, *Treatise Concerning Heaven and Hell*, no. 148.
[2] Emanuel Swedenborg, *Wisdom of Angels Concerning Divine Providence*, London 1790, no. 83.
[3] Emanuel Swedenborg, *op. cit.*, nos. 83 & 298.

> O Swedenborg! strongest of men, the Samson shorn by the
> Churches,

and criticized him for classifying souls mistakenly.

> Shewing the Transgressors in Hell, the proud Warriors in Heaven,
> Heaven as a Punisher, & Hell as One under Punishment,
> With Laws from Plato and his Greeks to renew the Trojan Gods
> In Albion, & to deny the value of the Saviour's blood.
>
> (Keynes, p. 506)

On plate 32 he shows an angelic world appearing to Milton
in a dream. The Seven Angels of the Presence discourse with
him and declare,

> We are not Individuals but States, Combinations of Individuals ...
> Distinguish therefore States from Individuals in those States.
> States Change, but Individual Identities never change nor cease,
> You cannot go to Eternal Death in that which can never Die.
> Satan & Adam are States Created into Twenty-seven Churches,
> And Thou, O Milton, art a State about to be Created,
> Called Eternal Annihilation, that none but the Living shall
> Dare to enter, & they shall enter triumphant over Death
> And Hell & the Grave: States that are not, but ah! Seem to be.
>
> (*Ibid.*, pp. 521–2)

Here Blake seems to be warning Swedenborgians against the
temptation to confuse souls with the states they may temporarily enter, and to be protesting against the predestinarian
tendency he had earlier complained of in *Angelic Wisdom Concerning the Divine Providence*. Indeed he seems to reject the idea of
eternal damnation entirely. Above all he affirms that state which
the mystics were familiar with, the truly living souls. The
'self-naughting' which he calls 'Eternal Annihilation'. Blake's
doctrine of 'States' is thus much more original and far deeper
than Swedenborg's.

Notwithstanding the extraordinary impression Swedenborg
can be proved to have made on Blake's mind, from the time
when he annotated *Angelic Wisdom Concerning the Divine
Providence*, Blake was in revolt against him. And again, this is
not surprising considering that even within the 'New Church'

there were such violent upheavals and dissensions at the same period. Not only had there been the 'concubine' scandal, during which Charles Wadstrom, founder of the *New Jerusalem Magazine*, Augustus Nordenskjold and Robert Hindmarsh himself, were suspended from membership for a time. There was the schism over episcopacy and the balance of power among clergy and laity, which resulted in two separate General Conferences being held in 1793; one in Birmingham and the other in Great East Cheap. As we have seen, the schism lasted until 1807. But more than this, there were strange little cults within the movement itself. Spiritualism has been mentioned. In addition a curate of the Rev. Clowes at Manchester, William Cowherd, insisted on a kind of puritanism in the practice of 'receivers' and fostered strict vegetarianism and abstinence among his followers; undermining their health according to Robert Hindmarsh's criticisms. Later on, in 1817, one James Johnston, a working man from Salford with a highly apocalyptic vision, revealed in his *Diary Spiritual and Earthly*, started an even more peculiar sect. Blake's reactions may have been partly the result of his own powerful insight. But they were not unique.

Certain of Swedenborg's own personal limitations appear to have irritated Blake beyond endurance. There does sometimes come into view a worldliness, a snobbery and a materialism in Emanuel Swedenborg's writings which are unworthy of a genuinely spiritual teacher. These Blake detected.

I have already suggested that in spite of his great gifts there clung to Swedenborg's character some of the smugness and self complacency which distinguished his father the Bishop and that his mental horizons were limited in a similar way. The voice of the father speaks in the son in this 'Memorable Relation', (The Third) from *True Christian Religion*.

I once observed, in the Spiritual World, a Concourse of People at a Distance, with Hats on their Heads; the Hats(*m*) of some were tied about with silken Girdles, and those were of the Ecclesiastic Order; the Hats of others had their Borders edged with Gold

Lace, and those were of the Civil Order, all of them Men of deep Learning and Erudition; besides these, I observed others who wore a sort of Bonnet on their Heads, and these were illiterate Men, of no particular Order, or Profession. As I drew near, I heard them conversing together about the Unboundedness of the Divine Power, urging, that if it proceeded according to any appointed Laws of Order, it would not in such case be unlimited, but limited; and consequently would only be Power, but not Omnipotence . . . Several of them then, observing me approach, came running to me, and with some Earnestness exclaimed, 'Art thou the Man who hast circumscribed God with Laws, as with Bonds? How rash, and unbecoming in thee to do so? . . .' On hearing these Words I opened my Mouth, and said with a loud Voice, – 'Learn ye the Laws of Divine Order, and after that disclose your Faith, and ye will see, as it were, a vast Desart, and Leviathan therein, with a large and writhed Body . . . but do ye, as Alexander is reported to have done, when he saw the Gordian Knot, and drew his Sword, and cut it in Pieces . . .' – As I uttered these Words, the Congregation bit their Tongues, with an Intent to sharpen them for Scoffery and Abuse . . . On this I said, – God created the Universe from Himself, as from Order, in Order, and for Order; in like manner he created Man, in whom he fixed the Laws of his own Order, by Virtue whereof he became an Image and Likeness of God; the Sum and Substance of those Laws are, that Man should believe in God, and love his Neighbour; and in proportion as he practiseth those two Duties by his own natural Powers, in the same proportion he maketh himself a Recipient of the Divine Omnipotence, and God joineth Himself to him, and him to Himself, whereby Man's Faith becometh a living, and saving Faith, and his Actions become living and saving Charity . . . On hearing these Words, they that wore ' Hats departed, with their Hats under their Arms, praising God; for in the spiritual World the Intelligent wear Hats as a Covering for their Heads; but they who wore Bonnets gave God no Praise, because they were bald, and Baldness signifies Stupidity, and Dulness; wherefore the latter went away to the left Hand, and the former to the Right.

(m) P. 99. That the Particulars of the Dress of Spirits correspond unto the Particulars of their several States, See No. 177 & seq. of the Treatise on Heaven and Hell.[1]

---

[1] Emanuel Swedenborg, *True Christian Religion*, no. 74, p. 95.

Here the tendency to self dramatization is apparent. Swedenborg takes the floor and sweeps all before him. Another unpleasant feature of this passage is the triumph of learning and
position over the 'plain man'. The more common Christian
attitude has been to suspect learned ignorance and respect
simplicity. Then Swedenborg's strange preoccupation with
the details of dress must have struck Blake. There is one
description, on plate 12 of Blake's *Europe: a Prophecy*, where he
too makes use of garments as a symbolism. It is a reference to
Lord Thurlow, forced by Pitt to relinquish the office of Lord
Chancellor, and the Chancellor's robes of office have become
fused with his flesh; his office identified with his person.[1]

> Above the rest the howl was heard from Westminster louder &
> louder:
> The Guardian of the secret codes forsook his ancient mansion,
> Driven out by the flames of Orc; his furr'd robes & false locks
> Adhered and grew one with his flesh, and nerves & veins shot
> thro' them.
> With dismal torment sick, hanging upon the wind, he fled
> Groveling along Great George Street thro' the Park gate . . .
> (Keynes, p. 242)

But it is above all in Blake's prose prophecy, *The Marriage of
Heaven & Hell*, that his comment on Swedenborg's whole
system is to be found. The idea had been forming in Blake's
mind for some years. Already, against a passage on the brain in
Wisdom of Angels Concerning Divine Love and Divine Wisdom,
page 458, Blake has set the statement,

> Heaven & Hell are born together.

And earlier in the same book he has annotated a discussion on
'the Action of God . . . and the Reaction of Man' with a sentence
that perfectly expresses the thought of his own prophecy.

> Good & Evil are here both Good & the two contraries Married.

The chief object of Blake's satire is Swedenborg's teaching
on angels. This must have riled Blake more than anything else

---

[1] David Erdman, *Blake Prophet Against Empire*, p. 200.

in Swedenborg's system. One book in particular, the *Treatise Concerning Heaven and Hell*, contains little consideration of God or Man. The work is almost entirely taken up with angels. These are formed into very exclusive societies, belonging to the 'celestial' or inmost heaven, the 'spiritual' or 'natural' heaven. Not only are these angels uncommonly snobbish – heaven, according to Swedenborg, is a kind of paradise for social climbers – but they live in a continual state of horror at the stupidity and ignorance of men, especially at their belief in such notions as the resurrection of the body. The curious refusal to admit any essential difference between body and soul which seems to accompany so often belief in a 'Spiritual Body', comes out in his description of Hell in the chapter entitled 'Of the Appearance, Situation and Plurality of Hells'. Swedenborg's hell is a completely prosaic one. It has none of the poetic grandeur of Dante's. The same refusal is at the back of the idea of angels as promoted or demoted men. There is no essential difference between men and angels, or fallen angels. Altogether the *Treatise concerning Heaven and Hell* must have been a book which moved Blake to exasperation and fury. He took his revenge in the scathing treatment of angels as smug idiots which is a feature of *The Marriage of Heaven and Hell*. This prophetic book is really a combined attack on *The Treatise* and the *Apocalypse Revealed*, as well as on Swedenborg's chief study of marriage, *The Delights of Wisdom pertaining to Conjugial Love*, *after which follow The Pleasures of Insanity pertaining to Scortatory Love*. The *Apocalypse Revealed* in particular contains a 'Memorable Relation' – the expression Swedenborg uses when he draws a lesson from one of his many paranormal experiences – which is obviously the inspiration for the 'Memorable Fancy' in Blake's work, of the philosophic Mill, and indeed the source of Blake's peculiar use of the mill symbol in his later writings.

> I once heard there a Sound as it were of a Mill, it was in the Northern Quarter; I wondered at first what it could mean, but I recollected that by Mill and grinding in a Mill in the Word is meant to collect from the Word what is serviceable . . . therefore

I went to the Place, where the Sound was heard, and when I came near, the Sound ceased and then I saw something like the Roof of a House about the Ground, into which there was a Passage through a Cavern; on seeing which I descended and went in, and behind there was an Apartment, in which I saw an old Man sitting amongst Books, with the Word before him, and collecting out of it Passages in support of his Doctrine; there were Papers lying about him, upon which he wrote down the Passages that made for his Purpose; in the next Room there were Scribes who collected the Papers, and copied them in a Book . . .[1]

This is very reminiscent of Blake's 'Printing house in Hell . . . in which knowledge is transmitted from generation to generation'. Especially of the sixth chamber where were men who received the ideas and they 'took the form of books and were arranged in libraries'. (Keynes, p. 155.)

Also of the trip with the angel who,

took me thro' a stable & thro' a church & down into the church vault, at the end of which was a mill: thro' the mill we went, and came to a cave: down the winding cavern we groped our tedious way, till a void boundless as a nether sky appear'd beneath us, & we held by the roots of trees and hung over this immensity.

Eventually after many adventures they return to the Mill.

. . . we went into the mill, and I in my hand brought the skeleton of a body, which in the Mill was Aristotle's Analytics. So the Angel said: 'thy phantasy has imposed upon me, and thou oughtest to be ashamed'. I answered: 'we impose on one another, & it is but lost time to converse with you whose works are only Analytics.'

(*Ibid*, pp. 155–7)

After an examination of Swedenborg's system and Blake's reactions to it one can well understand such remarks as this one:

I have always found that Angels have the vanity to speak of themselves as the only wise . . .

(*Ibid*, p. 157)

[1] Emanuel Swedenborg, *Apocalypse Revealed*, Manchester 1791, Vol. I, no. 484.

and especially the challenging declaration which is embedded in the *Marriage of Heaven and Hell:*

> Thus Swedenborg's writings are a recapitulation of all superficial opinions, and an analysis of the more sublime – but no further.
>
> Have now another plain fact. Any man of mechanical talents may, from the writings of Paracelsus or Jacob Behmen, produce ten thousand volumes of equal value with Swedenborg's, and from those of Dante or Shakespear an infinite number . . .
>
> *(Ibid,* p. 158)

Blake's attitude to Shakespeare could be critical. He includes in his ironical version of Dr Thornton's Lord's Prayer the line, 'lead us not to read the Bible, but let our Bible be Virgil & Shakespear:' *(Ibid,* p. 789). And his reactions to Dante were even sharper, ' . . . he has made This World the Foundation of All & the Goddess Nature Mistress . . .' *(Ibid,* p. 785). (Swedenborg comes under the like censure in these notes on the Illustrations to Dante's *Divine Comedy.*) 'Swedenborg does the same in saying that in this World is the Ultimate of Heaven.' *(Ibid.,* p. 785.)

Nevertheless, it is clear that Blake was deeply influenced by both Dante and Shakespeare. As for Paracelsus and Boehme, their names might be said to give the key to Blake's real derivation. By comparison the effect of Swedenborg's system on Blake's mind, though more obvious, was less profound. However, he was in contact with that system for a good many years of his life. Edwin Ellis and Morris maintain that not only was Blake's father a follower of Swedenborg, but his brother James also, and I have pointed out that this is within the bounds of possibility. At any rate if the 'William' and 'Catherine Blake' listed are those we are concerned with, we can say that by his attendance of the First General Conference at Great East Cheap in 1789, Blake shows himself to have been a member of the New Church at that time. It is important to remember as well, that before the freethinker, Joseph Priestley, published his challenging *Letters to the Members of the New Church* in 1791, he had caused Hindmarsh to send round copies of Swedenborg's works to Joseph Johnson, the bookseller's shop, for him to study. And J. G. Davies is no doubt right in suggesting that the authors who were associated with Johnson at that time, such men as Dr Richard Price, the preacher who so much impressed the philosopher William Godwin, Joseph Priestley, Fuseli the artist, Godwin himself and Blake, are likely then to have discussed Swedenborg's doctrines with some heat.[1] Later, whatever his own views, Blake remained on very friendly terms with both Flaxman and Thomas Butts, one of his kindest patrons and, like Flaxman, a constant and devout member of the New Church. Richard Cosway, Blake's miniaturist friend, was, it is worth recalling, such an ardent Swedenborgian that he asserted he had seen the Blessed Virgin, and sketched her, and had had conversations with Christ and with God himself.[2] Finally in his *Descriptive Catalogue*, issued for the exhibition of his paintings held in the Broad Street house in 1809, Blake gives the title of picture VIII as 'The Spiritual Preceptor' and explains that,

> The subject is taken from the Vision of Emanuel Swedenborg, Universal Theology, No. 623 . . . The works of this visionary are well worthy the attention of Painters and Poets; they are foundations for grand things . . .
>
> (Keynes, p. 581)

So that in spite of the reservations he made, we may take this as Blake's last word on the matter.

Apart from his very interesting influence upon Blake's thought, the whole appearance of Swedenborg on the eighteenth century scene is an extraordinary phenomenon. His teaching attracted the same type of men as we have encountered earlier in the century; prosperous citizens of varying social status, clergy and some gentlemen and scholars, many of them Londoners and some already devotees of Jacob Boehme and William Law. There were of course some Swedish followers of the Baron, who happened to live in London, just as Freher's

---

[1] J. G. Davies, *The Theology of William Blake*, p. 50.
[2] Mona Wilson, *The Life of William Blake*, pp. 361–2.

German friends were to be found in his London circle a generation before. If Blake, Flaxman and Cosway were drawn towards Swedenborg, so the artist Leuchter had been a disciple of Freher's. And in his symbolism Emanuel Swedenborg drew upon the same fountain-head of Neo-Platonic thought and Kabalah as did his predecessors. There is to be found within it the same odd combination; a rejection of the material body in favour of a 'spiritual' one, with refusal to distinguish between body and spirit, nature and super-nature; the same Montanism and Gnosticism, Pantheism and Monism that we have met before so often; and which left a mark on Blake's own vision. Yet since Swedenborg was a scientist, and very much a man of his own century, all this is presented in a fashion more acceptable to his contemporaries by reason of those same limitations I have criticized. For the most perceptively spiritual of the men and women who came within the influence of his thought towards the end of the eighteenth century, he was insufficient, unsatisfying; and William Blake was one of these. We shall encounter others. For them he had no real answer. Rather, Swedenborg was like some strange spiritual red herring. Distracted for a time by his appearance, they continued their course in another direction.

CHAPTER IX

The Late Eighteenth Century

*

The impetus which Law had given to spirituality in eighteenth-century England was certainly not spent at the time of his death. There is a good deal of evidence, though it has been very seldom drawn upon, to show the continuing strength of his influence; the existence within certain circles of that pre-occupation with the mystics, combined with respect for a 'theosophy' deriving from Renaissance Neo-Platonism and Kabalah, which distinguished Law's outlook. Apart from such men as the Rev. Duché and Thomas Hartley, whose interest eventually turned to Swedenborgianism, there were many others who held by William Law's own position and regarded the New Church with impatience. Outstanding among these, and in a sense the key to the whole situation, was that Henry Brooke who has earlier been quoted.

We owe to Henry Brooke's thirst for knowledge of the mystics, and to his position as an Irishman who wished to be kept in touch with fellow spirits in other parts of the British Isles, valuable information about many figures who would otherwise have passed quite unnoticed. For his correspondence was copied out by a son-in-law (the same F. H. Holcroft responsible for the volume of Boehme's works published in Dublin), and this copy now reposes in the Dr Williams Library, London.[1] It was drawn upon by Christopher Walton and parts extracted for the footnotes to his *Notes and Materials for an adequate Biography of William Law*. But otherwise these precious letters have lain untouched and with them a whole world remained closed to students of the period. Since the men

[1] Dr Williams' Library, London, Walton MS. I. i. 43.

and women whom Brooke contacted were admirers of Law and sometimes had been disciples of his, they thought and read along the same lines as the earlier figures we have studied. Most were ardent enthusiasts for Jacob Boehme; some still recalled the Philadelphian movement. Those Catholic mystics Law had reverenced also commanded their respect. A few interested themselves in the writings of the Commonwealth period and one, the Richard Clarke I have already alluded to, was a Hebraist, a student of the Kabalah after the manner of Francis Lee, and had some knowledge of Alchemy also. Quite a number were visionaries and liked to compare their spiritual experiences with those of others. These personalities come to life in a remarkable way in their letters. And, as Brooke was himself a notable person from a distinguished Anglo-Irish family, the story of his strange spiritual quest should, perhaps, be told from the beginning.

The truth is that Henry Brooke was a man with a passionate hunger of the soul. His mind turned to religion early in life, which was perhaps natural with his family background, and he never ceased from the most determined efforts to contact those who might have real mystical insight, to win their guidance and to press forward in the life of prayer himself. For a man of his bent there was little alternative in that age to the movement centering upon Law in England, drawn originally, as we have seen, from an earlier tradition and possibly making its impact upon Ireland at a slightly later date. I have said that Brooke's family helped to predispose him towards spirituality. Its climate of thought was unusual and it numbered several very exceptional members. Both Brooke's grandfathers were clergymen, and his parents were first cousins. According to Isaac D'Olier, another son-in-law who was his biographer,

> His paternal grandfather was the Rev. William Brooke of Rantavan, Rector of the Union of Mullogh, in the diocese of Kilmare, who married Miss Digby.[1]

[1] Isaac D'Olier, *Memoirs of the Late Excellent and Pious Mr. Henry Brooke, Collected from Original Papers and other authentic Sources* . . . Compiled and edited by Isaac D'Olier, LL.D., Dublin 1816, p. 1.

Henry Brooke's father, Robert Brooke, seems to have been overshadowed by his very brilliant brother, Henry. This elder Henry Brooke was a barrister, but made his name as a writer. His play, *Gustavus Vasa*, celebrating the struggle for Swedish liberty, greatly alarmed the British Government. The ideals expressed were seen to have all too clear a bearing on the Irish situation, and just as a performance at Drury Lane had been arranged it was banned, much to the disappointment of Garrick.[1] Brooke was the protegé of Pope and Swift who hoped great things from him. But after his disillusioning experience in drama he retired to Dublin and concerned himself more directly with Irish politics for a while. He wrote the *Farmer's Letters*, a discussion of the country's affairs from a very Protestant point of view, in which he accuses the Irish peasantry of a native love of violence. And, in turn, this plunged him into controversy with a notable Catholic antiquary, Charles O'Connor, who rated him in these terms.

> Ungenerous poet! . . . shame upon the Man whose breast nature has formed to glow with the generous flame of freedom, and whose soul sinks with a debased vitiated taste, into the interests of a narrow minded party, who loves the freedom of every country but his own . . .![2]

His contact with O'Connor caused Brooke to swing over towards a pro-Catholic position; though O'Connor and his friend Dr Curry, who often discussed him in their letters, felt he never entirely shed his Protestant prejudices. At any rate in 1762, Brooke published his *Tryal of the Roman Catholics*, a heartfelt plea for the abolition of the penal laws.

Indeed, we find Brooke complaining to O'Connor of the heavy load he has taken upon himself on behalf of the Catholic cause.

> I have you to blame, particularly, for the extraordinary pains I am obliged to take in the case of the Roman Catholics. Had you not

[1] Charlotte Brooke, 'An Account of the life of Henry Brooke Esq', Volume I, *The Poetical Works of Henry Brooke*, Dublin 1792, iii–xix.

[2] Rev. C. O'Connor, D.D., *Memoirs of Charles O'Connor*, Dublin 1797, pp. 208–10.

written so well on the subject, I might have treated it at my ease, and I truly assure you that you have compelled me to very hard labour.[1]

Towards the end of his life Brooke became occupied with a long novel, *The Fool of Quality*, after the pattern Richardson had made so fashionable in England. And this, which had considerable popularity, bears marks of the absorption in Jacob Boehme's system that became Brooke's chief interest during the years before his death.[2] And the interest was certainly passed on, for it reappears in the preoccupation with the mystics of his daughter Charlotte, his only surviving child, as D'Olier makes plain.

> This amiable author died in the bosom of his family, his fine understanding worn out with mental exertion, and his body with the weight of years. He had a great number of children, but they all died young, excepting one daughter that lived to survive him, Miss Charlotte Brooke, who inherited a large proportion of her father's talents. This ingenious and accomplished lady, gratified her country and the literary world, with that national and elegant performance 'Relics of Irish Poetry'; and shortly before her death, published a new and corrected edition of her father's Poetical Works.[3]

Certainly Charlotte, the remarkable child who remained to Brooke out of the twenty-two that had been born, can be regarded, with Charles O'Connor, as one of the most distinguished Irish scholars of the age. She helped to pioneer the rediscovery of Gaelic literature which took place just as the tradition of Irish verse writing itself was dying out, and her editorial labours on her father's works were much appreciated by all her friends. But they were not so pleased with her mystical tastes. They felt she was indulging in sensationalism,

[1] Rev. C. O'Connor, *op. cit.*, p. 406.

[2] Henry Brooke, *The Fool of Quality*, or *The History of Henry Earl of Moreland*, London 1777. See for example Vol. III, pp. 194f.

[3] Isaac D'Olier, *Memoirs of the Late Excellent and Pious Mr. Henry Brooke*, p. 2.

misled, perhaps, by cranky nonsense. She met their criticisms with calm assurance, as in this letter.

You seem to think the mystic writers too much taken up with *speculative* religion, to the neglect or omission of those points of doctrine which would lead to the *practice* of it . . . In the nature of things, it cannot be that we should reign without first we suffer . . . And how is nature to be convinced of that? – By learning to know herself. – This truth and this knowledge is taught by the mystics beyond any other writers that I ever have read.[1]

Sharing this family bent, we find one of Charlotte's cousins, Thomas Digby Brooke, a brother of the younger Henry Brooke, who passed a life-time in devotion to the mystics, actually translating some of Mme Guion's works into English. This young man was associated with another family project, launched by his elder brother Captain Robert Brooke. The latter had spent a very adventurous career accumulating a fortune in India. But he felt keenly the poverty of his Irish countrymen and, in an effort to provide employment, he built the town of 'Prosperous' in County Kildare, to establish the cotton industry for the first time in Ireland. Unfortunately his venture was a failure and he lost his money. Thomas Digby is said to have died of a broken heart after the collapse. But his brother was appointed Governor to the Island of St Helena as a compensation for his losses, and a reward for his public-spiritedness.

Born into this gifted and original family, in November 1738 – a family remarkable also for its strong social con-science – it is not surprising that Henry Brooke the younger should have developed these inclinations towards spirituality which were to dominate his whole life, and at a comparatively early age. We have the history of this development in a long letter to John Wesley, written in April 1765. For just as Henry Brooke took an interest in the Swedenborgians and some of his correspondents were actually members of the New Church, so he followed the Wesleys' evangelical movement with keen

[1] Charlotte Brooke, *Reliques of Irish Poetry*, Dublin 1788, pp. cxiv–cxvi.

sympathy, becoming finally a close friend of John Wesley's. The story he tells runs according to a familiar pattern. 'Both my father and mother were children of the clergy,' he says, 'and intended me for the church. They bred me up very religiously, and brought me to the Sacrament when about fourteen. I remember I had at that time deep convictions and repentance for some actual sins; but whether I was convinced of the depravity of my nature, I do not recollect; however, I remember to have the accusation and guilt of those sins entirely taken away, and peace and joy succeeded . . .' But the giddiness of youth brought him, apparently, into a more worldly frame of mind. Fear of offending his family prevented him from going too far, and reading his father's copy of Law's *Serious Call to a Devout and Holy Life* occasionally recalled him to his senses; sometimes, indeed, he was overwhelmed by guilt, 'in agonies of grief'. He was distracted from these pious fits, however, by 'a jaunt to England' and there material difficulties and the shock of parting from his family made him turn once more to Law's *Serious Call*. This book did not satisfy him, however, and it was not till he bought a copy of *The Spirit of Prayer* that he made any progress. But then, as he puts it,

> The light began to dawn; I saw something I knew not what, but was delighted beyond measure at the promise of the day. Some persons began to ridicule me on my growing so serious, and reading the fanatic, Mr. Law, saying, they supposed I should presently be deep in Behmen. They excited my curiosity to obtain some of his works; but was for some time lost in the labyrinth.
>
> One day reading Mr. Law's 'Spirit of Love', my heart expanded, my eyes were opened; I saw, and felt that God is love. Need I attempt to describe unutterable things?
>
> . . . I now dwelt alone, and solitary as in a desert, though in the populous city of London; I had no one to speak to; all regarded me as a monster: my heart yearned, and I often wept over the busy throngs that crowded the streets, hurrying up and down the broad way . . . As I passed by the Tabernacle, in Moorfields, I heard them singing; I stepped in, my heart melted, my tears flowed, and I joined them sincerely. But when the preaching began I was disgusted; I left the house, my heart was heavy. Oh!

said I, the multitude perish for lack of knowledge; they follow the cry of 'Lo! Christ is here; and there is Christ,' and know not that the kingdom of heaven is within them. I went two or three times to hear the hymns, but never stayed for preaching. I continued thus a new creature for about nine months, when family affairs obliged me to return to Ireland.[1]

This description is notable in several ways. Like Duché's letter to Mr Paine, quoted in the Introduction, and included in Holcroft's copy of Henry Brooke's correspondence,[2] it reveals the profound effects of William Law's books, especially the mystical ones, upon the most sensitive minds of the age. The general attitude to Law and Boehme is made equally clear, however, and when Brooke began to contact the Evangelical movement his attraction towards it is made plain, but at the same time his dissatisfaction with the lack of interior spirituality. Any disciple of Law would have found this disturbing and it was, in fact, the basis of a life-long disagreement with John Wesley. For though, when Henry Brooke returned to Ireland he joined the Methodists, yet, as he explains to his cousin Charlotte Brooke in one of his last letters,[3] he felt obliged to make reservations.

> You know I was not born (so to say) a Methodist; yet have I lived among them between twenty and thirty years, and opposed (with meekness) even Mr. Wesley when I thought him wrong. They continue to love and esteem me; and we agree to disagree on some points.

In Ireland, then, during the latter part of the eighteenth century, there flourished within one family at least, the spirit that had moved William Law earlier. And it is important to remember that during the seventeenth century Dublin had been the home of Edward Taylor who composed there his book, *Jacob Behmen's Philosophy Unfolded*, so much praised by his

[1] Isaac D'Olier, *Memoirs of the Late Excellent and Pious Mr. Henry Brooke*, pp. 32 f.

[2] Walton MS I i 43, pp. 199–208.

[3] Isaac D'Olier, *Memoirs of the Late Excellent and Pious Mr. Henry Brooke*, p. 180.

publisher, Thomas Salusbury. Arthur Hopkinson, indeed, quotes some verses from the poems of Henry Brooke the elder which are obviously based on the panegyric upon Boehme in the publisher's preface to that work.

> Whate'er the *Eastern Magi* sought
> Or *Orpheus* sung, or Hermes taught
> Whate'er *Confucius* would inspire,
> Or *Zoroaster's* mystic fire;
> The symbols that *Pythagoras* drew,
> The wisdom God-like *Plato* knew;
> What *Socrates* debating proved,
> Or *Epictetus* lived and loved;
> The sacred fire of saint and sage,
> Through ev'ry clime, in every age
> In *Behmen's* wondrous page we view,
> Discovered and revealed anew . . .
> The trumpet sounds, the Spirit's given,
> And *Behmen* is the voice from heaven.[1]

This would seem to be Brooke's eighteenth-century version of the original Renaissance tradition. His nephew was not fortunate enough to contact William Law himself upon his own spiritual awakening; the great Non-Juror had died in 1761. But, as we have seen, he did the next best thing which was to start a correspondence with Thomas Langcake, Law's disciple. His opening letter was written in December 1776, addressed to Langcake at 'Paddington near London', and one can gather the nature of his enquiries quite easily from the reply, dated 29th December 1776. Langcake begins by explaining the rather limited nature of his contacts with Law.

Though I had the honor and happiness of being several years intimate with the divine and blessed man you write about, yet it was rather in a way of correspondence than by personal inter-course, and at those times I visited him, nothing passed in con-versation but what might have occur'd with any other of his disciples, it chiefly turn'd upon his own writings at my going down the first time, and I well remember that walking together

[1] A. Hopkinson, *About William Law*, p. 119.

in his Garden, and talking of objectors to them, he said the abler the adversary, the better he should be pleased, but that his principles could not be overthrown without tearing up the whole Christian religion by the roots.

The primitive Quakers and their writings Mr. Law had a regard for, but as to Isaac Pennington I do not recollect to have had any converse about him: though after Mr. Law's death, I was myself satisfied, he had read him with great approbation, I never heard him mention a word about Engelbrecht; but a friend told me that he said Swedenburgh was very voluminous & that was not his worst fault . . . – But to proceed. You ask me whether I have met with any one, passed into the unitive life since the death of Mr. Law. My answer is, I hope many dear Souls longing after an increase of the divine birth, and I ground my hope upon this comfortable assertion of Mr. Law's, said to a friend 'that the Highest state of a mystic was the Lowest state of a penitent to wit Union'. As soon as the desire of the heart is turn'd towards God, he enters into that heart, and so an immediate Union and communion is open'd between God and the creature . . . This desire continued, the divine birth gradually grows up in us, and passing thro' various states we at last happily arrive to a full maturity in the Divine Life but as I do not know the invisible workings of others' minds, so I do not know what progress any particular person may have made towards perfection. In some simple Souls, the great work of regeneration goes on in them very surely though imperceptibly, others feel many conflicts, passing through a variety of states of Light and darkness; and perhaps no two persons are constructed exactly in the same manner . . .[1]

After these very sane remarks Langcake concludes:

P.S. I cannot form a true estimate of Dr. Pordage and Jane Lead. I know those who greatly esteem them, I am not much conversant in their writings.

This letter of Langcake's reveals several important facts. First of all, it was written in reply to an enquiry which had the intention of discovering whether there were men and women at the time of writing who were not only interested in mysticism but who actually practised it. We shall see that Henry Brooke's curiosity on this point did lead him to make some discoveries.

[1] Walton MS. I. i. 43, pp. 1–4.

An interesting light is thrown on Law's own reading and opinions. His rather acid comments on Swedenborg are illuminating. Langcake's own views on states of soul are examples of the balanced attitude Law seems to have encouraged, and then again Henry Brooke's curiosity about Pordage and Jane Lead is very significant. Possibly he may have been impelled to write the letter at the time he did by the account of a visionary experience which was sent to him in Dublin in the same month. The letter relating this is not precisely dated. It is from a Mrs King and the vision took the form of a dream which conveyed a warning of the troubles which were likely to come upon 'this unhappy Land'.

> I thought I went out of my door to look out for a rainbow, on looking up to the sky which I think was dark, instead of a rainbow I saw a sword drawn, which reached from near the place I stood in, across the Earth, further than I could see the end of. The shape of the sword was in an Arch, a broad sword with two edges and a rising in the middle, the handle of the sword was made in the form of a Cross, on the right hand side of which stood a short candle, lighted which gave a bright light upon the entire right side of the sword whilst the left side was left in total darkness.

Mrs King then heard words explaining that the lighted candle was short because the time when troubles would be coming on the earth was near. The dark side of the sword represented the wicked, while the light showed that the good would be supported and comforted. Again she received a locution; 'You are looking for peace and safety, But behold swift & sudden destruction cometh.'

Henry Brooke had also preserved another similar letter of an earlier date, this time from a friend of his, Alexander Boswell, in Osbertstown, Northern Ireland. On Good Friday, 1763, Boswell dreamt that he was in the parlour with 'Mr. Brooke' (possibly Brooke's uncle the elder Henry Brooke), when they both saw 'it grew dark as pitch' and then 'the constellations in great fury with one another'. They imagined that the last Judgement had come.

O says Mr. Brookes (in a great fright) this is the day of Judge-ment, then I thought I heard the Righteous crying out in great Joy, 'Here comes the comforter, which none can pluck from us,' I thought I was greatly frighten'd as to my Sins, I began to be sincerely sorry for them but there was no help for it. I thought that besides the eyes of outward Nature, I had also the eyes of the dark property, which I thought I then understood, and imagined was near being open'd . . . In the midst of this Horror I thought I awoke in church, and found myself standing in the gallery, they were all standing too, but I thought the minister was doing nothing, & it seem'd to be like an examination, I was greatly surpriz'd at this and in the midst of Terror & amazement I awoke. When I awaken'd I found myself in a great sweat and a fit of shaking which I imagined was the ague . . .

The important part about poor Mr Boswell's dream is its imagery, and the very Behmenistic terminology used to describe it; 'the eyes of outward nature', the 'eyes of the dark property', the anticipated 'opening' of this property. The letter seems to point to circles in Ireland where people thought in these terms.

By the 1780's Langcake is writing to Henry Brooke telling him of visionaries within his own experience. He writes from Bristol, where he is staying with a Mrs Field in Hillgrove Street, and begins with a note about an enclosure.

In. Septr. Gentlemans Magazine I inserted a letter of Dr. Byrom with a Note of my own. There is just come out the divine Visions of John Engelbrecht, a most extraordinary Character indeed! One Mr. Stephen Penny an accountant of the City is lately dead, an intimate friend of mine. He has left a very striking letter behind him, which he directed to be printed just before his death. I have had a printed Copy of it presented me.

Further light is cast on happenings in Bristol in a later letter to a Mr Tighe, staying with the Rev. Okely, a Moravian Minister, author of a life of Boehme, at Northampton.[1]

Mrs. Field's daughter, who I believe you saw when you visited me, has lately had a divine Vision a transient view and Taste of

[1] Walton MS I i 43, pp. 26-8.

the Glory of the Heavenly City and the happiness of the saints in bliss: And her overflowing love to her fellow creatures, prevail'd on her to make it public in a small Pamphlet. There were numbers of them sold in this City; but the second edition does not go off. Perhaps they would some of them be sold if they were sent to a bookseller at Northampton. Please to intimate to me your Opinion here-in, and if you think it advisable together w. worthy Mr. Okely I will send some down to you . . .

P.S. . . . The Pamphlet is Entitled – The Glory of the Heavenly City and blessedness of Departed Saints graciously manifested in a Vision to a Young Lady of Bristol in the 10th Oct. 1781 as related by herself. Price 6d.

This strange mixture of enthusiasm and hard business sense is typical of Thomas Langcake's personality. Both he and Henry Brooke seem continually to use the terminology of St Teresa of Avila, and evidently regard the mystical experience very much from her point of view. Steeped as he was in the great Catholic mystics, after the example of William Law, Henry Brooke found it a great sorrow that John Wesley, for whom he had so much respect and affection, did not share the great respect he himself also felt for Boehme's teaching. And Brooke was not the only one to deplore Wesley's attitude to Boehme. A certain W. Smith, writing to Brooke from Manchester, confirms this sad lapse on Wesley's part.

We have had Revd. Mr. Wesley at Manchester this week he cannot help yet condemning the Pious Behme and Law, yet he says he hopes to meet them in Heaven. Indeed all that Mr. Wesley can say of Christian perfection was said by John Sparrow in the Preface to Behme's Aurora w^h he published in 1656. – It is not in his power in all his publications to say anything but what may be found in Behmen.

There was another individual, however, who disconcerted Wesley even more than the deceased Boehme and Law, and who was acquainted with an even more formidable number of visionaries and mystics than Langcake or Brooke – the extraordinary Mr Ralph Mather, whose later activities in favour of the Swedenborgian 'New Church' we have already noted. Henry Brooke received many lengthy letters from Mather, mostly discussing the state of his soul. Some are definitely hysterical in tone. He describes how, on one occasion he had intended to commit suicide but was saved because the chemist gave him salts of lavender instead of laudanum! Mather regarded this as a dispensation of Providence. His correspondence with Brooke no doubt arose from a common contact with Wesley; for he is mentioned several times in Wesley's Journals and letters. And Brooke replied to Mather's agitated letters with a calm and friendly sanity which must have done him good. Mather evidently had great powers of rousing religious fervour in others, for in Wesley's Journal he is shown as inspiring real changes of heart among the boys at the Kingswood School near Bristol. In August 1773 Wesley set out for Exeter 'with Ralph Mather, then a humble scriptural Christian', returning to Bristol in September. On his visit to the School Wesley made the following comments:

I waited a few days before I set down what has lately occurred among the children here. From the time God visited them last, several of them retained a measure of the fear of God. But they grew colder and colder, till Ralph Mather met them in the latter end of August. Several then resolved to meet in class again, and appeared . . . to be greatly humbled. At five all the children met in the school. During an exhortation then given, first one, then two or three were much affected. Afterwards two more were taken apart, who were soon deeply distressed; and one of them (James Whitestone), in less than half an hour found a clear sense of the love of God. Near seven, they came down to the boys in the school; and Mr. Mather asked, 'Which of you will serve God?' They all seemed to be thunderstruck, and ten or twelve fell down upon their knees. Mr. Mather prayed, and then James Whitestone. Immediately one and another cried out; which brought in the other boys, who seemed struck more and more, till about thirty were kneeling and praying at once. Before half-hour past nine, ten of them knew that they were accepted in the Beloved. Several more were brought to the birth; and all the children, but three or four, were affected more or less.

239

Mather had an equal success at the Misses Owens' girls' school at Pensford.

> After Mr. Mather had preached at Pensford, he met the children there. Presently the spirit of contrition fell upon them, and then the Spirit of grace and of supplication, till the greater part of them were crying together for mercy, with a loud and bitter cry; and all Miss Owen's children, but one (two-and-twenty in number) were exceedingly comforted.[1]

One can imagine the disgust with which Law would have viewed these emotional outbursts. It would not have been greater, though, than the suspicion Wesley entertained for mysticism. The next reference in the Journal is for 29th January 1774.

> ... several times in the following week, I had much conversation with Ralph Mather, a devoted young man, but almost driven out of his senses by Mystic Divinity. If he escapes out of this specious snare of the devil he will be an instrument of much good.

Later in March he is commenting disconsolately,

> I went over to Kingswood, and put an end to some little mis-understandings which had crept into the family. At this I rejoiced; but I was grieved to find that Ralph Mather's falling into Mysticism and Quakerism had well nigh put an end to that un-common awakening which he had before occasioned among the children. But next day I found the little maids at Publow, who found peace by his means, had retained all the life which they had received, and had indeed increased therein.[2]

The tension which existed between Wesley and Ralph Mather on the subject of mysticism makes it quite clear why such a close bond was soon forged between Mather and Brooke. But John Wesley could not help appreciating the rare qualities which Mather displayed. There is a surprising letter to Charles Wesley in which he admits;

[1] *The Journal of John Wesley*, edited by Nehemiah Curnak, Vol. V, pp. 523–5.
[2] *The Journal of John Wesley*, Vol. VI, pp. 10–11.

To tell *you* my naked thoughts (which I do not tell to everyone),
I have talked with Ralph Mather again and again. I think verily
I have never met with such another man. I am much inclined to
think (though he is not infallible, neither of an uncommon natural
understanding) that he is now as deep in grace as G. Lopez
was . . . When I talk with Ralph Mather, I am amazed and almost
discouraged. What have I been doing for seventy years![1]

This is an amazing tribute by a famous man to an extraordinary one. Even more astonishing is the document which
Mather addressed to Henry Brooke in November 1775,
entitled *A List of some names and the places of abode of those in
whose minds the Light of God has arisen or is graciously arising. Sing
Praises*. The paper is a Baedeker's guide to mystical Britain and
begins with Ireland.

Carrickfergus. E. Pendril shoemaker a married man who under
great persecution lives in continence & abstinence from animal
food. Visited about five years since. He is a tender mind. He was
with the Quakers but now fully believes in restitution & the
Universality of God's Power and Love.
Belfast – William Forde (Hercules Lane) a poor man he is not so
solid as E.P. but teachable and lives on roots & water, there is
another In that debauched Town but I wait to see if it will prove
more as the seed sown in good ground.

Moving to England Mather commences with Liverpool; a
useful point of departure. There Brooke could find a relative of
his, one R. Sedden, a Methodist. 'My Sister also married his
relation, but she poor thing & her Husband a Capt. of a Ship,
are in the dark World.' Passing on to Warrington and Leigh
nearby, Brooke could meet

Wm. Crompton Farmer & . . . R. Darwell . . . J. Marsh, poor
people love J. Boehme and Wm. Law . . .
Bolton. E. Hughes   passed unto God.
    M. Owen   greatly advanced
    W. Winkbridge 15 yrs in purifications.
several more coming on, these I think are in general but low in the
World, but 'tis a school of female Philosophers. O how gladly

---

[1] *The Letters of John Wesley*, edited by John Telford, Vol. VI, p. 78.

would they see a mind desirous to get out of the dark World. But these Angelic Souls are as the filth of the World and scouring of all things.
Chester (I forgot)
enquire for Eliz. Letsham at H. Riders she has a most tender mind. She was with the methodists, and tho' a worthy handsome annuity, sits alone and keeps silence . . . J. Leadbetter a painter and many (5 or 6) others have been visited, these are also held in derision as Mystics, but tho' some do not come forward as one would wish, yet they are not gone from simplicity;
Manchester. Sarah Lee in St. Anne's Square one highly elated in the world but of large experience. Thomas Clowes a rector of one of the Churches, a pious solid young man. – – A curate of another T.C.'s acquaintance, more in the fire yet would seem promising. Sam Mann Radcliffe St., has been about 18 years in the way. This dear man & his wife will shew the rest . . . Some others in this place who would feign the name of mystics I fear are deceiving themselves.

The Behmenist terminology used is notable in this account and the references to individuals who had a reverence for Boehme and Law. Also it will be seen that Mather's attitude is by no means credulous or uncritical,

Near Manchester there are three simple tender minds who have been seeking the true Life many years. Saml. Mann will therefore point them out – But there is another also M. Robinson who has the most exquisite talents, genius, intrepidity and docility of whom I am jealous lest the quakers hath got her into their society. If she escapes she bids fair for being a star of the first magnitude. She has been a sprightly, quick, and gay frequenter of all the scenes of pleasure.
Near Wellington in Shropshire lives – Hatton a preacher of the Episcopal Church. This man's compasssion writes to E. Letsham in a sweet broken strain. Not far from hence lives J. Fletcher. – But should not Leeds be too far from Manchester (40 miles) there is C. Cayley, the Widow Crosby & a young maiden . . . are preachers; & six miles from them lives M. Bosanquet who appears in Public also – I have been at her house, among the numbers of Methodists of which there are two or three thousand just in the neighbourhood some must be deeply touched. –

The Rev. John Fletcher of Madeley was widely respected as a

director of souls; much admired by Henry Brooke and John Wesley alike. And of course Mary Bosanquet was well known in Methodist circles. Having touched lightly upon Macclesfield, Mathers then goes on to describe the situation further south, beginning with Birmingham.

> Birmingham (see Wolverhampton) there is one if not more of whom I hear a thirst is in kindled for Spirit & Life. J. Behme & Wm. Law are favourite authors with one of them. – Banbury – Richd. Cooper the son of a timorous wealthy man has given himself up to much solitude. Providence may make way for converse. I know him not in person. But a young man at this place, a grocer who lived in Bristol professes a great veneration for the mystics but I've found more brokeness in fewer words; yet is he not in the spirit of the World. But another turn, over the wheel would lay the mind more deeply in the dust. –
> Worcester in this city there cannot but be some seekers, but Gloster is a dead place. I met with a man at Gloster calls himself the prophet, but on my querying closely, he used me with the greatest insolence & perversity, so I had no liberty to see him any more.
> Cheltenham Gloster. – enquire for Newman Schoolmistress she is brought down from her Calvinian notions, thro' some simplicity of a forlorn rector's wife who lives from her husband. But tho' the sister of this Schoolmistress with whom I had much conversation, is called the Phoenix of the Methodists in those parts, she cannot believe that as yet her sister knows aught of Religion.

Passing on from Stroud to Bristol, Mather refers to what he calls his 'spiritual mother', whom he presses Brooke to visit.

> I am persuaded God will give thee admittance to her (if yet alive) tho' none but those to whom her God & thy God shall direct her to converse with, can she by any means admit. O the angelic pleasure it must give! What is 500 miles to behold so pure, so sweet, so childlike a soul, – She is swallowed up in the Philanthropy of God. O that souls would but die, or rather. O that I may die! daily! till death is swallow'd up in victory! –

There follows a list of Bristol figures and a reference to the girls' school nearby that Wesley had mentioned his visiting.

> Also near Bristol there is a school of young girls kept by those

promising young women & sisters, their name is Owen: their brother is or was at the University. The youngest of these women a most devoted soul bids fair for a Teresa. The others are not yet prepared for such communications. –

Before leaving Bristol Mather produces a sharp classification of the Methodists in that city from the spiritual point of view.

– Amongst the Methodists of which sect there were in J.W.'s only 800 in the City of Bristol there is a handfull, travelling with another Spirit (as L. Cas is one of them) of this number J. Southest S. Johnston (an elderly Virgin) the widow Purnel &c. – might (if any) be ranked in the number. But the Bristol society is mixed up of 5 or 6 sorts! Here and there an inward mind. 2nd a few much wed to the prayer of meditation. 3rd a diversion of these less positive in their active state, 4th those who are passed into some consolations, and the extatic state. 5th some under the first convictions. 6th a large body of prating vain worldly minds, who can talk about God & the World like one who has to dictate to two writers, each writing on opposite subjects. But the hardest to convince, or bring into any true Union or Nearness to God & his purity are the 2nd & the last, for the one has got the spiritual and the other the temporal riches, neither of whom can in this whorish persuasion of Soul enter into the Kingdom of Heaven: But the first are sliding tho' painfully yet surely into God, the 3rd it's possible to rouse from their sensuality. 4 this is the gate to death – 5th is the ploughing and pruning season in order to bring forth fruit: But the 2nd and 6th Alas! how hardly shall those who have Riches (in sweetness in images in the World) enter God's Kingdom. With men it's impossible but Glory to God; all things are possible with him. –

Mather next mentions Bath and Bradford on Avon where is to be found 'Joseph Yerbury my dear brother and his sister', who 'are both drawing into the pure Nature of God'. In London the only person worth mentioning appears to be a 'Mary Roberts a methodist in Union Street Oxford market . . . She has some choice old matron with whom she converses. There are a few at the West end of the Town to whom I would hope mercy has been offered'. Apparently only so few qualify even for this! Barnstaple, Bideford and Bishop's Norton are also touched on, but more important is Northampton.

> Northampton at this Town a Moravian Preacher Okely professes
> great love to the mystics but at Loughboro' not far from thence
> near twenty are turn'd from Methodism to Quakerism. as this is
> the case prejudice may have shut up their hearts but to those, who
> can speak thee & thou, & wear a broad brimmed hat & who
> have learned their Phrases. So I am afraid it is with those at
> Barnstaple, as many of the Quakers has visited them: but all
> things are possible with God.

From these remarks it would appear that Ralph Mather was
not a Quaker at this time, as Wesley had supposed. And
whether he joined the Society of Friends later or not, we know
he ended as a Swedenborgian who helped to spread the
doctrine of the New Church in America. But at the stage when
his spiritual guide came into the hands of Brooke, no doubt all
this was in the future. Having brought his account so far,
finally he sums up.

> Should Providence lead thro' Salop, there are doubtless in that
> large Town, some serious Minds. But about Manchester & Bristol
> the spring of Truth would seem to open most of anywhere that
> I know. In Bolton . . . they are universally hated, derided and
> treated with evil reproaches, and in Bristol as Whimsical dreaming
> enthusiastical Visionarys. If therefore we are persecuted & suffer
> for righteousness sake, happy are we: It is then that the Spirit of
> GOD and of Glory rests upon us . . .

Ralph Mather's *Account* is a document of great historical
importance; particularly because he reveals the preoccupations
with mysticism, mystical literature, visionary experiences and
theosophy of many obscure individuals who might otherwise
never have been heard of, as well as of some notable figures, up
and down the country. Since he is careful to give their social
standing in each case, one can see that they represented a fair
cross-section of the population but that the majority came from
precisely that social level to which Blake himself belonged.
Mather reveals, indeed, just that part of eighteenth-century life
which has been missing from the picture. His survey throws

a flood of light upon the true interests of a very lively minority, in an age supposed to be given over entirely to rationalism and materialism.

Henry Brooke himself was not only interested in the mystics and theosophists of his own time but also in those of the past. He made repeated enquiries with Langcake about references to the Philadelphians in Law's correspondence. At last Langcake was able to find him one letter, (to the Mr Stephen Penny, who, himself, left behind such a 'very striking letter', as we have seen) at the distillery by Castle Green Bristol, dated 8th April 1747, and containing this not very flattering passage.

> Many persons of learning in the last century read J:B: [Jacob Boehme] with great earnestness, but it was only as it were to steal from him certain mysteries of Nature, and to run away with the Philosopher's Stone – And yet no where could they see the folly & impossibility of their attempts so fully shewn them as by J:B: himself. In the beginning of the century a number of persons, many of them of great Piety, formed themselves into a kind of society by the name of Philadelphians. They were great readers, and well versed in the language of J:B: and used to make eloquent discourses of the mystery in their meetings. – Their only Thirst was after Visions, openings and revelations &c and yet no where could they see their distemper so truly described, the causes of it proceeded from, and the fatal consequences of it, as by J:B: – He often truly says that in his writings are to be found all that the Heart of Man can wish to know of God, Nature, and Creature &c. but then he as often says & proves, that all is barred and locked & bolted up from all those, that by Art and reason, & self ability would enter into it.

Not only did he satisfy his curiosity about Law's attitude to these English Behmenists of an earlier age, through Langcake's good offices, but, later, Brooke was to make enquiries about one of his own correspondents; that Rev. Richard Clarke whom I have mentioned as a survival from the radical theosophists of the seventeenth century and as a Cabalist in the tradition of Francis Lee. He knew Clarke was an admirer of William Law, who had met him, and that he was friendly with Thomas Langcake. He also mentions in his letter a Mr

Winchester; surely that Elhanan Winchester from America, who distinguished himself by producing *A Defence of Revelation in Ten letters to Thomas Paine; Being an Answer To His First Part of The Age of Reason*?[1] It is a point of some importance that Richard Clarke, too, joined in this controversy and brought out an answer to Tom Paine. And Blake, we know, followed the published reaction to Paine's radicalism with passion.[2] However, though Langcake can supply background information to Brooke on Richard Clarke, he is quite ignorant of Elhanan Winchester. He writes, referring in his reply, dated 1st August 1790, to Clarke's belief in Universal Salvation; a belief which he shows, in the same letter to Henry Brooke, seems to have been privately shared by William Law himself.[3]

As to Mr. Clarke he was a visitor in this City in '88 and preaching Universal redemption, it stirred up the Preachers against him. The sectaries were ready to tear him out of the Pulpit; and one person called out when preaching at Temple Church, This man preaches false doctrine, Mr. C – told him (when summoned into the Vestry-room) He would find his Doctrine True in due Season, or words to that effect & so gently dismiss'd him. As to Mr. Winchester I know nothing of him. Mr. Clarke may inform you how he does. Mr. C. lives now at Limehouse near London. I saw a gentleman last week who lately made him a Visit . . .

By this late date in his correspondence with Langcake, Brooke had also been corresponding with Richard Clarke for many years. He must first have approached Clarke himself, praising him for some of his writings, for he received a letter from him, marked 'Chelsea near London Mar: 20th 1772', beginning, 'I rejoice, if what I have wrote, has been instrumental in the hands of providence, to awaken in you the seeking of that Kingdom of Life & Glory'. The reply obviously mistakes Brooke for his

[1] Elhanan Winchester, *A Defence of Revelation in Ten Letters to Thomas Paine; Being An Answer to His First Part of The Age of Reason*, London 1796. (After previous publication in New York.)

[2] See Blake's annotations to *An Apology for the Bible in a Series of Letters addressed to Thomas Paine by R. Watson, D.D., F.R.S.* Written in 1798.

[3] Walton MS. I. i. 43, pp. 194–7.

more famous uncle, and it is interesting that throughout this letter Clarke takes up a very independent position, almost a non-sectarian one, despite his Anglican orders, and reminiscent of the Levellers of Cromwellian days. He writes, as he imagines, to the well-known author Henry Brooke, because he believes him to have a bent towards spirituality, and yet sufficient worldly fame to enable him to further the cause of those who care for the life of the spirit. Also, because he has heard, he says,

> that there was some kindlings of divine fire in Ireland, but [Clarke insists] I have no connection with any party, or systems which are still adhered to, by which both the letter and spirit of the sacred oracles are depressed and subjected to men. They do not raise themselves to the gospel but lower that to their apprehensions . . . – The religious societies cling to the doctrines of men, who are not themselves enlightened, and therefore cannot understand the very language of scripture, expressing states and processes in the soul; for a child may as well understand conjugal and parental love, before these affections are stirred up by their proper objects, as any man understand the words of the gospel and law, (which speak to states) who have not had these states awakened in them.

Clarke goes on to explain why he cannot favour the Evangelical movement, then so vigorous, and makes mention of the most popular among his own published works.

> The Methodists have used me, and Mr. Law before, in an unbecoming manner, reviling me as more mad than Law, or Behmen: which I am sorry for, because it prevents many from reading the spiritual authors, who might probably receive great comfort and edification from them. – Some, however, amongst them have broke the chain of implicit confidence in man, and both read and come to hear me preach, & I believe, are not sorry for their having had so much resolution. – My 'Daily Service of the Temple', I find has been thought to open more the Regeneration, than any other tract . . .

But before he ends the letter Clarke takes the opportunity to air his particular preoccupations; his theories on the critical stage reached in world history at that date. The present age he equates with that period of time announced by the seventh trumpet of St John's Apocalypse, and in explaining this uses the phrase 'the everlasting gospel', so dear to the seventeenth century Ranters, and also the very Blakean expression, 'the spirit of prophecy'.

> The signs external are sufficient for the serious: the internal, is the spirit of prophecy, opening the *everlasting* gospel, which the Angel flies thro' Heaven & preaches to every creature.

Just because there are quite a number of parallels between Richard Clarke's language and symbolism and those used by Blake – and it would not have been at all impossible for them to meet, since Clarke spent years in London and had been bringing out books before Blake started to write – the question of Clarke's life and character has to be examined. Yet it is a difficult one, with many gaps and puzzles. From his letters it appears that he was educated at Oxford. And a certain 'Richard Clarke, son of Henry, of Winchester (city), gent.' is listed as matriculating at University College on 17th December 1741, aged eighteen.[1]

The title page of his *Gospel of the Daily Service*, published in 1767, describes him as 'Curate of Cheshunt, Hertfordshire'. William Robinson, the author of the *History & Antiquities of the Parish of Stoke Newington*,[2] has Clarke's name down under the list of 'Lecturers' for the Parish Church.

> Richard Clarke M.A., Formerly Rector of St. Philip's in Charles Town, South Carolina (Author of an Essay on the Number Seven, and other mystical works), was elected about April 1769, resigned 1776, and died 31st July 1802, aged 83.

If the account here is correct then obviously there must be a mistake in Clarke's age at the time of matriculation, assuming this to be the same Richard Clarke. Still earlier, we hear of Clarke in connection with William Law himself. Writing to

---

[1] Joseph Foster, *Alumni Oxonienses*, Vol. I, London 1887, p. 257.

[2] William Robinson, *The History and Antiquities of the Parish of Stoke Newington*, London 1820, p. 147.

Thomas Langcake on 29th August 1756, Law makes these frank remarks.

> Your friend Clarke's piece will have its place among those books that at certain times, help to kindle my fire. This is not through contempt or disregard of him or his pen, but because I know no better use of such materials. It is all the good that I can have from them. If the public should have as bad a taste as I have, he must, as he says, lay aside his pen.

Later, on 3rd December 1759, Law, writing again to Langcake, mentions an edition of his own letters that it seems Clarke was editing, as well as the book which had been so very influential in his own spiritual development, *Fides et Ratio.*[1]

> . . . The name of the author of *Faith and Reason*, is Mittenach, a German count. All his Latin works are in a book called *Fides et Ratio*, they are chiefly translations from Madam Guion . . . I wrote a letter to Mr. Clarke in answer to one of his . . . I know not how far he has proceeded in preparing some of my Letters for the press, or whether you are still in the opinion of publishing them.

Despite the disappointment of finding that the Henry Brooke who had written to him was not the famous novelist, Richard Clarke soon began to correspond with him enthusiastically. He again stresses the importance of 'the spirit of prophecy' in his letter addressed from Chelsea, and dated 24th April 1772.

> The spirit of prophesy will be despised, as it was allways before; yet Daniel says the wise and the enlightened of God, shall understand the times and seasons, and the signs of the times, both in nature and revelation.

A list of his own books is given, published by 'J. Townsend printer in London Street, Mark Lane London', so that Brooke can insert an advertisement in a Dublin paper. And then comes a revealing piece of gossip.

> Swedenburgh is dead lately: he ridiculed all the mystics: nor do I know one of the readers of the mystical authors, who can bear his

[1] See Stephen Hobhouse, '*Fides et Ratio*, The Book Which Introduced Jacob Boehme to William Law', *Journal of Theological Studies*, Oxford, October, 1936, p. 359.

extravagancies. Mr. Law thought him the greatest visionary he ever read.

In his next letter, of 30th June 1772, still from Chelsea, Clarke continues in his efforts to 'preach the *everlasting gospel* to *every creature* in the words of St John'. He discusses the symbolism of the human blood, a concept obviously Jewish in origin, and says,

> The wonderfull element of our earthly blood, will employ the wisest man for his whole life, and leave him puzzled at the last . . . What then must the blood of the everlasting covenant be, wherein the eternal spirit works the wonders of the endless life and all its feelings of Joy. Blood is the chariot of fire, whether in beast, or seraph, only the one is earthly, and reaches only the elementary fire of the sun: the other is heavenly and is centered in the glorious corporeity of the diety. But not amazed that I give body to the deity; the sea of glass mingled *with fire*, is the glorified visibility of God; it is the *pillar* of *fire* the *cloud*, what is a cloud, but the *water* of *life*, with its holy fire thro' and thro': and who among the *clouds*, can be compared unto our God? whose glassy sea, whose resplendant corporeity, is equal to the Lord our God? . . .

He ends,

> I must stop now: perhaps this may seem strong meat; but I am moved to give it, and can write no more, but that I am a poor wanderer in the wilderness of sin, and hope my steps are yet going forward to the new Jerusalem, the mother of free children, whose bodies never know death; as the mother below brought us into . . .

This doctrine of 'divine corporeity' was a favourite one with William Law and obviously bears relation to the Renaissance concept of the 'spiritual body'; 'a certain shining pure body like a star, which being immortal and eternal, could never be detached nor torn away from the soul and without which the soul could not be become an inhabitant of this world'.[1] Again, the distinction between Clarke's 'new Jerusalem, the mother of free children' and 'the mother below' is just the one Blake makes between his Jerusalem and Vala, or the 'Mother of my

[1] See D. P. Walker, 'The Astral Body in Renaissance Medicine', *Journal of the Warburg and Courtauld Institutes*, London 1958, pp. 119f.

Mortal part' as he puts it in the lyric 'To Tirzah'. It is also the distinction between the sephiroth, Binah and Malkhuth of the Kabalah; the Upper and Lower Gardens, or Paradises, the Shechinah manifested at different levels.

From December 1772, Clarke's letters are addressed from 'More Street, Hackney, near London'. During this time he was still 'Lecturer' at Stoke Newington and it is interesting that this particular church is described by William Robinson as 'in the peculiar jurisdiction of the Dean and Chapter of St Paul's'. So perhaps Clarke had then some connection with the cathedral. We find him, in October 1773, confessing himself to be 'under a strong impulse to deliver a message to the Jews'. While in 1778, after he had resigned the Stoke Newington lectureship, he writes to tell of his latest work, a commentary upon the 68th psalm, and hints at various difficulties he has been labouring under.

> I have been exercised with so many outward and inward troubles and difficulties, that for several months past, I have not had the least inclination to correspond with any friend or brother. But still I keep my heart warm towards them all; and I trust even towards those, who like Joseph's brethren, put patience to its hardest tryal, by malignant opposition and envy, and obloquy against the glorious truths of God's everlasting love and mercy in Christ to all mankind. I have just finished a large comment on the 68th Psalm.[1]

It is not at all surprising that Clarke encountered opposition, for many of his ideas must have seemed quite astounding to the comfortable churchmen of the day. As he made clear himself from the start to Henry Brooke, Richard Clarke was an independent spirit and expected disagreement, but unfortunately the practical consequences of it could be embarrassing and he confides his worries in an earlier letter to Brooke, written at a time when he was also obviously having difficulties. Sent from Hackney, December 1772, it reveals his passionate universalist convictions, his proud temper and his radical views.

[1] Walton MS. I. i. 43, pp. 287-8.

I wish to be entirely free from all church connection; for the light I have received, is beyond any private system or community, I shall speak it to more effect, in a general and unconfined way, for the children of the kingdom are scattered . . . I return you and your good father my sincere thanks for your kind affection to me, and beg both your prayers; for the prayer of one heart in the full love of the redeeming blood of the Lamb, is more availing, than ten thousand hearts praying in the spirit of Cain, who thro' envy killed his brother's body; but what are they who cannot will, and rejoice in the salvation of all men? Soul-murderers must stand in a higher rank of criminality before the Throne of Grace . . . But scorners and mockers must go before, and have a greater triumph than at present . . . they must have their day, and I hope & believe, it is near expiring, when a true community of spirit, will open a community of temporal things, as in the seventh year of the Lord, who never made the proud distinctions and divisions which the Babel of the World made . . . Poverty in this kingdom is connected with such low and debasing vices, because superiors cut off communications with inferiors, that the good dread it only for fear of ill consequences to the minds of their children, and indeed poor people in general, so forget their own nature and hold themselves so cheap, that they sell themselves for nought, and reap only misery for the wages of vice. And where there is no church to fill up the place of father and husband, to the orphan and widow, what can be expected but the same forlorn continuance of neglecting one another, and 'tis in this point I feel myself so vulnerable, and full of apprehension . . .

Clearly it was for this reason that Clarke never completely severed his connection with the Church of England, however impatient he might have felt with orthodoxy. The boldness of his own beliefs, which extended even to the point of communism, is equally plainly revealed. This was a man after Blake's own heart. At any rate, whether because of opposition nearer home, or for whatever reason, there is a long gap during the '80s of the century in Clarke's correspondence with Henry Brooke. Thomas Langcake replies to Brooke's enquiries about Clarke in the letter written from Bristol, on 30th April 1786, which has already been quoted, and describes him as living then at Limehouse. And the Reverend Mr Dodwell, librarian of the

Lambeth Palace Library, has suggested to me that earlier in the decade Clarke might have revisited America; for there is an 'R. Clark' listed in the *Digest of the Society for the Propagation of the Gospel Records*, as a missionary at Gagetown, New Brunswick, in 1783. Before that, however, whilst he was still in touch with Brooke, they had evidently considered the question of Alchemy. For Clarke supports this study in face of Brooke's more critical attitude, writing from London on 20th February 1779.

> ... whoever informed you about Alchemy, was much mistaken. I know the science to be true, but content myself without searching for it. Though most searchers into that mystery think I possess it; as they cannot conceive how I could write in the line I do, without that knowledge.
>
> I believe I know the whole, and found it if I see it right, in the Temple-service ...

These remarks are particularly revealing. They show an acquaintance with the subject on Clarke's part, if not a specialized knowledge, and the existence, even at that date, of people who were specialists. Evidently Richard Clarke accepts the attitude to Alchemy which had been current among those who were inspired by Renaissance Neo-Platonism, while Henry Brooke, or his informant, betrays the contempt for it that had become general by the eighteenth century.

It is with some relief that one reads the answer to another enquiry about Richard Clarke, this time from that Edward Fisher who was so solicitous in tracking down the real origin of all the papers in William Law's possession. The letter, written on 26th March 1789, was to Law's friend Miss Gibbon, who held a disapproving attitude towards Clarke and was even surprised to learn that he was in orders.

> It is true that the Reverend Mr. Clarke, (who is a regularily ordained Clergyman and has been so for many years,) came to Bristol, as he had been at other places, to preach; and also I believe, to try what he could get in the way of charitable donations, for the relief of his temporal necessities, which, I apprehend, were then very urgent upon him, as having a family of children,

together with himself to maintain, and very scanty and insufficient means to do it. As he formerly well knew Mr. Langcake, who has at one time lodged with Mr. Clarke at his house in Hoxton Square, London, he was much in his company at Bristol, but did not lodge in the same house. Mr. Clarke afterwards went to Winchester, on notice that an elder brother of his, who lived there in good circumstances, was in a very ill state of health, and not likely to continue long in life. That brother is since dead, and has left Mr. Clarke such a provision, as with economy and prudent management, may serve to set him above the pecuniary difficulties and distress he before had to struggle with.

Richard Clarke's family then, like that of the Clarke who was at University College, Oxford, in 1741, evidently were from Winchester.

At this period Clarke was able to bring out some more books, perhaps because of his improved circumstances. A collection of letters was published in 1794, to be bought at 'the Author, No. 19 Catherine Street, Strand'. And more important still, *Jesus the Nazarene, Addressed to Jews, Deists and Believers*, came out in 1795 and was on sale at 'No. 8, Little Queen Street, Holborn'. William Blake's own great epic, *Jerusalem*, was of course divided into four sections; dedicated 'To the Public', 'To the Jews', 'To the Deists' and 'To the Christians'. And at many points in the poem Blake uses the symbol of the 'Covering Cherub', just as he does in earlier prophecies. *Jesus the Nazarene* contains a very full treatment of precisely this biblical image, clearly a favourite of Clarke's and one that he had already developed. Using, again, the phrase 'a Sea of Glass', which William Law applies to the 'Spiritual Body', Nature perfectly united to the spiritual world, as Boehme taught it was before the Fall, and referring back to the Chariot Mysticism of the early Jewish tradition, Clarke had given the following exposition in a note to page 361 of *The Gospel of the Daily Service of the Jews*.

This World in its present *fallen* Condition is the *Materiality* of *Satan's Kingdom* and *Principality*, . . . for he cannot raise it up into a *Sea* of *Glass* mingled with Fire, wherein he once had a *solar*

Throne, a *cherubical Chariot* before the Ancient of Days. It is of this proud Archangel, . . . that the Lord speaks under the Figure of the *King* of *Tyrus*: 'Thou *sealest* up the *Sum* full of *Wisdom* and *perfect* in *Beauty*. Thou hast been in *Eden* the *Garden* of *God*, *every precious Stone* was *thy covering*. Thou art the *anointed Cherub* that *covereth*, . . .' The Fall of *Lucifer* who became *Satan* by transgression, the *old Dragon* or the *first Beast out of* the *Sea*, was known to all the ancient Philosophers; and the *Confusion* of *his Hierarchy* is continually mentioned by the *Vessels* of *Light* broken and fallen down into *Klippoth*, Cortices impuros, that is, among the Jewish Writers, understood of the *Elements* confused, and shut up into *hard* and *massy* Bodies, throughout the Face of degraded Nature . . .

The treatment of the Klippoth, the 'Shells' of Lurianic Kabalah, the impure dregs of the emanational system, shows Clarke's wide grasp of Jewish mysticism in general. His sources, indeed, are openly given in a passage, annotating *Jesus the Nazarene* and dealing with the Covering Cherub; discussing the three worlds 'called *emanation*, creation and formation' . . . 'which began in the fall of the *cherub*, and will finish in the restitution of *all things*'. And they are obviously in line with the tradition extending back to the Renaissance we have been studying. One notable point is Clarke's reference to the Edomite Kings of the Kabalah, the 'worlds of unbalanced force', an image which had also appeared in Blake's *Marriage of Heaven and Hell* where he declares,

Now is the domination of Edom . . .

on plate 3. Clarke begins by explaining why the Hebrew word for 'cherub' in *Ezekiel* 28 : 15, is used in the feminine gender.

. . . The *cherub* is not feminine, because the king of *Tyre*, (the rock) was immersed in pleasure, softness and luxury; but because this great king, wiser than *Daniel*, that sealed up the sum of wisdom, and perfect in beauty; who had been in *Eden*, and in the mountain of God . . . The truth is, this cherub, who was perfect in the day of his being created, was then the bride of God; and by pride and self-glory began the first divorce from the Superior Spirit, and the incubation and covering of his *living* lights and glories of his sovereign perfections. In him begin the deep sense of the *great whore* and all the branches of apostacy . . . Behmen in his *Aurora*; *Poirett* in his Œconomy of Divine Grace; Dr. Henry More, Bishop Rust's Lux Orientalis, Fludd's Mosaic Philosophy, Cheyné's Philosophical Principles of Religion, Ramsay's Philosophical Principles of Natural and Revealed Religion, and the Hebrew writers on the *Seven Kings* that reigned in *Edom*, before there was any king in *Israel*. They speak clearly of the *fallen materiality* of Lucifer, or the cherub's kingdom, sunk and bound up in hardness, thickness, dark and cold chains of adamantine compaction; in the whole system, planets included; which no power but divine can unlock, dissolve and purify, and reduce to the *sea* like *glass*, transparent, mingled with *fire* . . .[1]

The whole tone of this passage is strangely Blakean, as is Clarke's concept of 'Eden' as identical with Heaven. It is in this book, too, that the actual phrase 'the Covering Cherub' is quoted, on page 272, in a note on the head of rebellious angels.

This prince, or first head of rebellion, recorded in scripture, has several names descriptive of his lost glory and kingdom. He is cast under the character of *Nebuchadnezzar*, king of *Babylon*, (confusion) in Daniel; in Ezekiel, he is the *cherub*, *anointed* and *covering*. Thou sealed up the sum full of *wisdom*, and perfect in *beauty* . . . till iniquity was found in thee. Therefore I will cast thee, as profane, out of the mountain of God, and I will destroy thee, O *covering cherub*, from the midst of the stones of fire . . . We find this great son of God cast under the figure of *Pharaoh*, king of *Egypt*; whose name signifies to make *naked*. This relates to the same *cherub*, divested of his clothing of the ten precious stones, or the *ten* glories of the archangels, king and father-angels, (*Elohim*).

The title 'Elohim' continually appears, throughout the book. It may well be that here was Blake's most direct source for the term. And copious extracts are included throughout *Jesus the Nazarene* from some letters to Tom Paine which came out in *The Morning Advertiser*. *Jesus the Nazarene* is one of Richard Clarke's most serious and substantial books. (The only other to compare with it for influence is in fact the *Gospel of the Daily Service of the Law*.) It is in *Jesus the Nazarene* too, that the 'Account' appears 'of Books published from 1760 to 1795 by

[1] Richard Clarke, *Jesus the Nazarene: Addressed to Jews, Deists, and Believers*, London 1795, p. 130n.

the Author' and this provides us with the interesting information that Clarke's *Essay on the Number Seven* was 'published at the request of the late Dr Edward Young' who was, of course, the author of the poem *Night Thoughts* illustrated by Blake in 1796, for an edition published by a Bond Street bookseller in 1797. We also learn that *A Small Tract in Defence of Moses*, much praised in the *Monthly Review* for February 1784, was re-published 'with some Enlargements on the Thirteen Points' ... 'in 1795, in the *Morning Advertiser*, in Eight Letters, in Answer to *Paine's Age of Reason*'. Again, the second item of Clarke's *Series of Letters, Essays, Dissertations and Discourses*, (which, again, can be bought from 'the Author, R. Clarke, at his house, No. 20, South-Street, Manchester-Square') runs as follows:

> Letters to Dr. Priestley, in Defence of Drs. Reid, Oswald, and Beattie; and on Five Topics of his 'Appeal to the Serious and Candid Professors of Christianity'.[1]

There seems a strong probability, therefore, that Richard Clarke's work was known to that circle which, like Blake, had connections with Johnson, the bookseller.

What strikes one, almost, as a preliminary sketch for Blake's theory of Nature, as it is developed in his later prophetic books, appears indeed, complete in Clarke's *Gospel of the Daily Service*; the book which Clarke had originally recommended to Henry Brooke, and one that betrays an indebtedness to the seventeenth-century student of the Kabalah, Henry Ainsworth. Though he quotes often from Ainsworth, Clarke also disagrees with him on some points.[2] His commentary on St Paul's second epistle to the Corinthians, chapter eleven, expounds a view of material Nature as 'Enchantress' equivalent to Blake's Vala, and gives an identical doctrine of the sexes.

According to this Figure of the Law, the Apostle, writing in the

[1] Richard Clarke, *A series of Letters, Essays, Dissertations and Discourses on Various Subjects*, London 1792.

[2] Richard Clarke, *The Gospel of the Daily Service of the Law, preached to Jews and Gentiles*, London 1767, pp. 3–4.

Language of the pure Cabbala of the ancient Hebrews, espouses Christians as *Virgins* unto *Christ*; because he knew, that Christ would reveal his Power in this Form of Life, which must first be raised up, before the Entrance into the inmost, or *third* Heavens can be open, where they are all Males (*Zachar*,) having *one Name* as *Adam*, and two Natures or Essences, though the Woman lose herself in the *superior* Form of Life. This is a *great Mystery*, says the Apostle, where he passes over it, and veils it in a Manner, from the Profane and Carnal; because he knew, that there were *Gnostics*, *Nicholaitans*, *Moravians*, and *Antinomians*, that is, Teachers and People; one ready to preach, and the other to receive at that Day, and in all Days, any Doctrine that might be twisted to favour the strongest Passion in our *Aegyptian* Flesh, which binds us in a triple Chain to the strange Woman, that is, in the spiritual Sense, to the Senses and Appetites of *Adam's Body*, changed from Immortality to Mortality, from Spiritual to the *Coat* of *Skins*, or Flesh like the *animal* Creation. Take this Enchantress, this *Jezebel* out of our Nature, and all other Passions are moderate, and easily gratified.[1]

In setting out this doctrine Clarke has, ironically, fallen into the very errors of those Gnostics whom he condemns; men who were guilty not so much of sensuality as of contempt for Creation, or rather who so often swung violently from extreme asceticism to orgy in all those ages when their teaching had influence. Clarke, like Blake himself, was blind to this aspect of affairs, absorbed as he was in an energetic reaction away from the materialism of his time. His genuine piety continued to be appreciated by his friends and on 29th October 1792 we find Henry Brooke once more stimulating a correspondence.

Revd. & dear Sir,
I shall not say how long it is now, since I hoped and expected a letter from you – But I can no longer refrain, and I am assured (if possible) you will no longer keep silence.

What really provoked Brooke's approach to Clarke was an embarrassing and uncomfortable experience that had come to him, indirectly, through Clarke's influence. As he puts it,

Mrs. Pratt an acquaintance of yours wrote a letter in Jan^r. last.

[1] Richard Clarke, *op. cit.*, p. 212.

I answered it, and two or three others since: and not withstanding the rich vein of enthusiasm that flashed out here and there, I admired the piety and was much refreshed . . . But at length she asserted of herself such things as I could by no means silently listen to, lest my silence should be an acquiesance. – She asserts that she is the very first that has had the seventh seal opened; the first that enjoyed the resurrection Life, and the first that entered Paradise; and had free access to the tree of Life &c. &c. that Jehovah her spouse speaks by her mouth – that what she asserts – she asserts and cannot retract from. – being only the speaking trumpet of his impulse. –

(At this point Christopher Walton has interpolated a pencil note on the copy of the letter which runs, 'poor, simple, well-meaning reasonable Harry!') Brooke continues,

About one hundred & twenty years ago in London, Jane Leade, a mother in the Philadelphian society, asserted the very same things of herself, and had many friends, followers and advocates, such as Dr. Pordage, Dr. Ed^w Hooker, Mr. Roache, Bromley, &c. &c.: she even mentions particularly having passed the 7th seal – the foregoing death the consequent ressurrection – admission into Paradise – feeding on the tree of life – (gives a small treatise on the Laws and enjoyments of the paradisical World) – deification – the still eternity &c. &c. – I answered Mrs. P. very delicately – ['Very!!' says Christopher Walton] but declined any further correspondence fearing that her writing or speaking so much, might aggravate that malady which she was formerly subject to. ['This rather too bad but quite natural': Christopher Walton.]

Henry Brooke was shocked by this apparent duplicity on Mary Pratt's part. He also objected to her bitter criticisms of her own family. In a letter to him of 14th October 1792, she complains that she would like to publish an account of her experiences, but, she says,

I have a persecuting husband and an ungodly infamous son, who is allowed plenty of money, while I am dealt with like Hagaur the Israelite – kept without a shilling – but I want neither food or clothing, and my high priviledges brings me peace & content. Mr. Pratt is a strict follower of Swedenborg, that deluded society is spreading contagion in London; but why do I say contagion for it is no matter what persuasion people are of, till they feel the pangs of the new birth . . .

Blake would have completely agreed with these last remarks, and perhaps Henry Brooke would not have been too pleased if he had been 'kept without a shilling'. It is always easy to bear other people's troubles with Christian fortitude. Whatever one may feel about Mary Pratt's extravagant claims for her spiritual state a certain sincerity and eagerness comes through her letters. She clearly derived most of her ideas from reading the works of the Philadelphians and the Quietists – St Francis de Sales is the only orthodox mystic mentioned by her – but she may perhaps have so much identified herself with the earlier woman visionary, Jane Lead, as to have forgotten her borrowings here. It is interesting that in his response to Henry Brooke, Richard Clarke refuses to criticize Mary Pratt. He simply states, 'it were better in my judgement that correspondence cease'. He was much more anxious to discuss with Brooke a topic which was preoccupying him greatly at that time; the identification of Christ with the Primordial Man, the Adam Kadmon of the Kabalah. Writing to Brooke on 6th May, he explains this idea and insists – 'in the fourth century this truth was lost by the condemnation of Origen's works' – .

> 'It will be found,' says Clarke, 'that Messiah is the seed of the woman, generated and assumed to the throne of the *Ancient of days*, and become a *Lord God*, as the priests of Melchisedec in an order are. They are the holyness of Jehovah, and bear it on the forehead . . . Christ . . . sent first.'

He expands on the idea in one of his last letters to Brooke, sent on 24th April 1799.

> . . . observe that Jesus Christ is never Son of Man in the four gospels, But son of *the Man*, that is, the *Ancient of days*, by Hebrew church, the *Man* celestial, exemplar and prototype of all Perfect Men . . . twice is he called Son of Man in Rev. 1. & ch. 17 to point him out as the Bar Enoch of Daniel.

Enclosed with this letter is an opinion on the visionary,

Richard Brothers, whom Brooke had been asking about. He is quite cutting in his remarks.

> When a swineherd in Bavaria has ventured to declare, and has many disciples, that the Prophets and Saints of old are concentered in him; when the Illuminati (as they proudly call themselves) are spreading their deceptions; I shall not be surprised if a new Messiah should come forth. From Montanus who in the second century, had the pride & ignorance of calling himself the Holy Spirit which was promised, the Church had never witnessed such a character as Brothers, and his two witnesses Wright and Brian. If such a great man as Tertullian could at first be deceived by such a blasphemous pretence, we may allow some what to the learned Halhed in the present age.

It is quite likely that in his reference to Montanus Clarke is harking back to Francis Lee's *History of Montanism.* He himself, I have suggested, with his Hebrew learning, was very much in the line of Francis Lee. A curious note to Brooke, sent in July 1796, throws light on his personal circumstances in these last years.

> I shall be happy to hear of you – I get my bread by teaching Hebrew and the classics, expecting soon to see the Lord to take the Nations under his broad wings of life, light, & love – He can contain all, as well as his chosen few, compared with the whole seed of fallen man. Rev. 7. Isai: 25. Zeph 3 & 9.10.
>   He is Jesus, yea, yea, not yea & nay –
>   Love to you all
>   Ricd. Clarke.

During these years Richard Clarke seems to have become more and more concerned with the matter of prophecy. A letter of his dated 1st October 1794 and later published discusses the question of the return of the prophet Elias, quoting Dr Burnet for the belief that he would come as 'the great *peace-maker*', to prepare the Millennium. Clarke continues,

> *Henry More,* a great judge of the *prophetical* style and *typical* characters in persons and events, adopts the same sentiments, subjoining only *a zeal* and a spirit of rebuke to false prophets or teachers, in the fifth of his *Divine Dialogues.*

A reference to the Hebrew scholar Joseph Mede, and the Christian Cabalist, Hugh Broughton, follows, and the familiar phrase 'the Everlasting Gospel' is used.

> Let me add, *this spirit* will appear most probably in some converted Jews, as *Mede, Broughton*, and others think, who from *Sauls*, will become *Pauls* . . . *This gospel* of the *kingdom* shall be *preached* in *all the world* . . . The second witness to the same advent is this beloved disciple in Rev. xiv. 6. who sees the *angel* flying through the midst of heaven, having the EVERLASTING GOSPEL to preach unto them that dwell on the earth. . . .

Of course this kind of theme had been long in Clarke's mind, as can be seen from the titles of two books which appeared in 1760; *A Spiritual Voice to the Christian Church, and to the Jews* and *A Second Warning to the World by the Spirit of Prophecy*. But as the century drew on clearly a more general interest in the topic of prophecy also increased, and this is evident from Clarke's own study, posthumously published in 1812, *Prophetic Records of the Christian Era*, and his letter on 'the present Rage for Fragments of Prophecies, not founded on Scripture'.[1]

Meanwhile in *his* later years Henry Brooke had at last found his true spiritual master, the saintly Fletcher of Madeley, the figure most revered above all by John Wesley. The Rev. John Fletcher was another of those remarkable eighteenth-century ecclesiastical figures whose lives are such a challenge to popular misconceptions of the state of religion at that time. An Anglican clergyman, born in Switzerland, whose native tongue was in fact French, he was John Wesley's closest friend, for many years intimate with the Countess of Huntingdon, widely travelled and yet deeply devoted to his parishioners at Madeley. On his journeys abroad he not only visited French Huguenot families, but had long conversations with Italian priests and monks, 'in order that he might thoroughly know their sentiments concerning spiritual religion'. Fletcher's influence over Brooke is clearly revealed in his very last letter of 1806,

---

[1] Richard Clarke, *Prophetic Records of the Christian Era*, London 1812; *A Collection of Poems and Letters*, London 1777, item 5.

published by his son-in-law D'Olier in his biography, and addressed to another of Fletcher's admirers, a Mr Brackenbury of Raithby-hall.

> The blessing I was indulged with in the correspondence, conversation, public ministry and private friendship of that holy man of God Mr. Fletcher, is indeed a memorable epocha in my life.Oh! that it had fully answered all the gracious designs of God towards me, by so bright an example in private life and such powerful and precious instructions in his public ministry. But I have been but a dull scholar, a weak disciple, and an unprofitable servant; and reaped a very scanty harvest, during so prolific a season.[1]

Evidently Brackenbury shared with Henry Brooke a preoccupation with the question of prophecy, encouraged, perhaps by Fletcher, for in the latter part of his letter Brooke launches out into a study of the second and seventh chapters of the Book of Daniel; and one somewhat in Richard Clarke's style. It is not surprising that Blake, for instance, was so fascinated by a figure like Nebuchadnezzar, whom he has immortalized in his great colour print, when such speculations as these were in the air.

> I have not had much light into the x and xi of Daniel; the comparison of the ii and vii has engrossed my attention, since they correspond like the two sides of a tally; only the concluding events are more particularly enlarged upon, and enforced in the vii. 'Thou art this Head of Gold' gives the key to the figure, and marks the time of its commencement.
>
> The two chapters are a prophetical epitome of what was to succeed in the revolutions of monarchies, till the *period* of the present state of things in the world. Can any thing be more beautifully or exquisitely shadowed out, than the degradation of Nebuchadnezzar, by the plucking the wings of the Babylonian lion?
>
> Or his restoration, by his being lifted up from the earth, made to stand upon his feet like a man, having his bestial heart taken from him, and a human heart (perhaps renewed, converted, and so far divine) given to him?

[1] Isaac D'Olier, *Memoirs of the Life of the Late Excellent and Pious Mr. Henry Brooke*, pp. 140f.

The second or Persian kingdom, silver in the Image, of a lazy bearlike savage cruelty in the 7ch. 5v?.

The third, Grecian or brazen monarchy in the Image, and as a leopard in the 7 ch. having wings and four heads, the four kingdoms into which Alexander's government was divided?

The fourth or iron monarchy . . . the Roman kingdom represented by the fourth beast exceedingly terrible . . . I suppose that *Origen* and all the very early commentators on the Prophets and Revelations, have done like Madame Guion, Mr. Marsay, and some other modern writers, allegorized the predictions into the successive internal states of the soul . . .

But I must have done. Adieu my dear soul! I am too near eternity to write you many more letters; yet I shall be glad to hear from you before I go hence, and am no more seen . . .

There is something very touching in the thought that Henry Brooke eventually found his peace in the mystically inclined piety of John Fletcher, which he shared with such men as his friend Brackenbury. He deserved such a haven, too, for he was in his quiet way a remarkable man, and one who shared some characteristics with Blake; for he was an artist, pursuing, as Isaac D'Olier puts it,

with good success his profession as an historical and landscape painter and drawing master.

Not only the Methodists among whom he mixed but all his close friends recognized Brooke's real spirituality.

Mr. Brooke had an uncommonly sweet gift of extempory prayer; and in this act of divine worship, whether in the public congregation or in more private assemblies, the power of God was felt and acknowledged. Mr. Brooke was a man of habitual prayer, he entered into the spirit of it, and dwelling under a constant sense of the divine presence, he penetrated within the vail, and worshipped in the Holy of Holies.

What then is to be the final judgment upon that extraordinary group of men and women belonging to the late eighteenth century, revealed to us in Henry Brooke's correspondence? With William Law and his model, Jacob Boehme, as their inspiration, they certainly still used the tradition of thought derived from Renaissance times which had flourished so mightily in seventeenth-century England. The distinctive feature of their outlook was an absorption in Mysticism, with a substantial debt to the traditional Catholic mystics, but also a strong leaning towards Quietism. The doctrines of Swedenborg attracted some of them. Most did not consider these offered any real solution to their spiritual problems. The attitude to Swedenborg betrayed by the correspondence is on the whole a hostile one. Their ardent belief in the power of prophecy, and their capacity to live in an inner world of their own, is very close to Blake's. Indeed to me it seems quite clear that theirs is the background against which Blake's thought must be placed. As far as so independent a spirit had one, this was his mental milieu. And the men and women who figure in Henry Brooke's correspondence cannot be dismissed as cranks. Many were sincere, intelligent and remarkably well read. Even Ralph Mathers, the most hot-headed of them, made a deep impression upon John Wesley, who was prejudiced against all he stood for. And Thomas Langcake reveals himself as a balanced sensitive man, widely experienced in the life of the spirit. Through William Law and Boehme such minds as his had inherited a Neo-Platonism suffused with Christianity; very different from the revived paganism of Thomas Taylor. As long as the Christian element within it remained strong the movement retained considerable vigour. Those who kept closest to Christian orthodoxy showed also the greatest interior balance and most acute perception. And this would seem also true of the larger circle who formed the subject of Ralph Mathers's explorations.

The world of Mather's 'Spiritual Persons' might appear to us a strange one. But it was part of the wider world of the late eighteenth-century Britain about him. It is the nearest we can get to Blake's native climate, to the formative influences which worked upon him, and Blake was by no means the strangest figure in it. He was, however, the only genius. An amazingly receptive genius in some ways but necessarily adding another dimension. He brought to a tradition – one that had begun as a major part of Renaissance thought and ended as no more than a powerful undercurrent – an originality, a force and an independent vision which were new. His freshness has deceived critics into crediting him with more inventiveness than he possessed. But in reality his greatness is of a more serious order. It springs from a contact with those deeper levels existing within the civilization that produced him.

CHAPTER X

The Tradition in Retrospect

*

A Renaissance tradition of symbolism, embodying a special set of values, indeed a whole philosophy of life, has been traced from its beginnings with Gemisthus Pletho, Ficino and Pico della Mirandola down through devious routes to the circle of Henry Brooke's correspondents, in late eighteenth-century England. And its influence upon at least one major poet and painter traced, as well as upon many other men and women of note. I have tried to show how practically every aspect of European civilization was in some way affected by this tradition; the symbolic language used by the great artists, the efforts towards a syncretism of belief which occupied the minds of many brilliant philosophers and theologians, the practical decisions made by politicians, the art of ballet, new fashions in architecture, a whole apparatus of imagery for the poets, the beginnings of modern astronomy, medicine, chemistry and science in general, and finally the religious enthusiasm of seventeenth- and eighteenth-century England.

The main line of this tradition is most apparent, perhaps, in the continual reference to a particular set of names; the reverence paid to such ancient, and often semi-mythical, figures as Zoroaster, Hermes Trismegistus, Orpheus, Appollonius, Pythagoras, Plato himself, the Sibyls, the Druids, the Brahmins, and the famous Neo-Platonists Plotinus and Porphyry. With these Moses is often associated, especially in his capacity as unfolder of the secret wisdom, the hidden, unwritten law of the Jews. And of course there are many grounds for describing the Kabalah as a kind of 'Jewish Gnosticism'.

It seems to have grown up in the period when the early Christian heresies flourished and when classical paganism put up a last stand in the mystical philosophy of the Neo-Platonists, whose system, of course, deeply influenced St Augustine and other Christian thinkers. This thread of thought, composed of so many strands twisted together, was the one picked out and used by those Renaissance enthusiasts who revived the wisdom of the past and attempted to harmonize it with the basic Christian doctrines they had inherited from the Age of Faith. Once this process started one devotee would quote another; Pico della Mirandola refers back to Ficino, Giorgio to Pico, Archangelo to Giorgio, Cornelius Agrippa to all three. Paracelsus would hold up Ficino as his model of the priest-physician, the Boderie brothers translated Giorgio and were deeply steeped in Neo-Platonism as well. Boehme's debt to Reuchlin and Paracelsus, and the plainly Neo-Platonic basis of his thought have all been pointed out. Men like Robert Fludd, as also the English poets Spenser, John Donne, Ben Jonson and Joshua Sylvester, were widely read in all these directions. Robert Fludd indeed, can be said to be a seventeenth-century disciple of Giorgio, and his opponent in controversy, John Kepler, was almost as much preoccupied with theories of universal harmony. The Cambridge Platonists naturally concerned themselves with Neo-Platonic philosophy, and we have seen how deeply Henry More was drawn into a study of the Kabalah by François Mercure van Helmont and von Rosenroth, and how his friend, Lady Conway, also knew Boehme's works. The circle in which Milton moved was likewise affected by those currents of thought. Indeed it has only recently been demonstrated how the politics of the Civil War period in England were chiefly guided by the influence of three men; John Milton's friend Samuel Hartlib, John Dury, and the great Bohemian scholar Comenius. And each of these lived in a climate of thought conditioned by the Renaissance tradition which had sprung originally from the Italian academies.[1] They

[1] H. R. Trevor-Roper, 'Three Foreigners', *Encounter*, February 1960.

were in close contact, too, with Abraham von Frankenberg, Boehme's friend and biographer.

Particularly during the second half of the seventeenth century, mystical literature had a widespread and moving effect in England. Especially the works of Jacob Boehme, which, as I have explained, inspired something like a new sect in the country; because here at last was a Protestant mystic capable of standing comparison with the spiritual writers of the Catholic Church – writers whose works, nevertheless, also had a surprisingly wide currency; notably those of the Rhineland mystics and St Teresa of Avila. Dr Everard was meanwhile making available in translation, not only the writings of the Dominican Tauler, but the Hermetic Literature of the early centuries of this era in his *Divine Pymander*. Then, again, not only was the poetry and prose of such metaphysical writers as Henry and Thomas Vaughan, Traherne and Marvell having its influence – and much of it was mystical in feeling – but the humbler circles of the Ranters, the Levellers and the Familists were disseminating a philosophy based on Joachim of Flora, that medieval abbot who derived much from the Kabalah, and whose vision affected so many figures in the Rhineland, at a far later time, both Catholic and Protestant. Paracelsus was aware of this vision, Gnostic as it was in tendency, and definitely apocalyptic. There was a great deal of inter-action amongst all these groups and their thought survived on into the next century in a way that has scarcely been realized.

For the eighteenth-century picture the most important figure is undoubtedly the Non-Juror, William Law. But I have pointed out that Law's was not a particularly original mind. He drew heavily, first of all on the works of Jacob Boehme himself, to which he was introduced by the *Fides et Ratio* of Baron Metternich, recommended by the Scottish doctor, George Cheyne; a man who discoursed freely of his enthusiasm throughout London and who was friendly with Alexander Lord Forbes of Pitsligo, an intimate of the Baron's.[1] But this was not all.

---

[1] Stephen Hobhouse, *Fides et Ratio*, p. 359.

Law got his hands on the manuscripts of the German Boehme scholar, Dionysius Andreas Freher and of Francis Lee, the Hebraist and former Philadelphian, as Edward Fisher later discovered. And he was an omnivorous reader, following with devotion the orthodox Catholic mystics, St John of the Cross and St Teresa as well as books like the *Theologia Germanica*, *The Imitation of Christ* and those by the mystics of the Low Countries which were often popular among Protestants. He paid a regard likewise, though a critical one, to those Quietists such as Mme Guion and Antoinette Bourignon, who had also been much taken up outside the Catholic communion. Naturally William Law attracted round him fellow-spirits from all over the country. And his disciple John Byrom publicized their mutual interests even more widely than Dr George Cheyne had done in London. The collection of people who visited Law or corresponded with him shared a basic philosophy which was in spirit Neo-Platonic, having absorbed also the Kabalah and Boehme's own system, and was, in many respects, unorthodox. Although it had been so deeply suffused with Christianity and represented an extreme position always so attractive to spiritually minded Christians that few of them probably realized how unorthodox it was.

A number of William Law's followers survived him. And these in turn influenced some younger people who had not had the chance to know Law in person but who warmly sympathized with his position. We have seen how a record of their thoughts and feelings was preserved by the Dublin artist Henry Brooke, or rather by the devotion of his sons-in-law, F. H. Holcroft and Isaac D'Olier. And we have the evidence, too, of Richard Clarke's books. This passage from a work especially addressed to the Jews, *Signs of Times or a Voice to Babylon, The Great City of the World And to the Jews in particular*, which came out in London, in 1773, is enough to emphasize Clarke's antecedents, his line of descent in thought.

In the *Sabbatical* Year, which is a Sign and Standard of *Time*, under the *figurative* Dispensation, I have opened the spiritual

Sense, both as a Circle of Time answering to six great Years, of a thousand Years for each, concluding in a *seventh*, according to the *pure Cabbala*, or *traditional* Interpretation, defended by *Buddeus*, Dean *Allix*, Dr. *Henry More*, the great *Cudworth*, *Vitringa*, *Kircher*, *Erasmus*, *Huet* &c. and to the Doctrine of the Christian Church as shewn by Mr. *Mede*, *Broughton*, and Dr. *Burnet* of the Charter-house.[1]

The 'ancient tradition' that Blake draws upon, on plate 14 of his *Marriage of Heaven and Hell*, is again mentioned here, of course. And Clarke's thought is shown basically to stem from the Jewish Kabalah, the Cambridge Platonists and Christian Cabalists like Hugh Broughton, with a debt to other orientalists in addition. The references in the footnotes to yet another, early, work, *The Spiritual Voice to the Christian Church And to the Jews*, are also very revealing. The most frequently cited book is the Bible itself with Pistorius, Pico della Mirandola, Rittangelius and Ainsworth often appealed to; as authorities for its interpretation in a mystical sense. Abarbanel is a favourite, as is Maimonides.[2] The former figures prominently in *A Second Warning to the World by the Spirit of Prophecy* and it is interesting that the British Museum copy of this book is marked 'H. Brooke London 1762' and must have been bought by Henry Brooke, perhaps upon the visit when his 'conversion' took place. Signs of that absorption in the concept of fire and light, which Boehme shared with the cabalists and perhaps derived from them, appear in Clarke's crucial *Gospel of the Daily Service*, and in one passage, from the *Spiritual Voice*, he uses that curious expression the 'rolling Wheel' which so commonly appears in the language of the seventeenth-century Ranters and their fellows. 'Wherever Light is, there must be *Fire*, its hidden Root and *rolling Wheel*, in all Worlds, which our Bacon calls parallella Signacula, and which the Jews mean, when they say, that God set his Seal of *Sephiroth* so hard that he printed it

---

[1] Richard Clarke, *Signs of Times or a Voice to Babylon, The Great City of the World and to the Jews in particular*. London 1773, p. 2.

[2] Richard Clarke, *The Spiritual Voice to the Christian Church and to the Jews*, London 1760, pp. 5–6; 37; 87; 98; 109; 114–15; 124.

through the three Worlds.'[1] Clarke goes on to insist upon the meaning of the Archetypal World, with its 'Ideas and Forms', which, he says, '*Pythagoras* and *Plato* borrowed of the ancient Church of God'. In a further passage, where he is never far from that image of the candleflame the *Zohar* employs so vividly, Clarke sets out a doctrine of the sexes identical again with Blake's.

> The Kingdom of God rises in us by the Renovation of seven divine Spirits, which constitute the *Bride* to be united to the *Male*, who bears the stronger Glories, as the Female in the Physics of heavenly Powers is a reflected Image, a secondary Emanation, and a Vessel to the first, as Fire out of Fire, a Light from a light, Air or Water from another: the last is the Female, Likeness and Glory of the First, a Vessel to contain it, always adhering to the Cause or its Head, the Husband and Lord; more firmly embracing its Root, than two Plates of polished Glass stick together, *Face* to *Face*. This is the Mystery of the Female, with only this Difference, that what is a Vessel or a Subject to a superior Light, may be, and is a *Male*, a Head, an Husband to an inferior. This is sound Philosophy of *Moses* in the inner Ground of Things, from the highest to the lowest Scale of the Universe.

Here Clarke is saying that the system of the Kabalah by which the Divine Influence spreads out from sphere to sphere, works in this fashion. He proceeds to compare the seven lights with the seven-branched candlestick of the Temple.

> By these Powers he quickens and re-illumines the *perished Lights*, represented in the *first Sanctuary* by seven golden Lamps on one Candlestick, which were a Figure of the *first Eve*, the *Wife* and *Sister* of *Adam*, emaning out of the same physical Powers.

His feelings, though, on the uses to which the symbolism have been put are mixed. Just as he sometimes admits the value of such cabalistic practices as Notarion and Gematria, but at other times dismisses them as so much 'Hay and Stubble', so he attacks the position of the Gnostics, even though his own is really uncomfortably close to theirs.

> This Mystery of the Gospel was first corrupted by the Gnostics,

[1] Richard Clarke, *op. cit.*, p. 83.

who had stole the spurious Cabala of the Jews and Platonists, as our *Jezebel*, the Moravian *Prophetess*, has done with the same Materials, abusing the sacred Language to the most carnal and abominable Sense, as some impious Wits have done by the *Song of Songs*.[1]

One of the concepts which fascinated Clarke most was the doctrine of the Shells, the 'Klippoth', developed by Isaac Luria. By means of the Shells, the husks of the material world, Luria believed that Evil was disentangled from Good in the world and given an objective existence. And when the 'Covering Cherub' had fallen he was associated in Clarke's mind with the same hardening and thickening process, becoming a block to Truth rather than its vehicle. This is in perfect accord with Blake's own symbolism. Certainly the theory of the 'Klippoth' is presented within Clarke's *Spiritual Voice*, in a way extraordinarily reminiscent of Blake's picture of Albion, the Universal Man, asleep on the rock of death. This passage (from page 20 to 22), for instance, alludes once more to the Seven Lights.

> This inner and hidden Kingdom consists of seven glorious Lights, which *Adam* lost; and which were preserved in Type by the *Seven golden Lamps*, their *Oil* and their *Fire*, and *Light* in the *holy Place* of the *Tabernacle*. These the Cabbalists call the seven Lights, and their Vessels broken away from Union with the superior Lights, and fallen down among the *Klippoth*, the Dregs of *Matter* compacted into Hardness and Thickness. These perished Powers, *Jesus Christ*, who is the High Priest of the heavenly Temple building up in fallen Man, must bring to Life again, and raise them up from their Death and deep Sleep, into their first Might and Glory, Strength and Majesty.

Here the last sentence recalls Blake's majestic vision of the sleeping Albion on Plate 15 of *Milton*.

> First Milton saw Albion upon the Rock of Ages,
> Deadly pale outstretch'd and snowy cold, storm cover'd,
> A Giant form of perfect beauty outstretch'd on the rock
> In solemn death: the Sea of Time & Space thunder'd aloud
> Against the rock, which was inwrapped with the weeds of death.
> (Keynes, p. 497)

[1] Richard Clarke, *op. cit.*, pp. 134-5.

And with it that dramatic and terrible passage on plate 95 of
Jerusalem where Albion awakes.

> The Breath Divine went forth over the morning hills. Albion rose
> In anger, the wrath of God breaking, bright flaming on all sides
>   around
> His awful limbs; into the Heavens he walked, clothed in flames,
> Loud thund'ring, with broad flashes of flaming lightning & pillars
> Of fire, speaking the Words of Eternity in Human Forms . . .
>   (Keynes, p. 742)

The resemblance between Richard Clarke's symbolism and
William Blake's is surely too close to be entirely coincidental.
And the points of contact in interest and personal acquaintance
add up to something fairly considerable. Clarke had, after all,
been a friend of Edward Young's and had written his *Essay
on the Number Seven* for him. He had engaged in public controversy with Tom Paine and Joseph Priestley among others.
Most of his later life was spent in London and from there he
issued a stream of books which came out during Blake's most
formative years, embodying just that vision of nature and the
relation between God and Man, and between the sexes, that
Blake later expressed in his prophetic poetry, and using some
identical images. He was known as a Hebrew scholar and
taught the language. Blake later learned a little Hebrew himself.
And Clarke was always a conspicuous personality, as the
incident in the Bristol Temple Church recounted by Langcake
reveals. A letter of his to Brooke written on 20th January 1795,
describes another, apparently rather hare-brained, scheme of
his for publicizing his prophetic message. – A circular letter is
being passed round. He writes to Henry Brooke,

> – The letter to the Bishop you will please to have delivered – I
> knew him when I was at (Winch?) college; he is learned but farther
> I know not: meer learning at best is but a handmaid, and not a
> mistress, as often seals up the eye from spiritual wisdom, . . . as it
> opens it . . . – I have sent to all the Bishop's, Nobles and com-
> moners of this Kingdom, what I am directed to do.

(The then Archbishop of Dublin, Robert Fowler, was up at
Trinity College, Cambridge, in 1744.)

Evidently Clarke intended to contact not only all Members of Parliament but the bishops and peers as well. But a man of his sort would be bound to acquire some notoriety. Moreover Clarke had been in contact from the beginning with the circle surrounding William Law, through the friendship he kept up with Thomas Langcake, and he may well have been known, for instance, to the Moravian minister, Francis Okeley; the man to whom Law confided the account of his original attraction towards Jacob Boehme's system.[1] At any rate one can sum up the situation by saying that anyone in London who, by the 1790's had become closely interested in the doctrines of Boehme, and aware of the cult of them which flourished among Law's followers and the considerable group of disciples who survived him, could hardly have remained unaware of Richard Clarke's existence for very long.

In his enthusiasm for social justice which made him look towards a communism in material goods, and in his suspicion of established religious institutions, as in his passion for apocalyptic prophecy, Clarke looks backwards towards the seventeenth-century radicals of the Commonwealth period. So did his devoted friend, Mary Pratt, to whom it is worthwhile to return for a moment. In one of her splendidly breathless and fervent letters to Brooke she writes, excusing herself for a gap in their correspondence due to practical difficulties,

Honoured and Dear Sir,
I beg to be exculpated from the odium of ingratitude or neglect, to a gentleman I know as a Christian, & love as a friend; accept if you please the following reasons for my omission; our house in Portland St. is undergoing a thoro' repair, and while we were; removing our furniture to the Country, every one of the family was taken ill of a violent fever that raged in this neighbourhood, but they were peculiarly favoured as my neighbour a Lady of Fortune had her four amiable daughters taken off, & all lay dead in the house at one time. Truly dear sir, I feel humbly thankfull for my deliverance.
The book which I intended sending, was *Molinos*, a translation

[1] Stephen Hobhouse, *Fides et Ratio*, p. 351.

from the Italian: but in conversing with dear Mr. Clark, he told me that you had most certainly got it, with every other mystic book, that is extant . . .

There is a very choice author, which I delight in, could I purchase any of his works, a Welsh minister, his name William Erbery, he suffered much persecution; and I think lived in Oliver Cromwell's time; I have a sermon of his, which is clear as the sun, to a spiritual eye: perhaps you may have heard of him. Peter Sterry is quite in the Love Principle he also wrote with all the love and sweetness of William Law's who translated part of Behmen's works: but books are dry and insipid, unless illuminated by the spirit of God while we read them.

Proceeding from his Southwark home, where he was born in 1613, Peter Sterry went up to Emmanuel College, Cambridge, and was one of those young men there exposed to the full influence of Benjamin Whichcote and John Smith, with their fellow Platonist Ralph Cudworth. He was indeed elected to a Fellowship of the College in 1637 but resigned this to become chaplain to Robert Greville, Lord Brooke, heir to Fulke Greville, whom we have seen figure in the group which has been named the 'school of night' and in connection with Giordano Bruno. Lord Brooke was said to have foreseen his death in the assault upon Lichfield in 1643 and to have ordered his chaplain to preach on Esther's words, 'If I perish, I perish'. Recognized by then as among the foremost of the Puritan divines belonging to the 'Independents', Sterry was appointed chaplain to Cromwell's Council of State in 1649, and worked at Whitehall where he must have been in contact with Cromwell's secretaries, the poets Milton and Marvell. After the Restoration Sterry lived at Richmond under the protection of Lord Lisle, settled with his family at Sheen Priory until his death in 1672. When his library was eventually sold it was found to contain, not only the works of the Neo-Platonists Plotinus, Porphyry, Iamblichus, Proclus, Ficino and Henry More, but also those of Dionysius the Areopagite, Maimonides and Scaliger. His commonplace book cites also Jacob Boehme, several of whose books he possessed, as he did those of

Nicholas of Cusa. His own works, sermons and theological treatises for the most part, reflect these kinds of influences. They are rare, but have rightly been praised for the magnificent prose of which he was master. John Byrom possessed a copy of Sterry's *Rise, Race and Royalty of the Kingdom of God in the Soul of Man* and Professor Pinto has pointed out that a volume containing some of his prayers was reprinted in 1785.[1] It is not surprising then, that Mrs Pratt was aware of Sterry's value, but at this stage of her life interior experiences absorbed her more than books. She continues,

> When the seventh seal is opened in the soul, then every line of the Word of God, appears in a new light; and that scripture is verified, which says that eye hath not seen, neither hath ear heard the things that God hath prepared for them that love him. This great mystery it has been the good will of Jehovah to bestow upon me, mere dust, and ashes!

Mrs Pratt goes on to explain what she means by this extraordinary statement.

> No man can see the face of God and live, but the dead see him; those who have died the spiritual death, they see him; this is the first resurrection; – but not after the manner of the deluded Swedenborgians; they grasp at shadows; – My partner in life is an adherent to these wild doctrines; – who call themselves the New Jerusalem church and are building chapels to preach the Baron's doctrine in; poor hoodwinked mortals, led blindfold by the seducer, to their own destruction: this is the prophecy mentioned by Daniel, when ye shall see the abomination of desolation standing in the holy place, then let him that readeth understand . . . I shall be delighted to find your spirit *abandoned* to God – like Esther before Ahasuerus saying, If I perish! I perish![2]

Two notes attached to the transcript of this letter are interesting; one by Holcroft, the transcriber, 'Mrs Pratt I conjecture a Methodist . . .', and the other a pencil scribble by Christopher Walton,

> . . . arrived at the *Divine flower* or summer of the regeneration – of course reason thinks her a fool. I think her a true Sophian child.

[1] V. de Sola Pinto, *Peter Sterry, Platonist and Puritan*, p. 4.
[2] Walton MS. I. i. 43. See correspondence, pp. 320–68.

In her next letter, of 25th August 1792, Mary Pratt makes even more astonishing statements.

> My own experience, (before I was in this glorified resurrection state) was to believe contradictions, impossibilities, and by that means the Lord instructed me in revelation. There is no book extant that speaks of my experience; because I am the first, who ever had the honour to have the seventh seal opened to them: The time was not *come*, till it came to me; be not staggered dear Sir, at my saying so; nor look upon the meanness of the instrument . . .

But Henry Brooke *was* staggered as we have seen. In fact he had already been considerably disturbed by the claims Mary Pratt had made for herself. In an earlier letter, where she hinted she could offer Brooke a helpful spiritual guide (the Quietist, Molinos as we have seen), she has this to say of her experiences,

> . . . the undefiled, righteousness of Jesus the Anointed, Jah – Jehovah has clothed me and I see and rejoice in my own beauty: not by attainments; not by my sufferings – tho' grievous and most terrible; not by watchings for twenty years, nor by fasting, abstraction, or prayer –
> No – it was the Lord's free gift, he made me see my own darkness, impotency, insufficiency, and extreme poverty, and nakedness – and then (Glory for ever to his adorable love) he took me into his bosom, I became his bride . . . I was one of the ugliest, dirtiest, raggedest objects, you ever saw, and yet Love took me in, & set me upon a Throne; ordered my goings, put a new song in my mouth: and I live only to praise him. – I have filled the paper. Please to let one know any conveyance and I will send you a book clearer than Behmen, also Mr. Clarkes books if you chuse them.

It is certainly true that Mary Pratt must have been under the influence of Jane Lead's works, as Brooke points out, and she did not acknowledge this in her letters to him. When one returns, for instance, to the Ninth Commandment of Jane Lead's *Laws of Paradise*, the extent to which Mary Pratt drew on her, and Richard Clarke, for that matter, becomes obvious.

> So here you may see who is that true Worthy Neighbour, whom you are obliged to bear witness *to*, and *for*, and not *against*;

stedfastly bearing Record of the Truth, from the Spirit of God's Wisdom dwelling in you, which is the only True Prophet, and Witness for Jesus in Thee. Verily there are intruding Spirits, that would come in as False Witnesses, of whom be thou aware, and be not found in the Conspiracy with them, who would condemn that Just One again, and Crucifie the Life afresh, that is risen out from the Morning Womb of God's Virgin, to be the Anointed Nazarite. Against whom out of thine own Nation, false Prophets will arise to seduce, and if possible, deceive my Elect and precious Seed, now formed into Heavenly Similitude. But I am come to give thee Light from my Celestial Glass and Globe, that in it thou mayest see all the false transforming Spirits that would subtilly bring in old Traditional things; instead of, and in opposition to my Pure and Unmixed Doctrine, the which I do into the Clean and Gold-refined Vessels never fail to pour: That so by it thou mayest be Tinged throughout, and in thy self feel a might Burning Oyl, spiriting thee for Infallible Prophesie.[1]

Jane Lead's work is full of references to the 'Celestial Glass and Globe', and especially, of course, to the Tree of Life and its fruit, which is associated with a spiritual death and a re-awakening to the Vision of God. Her *Fountain of Gardens* often mentions this theme, for example.[2] People who have very clear cut spiritual experiences all tend to regard themselves as unique, and this may explain Mrs Pratt's failure to give credit to her predecessor. But it may also be true that she did just this in some of her other writings. (She does, in her correspondence with Brooke, mention having read the 'Philadelphians', though with no reference to Jane Lead. She says that the writers she had examined only had 'glimpses'. They had not really passed through the 'gulph' of spiritual deaths.) For Christopher Walton was so impressed by her quality that he went to the trouble of trying to track down these papers. Her works had apparently been most voluminous in manuscript, but, according to an E. Rich who visited Mary Pratt's daughter in Chelsea in 1852, all the papers and diaries had by then been destroyed.

---

[1] Jane Lead, *Laws of Paradise*, London 1695, pp. 33–5.
[2] Jane Lead, *Fountains of Gardens*, London 1696–1700, Vol. I, pp. 247–51; Vol. II, pp. 94 & 105; Vol. III, p. 74.

They did not know what to do with them, so used them for lighting the kitchen and copper fires.[1]

Apart from the group we have been immediately concerned with, there were other figures conspicuous for their pre-occupation with the same subjects, during the same period, whose interest was dictated either by a passionate partizanship or equally passionate disgust. And these cannot be entirely ignored. The earlier work of the Rev. Thomas Hartley, for instance, is important. This was the gentleman who came up to London in 1769 with a Quaker friend Thomas Cookworthy, who had introduced him to Swedenborg's writings, in order to visit the Baron. Hartley became an enthusiastic supporter of the Swedenborgian doctrines and helped to translate the originals into English. But in 1764 he had already published a book very close in spirit to William Law's teaching, to the position of the Philadelphians, and to that adopted by Richard Clarke in his turn; *Paradise Restored: or a Testimony to the Doctrine of the Blessed Millenium; With some Considerations on its approaching Advent from the Signs of the Times. To which is added, a Short Defence of the Mystical Writers.* For just as Richard Clarke taught the doctrine of 'the Great Sabbatical Year', defined in the summary to his *Signs of the Times,*

> the Messiah is proved to have been the *Son* of the *Woman* before the *Fall* of *Adam*; at which Time he became from the *Womb* of his Mother, the Nazarite. Rev. xxi, 5, 6, 7. Dan. vii. 13, 14.
> A Testimony by the Spirit of Prophecy to their Conversion near at hand, and to the *great Sabbatical Year*, when all *Nations, Languages, Kindreds* and *Peoples* will serve the LORD and his CHRIST under the *Cloud* of *Glory* . . .[2]

So Hartley believed there would be 'a kingdom of perfect righteousness' on earth. He quotes, too, exactly the same authorities that Clarke drew upon, praising 'Dr. *Henry More*, that wonder of his age', 'the excellent Mr. *John Smith*', as well as 'the learned Mede' and 'Dr. Everard'. Hartley was clearly a

[1] Walton MS. I. i. 43, pp. 370f.
[2] Richard Clarke, *Signs of Times*, summary of contents, title page.

devoted Behmenist who recommends to the reader '*Jacob Behmen's* Theosophick Philosophy unfolded, shewing the verity and utility of the doctrines contained in the writings of that divinely instructed Author, by *Edward Taylor*, Gent'. He pays due tribute also, to Thomas Bromley, the Behmenist from All Souls College, Oxford, 'the pious and excellent Bromley in his *Sabbath of Rest*', and he vigorously defends, with him, William Law whom he describes as 'that eminent Mystic of our church', deploring, like Henry Brooke, John Wesley's attitude to Jacob Boehme.

> He had taken pains to represent in a reproachful manner the work of that wonderful man *J. Behmen*, which he never understood . . .

Just a little later than Hartley's book, in 1776, there appeared a similar work, *Horae Solitariae or Essays Upon Some Remarkable Names and Titles of Jesus Christ, Occurring in the Old Testament*, by Ambrose Serle. Here the emphasis is upon the Cabalistic rather than the Neo-Platonic aspect of the tradition, but it is obvious Serle is well informed, though perhaps rather too anxious to place a Christian interpretation upon the Kabalah in its Jewish form. He states, in his Introduction,

> The learned *Kircher* is of Opinion, for which he gives many Reasons, that the antient Jews and the later Cabalists derived their Knowledge of the Trinity, and consequently the Sense and Import of the divine Names which contain it, by a continued Tradition from the *first* Patriarchs; and he cites the *Jetzirah* (a Book which the Jews ascribe to *Abraham* himself; but which, however *that* be, is considered of extreme Antiquity) where the *first* Person or Hypostasis is described as . . . *Kether*, the *Crown*, or the admirable and profound Intelligence; the *second* Person . . . *Chochma*, *Wisdom*, or the Intelligence illuminating the Creation, and the second Glory; and the *third* Person . . . *Binah*, or the sanctifying Intelligence, the Worker of Faith, and the Father of it, because from his efficacious Agency it wholly proceeds.
>
> The most learned Divines and Expositors among the Jews, who preceded the Advent of *Jesus Christ*, plainly indicated their knowledge of this mysterious Truth, and expressed it nearly in the same Terms with us. They believed, taught and adored three *primordial Existences* in the Godhead, which they called some-

times . . . *Middoth* or *Properties*, and sometimes . . . *Sephiroth* or *Numerations*. The later Jews, who are only Deists, wish to resist this Evidence, by saying, that this *Sephiroth* were only meant for *Attributes*; but their Attempts have been very lame, and they are particularly puzzled to explain away the above Cabalistical Scheme, which was invented for the very Purpose of expressing the three Hypostasis in one Essence. Nor have they better Success in averting the Force of some of their most esteemed Comments upon the sacred Writings, which declare the same Doctrine. Thus R. *Simeon*, and the famous *Jonathon*, treating upon the *Trisagion* or *thrice Holy*, in the 6th Chapter of *Isaiah*, say, That the *first* Holy implied the FATHER, the *second* Holy the SON, and the *third* Holy the HOLY GHOST. And it was almost an Adage amongst them, that . . . *Aleph* by . . . *Beth* . . . created the World . . .

With such books as Hartley's and Serle's on the market it is not perhaps surprising to find the opposition also in action. Richard Graves, afterwards Regius Professor of Divinity in the University of Dublin, brought out his *The Apostles were not Enthusiasts* in 1798. This work contained an appendix which is a positive mine of information on everything from the Koran to the writings of the Neo-Platonists. The cases of visionaries, both non-Christian ones like Iamblichus, and saints like St Francis, St Benedict, Julian of Norwich and St Ignatius are examined, and all these great figures are referred to as 'celebrated fanatics'. Turning to more modern examples Graves points out, in his Appendix, that . . .

About the end of the 16th century, there arose in Savoy a sect of enthusiasts who pretended to be prophets, and who afterwards made many disciples in London, where they were patronized by Sir Richard Bulkeley, a man of some note and learning, on whom they had wrought a cure, which he conceived to be supernatural. A very particular and curious account of them was published in 1709 at London, and annexed to the 4th edition of Dr. Hickes' Spirit of Enthusiasm exorcised . . .

(Francis Lee's contribution to this book is singled out for mention.) The case of the visionary Brothers and his appeal to the scholar Halhed, is brought in; incidents occurring in Lady Conway's household are mentioned; the French Quietists discussed; Manichean doctrine explored and oriental practices drawn upon, in quotations from Bayles' Dictionary.

> The Brachmans of Bengal lead a very austere life; they go bare-headed and bare-footed in burning sand, and live only upon herbs. They have very odd opinions about nothingness; and a morality which has a great affinity with the visions of our Quietists. . . .

And from Kempfer's *History of Japan*, Graves produces,

> . . . Jummabos, a religious order in Japan, who spent most of their time in going up and down holy mountains, washing themselves in cold water in the midst of winter.

Curios readers, following up Richard Graves' references, would have been led to a good deal of literature concerned with the theory of emanation, whether Gnostic or Neo-Platonic, amongst other strange pieces of information.

The eighteenth century was distinguished for the number of compilations, encyclopaedic volumes, dictionaries of miscellaneous information which appeared on every conceivable subject. Some collections which would have given a mind like Blake's, for instance, a real insight into the Kabalah, Neo-Platonism, the various Gnostic schools and different forms of Eastern religious symbolism, were Thomas Maurice's *Indian Antiquities*, his later *Dissertation on the Oriental Trinities*, and Beaval de Basnage's *History of the Jews*, in the translation of Thomas Taylor, the earlier Cambridge Platonist.[1] Basnage's account of the Kabalah is full, with many quotations, and on the whole correct. He differed from the Renaissance writers in maintaining that the Jewish tradition derived from Egypt. He also draws many parallels with the Greeks and the Gnostics and takes no trouble to disguise the heresies latent in the system. At any rate, if Richard Graves was impelled to uphold the more general eighteenth-century scepticism it was only because the forces stemming from the preceding century were

[1] Beaval de Basnage, *History of the Jews*, translated by Thomas Taylor, London 1709.

still very much to be reckoned with. There had already appeared, for example, a book entitled *Theological and Practical Divinity: With Extracts of several Treatises written by Jacob Behmen*, 'Published by a Gentleman retired from Business',[1] where the following forthright remarks are set out in the Preface.

> It is a great pity that many well meaning persons, great friends to the letter of christianity, are such enemies to the sprint of it, as to fly out against all internal operations on the soul; calling them Enthusiasm, Fanaticism, and whatever their spleen and aversion can suggest! All the . . . ill names given to revealed religion by Deists and Atheists are employed by some against what they call Mysticism, as the worst name they can invent.

Here the author is taking the same line as Richard Clarke did in his *Jesus the Nazarene*. During one of his passages insisting on the 'evangelical baptism of heavenly fire to be poured out on all flesh' after 6,000 years, Clarke pauses to remark upon the word 'mystery', suggesting it has gathered unfortunate associations, quite undeservedly.

> As mysticism (which is the explaining of the figures of the law realizing in man, in his body, the temple and house of God, in *Paul's view*) is looked upon to be as evil as *magic*; and they who open the mysteries, or spiritual truths of the gospel in consonance to the figures of the law, are regarded as fanatics and enthusiasts, by the wise and prudent . . . the interpreters of the *oral* law, called *Cabbalists*, are, by ignorant men, supposed to be deficient in teaching moral duties, as much as the *Mystics* of the Christian Church. But it is a mistake and a calumny. To mention a few of our country, and of modern times, *Everard, Rous, Sterry, White, Sadler*, author of *Olbia, Smith*, of *Cambridge*; Chief Justice *Hale*, in his *Magnetismus Magnus*, and *Whichcot*. Who are better preceptors of all moral and social duties than *Bromley, Robert Gell, Roach, Norris* and the late *William Law*?[2]

---

[1] *Theological and Practical Divinity* . . . Published by a Gentleman retired from Business, London 1769, pp. vi–vii. (There is an entry against this title in the index to the contents of the Walton room, Dr Williams' Library; 'Dr. Chaloner'.)

[2] Richard Clarke, *Jesus the Nazarene*, London 1795, pp. 88–90n.

Once more the line of descent is clearly traced. And here it goes back to the Cambridge Platonists, the Philadelphians like Bromley and Roach, and to those figures such as Everard and Law who in England were outstanding for their preoccupation with mysticism. They had their own descendants, clearly, rather more numerous ones than has been imagined, and these were conspicuous especially in certain regions. We have seen how a lively circle of them flourished in Ireland. Ralph Mathers reports much activity in the West Country and we know how active Richard Clarke was in London and how ardent the fervour of his friend Mary Pratt. But above all, in the North around Manchester and Bolton the numbers of people who studied Jacob Boehme's writings, who were attracted to a vision of life really based on Neo-Platonism and who were well read in the Catholic mystics, being as much drawn to the Quietists as to the Evangelical movement affecting their own country, was particularly large. It is interesting to note that Christopher Walton, indefatigable collector of the material that remains to us on William Law and his circle, came from Worsley in Lancashire, though he was settled in London from 1830 onwards, working first as a silk mercer and then as a very successful goldsmith at Ludgate Hill. Born in 1809, he comes of a later generation than those groups we have been dealing with. Yet in his youth books like Isaac D'Olier's *Memoirs of the Late Excellent and Pious Mr. Henry Brooke*, and Holcroft's edition of Boehme's remaining works in English were still coming out. He is said to have been attracted to William Law's works through Wesley, for he was a Methodist and John Wesley had the fairness to include extracts from Law in his *Christian Library*. These whetted Walton's appetite and led him eventually to produce his formidable *Notes and Materials for an adequate Biography of the celebrated Divine and Theosopher William Law*. His book has been quite naturally criticized. The 'microscopic print, which makes careful study a torture to the eyes', the absence of a 'sense of values . . . so that authors whose insanity is conspicuous are quoted on a level with trustworthy and authoritative writers', all these have been complained of.[1] Yet one must remember that Walton did not pretend to have done more than assemble material. He looked for a qualified biographer to complete the task. And also the greater one's own knowledge of those authors whose insanity is supposed to be so conspicuous, the more one respects them in fact. They may have been enthusiastics in the seventeenth-century sense, but there was always something serious and important in their outpourings. Of these Christopher Walton should perhaps be regarded as the last survivor. He was a young contemporary of Blake, and from a comparable social background, and his outlook shows that combination of interest in the Evangelical movement and the mystics, which was typical of the whole group. An interest which, however, was just as much centred upon the Quietists, Molinos, Guion and Poirett, just as much devoted to Fénelon's works, as to the *Imitation of Christ* and to the acknowledged masters of orthodox Catholic mysticism, St Teresa of Avila and John of the Cross. And just this attitude is reflected in the passage from *Jerusalem*, plate 72, on the Four Gates of Los, where a succession of figures is mentioned, not usually associated together, that has caused some speculation.

> And a Son of Eden was set over each Daughter of Beulah to guard
> In Albion's Tomb the wondrous Creation, & the Four-fold Gate
> Towards Beulah is to the South. Fenelon, Guion, Teresa,
> Whitefield & Hervey guard that Gate, with all the gentle Souls
> Who guide the great Wine-press of Love.
>
> (Keynes, p. 712)

Here two Evangelicals, both with rather Calvinist leanings, Whitefield and Hervey, author of *Meditations among the Tombs*, are set among Fénelon and his protegé Mme Guion, and with the great Teresa of Avila. In the Preface to Chapter 3 of *Jerusalem* it is worth noting that Blake takes the opportunity of defending Whitefield and the Methodists against the Deists.

> Voltaire, Rousseau, Gibbon, Hume, charge the Spiritually Religious with Hypocrisy; but how a Monk, or a Methodist

[1] Arthur Hopkinson, *About William Law*, 1948, p. 117.

either, can be a Hypocrite, I cannot conceive. We are Men of like
passions with others & pretend not to be holier than others . . .
Foote in calling Whitefield, Hypocrite, was himself one; for
Whitefield pretended not to be holier than others, but confessed
his Sins before all the World . . .

(*Ibid.*, p. 682)

Here it is almost as though Blake were ranging himself beside
the Monks and the Methodists. 'The Spiritually Religious'
with whom Blake may be said to belong were just those men
and women Christopher Walton describes, being himself a late
representative of their way of thought. Blake's own thought
certainly has in it all the same ingredients, and there were many
among these people as fiercely critical of religious organization
as ever Blake was. Theirs was a spiritual climate in which he
would have been completely at home.

If we concede, then, that this traditional way of thought, this
symbolic language, was still in existence during the late
eighteenth century, and surprisingly vigorous, how is it to be
finally judged? What is its value? As this philosophy found an
outlet during the eighteenth century it was clearly a protest
against the prevailing materialism, Deism and general indifference to the interior life. But the Renaissance source had
been a passion for exploring new mental universes – we have
traced the way the scientific investigation of the natural world
was bound up with this too, from its beginnings – and above
all, for integrating the Christian mode of thought with the
Jewish, the Greek and the oriental. The supposition always
being that Wisdom is from the East and that the classical
authors' main value was as vehicles for an insight, purer at its
source, which was somehow shared, too, by our Celtic
ancestors the Druids. Incidentally, the tradition contained
within it a mass of esoteric material; the Jewish Kabalah, with
its mystical interpretation of the scriptures, Alchemy, Neo-
Platonic theories of Harmony, Hermetic literature and the
vision of such great medieval figures as Raymond Lull and
Joachim of Flora. All drawn upon and used for fresh purposes

288

by the Renaissance giants Paracelsus and Boehme, by their followers, and by the Cambridge Platonists. The appearance of this tradition in any kind of literature, is always heralded by reference to a list of venerable authorities which varies little from the age of Ficino to the time of Richard Clarke. Except that the list grows. Those who earlier cited Hermes Trismegistus, Zoroaster, and Plotinus, like Pico della Mirandola, his master Ficino, Giorgio and Cornelius Agrippa, begin themselves to be added to the train. But the essence of the whole movement is a Christian piety, an impulse towards catholicity. There seems to have been little esotericism for its own sake, little of the secrecy that hung round Freemasonry or Rosicrucianism, in the early stages, though the whole matter was, by definition, the preserve of the thoughtful and the scholarly. As long as contact with the Christian vitality which inspired the tradition was maintained it flourished; especially as the Neo-Platonic philosophy has been, since the time of St Augustine, as it were naturalized into the Christian faith, and has always coloured the outlook of the most spiritual members of the Church, particularly the mystics. But within the Church it was held in tension with another, more Aristotelian, mode of thinking and the extremes balanced. Once the links with the Church were snapped the weaknesses behind the Neo-Platonic positon became more and more apparent. It is in the conception of a relationship between Soul and Body, between Heaven and Earth, the Supernatural and Nature, that the most dangerous flaw is to be found. William Law's teaching of Man as a fallen angel gives the conception classic expression.

> He was created an Angel, both as to Body and Spirit; and this Angel stood in an outward Body, of the Nature of the outward world; and therefore, by the nature of his State he had his Trial, or *Power* of choosing whether he would live as an Angel, using only his outward Body as a means of opening the Wonders of the outward World to the Glory of his Creator; or whether he would turn his Desire to the opening of the bestial Life . . .[1]

[1] William Law, *The Spirit of Prayer*, London 1750, p. 10.

Above all it is most important to remember that the root idea behind this position is what Francis Lee describes in the *Historical Account of Montanism* as 'the First and Fundamental Lie on which all the rest do hang, . . . *the Consubstantiality of Spirit with Matter*'. This is the reason why Lee traces a record of the various Gnostic sects under the title of a history of Montanism, although the beliefs of the early heretic Montanus might seem to have been in direct opposition to the Gnostic ones and his supporter Tertullian, mocking the Neo-Platonists, called Plato the 'Patriarch of the Gnostics'. Yet Lee, whose learning was profound and who had in addition some first-hand experience of such cults, knew what he was talking about when he linked Montanism to Manicheism.

Thus then *Manicheism* spread itself, after it had been midwif'd and nourished by *Montanism*, and fill'd great part of the World.[1]

So, though it may seem strange that a movement which was largely a reaction away from materialism, should actually stem from a kind of materialism, yet that is what happened. Lee is right, too, in comparing an idea of God which incompletely expresses what is meant by Christ's saying 'God is a Spirit', with the '*Parabrama* of the *Indian Brahmins*'. In all these systems a certain contempt for Nature seems to exist side by side with a failure to disassociate Nature from God. Indian religion has therefore been described as pantheistic with much truth. And even Boehme held firmly by an Eternal Nature. Again, for this reason the Montanists, and those groups which flourished so conspicuously in the sixteenth and seventeenth centuries, like the Adamites and the Christadelphians, who put great stress on the body, were not in real opposition to the philosophy of the Neo-Platonists and Cabalists. The two things were simply opposite sides to the same medal. Therefore such statements as Blake's,

Man has no Body distinct from his Soul; for that call'd Body is a portion of Soul discern'd by the five Senses, the chief inlets of Soul in this age . . . (Keynes, p. 149).

[1] Francis Lee, *An Historical Account of Montanism*, London 1709, p. 316.

from *The Marriage of Heaven and Hell*, plate 4, are hardly as much in contradiction to his later impatience with the bonds placed upon the spirit as might be imagined. Naturally some allowance must be made for Blake's age at the time when *The Marriage of Heaven and Hell* was composed. His enthusiasm, then, at the peak of his manhood's vigour, for 'Energy . . . the only life' is understandable. And he always remained, as a poet and painter supremely sensitive to impressions from the outside world, a point which is often forgotten by critics. Yet at the same time there is in Blake's mythological system just that curious inability to imagine the spiritual except as in some way corporeal, that distinguishes Swedenborg's outlook and is to be found quite often within the tradition we have been following. And there co-exists the fear of Nature as exerting a kind of downward pull, the desire to assert Man's angelic origins, the outright hostility to matter that Law and Boehme both display. Except that he is also influenced by Milton's dramatic vision of the Fall, Blake presents just the very picture of creation as a fall, shows the identical repugnance towards matter that Jacob Boehme expresses. As Boehme's original Adam was seduced by the charms of earthly Nature, the Enchantress, as Clarke calls her, so Blake's Luvah is condemned to corporeal existence in these terms,

> . . . Go & die the Death of Man for Vala the sweet wanderer.
> I will turn the volutions of your Ears outward, & bend your
> Nostrils
> Downward, & your fluxile Eyes englob'd roll round in fear;
> Your with'ring Lips & Tongue shrink up into a narrow circle
> Till into narrow forms you creep.
> (*The Four Zoas*, Night the Third, II.85-9. Keynes, p. 294)

Though it is true Blake saw 'Time as the Mercy of Eternity' and considered the embodied life could be used redemptively, he always regarded it as making the best of a tragedy, as the effect of a cosmic fall.

There is in this whole outlook a protest against the fundamental human condition, with which one cannot help but sympathize. For the tensions Man is subject to, by virtue of his partly spiritual, partly material nature are almost unendurable. This it is that gives human life its peculiar drama. The men of the Renaissance, reacting against the enormous influence of Aristotle, swung over to the Platonic point of view and in this impulse expressed their particular protest. Those minds in the eighteenth century, disgusted, like Law and Blake, with the prevailing materialism, so unimaginative and mechanical, used the language of an earlier tradition framed for just this purpose. During the nineteenth century a further shock was administered with the Darwinian theory. It appeared that Man, far from being an angel, was actually a monkey. Yet it is precisely from this evolutionary approach, belonging as it does to the Aristotelian aspect of things, that the most exciting and inspiring twentieth-century theory of Man, that of Pierre Teilhard de Chardin, has arisen. Describing his own revelation Chardin puts the matter in these words.

> ... I doubt whether there is a more decisive moment for a thinking being than when the scales fall from his eyes and he discovers that he is not an isolated unit lost in the cosmic solitudes, and realizes that a universal will to live converges and is hominized in him.
> In such a vision man is seen not as a static centre of the world – as he for long believed himself to be – but as the axis and leading shoot of evolution, which is something much finer.[1]

I believe that it is. The vision of Man as 'thinking dust' is to me more moving than the aspirations of the Neo-Platonists because it is more realistic and more universal. Man is no longer lost and trapped in an alien order. He is the growing point of its whole life; a painful thing to be, but wonderful. There is an imbalance in the Neo-Platonic position which was detected and gave rise to an ever-increasing suspicion of the spiritual life; in itself a European tragedy. Why is it that the great mystical tradition of the West died down in the eighteenth century? Although it had Fénelon as a powerful defender, by the time of Bossuet mysticism had been put into disrepute, precisely

[1] Pierre Teilhard de Chardin, *The Phenomenon of Man*, p. 36.

because, and especially through the influence of the Quietists, it had become associated with the weaknesses of the Neo-Platonic standpoint. Bossuet, an irritating and obtuse man in many ways, yet perceived a desperate danger to the Christian inheritance. For after all Christianity is basically an Incarnational religion. It would have been better if Bossuet had troubled to disentangle the false mysticism from the true, if he had seen that the Neo-Platonic influence represented a good impulse gone to extremes. But he was right to sense the danger, all the same.

I have already stressed the disintegration of the tradition which took place when its very close links with the Church were snapped. A process that began in the seventeenth century when the symbolism was used more and more by groups of religious enthusiasts with a tendency to hysteria, and by secret societies. During the eighteenth century it passed into the hands of pious individuals, who were either cut off from the Church by force of circumstances, as Law was, being a Non-Juror, or by the kind of disapproval that Richard Clarke felt for organized religion. Otherwise they were members of splinter groups, Methodists like Brooke or Swedenborgians as Ralph Mather became. Although these men and women had distinction and seriousness, they were exposed to the charge of eccentricity, one that cannot be entirely denied. And the curious fact is they were split among themselves. Renaissance scholars who made use of Neo-Platonic theories of harmony, the Kabalah or Alchemic symbolism may have quarrelled with one another on particular points, but they all accepted a common language, a framework of reference. We have noted though, how Law was suspicious of Clarke's Hebrew symbolism and critical of Swedenborg, how Clarke inveighed against the visionary Brothers and against the 'French Prophets', how Henry Brooke felt uncomfortable about Alchemy and how Mrs Pratt's Swedenborgian husband was scandalized by her devotion to seventeenth-century spiritual writers. It is as if each were trying to establish his essential soundness in refusing to be linked with what others might regard as spurious. There is no doubt that by the early nineteenth century the tradition was losing its genuineness, and when it reappears later, in the time of Mme Blavatsky, Eliphaz Levi and W. B. Yeats, 'Theosophy' has turned into a cult marred by sensationalism, false mystification and undigested oriental material. The appearance of this kind of theosophy in Christopher Walton's book has prejudiced many readers against an earlier tradition, organically united with the Christian civilization from which it sprung.

Perhaps one can say that the wheel had come full circle with the arrival of the Neo-Platonist scholar, Thomas Taylor. Just as the philosophy of the Florentine academy was inspired by the advent of Gemisthus Pletho from Greece, a figure of doubtful orthodoxy who was interested in a revived paganism of the kind Julian the Apostate had hoped for after Constantine, yet whose ideas were taken over in the most pious spirit by the devout Ficino. So the appearance on the eighteenth-century scene of Thomas Taylor, a brilliant mathematician and Greek scholar, and a close friend of Flaxman the sculptor, heralds the beginning of the end of that Neo-Platonism, suffused with the Christian spirit, which had given so much to Europe from the time of Pico to the Cambridge Platonists. Isaac D'Israeli, Lord Beaconsfield's father and a considerable patron of Blake's, draws a parallel, in fact, between the two figures of Pletho and Taylor in an article called 'A New Religion', part of his *Curiosities of Literature*, where he quotes George of Trebizond on the first of them.

> His common name was *Gemistus*, but he assumed that of *Pletho* . . .
> He has written with wonderful art and with great eloquence . . .
> It is certain he was so zealous a Platonist, that he entertained no other sentiments than those of Plato, concerning the nature of the Gods, Souls, Sacrifices &c. . . .

D'Israeli continues,

> I cannot quit this article without recollecting some similar works even of the present day! The ideas of the phrenetic *Emanuel Swedenburgh* are warmly cherished by a sect, who have so far

disgraced themselves as to bestow on their society the name of this man. Mr. *T. Taylor*, the Platonic philosopher and the *modern Pletho*, consonant to that philosophy, professes Polytheism.[1]

Nothing would have infuriated 'Mr. T. Taylor' more than to be mentioned with Swedenborg. Speaking of modern commentators upon the Theogony of Hesiod, in his *Dialogues of Plato*, Taylor contrasts his own interpretation with theirs.

> . . . his Theogony, when considered according to this exposition, will be found to be beautifully consistent and sublime; whereas, according to modern interpretations, the whole is a mere chaos, more wild than the delirious visions of Swedenborg, and more unconnected than the *filthy* rant of stool-preaching methodist.[2]

Taylor seldom misses an opportunity to sneer at the Christian faith. In the time of the ancients, he explains, before Constantine,

> . . . the generous ardor of unbounded liberty was not yet extinguished by the frozen hand of despotic usurpation. The Roman manners and *religion* were not yet destroyed; and nobility was not contaminated by the sordid occupations of traffic. *Meekness* was not esteemed a *virtue*, nor *merchandize* an *honour*!!![3]

And his criticisms do not stop at the dissenters of his own day. He continually inveighs against the more orthodox Cambridge Platonists for their views on a Christian Trinity which he considers merely a perverted version of the Platonic Triad. The interest of Thomas Taylor's writings rests not, however, on his opinions about Comparative Religion, but on his presentation of Greek myth in a very full manner, from a Neo-Platonic point of view. It is very likely, as Kathleen Raine has suggested, that Blake used this apparatus to provide the machinery of his own myth. All poets need such a framework and few of the greatest have been so entirely original as to have done without

---

[1] Isaac D'Israeli, *Curiosities of Literature*, London 1794, Vol. I, p. 435.

[2] Thomas Taylor, *The Cratylus, Phaedo, Parmenides and Timaeus of Plato*, London 1793, Introduction to the *Parmenides*, p. 290n.

[3] Thomas Taylor, *The Philosophical and Mathematical Commentaries of Proclus on Plato*, London 1789, Vol. II, p. 223.

it. But while Blake must have realized the affinity to early Neo-Platonism in much of the traditional material he drew upon, he clearly saw that Thomas Taylor's Neo-Paganism was untenable. Such an outlook would be plain idolatry to a man who well realized that not until the coming of Christianity was the true meaning of the Greek gods understood.

> These gods are visions of the eternal attributes, or divine names, which, when erected into gods, become destructive to humanity. They ought to be the servants, and not the masters of man, or of society. They ought to be made to sacrifice to Man, and not man compelled to sacrifice to them ... (*A Descriptive Catalogue*. Keynes, p. 571).

Blake was very definite about the distinction between the Bible and Greek myth. And he subscribed to the Renaissance concept of the classical authors as vehicles of a truth greater than their own and from a purer source.

> 'Let it here be Noted,' he said, 'that the Greek Fables originated in Spiritual Mystery & Real Visions, which are lost & clouded in Fable & Allegory ... while the Hebrew Bible & the Greek Gospel are Genuine, Preserv'd by the Saviour's Mercy ...'
> (*A Vision of the Last Judgment*. Keynes, p. 605)

And again from the same part of his notebook is another statement to the same effect.

> ... Apuleius' Golden Ass & Ovid's Metamorphosis & others of the like kind are Fable; yet they contain Vision in a sublime degree, being derived from real Vision in more ancient Writings.
> (*Ibid.*, p. 607)

William Blake gave the derivation of his own vision of life, as opposed to the framework of mythological machinery he used for his prophetic poems and epics, himself; and in perfectly plain terms. He was inspired by the Hebrew prophets, who expressed the spirit not the letter of the Law, the mystical Ezra of the Apocrypha, beloved by the Cabalists, as well as the great Isaiah; by the poets also, and by Paracelsus and Boehme. He stands within the tradition which gave so much to our civilization between the time of Gemisthus Pletho and Thomas Taylor. He stands a rebel, sensitive also to the revolutionary movements of his time. But he stands a Christian. Let him speak for himself.

> Now my lot in the Heaven is this, Milton lov'd me in childhood
> & shew'd me his face.
> Ezra came with Isaiah the Prophet, but Shakespeare in riper years
> gave me his hand;
> Paracelsus & Behmen appear'd to me, terrors appear'd in the
> Heavens above
> And in Hell beneath, & a mighty & awful change threatened the
> Earth.
>
> (Keynes, p. 799)

CHAPTER XI

Conclusion

*

Critical judgments of some severity have been passed on the tradition under examination; upon its value. Is this completely fair? Has justice been done to the quality of mind and spirit encouraged by it? One has to remember that respect for spirituality should never be despised. A noble impulse undoubtedly lies behind the tradition. And none of its doctrines is entirely false. Man *is* in some respects an exiled being. He does live in 'a vale of tears'. The 'Great Amphibian' is not entirely at home in his watery element. He harks always after a new life on land. There is no doubt that the 'Fall' of Man introduced a discord into the original harmony of things which may have affected his whole environment, and it is probably true also that he sank into a more material and less spiritual state than he had rested in at the beginning. The original syncretism of the Renaissance, too, was thoroughly Catholic in quality. It was an essentially healthy movement, even if it went astray. If the Christian heritage was threatened by an over-enthusiasm for Greek philosophy or Jewish mysticism, the attempt at a synthesis had to be made. Indeed the new mental horizons which opened up at that time were narrow compared with those we face today. The whole of Asia and Africa lies before us. We have to come to terms with an entirely foreign way of thinking. Intellectual adjustments that would have staggered the men of the Renaissance are forced upon us.

John Henry, Cardinal Newman foresaw the necessity; being, in this respect, far ahead of his contemporary fellow Christians, whatever their persuasion. He presents a vision of the Church that Ficino would have sympathized with; seeing her, as Martin

D'Arcy has insisted, as one that,

> looked round upon the earth, noting and visiting the doctrines she found there. She began in Chaldea, and then sojourned among the Canaanites, and went down into Egypt, and thence passed to Arabia, till she rested in her own land. Next she encountered the merchants of Tyre, and the wisdom of the East country, and the luxury of Sheba. Then she was carried away to Babylon, and wandered to the schools of Greece. And wherever she went, in trouble or in triumph, still she was a living spirit, the mind and voice of the Most High; 'sitting in the midst of the doctors, both hearing them and asking them questions'; claiming to herself what they said rightly, correcting their errors, supplying their defects, completing their beginnings, expanding their surmises, and then gradually by means of them enlarging the range and refining the sense of her own teaching.

Because the Church must now visit the Indian sages and incorporate Far Eastern traditions into her own, we, in our present situation, can look with sympathy upon the efforts of our ancestors and appreciate the daring scope of a Renaissance movement which adventured upon a similar enterprise. It is interesting to notice the parallel efforts of a highly original modern mind, and one that has fallen into some of the same Gnostic traps; Simone Weil.

There are indeed passages from such a work as Simone Weil's *Intimations of Christianity Among the Ancient Greeks*, that read very like Blake, or could be extracts from Pico della Mirandola, from Cornelius Agrippa or Thomas Vaughan. She explains in her chapter upon the Pythagorean Doctrine that,

> The roots of Pythagorean thought extend far into the past. In expounding the concept which is at the centre of that doctrine, Plato evokes a very ancient revelation, which is perhaps the primal one. (*Philebus*.) Herodotus says that the Pythagoreans borrowed a large part of their beliefs from Egypt. Another ancient historian, Diodorus Siculus, I believe, points to the analogies between Pythagorean thought and Druidic thought, which, according to Diogenes Laertius, was considered by certain people as one of the sources of Greek philosophy. This, be it said in passing, obliges one to regard the Druidic religion as of Iberian origin, just as the

metaphysical and religious part of Greek civilization comes from the Pelasgians.

If this be so, perhaps the fantasies of Boderie's *La Galliade* are nearer the truth than has been imagined. At any rate, except that he is speaking of the Jews, not the Greeks, Blake speaks with the same voice in the Preface to Chapter II of *Jerusalem*.

> Your Ancestors derived their origin from Abraham, Heber, Shem, and Noah, who were Druids, as the Druid Temples (which are the Patriarchal Pillars & Oak Groves) over the whole Earth witness to this day.

Simone Weil puts forward the following proposition, from the *Philolaus*, as the fundamental text of Pythagorean thought.

> All realities are necessarily either limiting or unlimited, or else limiting and unlimited. Unlimited alone they cannot be, since it is manifest that realities proceed not only from what limits, nor only from what is unlimited. Clearly the order of the world and of things contained therein has been brought into harmony, starting from that which limits and from that which is unlimited.

She explains the proposition in her essay on 'Divine Love in Creation'.

> The Pythagoreans said, not the union of the limited and the limitless, but what is much more beautiful: the union of that which limits and the non-limited. That which limits is God. God who says to the sea: Hitherto shalt thou come, but no further . . . That which is unlimited has no existence except in receiving a limit from outside. All that exists here below is similarly constituted; not only all material realities but all the psychological realities in ourselves and in others as well. So in this world there are none but finite joys and sorrows. The infinite joys and sorrows which we think of as existing in this world, and which furthermore we necessarily situate in the future, are absolutely imaginary. The desire for infinite good which dwells at every moment in all men, even the most degraded, has its objective outside this world, and the privation of this good is the only ill not subject to limitation.

Blake is using the same language when he describes Reason as 'the limiting power'; though as a matter of fact, he is ironically reversing the orders of value implied when he does so.

There is no doubt the whole Renaissance theory of harmony is based on the concept Simone Weil presents of the Platonic Model, from the *Timaeus*.

'Proportion and harmony,' she says, 'are synonyms. Proportion is the bond established between two numbers by a mean proportional; thus 3 establishes a proportion between 1 and 9, that is $\frac{1}{3}=\frac{3}{9}$. Harmony is defined by the Pythagoreans as the unity of contraries. The first couple of contraries is God and the creature. The Soul is the unity of these contraries, the geometrical mean which establishes a proportion between them: He is the mediator.'

'The Model, having eternal life, has tried to give as much as possible of that life to the universe also. Now the nature of the living (Model), being eternal, could not be absolutely given to that which is begotten. So he conceived the idea of creating a mobile image of eternity. At the same time as he established the order of heaven, he created a thing which, revolving by the law of number, is the eternal image of that eternity which is fixed in unity. That image is what we call time.'

Again, this is the Time that Blake called 'the Mercy of Eternity' And that 'law of number' was the inspiration of men like Giorgio. In the same way Henry Vaughan no doubt had this passage from the *Timaeus* in mind when he composed his moving lyric 'I saw Eternity the other Night'. Blake himself may be echoing it at the close of *Jerusalem* where he writes,

> . . . all,
> Human Forms identified, living, going forth & returning wearied
> Into the Planetary lives of Years, Months, Days & Hours; reposing,
> And then Awakening into his Bosom in the life of Immortality . . .

in one of the few passages that seem to suggest a 'Revolution of Souls'. Simone Weil is right to say,

Here is the source of the idea of microcosm and of macrocosm which so haunted the Middle Ages. Its profundity is almost impenetrable. The symbol of the circular movement is the key to it . . . The movements of the celestial bodies which divide our life into days, months and years are our model in this regard, because their rotations are so regular that for them the future in no way differs from the past. By contemplating this equivalence of the future and the past we pierce through time right to eternity . . .

But she is wrong to blame the natural human 'desire orientated towards the future' and call this effort of the imagination 'the unique source of error and untruth'. Although it can never be completely satisfied except in Eternity, this desire is a God-implanted thing, with uses in this world as well as the next. Not desire as such, but spiritual pride is the true source of evil and the Gnostic tendency to attack desire and make it the chief culprit, the cause of the soul's descent into matter, is itself an example of pride. According to this kind of philosophy no explanation can ever be given for Creation, except that it is either meaningless or a mistake. No room for Providence in the shaping of the world can ever be found. And of course it will not do to reduce God the Son to a geometrical proposition half-way between Godhead and the creature. He is the Co-equal Son, the only begotten of the Father from all eternity. Nevertheless, whatever faults we may find with Simone Weil's position, or with the Renaissance outlook to which it is so close, perhaps we can learn from the mistakes in these philosophies. An attempt in the same direction, but carried out with greater wisdom, must without fail be made.

At all events, regardless of the particular attitude we may bring to it, an understanding of the tradition is essential to an understanding of European life and art. Only an incomplete conception of the work of Leonardo da Vinci, Dürer, Michelangelo, Edmund Spenser, John Donne and Palladio, to mention just a few names, can be arrived at without some grasp of the symbolic language they all used. And certain enigmatic figures, Paracelsus, Jacob Boehme, Robert Fludd, even John Kepler can hardly be appreciated at all without it. Their thought remains for the most part inaccessible. Moreover the history of particular trends; Neo-classical architecture, the development of the Ballet, even the appearance of the new science of Chemistry, cannot be explained without reference to Neo-Platonic theories of harmony, and the material from the Kabalah and other sources, with which these were bound up. But among all the geniuses and men of note whose work demands an appreciation of the tradition, if full justice is to be done to it, Blake stands out as an extreme case. For that very reason I have applied the traditional symbolism to his system throughout the book, as an example of the illumination this can shed. For when considering Blake's work, especially the prophetic poetry, without a knowledge of the tradition upon which he drew, the reader is in rather the position of an intelligent Mongolian Buddhist attempting to fathom *Paradise Lost* without any knowledge of the Bible, any acquaintance with European letters, or any understanding of the Christian vision. Such a man might make inspired guesses at the epic's meaning and appreciate many of its qualities, but on the whole he would be baffled. And many readers of Blake have been left bewildered by his poems. Some have tried to make sense of them by using a psychological approach. Others have read into them episodes from his own life. And of course it is possible to show a great many reflections of events in contemporary England within Blake's work. He was a man essentially *aware*. But the key to an understanding of Blake's mental world is the realization that it was coloured by influences from no single author or artist, but from a combination of like-minded ones; from a shared tradition.

I believe Blake to have been influenced not only by the enormous figures of Paracelsus and Boehme whose thought was so important that whole literatures grew up around it and generations of men and women in Europe were affected by it: but by some of their humbler followers also. Notably by those in the direct line of descent from the English Philadelphians. Even such a strange character as Jane Lead herself may have left a mark on his mind. Blake's special using of the biblical name 'Beulah', from Bunyan's *Pilgrim's Progress* has already been noted. It is the allegorical state, the place where 'the babes of love lie hid'. Jane Lead, too, gives the word her own meaning in the visions she recounts within her *Fountains of Gardens*.

> Know then that there is a secret hidden Garden, within that land called *Beulah*, in which grow all Physical Plants, where the River

Pison doth water . . . Here are hid within the Bowels of this Holy Ground, the Veins of Pure Gold, with all Oriental Pretious Stones . . .

Nor must the religious enthusiasts of her type be regarded with too patronizing an air. After composing a masterly study of their weaknesses, Ronald Knox, for instance, freely paid this tribute to the visionaries he had been examining, warning us that we cannot afford to be over-suspicious of what they represent, we who are so lukewarm and unenthusiastic.

> . . . the fires of spirituality burn low, and we go on unconscious, dazzled by the glare of tinsel suns. How nearly we thought we could do without St. Francis, without St. Ignatius! Men will not live without vision; that moral we do well to carry away from contemplating, in so many strange forms, the record of the visionaries. If we are content with the humdrum, the secondhand, the hand-over-hand, it will not be forgiven us . . .

Nevertheless it would be dishonest to deny that the particular symbolism William Blake adopted, the interpretation of the universe he took over from the Neo-Platonists, was an obstacle to him, in many ways, in his own spiritual progress. I have already touched on this subject and can only continue to insist that Blake's failure to grasp the full implications of Incarnational Christianity placed him, in the end, in an impossible position. For his aspirations were lofty. His thirst of the soul as vehement as any St John of the Cross could experience. Yet the *Todo Y Nada* of that great saint, the Negative Way which has always been regarded in Christian Tradition as the quickest and most direct path, was not his path. The nature of this way has been brilliantly expressed in T. S. Eliot's *Burnt Norton.*

> World not world, but that which is not world,
> Internal darkness, deprivation
> And destitution of all property,
> Desiccation of the world of sense,
> Evacuation of the world of fancy,
> Inoperancy of the world of spirit . . .

Brought up in a Protestant environment, himself in protest against the legacy of Puritanism, Blake turned away from an

304

kind of asceticism. Moreover, Blake was an artist, and though less dependent on direct sense impressions than many, he obviously could not follow the Negative Way literally, the path of the rejection of images.

Was he then called to pursue the Affirmative Way, to become an Immanental mystic? He could have taken up Traherne's position, and proclaimed that,

> The brightness and magnificence of this world, which by reason of its height and greatness is hidden from man, is Divine and Wonderful . . . the Goodness of the Lord filleth the World, and His Wisdom shineth everywhere within it and about it . . .

Indeed there are signs that he was drawn to this path. Blake was, after all, the poet who believed it necessary to 'cleanse the doors of perception', who spoke of seeing 'a World in a grain of Sand' and who had such a sensitive regard for,

> The ground Spider with many eyes, the Mole clothed in velvet,
> The ambitious Spider in his sullen web, the lucky golden Spinner,
> The Earwig arm'd, the tender Maggot, emblem of immortality . . .

Yet he was also the man who attacked Wordsworth as an idolator.

> I see in Wordsworth the Natural Man rising up against the Spiritual Man Continually, & then he is No Poet but a Heathen Philosopher at Enmity against all true Poetry or Inspiration.

Blake sensed Wordsworth's basic pantheism and resented it. But he fell himself into another and related heresy. He failed to see creation as the work of God's hands, intended to be what it is, material; with an immortal destiny, however, when it is supernaturalized by the spirit. There is a difference between believing that the divine handiwork has since been marred by Man's sin and conceiving of the world as the result of a 'Fall' into matter. Certainly, according to Blake, matter saved Man from non-entity. It gave him a chance to work his way up again, back to his original condition. Yet, in the interpretation of life put forward by the philosophy Blake adopted, material forms are simply gross and at the same time, diminutive

versions of their spiritual originals. From the beginning the
'Eternals' could expand or contract themselves as necessary.
Fallen beings are those who have become fixed in contraction.
The transcendant, perfect state is described by Blake in the
Four Zoas, Night the First,

> Then those in Great Eternity met in the Council of God
> As one Man, for contracting their Exalted Senses
> They behold Multitide, or Expanding they behold as one,
> As One Man all the Universal family; & that One Man
> They call Jesus the Christ, & they in him & he in them
> Live in Perfect harmony, in Eden the land of life . . .

(Keynes, p. 277)

This is the condition from which Man fell into the world of
'multitude'; a world which is primarily a state where 'strong
energies' are condensed 'into little compass', under the
dominion of the Elohim, on the side of Rigour, which is the
aspect of terror, even though terror is itself an aspect of the
divine. The scales of value are heavily weighted against the
Space-Time world in Blake's system, and with this distrust of
Nature how could he follow, as a mystic, the Affirmative Way?
Therefore he was trapped, trapped into a state which belongs
neither to the mystic nor to the artist proper. But to the
magician. The prophetic books are the record of his struggle
to escape from this trap, and in the bitterness of his conflict he
lashed out against Nature and against Woman, powers that he
felt were keeping his soul in bondage.

Paradoxically, contempt for Nature and the Feminine always
impels a man towards Magic, the force which really held
William Blake enslaved. An insistence upon a masculine,
aggressive approach in preference for the surrender of the soul
in love, when it is expressed in spiritual directions, inevitably
leads to the state of the magician; to the seeking of power and
knowledge for its own sake. This is not a condition completely
to be despised, though obviously dangerous. Evelyn Underhill,
in her study of Mysticism, does it full justice.

Magic, in its uncorrupted form, claims to be practical, intellectual, highly individualistic science; working towards the declared end of enlarging the sphere on which the human will can work, and obtaining experimental knowledge of planes of being usually regarded as transcendental. It is the last descendant of a long line of teaching, in fact, of the mysteries of Egypt and Greece – which offered to initiate man into a certain secret knowledge and understanding of things.

She rightly explains magic as depending on analogy, on,

> an implicit correspondence between appearance and reality, the microcosm of man, and the macrocosm of the universe, the seen and unseen worlds . . .

and she quotes Sir Thomas Browne who, she observes,

> spoke for more than himself when he said, in a well-known passage of the *Religio Medici*: 'The severe schools shall never laugh me out of the philosophy of Hermes . . . that this visible world is but a picture of the invisible, wherein, as in a portrait, things are not truly but in equivocal shapes, and as they counterfeit some real substance in that invisible framework.' Such a sense of analogy, whatever the 'severe schools' may say, is indeed the foundation of every perfect work of art.

Her last comment is crucial. There is a sense in which every artist is a magician, and ought to be. But he must be one in all humility, acting under God, and so save himself from that cardinal error which Evelyn Underhill rightly discerns to be the chief danger, even on the highest levels.

> . . . Even on these levels, [magic] is dogged by the defects which so decisively separate the occultist from the mystic. The chief of these is the peculiar temper of mind, the cold intellectual arrogance, the intensely individual point of view which occult studies seem to induce by their conscious quest of exclusive power and knowledge, their implicit neglect of love.

Still, while she passes these strictures, Evelyn Underhill makes quite clear that an element of the magical is present in all religion, and that, conversely, magic is linked with mystical illumination.

> The best of the Hermetic philosophers, indeed, are hardly ever without such mystical hankerings, such flashes of illumination; as

if the transcendental powers of man, when they are roused from sleep, cannot wholly ignore the true end for which they were made.

And she warns us of the dangers of dismissing this philosophy with contempt. Especially indeed, for Christians, is it unwise to withhold due deference from what can be a path to truth itself.

In magic, whether regarded as a superstition or a science, we have at any rate the survival of a great and ancient tradition, the true meaning of whose title should hardly have been lost in a Christian country; for it claims to be the science of those Magi whose quest of the symbolic Blazing Star, brought them once, at least, to the cradle of the Incarnate God.

The incarnate God should be the goal of every magician's quest, whether he works in paint or in words or on the mind of Man. And equally, it should be understood that all art, in its use of the image, is to some degree magical.

A twentieth-century poet and profound thinker who fully realized the implications of the artist's role, and who had studied magic himself, was Charles Williams. A mind armed against the dangers Evelyn Underhill points out by a sincere acceptance of the orthodox Christian tradition, yet one sensitively in touch with the undercurrents of thought in his own day, and those from earlier times. Charles Williams understood clearly that the poet, as represented by his own Taliessin, for instance, is a Mage, for he deals in images; and he puts forward a very touching and perceptive vision of the doctrine of the 'Affirmation of Images'. Yet he frankly regarded Witchcraft, not as a delusion, or an inoffensive pre-Christian cult much misunderstood, but as the 'Way of the Perversion of Images'. And he had enough contact with the 'occult' and with various modern forms of Theosophy to grasp that those who tried to brush aside the proper distinction between Matter and Spirit all too often only succeed in presenting spirit as a very, very thin kind of matter.

At the same time Williams appreciated the essential innocence of the body, expressing it in his essay on 'Natural Goodness'.

> Matter, certainly, is by definition the opposite of spirit. It is apparently as far the opposite of God (leaving will and morals out of the question) as God chose to create. But it did not therefore become less significant of Him than that less technical opposite which is called spirit. We have, in fact, only lost proper comprehension of matter by an apostacy in spirit. Matter and 'nature' have not, in themselves, sinned; what has sinned is spirit . . .

While Charles Williams was not a genius of the same order as William Blake they shared many characteristics; an understanding of spiritual pride and the arrogance of the intellect. Both were epic poets depending on myth; Williams using the great Arthurian legend that Milton had considered and rejected. Both are mainly concerned with psychological and spiritual events rather than with exterior ones in their writings and the poetry of both is very difficult and only just beginning to be clearly expounded and fully enjoyed. They possessed a bardlike quality in common, a prophetic spirit.

Yet in some ways Williams, with a less remarkable natural endowment, achieves a better balance just because he is in touch with the mainstream of Christian thought and was humble enough to realize that the concepts which have their place in Christian orthodoxy are in harmony with the stored wisdom of humanity; a wisdom more than purely human. It is because of this balanced judgment that such theosophical symbolism as appears in Williams's works, his essays, novels and poems, commands the reader's respect in a way that W. B. Yeats's assortment of images taken from the movement dominated by Mme Blavatsky and Annie Besant cannot in themselves. Many centuries of exploration must pass before the religious values of India and the Far East can be successfully integrated with those of the West. There is a real distinction between these and even the most extreme Neo-Platonic elements in the Western vision, and they should not be carelessly confused. And while

Yeats's poetic magic was able to transmute everything he touched to gold, there is a certain amount of hocus pocus in his symbolism that has been justly noted in Margaret Rudd's study of Blake and Yeats, *The Divided Image.*

One should not forget, however, that at the time when Yeats and his friends were so much affected by the system of Mme Blavatsky and Annie Besant, a number of American transcendentalists were borrowing heavily from Thomas Taylor's elaborate commentaries on Plato and the Neo-Platonists. George Mills Harper has pointed out in a recent book[1] that Alexander Wilder's edition of Iamblichus is very much indebted to Taylor, and has stressed the number of Taylor's works which were reissued during the late nineteenth century. He influenced Emerson, Thoreau, W. T. Harris, H. K. Jones, among others, and T. W. Higginson whose work affected Emily Dickinson's Greek studies so deeply, collected manuscripts of Thomas Taylor. While in England, Coventry Patmore owned Taylor's *Five Books of Plotinus* and Lionel Johnson and E. J. Ellis, both members of Yeats's circle, were interested readers of Taylor's books.

The Platonism of Thomas Taylor in the eighteenth century represented, of course, an attempt to return to the pre-Christian system of Plato himself and his sources, and of Plato's followers in Alexandria, the original Neo-Platonists. This was taken up in the nineteenth century by many thinkers who were in reaction from Christianity or who preferred a more authentic type of Platonism to the Christianized version. I have said it is very likely that Blake knew Taylor, who was in close contact with Blake's sculptor friend Flaxman, and that he found Taylor's presentation of Greek myth from a Neo-Platonic point of view helpful in providing him with an apparatus for his myth. It does seem to me, though, that Taylor's Platonism as a philosophy was tried and found wanting by Blake, though it influenced him, probably, as strongly as the doctrines of Swedenborg had done.

[1] George Mills Harper, *The Neo-Platonism of William Blake,* pp. 29–30.

Again, whatever one may think of the 'theosophical' imagery of the Yeatsian group, the better informed and more reputable outlook of Ouspensky and Gurdjieff, deriving from the Society called 'Seekers after Truth' which organized expeditions into Persia, Afghanistan, Turkestan, Tibet and India, from 1895 onwards, would seem to deserve more serious consideration. There is a curious correspondence between the ideas that Gurdjieff expressed on ancient art and Blake's theories on the subject.

> No man can believe that either Homer's Mythology, or Ovid's, were the production of Greece or of Latium; neither will anyone believe that the Greek statues, as they are called, were the invention of Greek Artists: perhaps the Torso is the only original work remaining; all the rest are evidently copies, though fine ones, from greater works of the Asiatic Patriarchs . . .
>
> The Artist having been taken in vision into the ancient republics, monarchies and patriarchates of Asia, has seen those wonderful originals called in the Sacred Scriptures Cherubim, which were sculptured and painted on walls of Temples, Towers, Cities, Palaces, and erected in the highly cultivated states of Egypt, Moab, Edom, Aram, among the Rivers of Paradise, being originals from which the Greeks and Hetrurians copied Hercules Farnese, Venus of Medicis, Apollo Belvidere, and all the ground works of ancient art.
>
> (*Descriptive Catalogue* No. 1. Keynes, p. 565)

This is the standard concept that classical art and literature derived from more ancient sources farther to the East, which we find asserted over and over again from the Renaissance onwards. According to Gurdjieff the cathedrals of the West, the Taj Mahal and the Temple of Heaven in Peking, are all products of esoteric schools and he insisted that the Egyptian Sphinx was a copy of one in Babylon eight thousand years old. Gurdjieff accepted the idea that great works of art and architecture depended on a knowledge of rhythm and proportion which he pointed out that Pythagoras had understood and taught. And he quoted a cosmology in legend that he said had come through the Greeks, who got it from the Egyptians, and

311

the Egyptians from the ancient Babylonians and Summerians. Similarly he taught the descent of messengers from the divine world to the human race.[1]

At the same time the picture of Eastern thought presented by the system of Ouspensky and Gurdjieff is highly selective; all those elements which do not fit with these men's idealized version of Hinduism and Buddhism are simply left out. And the emphasis on developing inner powers betrays the same tendency towards activism that can be criticized in Blake himself. The masculine power drive is over-stressed and there is always the danger in this approach of just that 'cold intellectual arrogance' which Evelyn Underhill sees induced by a 'conscious quest of exclusive power and knowledge' and an 'implicit neglect of love'.

The central point of the Christian Platonist's scheme has always been the Incarnation and it is by virtue of his respect for Christ that Margaret Rudd, for instance, can rightly support Blake's claims to a far greater spiritual authority in his message than can be accorded to Yeats, so often dominated by sensationalism. Charles Williams constantly shows the heart of all his thought to be this reverence for the Incarnation. How boldly he could assert it may be judged from his essay, 'The Redeemed City', where he is discussing the workings of tyranny.

> The thing that is common between us and our allies, and in dispute between us and our enemies, is the proper freedom of the flesh. No one can in fact, prevent a man thinking, or interfere with the motions the soul has in itself; what he can do is to prevent utterance. He can prevent the tongue speaking or the ear hearing; ... All these things are worked out in terms of flesh ... It is the outrage upon the physical Image of Christ; the physical vehicle of the Holy Ghost, which is the final impiety here.

Charles Williams tempered Platonic Idealism with an awe for the Word made Flesh and for the flesh which through this event is to be glorified, and so arrived at a deeply satisfying

[1] C. S. Nott, *Teachings of Gurdjief, The Journey of a Pupil*, London 1961, pp. 67–8; 130; 186; 188–90.

balance, which is apparent throughout his work and thought.

But alas, the conception of incarnation often became repugnant to those who followed the Hermetic philosophy. That is the whole tragedy. Yet, as far as Blake is concerned, it is not the whole story. For Blake was saved from the worst of the perils to which he was exposed, by an inborn need for love. The man who scribbled, of himself,

> Go little creature, formed for joy and mirth,
> Go love without the help of anything on earth . . .

could never remain the victim of intellectual arrogance for long. But there is no doubt he often felt himself menaced by an egotism of the mind continually rising up from within his own nature. It did not arise from cold reason, for Blake's strength was his intuitive faculty, but from the sinister aspect of that great imaginative power which was his glory. No-one has taught profounder doctrine on this subject than Blake, and Imagination is the only instrument through which the soul can be brought to the brink of mystical union, for its power is effective when reason's falls away; and the only means by which she can convey the effects of that union. This is why all mystics are poets, and art analagous to mysticism. Yet at the highest spiritual reaches Imagination must be discarded. If the soul is imprisoned within the domain of the image while she longs for what can only come about beyond it, the result is a frustration which is agony, a spiritual pain expressed in every page of Blake's prophetic books. But not only this is expressed. Before he was anything else Blake was basically a Christian and as such he was gaining in genuine spiritual insight all the time. His superb mental honesty, his firm belief in the Forgiveness of Sins, and in the necessity for self conquest, the subjection of the Ego, show this quite clearly.

Any assessment of William Blake as a man, and a poet and painter, must take into account the foundation of Christian values upon which all else was built. Long before Blake heard about the Kabalah, the unwritten law of the Jews, for instance, he had grown up with the Bible, understood in a quite straight-forward sense. I have necessarily over-emphasized the more unfamiliar aspects of his thought since it is those that the tradition illuminates. But the boy who saw God looking in at the window, who had a vision of angels in a tree, had lived since infancy in a world of biblical imagery and walked with Milton hand in hand. So close was he to the language of the Bible that a thorough examination of the way Blake used biblical names, expressions and concepts, in his poetry and art, would be a formidable undertaking; at least as weighty as a corresponding exploration of Milton's mental universe. And in particular Blake belonged to the prophets. To the prophets Isaiah and Ezekiel, and to Ezra of the Apocalypse in the Apochrypha, whom Francis Lee had dwelt on so lovingly and with such care. There are many senses in which Blake was himself a real prophet, even in the literal meaning of the word. During his story of creation, which parallels Genesis, in *The Four Zoas*, Night the second, he speaks of the weaving of the thread of life.

> . . . And all the time, in Caverns shut, the golden Looms erected
> First spun, then wove the Atmospheres . . .
> While far into the vast unknown the strong wing'd Eagles bend
> Their venturous flight in Human forms distinct; thro' darkness
> deep
> They bear the woven draperies; on golden hooks they hang abroad
> The universal curtains, & spread out from Sun to Sun
> The vehicles of light: they separate the furious particles
> Into mild currents as the water mingles with the wine . . .
> (Keynes, p. 284)

This passage in not simply vivid and moving. It seems to antici-pate the atomic conception of modern physicists in its reference to the separation of 'the furious particles Into mild currents'. And there are many other examples even more striking. In the same way just that kind of obscurity exists within Blake's poetry as in the writings of Isaiah, Ezekiel and Jeremiah. An obscurity that comes partly from delving into deep places, partly from the presence of many layers of meaning. However alluring it may be to interpret Blake's epics as stories dealing with the doings of certain mythological characters, one must never forget his own words in the famous letter to Thomas Butts.

> Now I a fourfold vision see,
> And a fourfold vision is given to me;
> 'Tis fourfold in my supreme delight
> And threefold in soft Beulah's night
> And twofold Always. May God us keep
> From Single vision & Newton's sleep!

Nothing has only one meaning. Nothing refers only to one event, mental or physical. A complete commentary to Blake's prophetic poetry would need to be at least four times as long as Northrop Frye's *Fearful Symmetry*, for instance. Just lately it has become the fashion to decry the use of the term 'prophetic books' applied to Blake's epics, since it was only after the titles of the early poems, *America* and *Europe*, that he placed the words, 'a Prophecy'. But in fact, it is foolish not to see that their whole tone is prophetic, that their terminology and general machinery owe much to Ezekiel's visions, to Isaiah, and Jeremiah's lamentations, and that their mood is apocalyptic; as much so as William Langland's *Piers Plowman*. No, the consideration of Blake as a prophet is completely necessary to an understanding of his individual vision.

For William Blake was a visionary, one of the most remarkable in human history, and visionaries are usually either the centre of a rather unhealthy cult, or else they are underestimated or even violently attacked. A kind of snobbism has grown up, among theologians especially, which plays down the visionary faculty. It is an embarrassing one and open to abuse, no doubt, but a faculty which deserves much more serious consideration than it has received. St Teresa's words on the subject show the sanity and perception for which she is so notable and make the most important point. Speaking of visions which come through the imagination, in her *Interior Castle* she rules, that

When they come from Our Lord they seem to me in some ways more profitable (than any others) because they are in closer conformity with our nature, except for those which the Lord bestows in the final Mansion, and with which no others can compare.

St Teresa always insists on conformity with our human nature; she protests in this passage from her autobiography,

. . . we are not angels and we have bodies. To want to become angels while we are still on earth and as much on earth as I was then, is ridiculous.

If one considers for a moment the illustrious train of men and women who have received such visions from God, according to the mode of a nature which has imagination for its characteristic quality, it appears at once how vitally important the visionary is in the history of religion. From the time of Enoch and Moses to St Paul's day, and from his to the age of Mahomet, of St Francis, and St Joan of Arc, down to our own epoch, which has witnessed the events of Lourdes and Fatima, it has been true that amazing spiritual progress often follows such revelations, and enormous benefits are conferred, not only on the visionary, but upon the whole human race. But an exploration of this theme demands much space. I have only been able to touch on it here, and to remark briefly on the problems of Blake's religious position. The rest must wait for a later book.

In the same way Blake's acute sensitivity to the events of his own day, his political consciousness, which was highly developed, and his powers of practical observation, have been only barely indicated. A substantial study has come out on this subject from David Erdman, and there is room for more. Blake can too easily be approached as a complete introvert, which is very far from the truth. He was a man of considerable shrewdness and surprising technical skill. And his use of myth, also, is very far from being confined to biblical material or Greek mythology seen from Neo-Platonic eyes. I hope to follow the present work with a study of his handling, among other things, of oriental sources, Celtic and Scandinavian mythology, the Atlantis story as it appeared in the eighteenth century; and above all an estimation of the religious values he stood by and the psychological insight he so marvellously expressed in his achievement as the creator of the earliest, and still the greatest, inward epics, which have ever been written. The characteristics of William Blake's own psychology are curious and interesting, and as the first epic poet who dared to set the scene of action purely in the human mind, he anticipated, in an amazing way, the great discoveries of Freud, Jung and Adler.

It is just because Blake *was* a prophet that he felt so much alone in his own time.

> O why was I born with a different face?
> Why was I not born like the rest of my race?

Truly, a voice crying in the wilderness. But it is because he was a prophet that he has come into his own in our time. For his message, and that of the entire tradition he drew upon, has a particular reference to the present age. Again, Nicolas Berdyaev – whose insight into the Renaissance dilemma I have alluded to at the start – understood this. His book, *The Meaning of the Creative Act*, has in its turn been called a prophetic work and certainly anticipates developments which have become much more obvious since it was written. Berdyaev was not particularly interested in Blake. Indeed, he was only barely aware of his existence. But he was devoted to Jacob Boehme, and fascinated by the way of thought Boehme exemplifies, and it is a striking proof of Blake's debt to that tradition that everything Berdyaev says may be applied directly to Blake's own system. He perceives Boehme as a mystic, 'supra-national as he is super-confessional', and sees his strength as lying in his Christology, 'Boehme's mysticism is all concrete, pictorial, bound up with the face of Christ and the face of man, all permeated by anthropological consciousness'. His anthropomorphic attitude, which Swedenborg affirmed and Blake never wavered from, is more extreme than the orthodox Christian position.

From all eternity the Son is born of God, the Absolute Man, the

Divine Man, the God-Man. The Divine Son and Man is born in heaven and on earth, in time and in eternity, above and below. Hence what is accomplished in heaven is also accomplished on earth. The drama of earthly man is also the drama of heavenly humanity.

Yet this extreme, this 'anthropological and concrete spirit of the mysticism of the Kabbala and of Jakob Boehme' does serve to offset what Berdyaev calls 'the abstract and formless spirit of the negative mysticism of India, of Plotinus and of Eckhart, which is purely Arian in spirit'.

It is this abstract Neo-Platonism, holding a great deal in common with Hindu thought, that is modified by the Jewish element in the Renaissance tradition to which Boehme's system belongs. And it is the concrete, devotional Christology, the heritage from the Bible, which formed a counter-weight to the Neo-Platonism present within the philosophies both of Boehme and of Blake. Berdyaev's virtue is that he understands this age to be a time when these two elements encounter one another on a cosmic scale. His conception, too, of their utterly different nature is distinct. As he puts it,

> The mysticism of India is all impersonal: it does not perceive human personality in its metaphysical individuality and its value to the very life of God himself: it is all something before the revelation of Man in God, the revelation of personality through the Son of God.

And he is right in finding 'the same denial of man in Neo-Platonic mysticism'.

> For Plotinus, Berdyaev says, neither plurality nor individuality have met a physical reality ... the consciousness of Plotinus is the exact opposite of that antinomic Christian revelation by which the plurality of being is not quenched but rather confirmed in the One, and God is not the denial of man and of the whole cosmos but rather their affirmation.

It was their inability to grasp this last truth that made the minds affected by the Neo-Platonic tradition so ill at ease with nature and the created universe.

Berdyaev clearly sees the dangers, as well as the benefits of the encounter he describes.

> It is a strange and terrible thing to say, but Christianity is becoming more foreign and less acceptable to the modern mind of Christian Europe than Buddhism. The popularization of occult doctrines is of enormous symptomatic significance for our times. The day is at hand when secret mystical doctrines will be manifested and objectivized. The way of positivism and rationalism, along which modern man has travelled, has already shown its terrible fruits, and man now yearns for a return to his secret and pristine sources.

But he also realizes,

> Man's hidden occult forces, always present but suppressed by sin, must be revealed, must be expressed . . .

He sees the true expression, though, in a positive creative approach to nature, which only Christianity can bring. The Yogi and the adept, the Cabalist and the Mage have to learn that,

> The mystical way to God will be transformed into a way to creation, to the plurality of being, to man himself. The passive inhumanism of both the old mysticism and the old magic must be overcome; to them there can be no return.

Just as he realizes the West needs the riches of Eastern Christianity, for which 'Christ is subject: He is within the human soul: the soul receives Christ into itself, into the depths of the heart', so he sees that Neo-Platonism and the ancient Wisdom of the East needs to be baptized. Because the Renaissance tradition whose fortunes have been followed in this book was an attempt in this direction, though we may be forced to say, an attempt that failed, it is of paramount importance for us now, at this moment of history. And just because in William Blake, as in a battleground, the issue between the different forces we have been examining was fought out, his is a mind that in our turn we are forced to respect and to explore. Whether he appeals or repels he cannot be ignored. Above all the apocalyptic vision with which, in an approach so deeply biblical, he ever viewed the world, is the vision we are compelled to accept in an atomic era. Only by such a vision can we save ourselves. At the dawn of the space age, too; when the secrets of the psyche begin to be penetrated, and when the past at last takes shape as one great whole; at a period when, in the figure used by Teilhard de Chardin, the human ship finally leaves the shelter of the Neolithic Age and puts out, for the first time, towards the open sea. At such a moment, only the vision that William Blake asserted would come when the doors of perception were cleansed, only this, can make life endurable to Man.

> The Sun has left his blackness & has found a fresher morning,
> And the mild moon rejoices in the clear & cloudless night,
> And Man walks forth from midst of the fires: the evil is all
> consum'd.
> His eyes behold the Angelic spheres arising night & day;
> The stars consum'd like a lamp blown out, & in their stead, behold
> The Expanding Eyes of Man behold the depths of wondrous
> worlds!

The Rosicrucian and Freemason Movements

*

The origin and early history of both the Rosicrucian and the Freemason movements has been the subject of much controversy. As far as the Rosicrucian Society is concerned the question is whether such a society really existed as a concrete, though secret organization, or whether it merely represented an ideal, a philosophy towards which certain scholars aspired. An article on Rosicrucianism in the *Encyclopaedia Britannica*, 1953, by H. Spenser Lewis, Former Imperator of the Ancient Mystical Order of the Rosy Cross in America, gives this account of its history.

> Popular opinion credits the foundation of the Fraternity of Rosicrucians as having occurred in Cassell, Germany, early in the seventeenth century when some pamphlets were issued entitled 'Allgemein unt General Reformation der ganzen weiten Welt', and the 'Fama Fraternitatis' believed to have been written by the theologian, Johan Valentin Andrea (1586–1654). Later investigation, however, revealed that although the family arms of Andrea contained a cross and perhaps a rose, he had no actual part in the revival of the Fraternity in Germany and that the pamphlets were published in various languages under the symbolical name of Christian Rosenkreuz (Christian Rose Cross). The pamphlet referred to the previous existence of the Fraternity in the Orient but for nearly a hundred years the historical background was considered mythical.
>
> Research during the past few years revealed that the Rosicrucian Fraternity had an actual organized existence long prior to what was only a revival in Germany.

Mr Lewis quotes references to the earlier existence of the Society from Benedict Figulus, an authority on mystical literature; Michael Maier, Kaiswetter and Cornelius Agrippa, but without giving details. He also cites a letter from Dr Landalf of Lyons to Cornelius Agrippa saying that he was acquainted with the organization in 1509, and a statement that Paracelsus was admitted into a Lodge at Basle in 1530. He speaks, too, of a rare collection of MSS in Cologne which give further proof of the antiquity of the Order. If these manuscripts could be made generally available to scholars no doubt the argument would be finally settled.

What is definite is the early existence of Rosicrucian symbolism. As Dr Pagel has pointed out in his study, *Paracelsus*, the portrait of Paracelsus in the first edition of his *Philosophiae Magnae*, 1567, shows the Jacob's ladder, the child's head appearing out of the earth, the figure with a single eye; all standard features of this system. Dr Pagel shows, too, that the *Horologium Sapientiae* of the mystic Suso, appearing in Cologne, 1503, bears a title page with figures whose left eye is barely outlined, or omitted altogether. Then, too, the Vitruvian figure on page 162 of Cornelius Agrippa's *De Occulta Philosophia*, 1531, is surmounted by a 'single eye'.

Likewise the question of the beginnings of the Freemason movement is a very puzzling one. Apart from the practical artisans, the groups of 'operative' masons who made up the original Freemasons' guilds, companies and lodges, there seem to have grown up other groups of 'speculative' or 'accepted' masons who associated themselves, in their own societies, with these lodges during the seventeenth century. Eventually some lodges became purely speculative. An examination of the London Masons' Company records for 1620 and 1621 has prompted one authority, Bernard Jones, in his *Freemasons' Guide and Compendium* (p. 90), to point out that men who were already 'on the livery' in 1620 appear in a further list of those present 'Att the making masons' in 1621.

> This is the most definite indication so far that the Company apparently contained within itself a fraternity only to be entered by being made a freemason.

In 1646 the well-known scholar, Elias Ashmole, who

interested himself especially in Alchemy and Astrology, was initiated into the Freemason Lodge at Warrington, and apparently even intended to write a history of Freemasonry. The movement can hardly have been new in his day. We have records, too, of the initiation of Sir Robert Moray or Murray, into Mary's Chapel Lodge of Edinburgh in 1641. Moray was a founder of the Royal Society and its first President, besides being patron of Thomas Vaughan, and according to Antony à Wood, himself 'a most renowned chymist, a great patron of the Rosie Crucians and an excellent mathematician'. The meeting of the lodge took place near Newcastle, 'at the time when General Hamilton's Scots army was about to invest the town'.[1]

This initiation draws attention to the habit of Scots lodges of admitting non-operative members, mostly from noble families. For instance, John Boswell of Auchinleck was admitted to the Mary's Chapel Lodge forty years before Sir Robert Moray, and the Charter Lodge of Scoon and Perth claims that King James VI of Scotland himself was 'entered frieman measone and fellowcrafte'.

It seems that during the early seventeenth century the speculative movement within Freemasonry adopted symbolism from the Kabalah and from Neo-Platonic theories of harmony, especially when this had architectural application, but there is nothing that should lead us to suppose this symbolism to have been originally confined to such movements as Rosicrucianism and Freemasonry. Bernard Jones explains that the use of three pillars, or else of three floor candlesticks, often in the Ionic, Doric and Corinthian modes, was quite common in old lodges. No doubt he is right in identifying these with the cabalistic columns of wisdom, strength and beauty. Though in other old lodges the use of two pillars, symbolizing Jachin and Boaz, at the entrance of Solomon's temple, was prevalent. And we have already seen that the Craft Legend always refers to two pillars, one which could not sink and the other which could not burn. As there were, then, five columns to be taken into account

[1] Bernard Jones, *Freemasons' Guide and Compendium*, p. 127.

all told, these could neatly be fitted to the five classical orders of classical architecture.

Long passages, not only in Du Bartas' *Devine Weekes*, but also in Guy Le Fèvre de la Boderie's *La Galliade*, use a kind of masonic symbolism.[1] The title-page of Joshua Sylvester's translation of Du Bartas's poem, where one pillar supports a terrestial and another a celestial globe, has already been noted. Illustrations of badges from the Phoenix Lodge in Dublin (Bernard Jones, Plates XI and XXV) reveal the same sort of motif, probably borrowed, as Bernard Jones points out, from 'the misleading woodcuts in the Geneva Bible of 1560'. This is the Bible for which John Bodleigh, father of Sir Thomas Bodley, took out a seven years' patent from Queen Elizabeth in 1561. (The relevant chapter is VII of the First Book of Kings, describing the building of the Temple.)

Quite full accounts of the history of Freemasonry in Elizabethan times appear in John Nourthouk's *History of Masonry*, London 1784, which also stresses the role of Inigo Jones in the early seventeenth century. We have noted his enthusiasm for the Italian academies and their system, and Ben Jonson's satire on this enthusiasm. However, Nourthouk has been held suspect, since he based his accounts on records he admitted were burnt at the beginning of the eighteenth century.

---

[1] See the play made with the figure of the 'Magus Maisonnier' in both cercles II and III of *La Galliade*, particularly p. 34 verso. And pp. 360 f. of *The Devine Weekes*, 1611.

Manuscript Notes to Pordage's *Theologia Mystica*

*

John Pordage, MD – *Theologia Mystica, or the Mystic Divinitie of the Aeternal Invisibles*, portrait and plates, 8vo. London. 1683. On the fly leaves are a MS account of Pordage, and a comparison of his writings with those of Jacob Behmen.[1]

'Doctor Pordage was endowed with Jacob Behmen's Caracter, who (he?) alltho perhaps read J. Behmen's writings with profit, yet has not only drawn from the same spring, but allso in a certain respect has penetrated higher. He died at London, whose two Tracts were published at Amsterdam Anno 1698 & 1699 turned out of English into the German Language, One called, Theologia Mystica; the other, Sophia. The first (and notable?) part of which was again published in English, has a preface profixed of Jane Lead, friend to the Author whilst he was living. He discovers new manifestations in God, a new world of Spirits, beginnings prior ('former' deleted) to the angelical & natural world, all (manner?) of (which?) unknown to Jacob Behmen, to the understanding of whose writings he furnishes some interpretations of great moment, not however touching upon his arguments; for he leaves of (at least in the small Tracts which hitherto have appeared, which nevertheless are the beginnings of his Books) he leaves of, I said where Behmen begins. Which thing indeed being spoken will not seem an Enigma to him who is willing to read over his writing. Dr. Pordage has left not a few Manuscripts, some & more imperfect ones to be added to the number, of which now some in the year 1704 are published in high Dutch at Amsterdam, which yet some judge amongst the first conceptions of the Author which in other Books afterwards he has either amended or more evidently & plainly expressed. Other Manuscripts, because some are more confused, are so digested by some knowing of these

[1] Catalogue of the Library of the late John Byrom, Esq. M.A., F.R.S. — *Chetham's Library* — 23748.

matters, & reduced into some methodical systems & bodys, yt. occaision and conveniency offering to their being published, not a few may then go forth, of the World, or Globe of Eternity; concerning eternal and pure Nature; of the Angelical World; of the dark World; of Paradise; about some other arguments small treatises, some being sent before by way of preface which manifest the light & key to all. But the aids which in matter and labour wh can contribute to this, are yet to be expected both English and High Dutch may be brought to light. I have seen all those treatises nor without admiration of the most divine and most deep mysteries, which ever appeared to anywhere, or can come into the mind of man. They snatch the mind beyond it self – above heavenly things. They are described in a common & perspicuous elocution. To the more obscure writings of Behmen they bring light necessary to understand them. It appears that the Author was taught by God in those misteries most singularly. But the Authors two Treatises published in high Dutch, Theologia Mystica, & Sophia and allso four others more imperfect remain at Amsterdam with the Wetsteins.'

(Under the last four lines are inscribed
'Joseph Fopps
his book 1685'.)

At bottom and left side this Latin Inscription (in, apparently, another hand):
'Exprimit Effigiem Tibi & Urbi Sculptor & Orbi:
ast. (est?) Animum Auctoris, ni sua scripta, nihil
sic asserit E.H. MA MP' (E.H. MA. MP.?)

At back of written title-page 'G. Holford' in a later hand. Page watermarked Crown surmounting 'G.R.' above a lozenge marked 'G.O.'

Remarks in text. (Apparently in same handwriting as fly-leaves.)

Against first ⎰ p. 12. 'Pure Unity ie pure Deity.'
2 paragraphs ⎱   'Gods name I am that I am Exodus 3.v.14.'

Against   'I answered, that these Scriptures speak of God as he hath introduced himself into apostatized and impure Nature's essence after the fall . . .'
'A Wonderfull distinction.'
(Fall) viz of Lucifer & Adam.'

p. 13.
Against   '. . . free from all impurity and imperfection whatsoever:

and in this high purity consists the righteousness . . . of God.'

'Righteousness one of the divine qualities of God.' A B. (Ann Byrom? Antoinette Bourignon?)

Against   . . . 'the Divine Essence . . . is all Eternal Goodness.'

'Goodness another divine quality of God' A.B.

p. 14.

Against 'For as they exist in the Eternal World, before and without Eternal Nature they are free from all Essences whatsoever and exist in their own eternal Liberty.'

'Explanation.'

p. 15.

Against . . . 'in which Love the Holy Trinity stand united, and are nothing but *Divine Love.*'

'Wonderfull!'

p. 111.

Against 'the Mystery is yet in the manner how God doth generate this abyssal Essence out of himself . . .'

'My father worketh hitherto & I work.'

Bibliography

*

MANUSCRIPTS

1. The Diaries of Ann Bathurst. Bodleian MSS. Rawlinson D.1263, 1338.
2. *The Correspondence of Henry Brooke*, copies by his son-in-law, F. H. Holcroft: Walton MS. I. i. 43. Dr Williams' Library, London.
3. Comments on John Pordage in John Byrom's copy of his *Theologia Mystica*, No. 23748 of the Byrom collection in Chetham's Library, Manchester.
4. Samuel Taylor Coleridge: Pencil notes on the fly leaf of *The Works of Jacob Boehme*, British Museum copy C.126. K.1, Vol. I. Notes on the fly leaf of *The Theological Works of Henry More*, British Museum copy, Ashley 5176.
5. Albrecht Dürer: 'About the proportions of Human Limbs', British Museum MSS. I. 32; I. 114; II. 114.
6. *Expositio Libri Jetesirae*, Bibliothèque Nationale, Hebrue 381, fol. 21.
7. Genealogy of the Pordage Family. Bodleian MS. Ashmole 851, fol. 200.
8. Francis Lee: *An Hundred Queries upon the Mosaick Cabala* (copy in William Law's Hand) Walton MS. 186. 17.(18.) Dr Williams' Library.
9. Guillaume Postel: *Zohar on Genesis*, Munich Staatsbibliotek, Cod. Lat. 7428; British Museum Sloane MSS. 1410.
10. Richard Roach: *Account of the Rise and Progress of the Philadelphian Society*, Bodleian MS. Rawlinson D.833.
11. Rabbi Reuben Ṣarphathi: Scroll of the Kabalah, *The Big Leaf* (Bodleian Huntington. Addenda D. [1949]). A commentary to this scroll of the Sephiroth also exists in the Bodleian, MS. Michael 35, No. 5, fol. 90–148, under the title *Explanation of the Big Leaf* [sheet or page].
12. Scroll of 'a Cabala of the Jewes' (Bodleian Huntington Addenda E. [2429]). An explanatory Latin letter, MS. Adds. C. 279, accompanied it.
13. Jean Thénaud: *Le Cabale Metrificé*. Bibliothèque Nationale; La

Bibliothèque de Roi, No. 7239, olim 526. (Prose version, Bibliothèque De L'Arsenal; MS. Français No. 167.)

14. Leonardo da Vinci: *Study in Human Proportions*, Accademia, Venice Quaderni V. 1, MS. R. 343.

PRINTED BOOKS[1]

Abarbanel, Judah (Leone Ebreo): *Dialoghi d'Amore*. English translation by F. Friedeburg-Seeley and Jean H. Barnes, London, 1937.

Agrippa, Henry Cornelius: *De Occulta Philosophia*, Cologne, 1531. *Three Books of Occult Philosophy*, London, 1651.

CRITICAL STUDIES

Morley, Henry: *Cornelius Agrippa, A complete biography*, London, 1865.

Orsier, Joseph: *Henry Cornelius Agrippa, Sa Vie et son Oeuvre d'après sa Correspondence*, Paris, 1911.

Zambelli, Paola: 'Cornelio Agrippa di Nettesheim', *Archivo di Filosofia*, Testi Umanistici su L'Ermetismo, Rome, 1955.

Ainsworth, Henry: *Two Treatises*, London, 1789.

Alabaster, William: *Ecce Sponsus Venit*, London, 1633. *Spiraculum Tubarum, Sive Fons Spiritualium Expositionum ex aequivocis Pentaglotti significationibus*, London, 1633.

Basnage, Beauval de: *History of the Jews*, translated by Thomas Taylor, London, 1709.

Baxter, Richard: *Reliquae Baxterianae*, London, 1696.

Berdyaev, Nicolas: *The Meaning of the Creative Act*, London, 1955.

Blake, William: *The Complete Writings of William Blake*, London, 1957. Edited by Sir Geoffrey Keynes.

CRITICAL STUDIES

Bronowski, J.: *William Blake, A Man Without a Mask*, London, 1954.

Damon, S. Foster: *William Blake: His Philosophy and Symbols*, Boston and New York, 1924.

Davies, J. G.: *The Theology of William Blake*, Oxford, 1948.

Erdman, David: *William Blake, Prophet Against Empire*, Princeton, 1954.

---

[1] For convenience the original work of an author has not been separated from critical studies on him. Where editions of original works and critical studies appear under one author, the author's name is printed in bold type.

Frye, Northrop: *Fearful Symmetry*, Princeton, 1947.

Gilchrist, Alexander: *The Life of William Blake*, edited by Ruthven Todd, London, 1945.

Harper, George Mills: *The Neo-Platonism of William Blake*, North Carolina, 1961.

Keynes, Geoffrey: *Pencil Drawings of William Blake*, London, 1956.

Pinto, Vivian de Sola: *The Divine Vision*, an edition of *Studies in the Poetry and Art of William Blake* (by Kathleen Raine and others), London, 1957.

Roe, Albert S.: *Blake's Illustrations to Divine Comedy*, Princeton, 1953.

Rudd, Margaret: *Divided Image*, London, 1953. *Organiz'd Innocence*, London, 1956.

de Witt James, Laura: *The Finger on the Furnace*, New York, 1956.

Wilson, Mona: *Life of William Blake*, London, 1948.

Witcutt, W. P.: *Blake – A Psychological Study*, London, 1946.

Blau, Leon: *The Christian Interpretation of the Cabala in the Renaissance*, New York, 1944.

Boehme, Jacob: *The Works of Jacob Behmen, The Teutonic Theosopher*, London, 1764–81. Edited by George Ward and Thomas Langcake. *An Apology and Reply upon Esaiah Steifel*, London, 1661. *XL Questions Concerning the Soule*, London, 1647. *Of the election of Grace*, London, 1655. *Von 177 Theosophichsen Fragen*, Amsterdam, 1693.

CRITICAL STUDIES

Frankenberg. Abraham Von: *De Vita et Scriptis Jacobi Bohmii* (with Boehme's Works edited by J. G. Gichtel, Amsterdam, 1682).

Hutin, Serge: *Les disciples Anglais de Jacob Boehme*, Paris, 1960.

Martensen, Hans L.: *Jacob Boehme*, edited by Stephen Hobhouse, London, 1949.

Muses, C. A.: *Illumination on Jacob Boehme*, New York, 1951.

Stoudt, J. J.: *Sunrise to Eternity, A Study in Jacob Boehme's Life and Thought*, Philadelphia, 1957.

Taylor, Edward: *Jacob Boehme's Theosophick Philosophy Unfolded*, London, 1691.

Bradbrook, Muriel: *The School of Night*, Cambridge, 1936.

Brice, Edmund: Translation of the *Centrum Naturae Concentratum* of Ali Pili, London, 1696.

Bromley, Thomas: *The Way to Sabbath Rest*, London, 1650. *An Account of the various ways of God's manifesting Himself to Man*, London, 1710. *The Journeys of the Children of Israel*, London, 1710.

Brooke, Charlotte: *Reliques of Irish Poetry*, Dublin, 1788.

Brooke, Henry: *The Poetical Works of Henry Brooke*, Dublin, 1792. Edited, with a biography, by Charlotte Brooke.

Broughton, Hugh: *Works*, edited by John Lightfoot, 1662.

Burnet, Gilbert: *History of the Reformation*, London, 1679–1715.

Byrom, John: *Selections from the Journals and Papers of John Byrom*, poet, diarist, shorthand writer, edited by Henri Talon, London, 1950.

Clarke, Richard: *A Collection of Poems and Letters*, London, 1777. *The Gospel of the Daily Service of the Law, preached to Jews and Gentiles*, London, 1767. *Jesus the Nazarene: Address to Jesus, Deists, and Believers*, London, 1795. *Prophetic Records of the Christian Era*, London, 1812. *A series of Letters, Essays, Dissertations and Discourses on Various Subjects*, London, 1792. *Signs of the Times or a Voice to Babylon, The Great City of the World and to the Jews in particular*, London, 1773. *The Spiritual Voice to the Christian Church and to the Jews*, London, 1760.

Conway, Anne, Viscountess: *The Principles of the Most Ancient and Modern Philosophy, Concerning God, Christ and the Creatures, viz. of Spirit and Matter in general whereby may be resolved all those Problems or Difficulties, which neither by the School nor Common Modern Philosophy, nor by Cartesian, Hobbesian, or Spinosian, could be discussed*. London, 1692.

Nicolson, Marjorie: *The Conway Letters*, London, 1930.

Coppe, Abiezer: *A Fiery Flying Roll*, London, 1650.

Coppin, Richard: *A Hint of the Glorious Mystery of Devine Teachings*, London, 1649.

Daniel, Samuel: *Apology for Rime*, London, 1603.

Donne, John: *Essays in Divinity*, Edited by E. M. Simpson. *LXXX Sermons*, London, 1640. *The Poems of John Donne*, edited by H. J. Grierson, London, 1942.

D'Olier, Isaac: *Memoirs of the Late Excellent and Pious Mr Henry Brooke, Collected from Original Papers and other authentic Sources*, Dublin, 1816.

D'Israeli, Isaac: *Curiosities of Literature*, London, 1794.

Ecton, J.: *Thesaurus Rerum Ecclestiasticarum*, London, 1742.

Erbery, William: *A Call to the Churches*, London, 1653. *Nor Truth nor Errour*, London, 1647.

Fludd, Robert: *De Supernaturali, Naturali, Praeternaturali et Contranaturali Microcismi Historia*, Oppenheim, 1619. *Mosaicall Philosophy: Grounded upon the Essential Truth or Eternall Sapience,* written first in *Latin*, and afterwards thus *rendered into Englisl.* By Robert Fludd, Esq., & Doctor of Physick, London, 1659. *Philosophia Sacra & vere Christiana Seue Metereologica Cosmica,* Frankfurt, 1626. *Utriusque Cosmi Maioris scilicet et Minoris Metaphysica, Physica, atque technica Historia,* Oppenheim, 1617.

CRITICAL STUDIES
Craven, J. B.: *Dr Robert Fludd,* London, 1902.
Hutin, Serge: *Robert Fludd,* Paris, 1953.

Ficino, Marsilio: *Sopra L'Amore,* Florence, 1594.
CRITICAL STUDIES
Forster, Joseph: *Alumni Oxoniensis,* Vol. I, London, 1887.
Jayne, Sears Reynolds: *Marsilio Ficino's Commentary on Plato's Symposium.* Text with Translation and Introduction. Columbia, 1944.
Kristeller, P. O.: *Philosophy of Marsilio Ficino,* New York, 1943.
Robb, Nesca: *Neoplatonism of the Italian Renaissance,* London, 1935.

Giorgio, Francesco: *De Harmonia Mundi, Venice,* 1536. *Francisci Georgii Minoritani, in Scripturam Sacram, et Philosophos, tria millia Problemata,* Venice, 1536.
CRITICAL STUDIES
Mersenne, Marin: *Questiones in Genesium,* Paris, 1622.

Gell, Robert: *A Sermon Touching God's Government of the World by Angels,* London, 1650.

Glanvill, Joseph: *Lux Orientalis,* London, 1662. *The Vanity of Dogmatizing,* London, 1661.
CRITICAL STUDIES
Cope, Jackson: *Joseph Glanvill Anglican Apologist,* St Louis, 1956.
Henry More: *Annotations upon Lux Orientalis,* London, 1682.

Harvey, Gabriel: *Three Proper and wittie familiar Letters: lately passed betweene two Universitie men: touching the Earthquake in Apriell last, and our English reformed Versifying,* London, 1580. *Gabriel Harvey's Letter Book,* The Camden Society, London, 1884.
Heydon, John: *The Harmony of the World,* London, 1662.
Hill, Oliver: *Epistola ad Anglos; Being an Introduction Out of a Larger Treatise into the Mysteries of the True Christian Religion,* 1698.
James VI of Scotland: *His Majesties Poetical Exercises at Vacant Hours,* Edinburgh, 1591.

Jamitzer, Wenzel: *Perspectiva Corporum Regularium*, Nuremberg, 1568.

Jung, C. G. & Pauli, W.: *The Interpretation of Nature and the Psyche*, London, 1955.

Kepler, John: *Harmonices Mundi*, Augsburg, 1619.

Knox, Ronald: *Enthusiasm*, Oxford, 1950.

Koestler, Arthur: *The Sleep Walkers*, London, 1959.

Khrypffes, Nicolaus (Nicolas of Cusa): *Prohemium*, Strasbourg, 1490.

Kircher, Athanasius: *Musurgica Universalis sive Ars Magna Consoni et Dissoni*, Rome, 1650. *Oedipi Aegyptiaci*, Rome, 1653.

Law, William: *An Appeal to all that Doubt or Disbelieve the Truths of the Gospel*, London, 1742. *The Spirit of Prayer, or the Soul Rising out of the Vanity of Time, Into the Riches of Eternity*, London, 1750.

CRITICAL STUDIES

Hopkinson, Arthur: *About William Law*, London, 1948.

Talon, Henri: *William Law, A Study in Literary Craftsmanship*, London and New York, 1955.

Walton, Christopher: *Notes and Materials For An Adequate Biography of the Celebrated Divine and Theosopher, William Law*, London, 1854.

Lead, Jane: *Enochian Walks with God*, London, 1694. *Fountains of Gardens*, London, 1700. *Laws of Paradise*, London, 1695

Lee, Francis: *An Historical Account of Montanism*, in George Hickes's *The Spirit of Enthusiasm Exorcized*, London, 1709. *Dissertations, Theological Mathematical, and Physical*, London, 1752.

Le Fèvre de la Boderie, Guy: *Discourse de l'Honeste Amour sur le Banquet de Platon, Traduit de Toscan en Francais*, Paris, 1578. *L'Encyclie des secrets de L'Eternité*, Antwerp. *La Galliade*, Paris, 1578. Also, 'Par ordre du Roi', Paris, 1582.

MacGregor Mathers, S. L.: *The Kabbalah Unveiled*, London, 1926.

Maritain, Jacques: *The Degrees of Knowledge*, London, 1937.

Mede, Joseph: *Clavis Apocalyptica*, London, 1627.

Menestrier, C. F.: *Des Ballets anciens et modèrnes*, Paris, 1682.

More, Henry: *Psychozoia*, in *Philosophical Poems of Henry More*, edited by Geoffrey Bullough, Manchester, 1931. *Defence of the Philosophick Cabbala*, London, 1662. *Appendix to the Defence of the Philosophick Cabbala*, London, 1662. *Theological Works*, London, 1708.

Milton, John: *The Poetical Works*, edited by H. C. Beeching, London. *Complete Prose Works*, edited by D. M. Woolfe, London.

CRITICAL STUDIES

Bailey, Margaret Lewis: *Milton and Jakob Boehme*, New York, 1914.

Fletcher, H. F.: *The Intellectual Development of John Milton*, Illinois, 1956.

Saurat, Dennis: *Blake and Milton*, London, 1935. *Milton: Man and Thinker*, London and New York, 1925.

Moller, Martin: *Praxis Evangeliorum*, 1601. *Manuale Mortis. Schedia Regia.*

Morton, A. L.: *The Everlasting Gospel*, London, 1958.

Muller, Ernst: *History of Jewish Mysticism*, Oxford, 1946.

Nanni, Giovanni Nanni da Viterbo: *Auctores Vetutissimi Nuper in Lucem editi*, Venice, 1498. *Commentaria fratris Joanni Anni Viterbensis . . . super diversorum auctorum de Antiquitatibus loquentium*, Rome, 1498.

O'Connor, C. D. D.: *Memoirs of Charles O'Conor*, Dublin, 1797.

Paracelsus; Philippus Aureolus Theophrastus Bombastus von Hohenheim: *Interpretatio alia Totius Astronomiae, Opera Omnia*, Geneva, 1659. *Archidoxis*, translated by J.H., London, 1660. *Aurora*, translated by J.H., London, 1687. *The Waterstone of the Wisemen* (ascribed to Ambrosius Siebmacher), translated by J.H., London, 1659. *Paracelsus*, edited by J. Jacobi, London, 1951.

CRITICAL STUDIES

Pagel, Walter: *Paracelsus. An Introduction to Philosophical Medicine in the Era of the Renaissance*, New York and Basle, 1958.

Postel, Guillaume: *Candelabri Typici Mosis Tabernaculo Jussu Divino Expressi Brevis ac Dilacida Interpretatio*, Venice, 1548. *Sepher Yetzirah*, translated into Latin, Paris, 1552.

CRITICAL STUDIES

Bouwsma, William J.: *Concordia Mundi, The Career and Thought of Guillaume Postel*, Harvard, 1957.

Porter, John Holland: *The Smoke of the Bottomless Pit*, London, 1651.

Reuchlin, Johannes: *De Verbo Mirifico*, Basle, 1494. *De Arte Cabalistica*, Hagenau, 1517.

Roach, Richard: *The Great Crisis*, London, 1727. *The Imperial Standard of Messiah Triumphant*, London, 1727.

Robinson, William: *The History and Antiquities of the Parish of Stoke Newington*, London, 1820.

Scholem, Gershom: *Major Trends in Jewish Mysticism*, London, 1955.

Secret, Francois: *Le Zohar chez les Kabbalistes Chretièns*, Paris, 1958. *Scechina e Libellus de Litteri Hebraicis*, Rome, 1959.

Spenser, Edmund: *The Faerie Queene*, with introduction by Professor J. W. Hales, Ernest Rhys's Everyman's Library, 1955.

de Sola Pinto, Vivian: *Peter Sterry, Platonist and Puritan*, Cambridge, 1934.

Swedenborg, Emanual: *Apocalypse Revealed*, London, 1791. *Treatise Concerning Heaven and Hell*, London, 1778. *True Christian Religion*, London, 1781. *Wisdom of Angels Concerning Divine Love and Divine Wisdom*, London, 1788. *Wisdom of Angels Concerning Divine Providence*, London, 1790. *A Philosopher's Notebook*, translated and edited by Alfred Acton, Philadelphia, 1931.

CRITICAL STUDIES

Beck Block, Marguerite: *The New Church in the New World*, New York, 1932.

Sigstedt, P. O.: *The Swedenborg Epic*, Upsala, 1952.

Toksvig, Signe: *Emanuel Swedenborg, Scientist and Mystic*, London, 1949.

Sylvester, Joshuah: *Bartas, His Devine Weekes and Works*, London, 1605, and London, 1608.

Taylor, Thomas: *The Cratylus, Phaedo, Parmenides and Timaeus of Plato*, London, 1793. *The Philosophical and Mathematical Commentaries of Proclus on Plato*, London, 1789.

Teilhard de Chardin: *The Phenomenon of Man*, London, 1959.

Thorndike, Lynn: *A History of Magic and Experimental Science*, New York, 1934–38.

van Helmont, François Mercure: *A Cabbalistical Dialogue*, London, 1682. *Seder Olam and Some Questions upon the Revelations*, London, 1694.

Vaughan, Thomas: *The Fame and Confession of the Rosie Cross*, London, 1652. *Magia Adamica*, London, 1650.

de Vigenère, Blaise: *de La Penitence*, Paris, 1587. *Of Fire and Salt*, London, 1649. *Prières et Oraisons*, Paris, 1597.

von Rosenroth, Knorr: *Cabbalah Denudata*, Sulsbach, 1677, and Frankfurt, 1684.

Wesley, John: *The Journal of John Wesley*, edited by Nehemiah Curnak, London, 1915–16. *The Letters of John Wesley*, edited by John Telford, London, 1931.

Winchester, Elhanan: *A Defense of Revelation in Ten Letters to Thomas Paine Being An Answer to His First Part of The Age of Reason*, London, 1796.

Wind, Edgar: *Pagan Mysteries in the Renaissance*, London, 1958.

Yates, F. A.: *A Study of 'Loves Labours Lost'*, Cambridge, 1936. *The French Academies of the Sixteenth Century*, London, 1947.

PERIODICALS

Gordon, D. J.: 'Poet and Architect', *Journal of the Warburg and Courtauld Institutes*, Vol. 12, pp. 152 ff.

Higham, Charles: Article on Duché, *New Church Review*, XXII, 1915.

Hobhouse, Stephen: '*Fides et Ratio*, The Book Which Introduced Jacob Boehme to William Law', *Journal of Theological Studies*, Oxford, October, 1936.

Holmyard, E. T.: *Nature*, 1929, No. 123, pp. 520 ff.

Lee, Francis: *Theosophical Transactions of the Philadelphian Society*, London, 1697.

Miner, Paul: 'William Blake's London Residences', *Bulletin of the New York Public Library*, November, 1958.

Murray, W. A.: 'Donne and Paracelsus', *Review of English Studies*, XXV, 1949, pp. 115–23.

Ruggiero, G.: 'Storia della Filosofia': *Rinascimento e Riforma*, Laterza Baii, Vol. I, pp. 117 ff.

Secret, François: 'Guillaume Postel et les courants prophétiques de la Renaissance,' *Studi Francesi*, Turin, 1957, III, pp. 375 ff.

Scholem, G.: 'Zur Geschichte Der Anfänge Der Christlichen Kabbala', *Essays Presented to Leo Baeck*, London, 1954.

Trevor-Roper, Hugh: 'Three Foreigners,' *Encounter*, February, 1960.

Walker, D. P.: 'The Astral Body in Renaissance Medicine,' *Journal of the Warburg and Courtauld Institutes*, Vol. XXI, 1958, pp. 119 ff.

Wittkower, Rudolph: *The Journal of the Warburg and Courtauld Institutes*, Vol. VIII, 1945, pp. 68 ff.

Yates, Frances A.: 'The Art of Raymon Lull,' *Journal of the Warburg and Courtauld Institutes*, Vol. XVII, 1954, pp. 115 ff.

Index

z

Harvey, Gabriel (1550?–1631), 78, 146, 332
Harvey, William (1578–1657), 153
Havilah, 159–60
Haydocke, Richard (Matrc. Oxford, 1588), 46
Hayley, William (1745–1830), 136
Hegel, Georg Wilhelm Friedrich (1770–1831), 83, 90, 176
Helmont, François Mercure Van (1618–1699), xiv, 154–6n, 162–5, 197, 269, 335
Helmont, Jean Baptiste Van (1577–1644), 154, 197
Hepburn, James (Fr Bonaventura) (1573–1620), 116
Henry III of France (1555–1589), 69, 74, 112
Hermes, Trismegistus, 16, 20, 22, 35, 56, 73, 79, 100, 111, 114, 123–4, 134, 136
Hermeticism, xiv, 20–2, 35, 57, 134, 138, 141, 270, 288, 307, 313, 329
Hervey, James (1714–1758), 158, 287
Heyden, John (d. 1667?), 142, 332
Hierophants, 25
Higham, Charles, 336
Hill, Oliver (Matrc. Cambridge 1648), 108, 332
Hindmarsh, Robert (1759–1835), 201, 208, 209, 213, 219, 224
Hobhouse, Stephen (b. 1881), 90n, 250n, 270n, 336
Holcroft, F. H., 97n, 193, 227, 233, 271, 286
Holmyard, E. J. (1891–1959), 123n, 336

Homer (9th cent. B.C.?), 16, 161n, 311
Hopkinson, Arthur, 184, 192, 234, 333
Hudibras, 171, 177, 180
Hunt, Leigh (1784–1859), 4
Hutcheson, Elizabeth (d. 1781), 97n, 193
Hutin, George, 109n, 168n, 330, 332
'Hyle', 135, 136, 152

Imagination, 14, 65–6, 97, 133, 313, 315, 316
Incarnation, The, 308, 312
Isaiah, 6, 262, 297, 314, 315

James VI of Scotland, I of England (1566–1625), 81–2, 112, 115, 117, 137, 323, 333
Jamitzer, Wenzel (d. 1588), 47, 332
Jayne, Sears Reynolds (b. 1920), 21n, 24, 27n, 332
Jerusalem, 54, 63, 95, 133, 136, 159, 186, 255, 275, 287, 301
Jerusalem, 251
Jerusalem, The New, 167, 200, 201, 213, 219, 251, 278
Joachim of Flora (1145–1202), 8, 72, 101–2, 270, 288
Jones, Inigo (1573–1652), 82, 113–15, 324
John of the Cross, Saint (1542–1591), 304
Johnson, Samuel (1709–1784), 181
Jonson, Benjamin (1573?–1637), 82, 113–15, 269, 324
Josten, C. H. (b. 1912), xi, 67n, 130n